HAWAII ACCESS®

W9-CXJ-393

Pacific Ocean

Princeville
Airport

Kauai

Lihue
Airport

Kaulakahi
Channel

Niihau

Kauai
Channel

Oahu

Honolulu
International
Airport

Orientation

Like a giant green comet blazing across the blue **Pacific**, the 132 tropical islands, reefs, and shoals of **Hawaii** form a graceful archipelago spanning more than 1,500 miles, yet they are so remote that even the ubiquitous gull is unable to traverse the 2,400 miles from the nearest continent. Moving northwest on the back of a lithospheric plate at a rate of four inches per year, the island chain is in a continual state of eruption and erosion, as vast amounts of molten earth emanate upward toward the surface from a stationary "hot spot" on the ocean floor, only to be beaten back down by the merciless elements. After 42 million years of this, just eight major islands—the **Big Island, Maui, Kahoolawe, Lanai, Molokai, Oahu, Kauai,** and **Niihau**—remain and serve not only as home to 1.2 million people but also as one of the world's most treasured vacation destinations—Hawaii.

The beautiful, enchanting tropical paradise that is Hawaii has inspired writers from Mark Twain to James Michener; volumes have been written on the majestic volcanoes, golden beaches, captivating sunsets, and lush rain forests. Hawaii continues to enthrall millions of tourists each year with its numerous rainbows, magnificent waterfalls, astonishing lava flows, endless summer days, and warm starry nights. It's the unstaged backdrop for such movie classics as *Blue Hawaii* and *South Pacific,* the birthplace of regal humpback whales and playful spinner dolphins, and the home of such world-famous surfing sites as **Sunset Beach, Waimea Bay**, and the **Banzai Pipeline.** It's a playground for golfers, scuba divers, hikers, mountain bikers, windsurfers, snorkelers, swimmers, deep-sea anglers, and sun worshipers of all shapes and sizes. In short, Hawaii has something for everyone, whether you choose to sip a cool mai tai under a palm tree or dive into the depths of the turquoise sea. Perhaps most importantly, the slow, mellow pace that characterizes the Hawaiian lifestyle tends to ease stress and anxiety, allowing each visitor to return home with something far more valuable than any postcard or souvenir—peace of mind.

Hawaii is not without its faults. In an already overcrowded island state where indigenous Hawaiians are becoming increasingly rare (pure-blooded Hawaiians make up less than .005 percent of the population), the expanding number of immigrants from the US mainland and abroad has spurred a rise in racial bitterness, occasionally culminating in violence and, more often, targeted theft. This, combined with a huge foreign investment in precious real estate and a recent surge in ethnic Hawaiian pride, has done little to alleviate the interracial resentment that has existed since Captain James Cook set foot on Hawaii in 1778.

A new age is beginning for Hawaii. After more than 200 years of pursuing things new, the people of Hawaii are reassessing the value of things old. A

Pacific Ocean

aiwi
hannel

Kalaupapa
Airport ✈

Hoolehua
Airport ✈ **Molokai**

Kalohi
Channel

Kapalua–
West Maui
Airport ✈

Kahului
Airport ✈

Lanai

Lanai ✈   Auau
Airport   Channel

Maui

Hana ✈
Airport

Kealaikahiki
Channel

Kahoolawe   Alalakeiki
Channel

Alenuihaha
Channel

Hilo
International
Airport

Keahole-Kona
International
Airport ✈

✈

**Hawaii
(The Big Island)**

Hawaiian renaissance of sorts is
emerging, with renewed interest in
ancient crafts, rituals, and dances,
and a rekindled passion for the values
of traditional island culture, including
native art and the Hawaiian language. This renaissance is a necessity, because
or Hawaii to prosper in the next century, it must learn from past mistakes.
As former Governor John Waihee sagaciously observed, "We need to ask
ourselves how our ancestors did so much with so little, and why we are
able to do so little with so much."

Arguably the closest thing we have to heaven on earth, Hawaii is a priceless
resource worth preserving. It reminds us not only how beautiful the world
can be, but also how much of that beauty can be found in life's simpler
things. Gaze down a mountainside, stroll barefoot along the beach, or just
watch the sky change colors as the sun disappears behind the sea—it's not
hard to find splendor here.

How To Read This Guide

HAWAII ACCESS® is arranged by island so you can see at a glance where you are and what is around you. The numbers next to the entries in the following chapters correspond to the numbers on the maps. The text is color-coded according to the kind of place described:

Restaurants/Clubs: Red   Hotels: Blue
Shops/ Outdoors: Green   Sights/Culture: Black
& Wheelchair accessible

Wheelchair Accessibility

An establishment (except a restaurant) is considered wheelchair accessible when a person in a wheelchair can easily enter a building (i.e., no steps, a ramp, a wide enough door) without assistance. Restaurants are deemed wheelchair accessible only if the above applies and if the rest rooms are on the same floor as the dining area and their entrances and stalls are wide enough to accommodate a wheelchair.

Rating the Restaurants and Hotels

The restaurant star ratings take into account the quality, service, atmosphere, and uniqueness of the restaurant. An expensive restaurant doesn't necessarily ensure an enjoyable evening; however, a small, relatively unknown spot could have good food, professional service, and a lovely atmosphere. Therefore, on a purely subjective basis, stars are used to judge the overall dining value (see the star ratings at right). Keep in mind that chefs and owners often change, which sometimes drastically affects the quality of a restaurant. The ratings in this guidebook are based on information available at press time.

The price ratings, as categorized at right, apply to restaurants and hotels. These figures describe general price-range relationships among other restaurants and hotels in the area. The restaurant price ratings are based on the average cost of an entrée for one person, excluding tax and tip. Hotel price ratings reflect the base price of a standard room for two people for one night during the peak season.

Restaurants

★	Good
★★	Very Good
★★★	Excellent
★★★★	An Extraordinary Experience
$	The Price Is Right (less than $10)
$$	Reasonable ($10-$15)
$$$	Expensive ($16-$20)
$$$$	Big Bucks ($21 and up)

Hotels

$	The Price Is Right (less than $100)
$$	Reasonable ($100-$175)
$$$	Expensive ($176-$250)
$$$$	Big Bucks ($251 and up)

Map Key

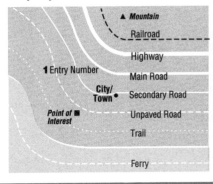

Area code 808 unless otherwise noted.

Getting to the Islands

Airports

Oahu's **Honolulu International Airport (HNL)** (836.6413) is Hawaii's hub, with connections made by more than two dozen international, national, and interisland carriers. Visitors from the mainland usually fly from Los Angeles, San Francisco, or Seattle, but it is possible to book nonstop flights from other major cities, like Denver or Chicago, to Oahu, Maui, or the Big Island.

For information on other island airports, interisland flights, and local telephone numbers for airlines, see the Orientation sections of the individual island chapters.

Airlines

Aloha	484.1111, 800/367.5250
American	833.7600, 800/433.7300
Canada 3000	888/226.3000
Canadian	839.2244, 800/426.7000
Continental	523.0000, 800/525.0280
Delta	800/221.1212
Hawaiian	838.1555, 800/367.5320
Island Air, interisland	484.2222, 800/652.6541
from the mainland	800/323.3345
Northwest, interisland	955.2255, 800/225.2525
from the mainland	800/441.1818
Qantas	800/227.4500

Quantas in Australia 13/13/13

TWA...800/221.2000

United 831.5225, 800/241.6522

Cruise Ships

An increasing number of cruise ships are stopping in Hawaii, despite the fact that, under US law, foreign ocean liners are not permitted to travel from one US port to another. Common itineraries include stops in Ensenada, Mexico, or trips to the South Pacific, Australia, or New Zealand after a stop on the Hawaiian Islands but before the ship returns to dock in San Diego or, in the case of **Cunard**'s (800/528.6273)

Queen Elizabeth 2 and *Royal Viking Sun,* Florida. **Royal Cruise Line** (800/327.7030) launches 10- to 15-day voyages throughout the Hawaiian Islands about twice a month, some that also go to Kiritimati (Christmas Island), others that begin and/or end in Vancouver, British Columbia; Seattle, Washington; Astoria, Oregon; or Victoria, British Columbia. Ports of call on the islands are: **Honolulu,** Oahu; **Kailua-Kona,** the Big Island; **Lahaina,** Maui; and **Lihue,** Kauai.

Alternatively, aspiring seafarers can go on a weeklong cruise on an **American Hawaii Cruises'** (800/765.7000) liner, a US-made craft that pulls into port in Kauai, Maui, and **Kona** and Hilo on the Big Island.

Local Lingo

In keeping with its cultural diversity, Hawaii has three languages—two official (English and Hawaiian) and one unofficial (pidgin). Virtually all islanders speak English, but it's usually infused with vernacular, sometimes to the point of incomprehensibility. The following list includes all the Hawaiian the average tourist needs to know, plus a few words and phrases in pidgin, a hodgepodge of languages originally developed to help traders communicate. However, to avoid becoming the humorous subject of a *pau hana* talk-story session (an after-work conversation among locals), visitors should probably limit themselves to "alohas" and "mahalos."

Aloha (ah-*low*-ha) Hello, good-bye, welcome, and love

Da kine (dah-*kine*) Pidgin for "that whatchamacallit" or anything else one doesn't know the word for or location of

Diamond Head East (as in: The library is Diamond Head of Bishop Street)

Ewa (*eh*-vah) West

Grinds Pidgin for food ("grind" is also used as a verb: to eat)

Hale (*hol*-lay) House

Hana (*hah*-nah) Work

Haole (*how*-lee) Pidgin for foreigner, normally used to refer to a Caucasian (sometimes in a derogatory sense)

Hawaiian time Pidgin for late (usually by about a half hour)

Heiau (*hey*-ow) Sacred temple, place of worship

J.O.J. Pidgin for tourists (stands for "Just Off the Jet")

Kamaaina (kah-mah-*eye*-nah) Native-born citizen (but usually refers to any resident or local)

Kane (*kah*-neh) Male

Kapu (kah-*poo*) Keep out, forbidden

Keiki (*kay*-key) Child

Kokua (koh-*coo*-ah) Help, assistance

Lanai (lah-*nigh*) Porch, balcony (also an island near Maui, pronounced lah-nah-*ee*)

Lua (*lew*-ah) Bathroom

Luau (*lew*-ow) Hawaiian feast

Mahalo (muh-*hah*-low) Thank you

Makai (muh-*kigh*) Toward the sea (used when giving directions)

Mauka (*mau*-kah) Toward the mountain (used when giving directions)

No ka oi (no-kah-*oy*) Is the best (as in: Maui *no ka oi*)

Ono (*oh*-no) Delicious (also a game fish)

Pakalolo (pah-kah-*low*-low) Marijuana

Pau (*pow*) Finished

Pau hana (pow *hah*-nah) After work

Puka (*poo*-kah) Hole

Pupu (*poo*-poo) Appetizer

Talk story Casual conversation

Wahine (wah-*hee*-nay) Woman or girl

Wikiwiki (*wee*-kee-*wee*-kee) Fast

Getting Around the Islands

Driving

Except on Oahu, public transportation in Hawaii is practically nonexistent. Unless you intend to stay at your hotel or prefer chartered bus tours, plan on renting a car to get around. The largest car-rental companies have booths at the main airports. The best deals are made in advance through mainland offices or as part of a vacation package; reservations are mandatory during peak seasons. Be prepared for a $2-per-day state surcharge and an optional Collision Damage Waiver (CDW) fee. (Some credit cards and personal insurance policies automatically cover you for collision damage and liability, so be sure to check in advance.) Also, many car-rental companies prohibit renters from driving cars on certain roads. Although the companies don't actually police the roads, they won't provide assistance if you break down on one or insurance coverage if you have an accident on one. For additional information on car rentals, see the Orientation sections of the individual island chapters.

The main roads are well paved almost everywhere on the islands, but heading out on unpaved terrain is highly recommended to those renting four-wheel-drive vehicles (they're available from many island car-rental companies—check first to make sure the four-wheel-drive capacity is connected). Often the end of the road is the beginning of the journey in Hawaii, especially on the isles with large wilderness areas, like Lanai and the Big Island.

Traffic jams have become commonplace on the most populated islands, so try to avoid driving during rush hours, as you'll rarely find alternate routes to the main roads (most of which follow the coastlines).

Also, keep in mind that it's a major *faux pas* to pass other cars at high speeds (some locals hate to be passed at any speed) or to honk your horn unless it's absolutely necessary (it's considered bad manners in the Aloha State). You'll also find other drivers motioning for you to go when they have the right of way (pay attention, or traffic will stop dead). And caution: Yellow traffic lights are heeded and the pertinent laws enforced.

Ferries

The only ferry operating in the Hawaiian Islands is *Expeditions* (661.3756, 800/695.2624), a shuttle between Lahaina on Maui and the island of Lanai. See the "Maui" or "Lanai" chapters for additional details.

Hiking

Hawaii was made for hikers. Whether you're in the heart of Honolulu or in the middle of nowhere on quiet Lanai, a trailhead is likely to be only a stone's throw away. You can climb an extinct volcano or tromp through the crater of a dormant one, hike into a desert or along a dramatic coastline, spend an hour on a well-maintained trail or a fortnight in the wilds. Wherever you hike, the trail inevitably leads to the island's heart and soul.

For information on specific trails, try **Hike Maui** (PO Box 330969, Kahului, HI 96732; 879.5270; www.hikemaui.com;), the **Molokai Ranch Outfitters Center** (PO Box 259, Maunaloa, HI 96770; 800/254.8871), or the **Sierra Club** (PO Box 2877, Honolulu, HI 96803, 536.6616).

Taxis

Cab service is available on all the islands, but it's not cheap, so first see if there's a shuttle headed your way. You can hail a cab at the airport or look in the yellow pages for local taxi companies (in **Waikiki** or Honolulu you may be able to hail one on the street). Fares are not regulated and can vary from company to company. Some cab companies charge a flat fee for long distances.

Tours

The top tour operators in the islands are **Robert's Hawaii** (539.9400), **Pleasant Island Holidays** (924.2286), and **Trans-Hawaiian Services** (566.7420). The first two offer vacation packages to Maui, Kauai, and the Big Island from Oahu that include flights, guided bus tours, lodging, and rental cars; the third offers bus tours of Oahu, Maui, Kauai, and the Big Island, but provides no air travel, car, or lodging. Among the sights included in most tours are the active **Kilauea** volcano on the Big Island, sunrise over the dormant **Haleakala Crater** on Maui, and Kauai's dramatic **Waimea Canyon.**

For information on bus, walking, helicopter, and other types of sight-seeing tours on each island, see the Orientation sections of the individual island chapters.

Walking

Hawaii's towns are well suited to walking tours. Be it Honolulu or **Kaunakakai,** Hilo or **Hanalei,** there's nowhere too big to explore in a day or two on foot. The only challenge is to slow your pace to Hawaiian time—tortoises will find more to savor in the small tropical towns than hares.

FYI

Accommodations

Peak tourist seasons are from June through August and December through February, when reservations for everything (especially hotel rooms and rental cars) are much harder to come by and more expensive. The rest of the year is considered off-season.

Bed-and-breakfast establishments are far more personal and private and often are in remote locations. A prominent bed-and-breakfast referral service is **Hawaii's Best Bed & Breakfast** (PO Box 563, Kamuela, HI 96743, 885.4550, 800/262.9912; fax 885.0559; www.bestbnb.com), run by longtime resident Barbara Campbell.

Villas of Hawaii (593.9660) rents luxury homes on Oahu, Maui, the Big Island, and Kauai for as little as a weekend and as long as a month. This can be a particularly affordable lodging option for families and groups. Most of the homes are on or near secluded beaches and have all the basic amenities and then some; guests often have pools, VCRs, water-sports equipment, exercise rooms, and kitchens with everything from microwaves to garlic presses at their disposal.

Accessibility for the Disabled

The **Commission on Persons with Disabilities** (586.8121) distributes a guide with accessibility ratings for most of the Hawaiian Islands' hotels, shopping centers, beaches, entertainment, and major visitor attractions. There's a nominal fee for the three-part guide. The commission also provides addresses and telephone numbers of support services on all the islands for visitors with disabilities.

Climate

Hawaii has basically two seasons. April through November is the warmer period, when the mercury usually hovers in the 75- to 88-degree range (although during August and September, the hottest, most humid months, temperatures frequently soar way up into the 90s). The coldest months are December through March, when evening temperatures can dip into the high 50s. The water temperature on all the islands is about 75 to 80 degrees, five degrees cooler during the winter.

Months	Average Temperature (°F)
December-February	78
March-May	80
June-August	85
September-November	82

Drinking

The legal drinking age in Hawaii is 21. In Waikiki on Oahu and Lahaina on Maui, the bar action starts at about 10PM and escalates until at least 2AM every night of the week. Places with cabaret licenses then fill up and stay that way until 4AM. The pace is far sleepier everywhere else. Throughout most of Kauai and the Big Island, bars begin to *close* at 10PM; on Friday and Saturday nights you may find one or two places where you can hang around and sip a beer until 1AM or so—but don't count on it. Grocery and convenience stores sell beer, wine, and liquor seven days a week.

Hours

Opening and closing times for shops, attractions, coffeehouses, tearooms, etc. are listed by day(s) only if normal hours (opening between 8 and 11 AM and closing between 4 and 7 PM) apply. In all other cases, specific hours will be given (e.g., 6AM-2PM, daily 24 hours, noon-5PM).

Money

All of Hawaii's banks take traveler's checks, and most stores and restaurants accept them as cash. For the real thing, there is a plethora of 24-hour ATMs scattered throughout the islands (except on Lanai). Banks are generally open Monday through Friday from 8:30AM to 3PM, although some branches stay open later on some days. Common foreign currency can be exchanged at most banks.

Personal Safety

Crime is not a big issue in the islands. That said, visitors should keep in mind that it isn't uncommon for cars at the islands' beach parks to be broken into while their owners are basking on the sand or riding the waves. Also be forewarned that Honolulu's **Hotel Street** area—as close as these islands get to a red-light district—is not the best place for an after-dinner stroll (although it's actually more sleazy than dangerous). Finally, be aware that local men in the **Waianae Coast** area of western Oahu, resentful of the imposition of the US way of life on Hawaiians, can sometimes be abrasive to tourists.

Publications

The two statewide dailies are *The Honolulu Advertiser* (a morning paper) and the *Honolulu Star-Bulletin* (an afternoon paper). *USA Today* and some other major mainland newspapers are sold in Hawaii also. Visitors can pick up free copies of a handful of weekly publications targeted at them, including *This Week Magazine, Drive Guide,* and *Spotlight Hawaii.* Each has editions for all the major islands, available at newsstands and convenience stores.

Honolulu, Aloha, and *Hawaii* are monthly magazines available at most newsstands. The first two cater to residents with features on business, entertainment, and lifestyles; the last targets visitors, covering local festivals, adventure travel, and attractions.

The monthly magazine *Island Lifestyles* is Oahu's primary gay and lesbian publication; it contains lists of events and local resources. Pick it up at **Hula's Bar & Lei Stand** (Waikiki Grand Hotel, 134 Kapahulu Ave, between Lemon Rd and Kalakaua Ave, Waikiki, 923.0669), the central gay and lesbian meeting place on Oahu.

Restaurants

Life in the islands is casual. In most restaurants, men look out of place in a jacket or tie. Reservations are recommended at elegant dining spots, however, particularly during the winter high season (December through February).

Shopping

People from everywhere but the smallest towns will probably find shopping for basic necessities cheaper and easier at home. But when it comes to locally made items, Hawaii really shines. Kona coffee, hardy tropical flower arrangements, koa wood bowls, macadamia-nut candies, tropical fruit jelly, muumuus, aloha shirts, and many other locally produced items all make good gifts or souvenirs.

Smoking
No smoking is permitted in Hawaii's public buildings, elevators, or movie theaters, and sections for smokers in island restaurants are rare.

Taxes
The state sales tax, paid in shops and restaurants, is four percent. A hotel tax tacked onto the bill at all lodging places adds another 6.17 percent to room rates.

Telephones
The area code for all Hawaiian Islands is 808. For interisland telephone calls, dial "1" and the area code before the number.

Time Zone
During standard time, it's two hours earlier in Hawaii than on the West Coast and five hours earlier than on the East Coast. Hawaii does not follow Daylight Saving Time (DST), so when the mainland is on DST (the first Sunday in April to the last Sunday in October), Hawaii is three hours behind the West Coast and six hours behind the East Coast.

Tipping
Standard tips are 15 to 20 percent for waiters, waitresses, and bartenders; $2 a day for maids; 15 percent of the fare and $1 per bag for cab drivers; and $3 to $5 for bellhops, depending on the extent of their burden.

Visitors' Information Centers
The Oahu office of the **Hawaii Visitors and Convention Bureau** (**HVCB**; 2270 Kalakaua Ave, No. 801, Honolulu, HI 96815, 923.1811; fax 924.0290) is the locus of island information. It's open Monday through Friday from 8AM to 4:30PM. For information on other **HVCB** offices, see the Orientation sections of the individual island chapters.

Phone Book

Emergencies
Ambulance/Fire/Police 911

AAA Emergency Road Service.............800/222.4357

Poison Control Center 800/941.4441

Visitors' Information
American Youth Hostels.........946.0591 (Oahu only)

Better Business Bureau ....536.6956 (Oahu only)

Handicapped Visitors' Information
....586.8121 (Oahu only)

Weather ....973.4381 (Oahu only)

Parades and Pageants in Paradise

If there's one thing Hawaii residents know how to do, it's celebrate. Perhaps that's because Hawaii is a melting pot of cultures and traditions, or maybe it's simply that with its endless summers, no one can think of any real reason not to. Whatever the reason, the 50th state has more official holidays than any of its 49 counterparts. Following are some of Hawaii's biggest and brightest events. For more details, call the number given at the end of each celebration's description. If none appears, contact the **Hawaii Visitors and Convention Bureau** (923.1811) for more information.

January
First Night The streets of **Honolulu** are packed with thousands of residents and visitors ringing in the New Year to the sounds of the top contemporary Hawaiian bands.

NFL Pro Bowl Early in January, the top teams from both conferences kick off the New Year with an all-star game at **Oahu's Aloha Stadium.** For more information, call 486.9300.

Chinese New Year Repair to **Chinatown** in Honolulu after the first lunar moon (between 21 January and 20 February) for lion dances, a fireworks display, and general merriment.

February
Mauna Kea Ski Meet Weather permitting, Hawaii's skiers take to the slopes of the **Big Island** volcano for this annual downhill race, held on a mid-month Saturday. Bring your bikini. For more information, call 943.6643.

March
Honolulu International Bed Race Teams from local restaurants, bars, and businesses compete to see who can push a bed on wheels over the **Waikiki** finish line first. The madness, which benefits area charities, usually takes place on the third Saturday of the month. For more information, call 735.6092.

April
Merrie Monarch Festival If you want to understand the deep spirituality of the hula, this **Hilo** event is one to plan a trip around. Lasting for a week at the start of the month, it gives onlookers the chance to see both *auwana* (ancient) and *kahiko* (modern) styles of dance in an awe-inspiring series of nightly performances. Tickets, though inexpensive, are sold out about a year ahead, so call the **Hawaii Visitors and Convention Bureau** in Hilo (961.5797) as far in advance as possible.

May
Lei Day "May Day is Lei Day in Hawaii," goes the singsong phrase chanted in playgrounds all over the state. The first of the month is a time to buy leis for your loved ones; the day is celebrated with pageants around the state. For more information, call 266.7654.

Hawaii State Fair Held in Honolulu on two weekends at the end of the month, this is much like state fairs everywhere, except that the refreshments may be unfamiliar. Try the passion-orange-guava juice (known as "POG") and *mochi* candy (a deep-fried rice-flour cracker in soy-sauce batter). It's a good opportunity to mingle with island residents on Oahu. For more information, call 488.3389.

June

Hawaii State Horticultural Show This is *the* event in the US for orchid lovers. Hundreds of different varieties are displayed in Hilo's **Edith Kamakawiwoole Stadium** during the third weekend of the month.

O Bon Japanese Festival Candlelight ceremonies and dancing are featured at this Japanese commemoration of the dead, held from the end of June into August throughout the islands. The festivities are especially colorful in **Haleiwa** on Oahu.

July

Run to the Sun Though the grueling 37-mile road race up the side of Maui's 10,023-foot **Haleakala** volcano is not a great spectator sport, it can be fun to hang out in surrounding **Upcountry** towns and greet the hundreds of runners after their ordeal. Would-be participants should pencil in the second Saturday in July. For more information, call 871.6441.

Parker Ranch Rodeo Hawaiian cowboys are called *paniolos*, but they ride like their mainland counterparts. They show their stuff at this rodeo, which takes place mid-month at the country's second-largest ranch in the Big Island town of **Waimea**. For more information, call 885.7311.

Prince Lot Hula Festival If you can't attend the **Merrie Monarch Festival** (see above), try this event at Oahu's **Moanalua Gardens** on the third Saturday of July. It isn't as big as the April festival, but tickets are easier to get, and you'll come away with insight into the Hawaiian people and their *mana* (spirit). For more information, call 839.5334.

Volcano Wilderness Marathon The rough-and-tumble wilderness around the Big Island's **Kilauea** volcano is the venue for a marathon and a 10-kilometer (6-mile) race, both usually held on the last Saturday of the month. If you've never run a marathon before, we don't suggest that you start with this one. For more information, call 967.8222.

Hawaii International Jazz Festival Held on Oahu for four days during the last week of the month, this annual event pulls in artists from Ukraine to Allentown. For more information, call 941.9974.

August

Trans-Pacific Race This LA-to-Honolulu sailboat race takes place during August in odd-numbered years. Yachts arrive throughout the month and converge on the **Ala Wai Yacht Harbor** on Oahu, where the password is "party."

Kona's Hawaiian Billfish Tournament The town of **Kona** on the Big Island teems with activity (an unusual state of affairs here) during the last week of August as sportfishers from the other islands and the West Coast compete. For more information, call 329.6155.

September

Aloha Week This is big stuff. Buy an Aloha Week ribbon and join in the parades, luaus, pageants, presentations, and other events celebrating the spirit of aloha on all islands. The festivities generally take place in mid-September. For more information, call 589.1771.

October

Ironman Triathlon Even if your last bike had training wheels, you can barely dog paddle, and the only thing you run is errands, watching the Big Island's **Ironman** competition, particularly at the finish line at about 10PM, is a moving experience. Senior citizens, the disabled, and couples are some of the thousands of people you'll see completing a 26.2-mile run, a 2.4-mile swim, and a 112-mile bike ride in the Kona heat on the first Saturday of the month. For more information, call 329.0063.

November

Hard Rock Cafe's Triple Crown of Surfing The top dogs on the surf circuit are drawn to the **Banzai Pipeline** and other amazing two-story waves to vie for big money and the chance to wave at Mom on TV. If you're on Oahu for this event (usually during the third week of the month), don't miss it. For more information, call 955.7383.

Honolulu International Film Festival If you don't mind subtitles, the Pacific Rim films screened throughout the islands during this annual event make novel and intermittently dazzling entertainment. For more information, call 528.HIFF.

December

Pacific Handcrafters' Fair For unique Christmas gifts, from flowered muumuus to woven mats to koa wood boxes, head for this crafts fair at **Thomas Square** in Honolulu; it takes place on one of the first two weekends of December. For more information, call 254.6788.

Honolulu Marathon The 26.2-mile race, held on the second Saturday in December, draws the third-largest field of any marathon in the nation. This wouldn't be a bad choice for a first marathon. For more information, call 734.7200.

KEELY EDWARDS

The Big Island

This southernmost isle is formally known as Hawaii, although it's commonly referred to as the Big Island to avoid confusion with Hawaii, the state. Despite its relatively enormous size—4,038 square miles—this is Hawaii's least-visited major island, with only about 1.1 million tourists a year. The low turnout is probably due to rumors that the island is covered with lava, has no beaches, and offers little or nothing to do after dark. This last may be partly true—party hounds and searching singles will fare much better on Maui or Oahu—but the rest is pure bunk. Lush vegetation covers most of the Big Island's windward side, and uncrowded white-sand beaches line the western coast. Unlike on Kauai, you can lose yourself for days here without seeing another soul; unlike on Oahu, no hordes of tourists or unsavory characters are around; unlike on Maui, nobody will want to sell you time-share deals. Another plus—because tourism has such a low impact on the resident population, which depends mostly on agriculture and livestock for income, the locals are particularly warm and receptive to visitors.

As any resident will tell you, the islands of Hawaii are vastly different from each other in character, and the Big Island is often viewed as the introverted sister, quietly earning recognition yet maintaining an unmistakable distance from the family of isles. Once understood and appreciated, however, the Big Island becomes an easy favorite among romantics, recluses, and adventurers.

The Big Island is frequently described as a miniature continent, with rain forests lining the windward coasts in the east, immense snowdrifts resting atop **Mauna Kea** volcano, grassy plains stretching around **Waimea**, and miles of desert and lava beds dominating the **Kohala Coast**.

What is so extraordinary about this environmental diversity is that it can all be witnessed in a leisurely three-hour drive from **Hilo** to **Kailua-Kona** (towns on opposite sides of the island) across the undeservedly maligned **Saddle Road** (which is actually a quite pleasant, albeit sometimes rough, route).

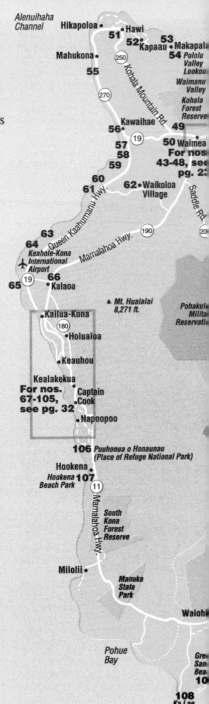

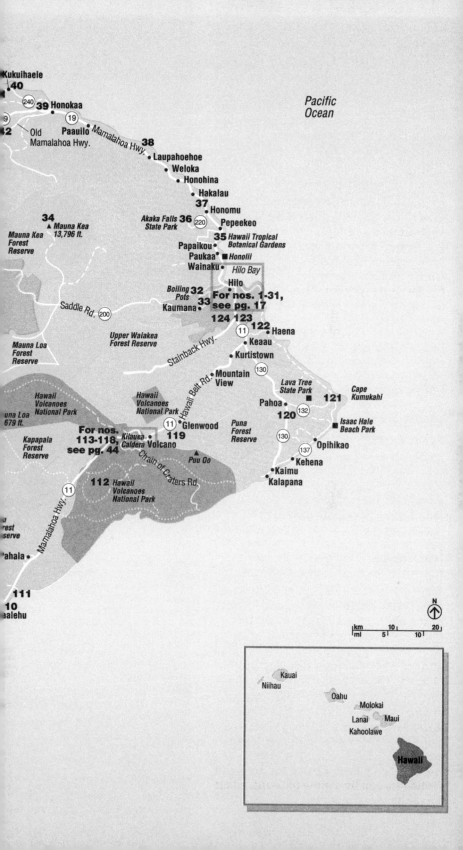

Pacific
Ocean

Kukuihaele
40

(240) **39** Honokaa

(19)

Old **Paauilo** Mamalahoa Hwy.
Mamalahoa Hwy.

38

Laupahoehoe

Weloka

Honohina

Hakalau

37 Honomu

34 Mauna Kea
13,796 ft.
Mauna Kea
Forest
Reserve

Akaka Falls **36** (220) Pepeekeo
State Park

35 Hawaii Tropical
Papaikou Botanical Gardens
Paukaa ■ Honolii
Wainaku

Hilo Bay

Boiling **32** Hilo
Pots
33 For nos. 1-31,
Kaumana see pg. 17

124 123

Saddle Rd. (200)

(11) **122** Haena

Keaau

Upper Waiakea
Forest Reserve

Kurtistown

Mauna Loa
Forest
Reserve

Stainback Hwy.

(130)

Mountain
View

Lava Tree
State Park ■ **121** Cape
Kumukahi

Hawaii
Volcanoes
National Park

Hawaii
Volcanoes
National Park

Pahoa **120** (132)

■ Isaac Hale
Beach Park

una Loa
679 ft.

Kapapala
Forest
Reserve

(11) **119** Glenwood

Kilauea
Caldera Volcano

For nos.
113-118,
see pg. 44

Puna
Forest
Reserve

(130)

(137) Opihikao

Kehena

Puu Oo

Kaimu

Kalapana

(11) **112** Hawaii
Volcanoes
National Park

Chain of Craters Rd.

Mamalahoa Hwy.

rest
serve

111
10
aalehu

ahala

N

km   10   20
ml   5   10

Kauai
Niihau

Oahu

Molokai

Lanai   Maui
Kahoolawe

Hawaii

Geologically, the Big Island, with Hawaii's only active volcanoes, is still in its youth. A little more than a million years old, the landscape has become more defined with erosion yet continues to grow with every volcanic eruption. Of the five volcanoes that make up the island, Mauna Kea would be the tallest in the world if measurements were taken from the ocean floor, and **Mauna Loa**, whose last eruption was in 1984, is the world's largest active volcano. But a significantly smaller volcano, **Kilauea** (pronounced *Keel*-oh-*ay*-ah), is the one that always steals the show. In a continual state of eruption since 1983, Kilauea has earned its title as the most active volcano in the world. Located within **Hawaii Volcanoes National Park**, the island's most popular attraction, Kilauea is also home to the Hawaiian fire goddess, a moody spirit known as Madame Pele (pronounced *Pay*-lay).

To properly tour this island takes at least one to two weeks, with two or three days devoted to each of its six main regions. Although each section is only a short drive from the others, all six are astoundingly different in climate and scenery, making it possible to condense several unique vacations into one. Start out in Hilo, a rural city ensconced in beautiful rain forests, and don't neglect neighboring **Puna**, an area where mainland refugees and retro-hippies make their home. Then pack up and drive to rustic Waimea, an island anomaly of green pastures, grazing cattle, weathered Hawaiian cowboys, and a few excellent restaurants and shops. Explore quaint and quiet **North Kohala**, then continue down the Kohala Coast to Kona, poking about the dozens of ancient ruins near the most sun-drenched beaches in the country. Head south to remote **Kau**, where the beaches are windswept and dramatic. For a grand finale, explore the Kilauea volcano and stay overnight in the rustic town of **Volcano** with its charming collection of buildings.

Area code 808 unless otherwise noted.

Getting to the Big Island

Airports

Hilo International Airport

Four miles east of downtown Hilo, this small, island-style airport has three attached buildings forming a single terminal. About 65 flights arrive and depart daily; no nonstop mainland flights land here.

Airport Services

Airport Emergencies	934.5801
Information	934.5839
Parking	969.6642

Airlines

Aloha	935.5771, 800/367.5250
Hawaiian	800/882.8811
from the mainland	800/367.5320

Since the Kilauea Volcano began its current phase of eruption in 1983, 181 homes have been destroyed and 35 square miles covered by 2,000-degree magma, but 500 acres have been added to the Big Island's landmass.

Getting to and from Hilo International Airport

By Bus

No public buses serve the airport, though the **Hawaii Naniloa Hotel** (see page 15) provides shuttle service for its guests.

By Car

The airport is a 10-minute drive from the heart of Hilo. Upon leaving the airport, turn right on **Route 11** to reach the downtown area; taking a left on **Waianuenue Avenue** will bring you to a handful of streets lined with restaurants and shops. Traffic isn't a problem. Reverse the directions to get to the airport from downtown.

The following car-rental companies have service counters at **Hilo International Airport.** They stay open until about a half hour after the last flight of the day lands.

Alamo	961.3343, 800/327.9633
Avis	935.1290, 800/331.1212
Budget	935.6878, 800/527.0700
Dollar	961.6059, 800/800.4000
Hertz	935.2896, 800/654.3011
National	935.0891, 800/227.7368

By Taxi

Cabs wait in front of the baggage claim area. Alternatively, call **Ace One Taxi** (935.8303) or **Hilo Harry's Taxi** (935.7091). The fare to Hilo is about $12.

Keahole-Kona International Airport

About seven miles north of Kona on the west side of the island, **Keahole-Kona International Airport** is a typical island airport: larger than a postage stamp and busier than a deserted island. The airport handles about 60 flights a day, most of them interisland.

Airport Services

Airport Emergencies	329.2855
Information	329.3432
Lost and Found	329.5073
Parking	329.5404

Airlines

Aloha	935.5771, 800/367.5250
Hawaiian	326.5615, 800/367.5320
United	800/241.6522

Getting to and from Keahole-Kona International Airport

By Bus

No public buses serve the small airport, but most **Waikoloa** hotels provide transportation for guests.

By Car

After leaving the airport, take a right on **Route 19** to go south into Kailua-Kona; take a left on Route 19 to head north to the Waikoloa resorts. Kona is a 15-minute drive away; Waikoloa, 25 minutes. There is no traffic. To get to the airport from Kona and Waikoloa, reverse the directions.

The following car-rental companies have counters at **Keahole-Kona International Airport.** They stay open until about a half hour after the last flight of the day lands.

Alamo	329.8896, 800/327.9633
Avis	327.3000, 800/331.1212
Budget	329.8511, 800/527.0700
Dollar	329.3161, 800/800.4000
Hertz	329.3566, 800/654.3011
National	329.1674, 800/227.7368

By Taxi

Cabs wait in front of the baggage claim area. The fare to Kona is about $20; to Waikoloa, about $40.

Interisland Carriers

Aloha Airlines and **Hawaiian Airlines** offer direct service between the Big Island and Oahu and Kahului on Maui (flights to other islands go through Honolulu).

Getting Around the Big Island

Bicycles and Mopeds

Mopeds aren't very common on the Big Island. The shoulders of the roads are narrow or nonexistent, so be sure you are willing to keep up with traffic (at least 30 mph) on the road that circles the island before checking into the offerings at **DJ's Rentals** (75-5663 Palani Rd, between Alii Dr and Kuakini Hwy, Kailua-Kona, 329.1700; harleys@aloha.net). **DJ's** has mopeds, and also rents motorcycles. **Hawaiian Pedals** (Kona Inn Shopping Village, 75-5744 Alii Dr, at Hualalai Rd, Kailua-Kona, 329.2294) rents mountain bikes. For a cycling vacation, contact **Backroads Bicycle Touring** (801 Cedar St, Berkeley, CA 94710, 510/527.1555).

Buses

The **Hele-On Bus** (961.8744) operates daily from 7AM to 6PM, running from Hilo to **Honokaa,** Waimea, Kau, and Kailua-Kona. But bus service is very infrequent and inconvenient here—even residents don't use it.

Driving

The Big Island's major roads are smoothly paved and inviting. The main "highway" (if you can call it that) circles the island, with many of the side roads accessible to four-wheel-drive vehicles only. Those who use such a vehicle (available through many island car-rental companies) will have no limit to their explorations. Saddle Road, a shortcut across the island, isn't maintained and is designated as off-limits in most car-rental contracts, although at press time the federal government was repaving the road. Kona has one main street, **Alii Drive,** which runs along the coast; Hilo, a less tourist-oriented town, is set up in a grid pattern. Unless you're four-wheeling, it's hard to get lost on this island. Car-rental companies at the airports are listed above.

Hiking

The prime destination for savvy hikers and back-packers is **Waipio Valley** on the island's north shore and neighboring **Waimanu Valley,** where the number of waterfalls usually exceeds the number of people around to gaze at them. Waimanu Valley is accessible only by foot or kayak, the latter only in the late summer when the sea is gentle. Less ambitious forays may be enjoyed in every corner of the Big Island, including **Hawaii Volcanoes National Park,** whose trails offer varying degrees of exertion and exhilaration.

Limousines

Few people take limos on the island because of its large size and casual atmosphere, but some firms do offer tours, including **A Touch of Class Limousines** (325.0775). Their rate is $83 an hour with a two-hour minimum.

Parking

Parking is no challenge. Rarely will drivers need to use metered spaces—in the towns large enough to warrant them (there's no charge on Sundays)—as free parking is available nearly everywhere.

Taxis

It's difficult to hail a taxi here; call **Aloha Taxi** (325.5448) on the Kona or Kohala coasts or **Ace One Taxi** (935.8303) in the Hilo area. Be sure to call at least a half hour before you want to depart—cab drivers run on "Hawaiian time."

Tours

Paradise Safaris (322.2366; parsaf@maunakea.com) runs daily seven-hour tours of the Mauna Kea volcano. A daylong tour that circles the entire island and covers its most popular attractions—**Puuhonua o Honaunau (Place of Refuge National Park),** a coffee plantation, Mauna Kea, a sugarcane plantation, the Kona Coast, **Punaluu Black Sand Beach Park, Parker Ranch,** and a macadamia-nut factory—is offered by **Robert's Hawaii** (329.1688). **Hawaii Pack and Paddle** (328.8911; gokayak@kona.net; www.hawaiipackandpaddle.com) offers half-day, full-day, and multiday kayak trips along the island's rugged western coastline, as well as boat rentals. Alternatively, **Waipio Valley Shuttle** (775.7121) runs a 1.5-hour driving tour of the valley in a four-wheel-drive vehicle. **Hawaiian Walkways** (885.7759) offers a variety of daylong hiking tours, including treks in **Hawaii Volcanoes National Park** and the North Kohala region. Custom hikes also can be arranged.

Contact **Captain Zodiac** (329.3199; seakayak@interpac.net) for a four-hour cruise from **Honokohau Harbor** to **Kealakekua Bay.** The boat hugs the coast, giving passengers a chance to see caves and the **Captain Cook Monument** before it stops for snorkeling.

Blue Hawaiian Helicopters (961.5600; blue@maui.net) at **Hilo International Airport** and **Hawaii Helicopters** (329.4700; hiheli@hawaiian.net) at **Keahole-Kona International Airport** are two of the several dozen flight-seeing tours that offer bird's-eye views of the island. **Waipio Na'alapa Trail Rides** (PO Box 992, Honokaa, HI 96727, 775.0419) offers horseback tours along Waipio Valley's rivers and streams, including the stunning **Hiilawe Waterfall.** A four-wheel-drive vehicle transports you a thousand feet down (on a steep road) and across the valley to the stables. Three-hour tours are offered Monday through Saturday. **Kings' Trail Rides O' Kona** (323.2890) in the country town of **Kealakekua** offers both beach and mountain half-day rides daily for all levels of equestrians; picnic lunches are included.

Walking

All towns on the Big Island are small enough to be explored end to end in a day or less. No real hills get in the walker's way either, although the midday heat in the summer can make lengthy hikes unpleasant.

FYI

Shopping

The shop-'til-you-drop strip in Kona is **Alii Drive,** a road that runs for several miles along the coast.

On the strip you'll find a collection of coffee and fruit vendors; booths offering muumuus and other alohawear; salespeople hawking tours and excursions; real estate offices; restaurants; and shops selling fashions made everywhere from Bali to Tibet, T-shirts, and surfwear and equipment.

In Hilo, the street to stroll is **Kamehameha Avenue,** anchored at one end by a farmer's market, and the other—a few blocks down—by a restaurant and bar called **Cronies** (see page 19). Also present are the ubiquitous superchains, **Wal-Mart, Kmart, Borders, Office Depot,** which unsurprisingly carry nothing unique to Hawaii.

Tickets

Tickets for most cultural events on the Big Island are available at **Mele Kai Music** in Kona (74-5467 Kaiwi St, between Kuakini and Queen Kaahumanu Hwys, 329.1454) and **Tempo Music** (Prince Kuhio Plaza, 111 E Puainako St, at Kanoelehua Ave, 959.4599) in Hilo.

Visitors' Information Centers

Offices of the **Hawaii Visitors and Convention Bureau (HVCB)** are in Hilo (250 Keawe St, at Haili St, 961.5797; fax 961.2126; gapplegate@hvcb.org) and in Kailua-Kona (Kona Plaza, 75-5719 Alii Dr, at Sarona Rd, 329.7787; fax 326.7563; gapplegate@hvcb.org). Both are open Monday through Friday.

Phone Book

Emergencies

Ambulance/Fire/Police	911
AAA Emergency Road Service	800/222.4357
Hilo Medical Center	974.4700
Kona Community Hospital	322.9311
Pharmacy	959.4508, 329.1632
Police (nonemergency)	935.3311
Poison Control	800/362.3585

Visitors' Information

Better Business Bureau	808/941.5222
Handicapped Visitors' Info.	961.8211, 322.0182
Time	961.0212

Hilo

The beaches are small, the shores are rocky, and the climate is wet, but this town—the island's largest, and the county seat—is full of beautiful, exotic blooms, has a lively seaport, and is the site of the Merrie Monarch Festival (see "Parades and Pageants in Paradise" on page 8). Hilo has been hit hard twice by tidal waves—in 1946 and in 1960—that inflicted very heavy damages on the waterfront district. Some of the old architecture remains, however, and a number of new shops have opened over the past few years.

1 Onekahakaha Beach Park With safe swimming, small tidal pools, picnic and camping facilities, and plenty of parking, this is the nicest beach in Hilo (especially for small children)—which isn't saying much. On the downside are dingy gray sand and a contingent of local homeless people. True beach lovers will want to head south for the Puna Coast, but this stretch of sand will do in a pinch. ♦ Onekahakaha Rd and Keokea Loop Rd

2 Arnott's Lodge $ Although it isn't listed with American Youth Hostels, this is mainly a backpackers' lodge. Close to the beaches but a long walk from shops and restaurants, the clean and friendly place has three three-bedroom dormitories (one for men, one for women, and one co-ed) that sleep a dozen people each, plus six two-bedroom suites (including kitchens) that sleep eight. All rooms and suites have shared baths; none have TVs or phones. There's no restaurant, but guests have free rein of the shared kitchen, a bonus for budget-conscious travelers. Tenting is another possiblity for those travelers who really want to save money. ♦ 98 Apapane Rd (between Onekahakaha and Keokea Loop Rds). 969.7097, 800/368.8752; fax 961.9638 &

3 Harrington's ★★$$$ Local seafood enthusiasts who come for the chowder, catch of the day, or fresh shellfish also get to admire the view of tranquil Reed's Bay. For Hilo, this is as romantic as it gets. ♦ Seafood ♦ Daily dinner. 135 Kalanianaole Ave (at Luana St). 961.4966 &

4 Hilo Seaside Hotel $$ The nicer of the 135 rooms have private lanais overlooking a picturesque lagoon. Nothing fancy here, but the pleasant accommodations have cable TVs and refrigerators. Some rooms are air-conditioned, and there's a good, inexpensive restaurant. ♦ 126 Banyan Way (between Kalanianaole Ave and Banyan Dr). 935.0821, 800/560.5557; fax 969.9195; www.sand-seaside.com/hilo.html &

5 Banyan Drive Named for the numerous banyan trees planted here by dignitaries and celebrities during the 1930s, the drive fronts a chain of hotels along Hilo Bay. Plaques at the bases of the trees reveal the names of donors, including such notables as Babe Ruth and Amelia Earhart.

5 Naniloa Country Club This flat, 9-hole course (par 35, 2,875 yards) is across from the **Hawaii Naniloa Hotel,** whose guests may take advantage of a substantial discount. ♦ Inexpensive greens fees. Daily; call ahead for weekend starting times.120 Banyan.Dr (between Kamehameha Ave and Lihiwai St). 935.3000

6 Hawaii Naniloa Hotel $$ The best of the limited choices in Hilo, this hotel commands a fine location, with views of Hilo Bay. Three wings contain 306 rooms and 19 suites, a health spa, a lounge, and one continental and one Chinese restaurant. The decor is Japanese, with lots of pink marble. ♦ 93 Banyan Dr (between Banyan Way and Lihiwai St). 969.3333, 800/367.5360; fax 969.6622; www.planet-hawaii.com/sand/naniloa &

6 Uncle Billy's Hilo Bay Hotel $$ Uncle Billy Kimi (who also runs **Uncle Billy's Kona Bay Hotel,** see page 37) believes in keeping prices down at the expense of ambience, hence the lobby video games. The 140 rooms serve their purpose; all have TVs, air-conditioning, and phones. There's a pool, restaurant, and shops. ♦ 87 Banyan Dr (between Banyan Way and Lihiwai St). 961.5818, 800/442.5841 in Hawaii, 800/367.5102; fax 935.7903; unclebillys@aloha.net; www.unclebilly.com &

7 Hilo Hawaiian Hotel $$ The views from the private lanais of the 268 rooms and 18 suites here are the best in Hilo, and the seafood buffet on Friday and Saturday is worth checking out. Baseball legend Babe Ruth planted the banyan tree in front of the hotel. Amenities include a pool, restaurant, bar, and shops. ♦ 71 Banyan Dr (between Banyan Way and Lihiwai St). 935.9361, 800/272.5275 in Hawaii, 800/367.5004; fax 961.9642; www.castle-group.com &

8 Liliuokalani Gardens Meditation mavens will find solace and harmony in this elaborate 30-acre Japanese garden, a popular picnic site. The manicured grounds contain pagodas, stone lanterns, bridges, and tidal pools. Follow the footpath to tiny Coconut Island for a sweeping view of Hilo Bay. ♦ Lihiwai St and Banyan Dr

9 Nihon Restaurant and Cultural Center ★$$ Although this authentically decorated Japanese restaurant and art gallery serves decent meals, your best bet is a round of sake and sushi at the lanai bar overlooking Hilo Bay, Mauna Kea, Mauna Loa, and **Liliuokalani Gardens.** ♦ Japanese ♦ M-Sa lunch and dinner. Reservations recommended. 123 Lihiwai St (between Kamehameha Ave and Banyan Dr). 969.1133 &

10 Suisan Fish Market Early risers can watch Hilo's fishing fleet unload its catch at what old-timers know as Sampan Harbor. The auctioneer uses a patois of English, Hawaiian, Japanese, and a bit of pidgin. Set the alarm and come experience a thriving bastion of local color. ♦ Free. M-Sa; auction 8AM. Lihiwai St (between Kamehameha Ave and Banyan Dr)

11 K.K. Tei ★$$ This is the Japanese restaurant of choice among many local residents. If you have more than six people in your party, reserve one of the *ozashiki* rooms overlooking the bonsai garden. Try the sukiyaki or the seafood specialties. Entrées range from good to gourmet, so consult your waiter before ordering. ♦ Japanese ♦ Daily dinner. Reservations recommended. 1550 Kamehameha Ave (at Manono St). 961.3791 &

12 Ken's Pancake House ★$$ Located on the way to the airport, this reliable place is the only 24-hour restaurant in Hilo. Have the macadamia-nut pancakes or one of the wild waffle combinations—ask for an order with bananas and macadamia nuts (they're mixed right into the batter). ♦ Cafeteria ♦ Daily 24 hours. 1730 Kamehameha Ave (at Kanoelehua Ave). 935.8711 &

13 Fiasco's $$ The large selection of Mexican, American, Chinese, and Italian food available here should take care of just about any craving you might have, though the quality of the food is touch and go. Treat yourself to one of the house-specialty fajitas. ♦ International ♦ Daily lunch and dinner. Waiakea Square, 200 Kanoelehua Ave (at Kuawa St). 935.7666 &

14 Waiakea Plaza Most of the outlets in this modern megacenter—like **Office Mart** and **Ross Dress for Less**—won't have much appeal to visitors, but there are notable exceptions. ♦ Daily. 301 E Makaala St (at Kanoelehua Ave). No phone &

Within Waiakea Plaza:

Borders Books & Music No. 205 of this highly successful national chain carries more than 10,000 books and nearly as many CDs. Despite its high prices, the cafe is a good place for those who want to page through a new purchase without delay. ♦ Daily. 933.1410 & Also at: 75-1000 Henry St (at Queen Kaahumanu Hwy), Kailua-Kona. 331.1668 &

Black sand is created when 2,000-degree lava hits cool water and explodes.

Restaurants/Clubs: Red   Hotels: Blue
Shops/ ⟁ Outdoors: Green   Sights/Culture: Black

ISLAND NATURALS

Island Naturals Market and Deli ★$ If you've been having trouble finding vegetarian or other healthy cuisine in Hilo, this grocery and deli—which features a by-the-pound gourmet bar and alfresco seating—is the place to visit. ♦ Health Food ♦ Daily. 935.5533 &

15 Prince Kuhio Plaza Fashion is a relative term at this $47.5-million shopping complex, which includes **Liberty House, Sears, Hilo Hattie, Safeway, Longs,** and many other retailers. There's not much typically Hawaiian here; this shoppers' haven could be any mainland mall. ♦ Daily. 111 E Puainako St (at Kanoelehua Ave). 959.3555 &

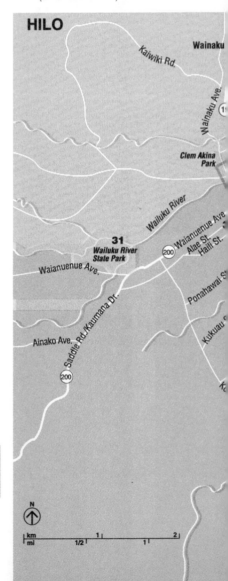

Home Style Japanese Cooking

16 Miyo's ★★$ Local Japanese-food aficionados (and Hilo is the town for them) assemble at this popular restaurant at the edge of Waiakea Pond. The dining room overlooks the pond, with parks and curved bridges in the distance. Specialties include *soba* (buckwheat noodles), *shabu-shabu* (a cook-it-yourself soup in an earthenware pot), sesame chicken, and broiled salmon. ♦ Japanese ♦ Tu-Sa lunch and dinner. Waiakea Villas, 400 Hualani St (west of Mililani St). 935.2273 &

17 Restaurant Miwa ★★★$$ One of Hilo's best Japanese restaurants is in one of the worst locations—in the corner of dilapidated **Hilo Shopping Center.** The simple interior is the perfect setting in which to enjoy the seasonal menu that includes Kona crab, Bangkok shrimp, *shabu-shabu,* sake-flavored steamed clams, and sushi. Sweet tooths will love the *haupia* (coconut) cream pie. ♦ Japanese ♦ M-Sa lunch and dinner; Su dinner. Hilo Shopping Center, 1261 Kilauea Ave (at Kekuanaoa St). 961.4454 &

18 Scruffles $ For a real taste of local cuisine, stop at this drive-in, take-out, sit-down eatery

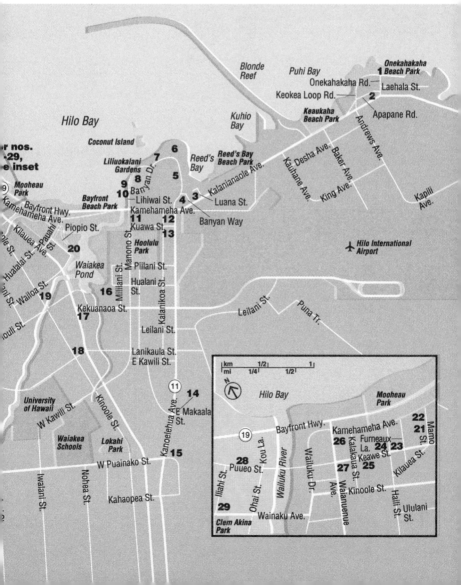

where Hilo families and business people munch fish tempura and a vast variety of sushi. ♦ Asian/American ♦ Daily breakfast, lunch, and dinner. 1438 Kilauea Ave (at W Lanikaula St). 935.6664 ♿

19 Sun Sun Lau ★$ Cantonese fare, including shrimp Canton, cake noodle, and fresh abalone soup, is served in a building optimistically designed for droves of customers. Extensive is the operative word for the dinner menu as well as the selection of "crackseed," a Chinese snack of preserved and seasoned fruits and seeds that's a favorite with local kids. ♦ Chinese ♦ M-Tu, Th-Su lunch and dinner. 1055 Kinoole St (between Mohouli and Wailoa Sts). 935.2808 ♿

20 Wailoa Visitor Center At this 10-sided building, the friendly staff will advise you on local activities. Then check out the 24 changing exhibitions on Hawaiian art, history, and culture, and the permanent photographic display of post-tsunami Hilo. ♦ Free. M-F. 200 Piopio St (east of Pauahi St). 933.0416 ♿

21 Royal Siam ★★$ This spotlessly clean, unpretentious little restaurant offers more than 50 consistently good Thai dishes at every spice level from mild to aaaahhhh! The basil chicken and yellow curry beef are especially good. ♦ Thai ♦ M-Sa lunch and dinner. 70 Mamo St (between Kamehameha Ave and Keawe St). 961.6100 ♿

22 Hilo Farmers Market Local color abounds at this festive fair. Come early for the best buys on fresh vegetables, flowers and plants, baked goods, and arts and crafts from more than 80 vendors. Truly an ethnic bonanza, the market offers *malasadas* (Portuguese doughnuts), pickled turnips, *warabi* (fern shoots), orchids, winged beans, papayas, and various other exotic items. A number of well-known Big Island artists got their start right here. ♦ W, Sa 6AM-2PM. Kamehameha Ave and Mamo St ♿

22 Reuben's Mexican Restaurant ★$ When you gotta have it, you gotta have it. Hilo's only Mexican restaurant serves such classic south-of-the-border fare as chicken *flautas* (fried corn tortillas) and steak ranchero. With festive posters on the walls and colorful tissue paper covering the ceiling, every day here is a fiesta. ♦ Mexican ♦ M-Sa lunch and dinner. 336 Kamehameha Ave (between Mamo St and Furneaux La). 961.2552 ♿

There are no snakes in Hawaii.

22 Cafe Pesto ★★★$$ A chic yuppie pizzeria, this restaurant has all the trimmings, including an open kitchen, wood-fired oven, black-and-white decor, and an outstanding menu. Try the artichoke pizza with fresh shiitake and oyster mushrooms and rosemary-gorgonzola sauce. If you're celebrating, splurge on an order of mango-glazed chicken. ♦ Pacific Regional ♦ Daily lunch and dinner. 308 Kamehameha Ave (between Mamo St and Furneaux La). 969.6640 ♿ Also at: Kawaihae Shopping Center, Rte 270 (west of Queen Kaahumanu Hwy), Kawaihae. 882.1071 ♿

23 Pescatore ★★$$$ Upscale Northern Italian dishes are served at upscale prices. Start with the *calamari fritti* (fried squid) and then dive into the *fra diavolo* (shrimp, clams, and fresh fish in a garlic and basil marinara sauce). Oil paintings and chandeliers add character to the intimate setting. ♦ Northern Italian/Seafood ♦ Daily lunch and dinner. Reservations recommended. 235 Keawe St (at Haili St). 969.9090 ♿

24 Spencer Health and Fitness Center Has wet weather spoiled your jogging schedule? Sweat out your frustration on the treadmills o Stairmasters, then lift some weights—and hit the beach to recover. ♦ M-F 5AM-9PM; Sa 5AM-3PM; Su 6AM-noon. 197 Keawe St (between Haili and Kalakaua Sts). 969.1511

25 Restaurant Satsuki ★$ The Japanese/ Hawaiian cuisine here is done with better tast than the interior decorating, but at such low prices, who cares? Always packed with locals (an auspicious sign at any restaurant), this is a sure bet for oxtail soup fans. ♦ Japanese/ Hawaiian ♦ M dinner; W-Sa lunch and dinner. 168 Keawe St (between Haili and Kalakaua Sts). 935.7880 ♿

26 Sig Zane Designs Designer Sig Zane takes simple Hawaiian motifs such as ti, breadfruit, or taro leaves and prints them on fabrics to create islandwear that is both elegant and educational. Each T-shirt, aloha shirt, muumuu, and pareu (wraparound skirt) imparts the spirit of Hawaii. Zane's wife, Nalan

Kanaka'ole, is a revered hula master. ◆ M-Sa. 122 Kamehameha Ave (between Kalakaua St and Waianuenue Ave). 935.7077 &

26 Cronies ★$ Young local resident Layne Oki had always wanted to operate a restaurant and bar, and when the longstanding gathering place known as **Lehua's** closed, he initiated talks with the owners about taking over the place. The menu is predictably twentysomething, running mostly to cheeseburgers and Buffalo wings, but the entertainment packs in the resident crowd as well as those visitors who find their way in on Tuesday, and Thursday through Saturday. Four TVs, a dartboard, video games, and a pool table make this a perfect stop for sports enthusiasts. ◆ American ◆ M-Sa lunch and dinner. 90 Kamehameha Ave (at Waianuenue Ave). 935.5158 &

27 Bears Coffee ★$ Always bustling, this classic establishment (pictured above) offers Belgian waffles, eggs, croissants, muffins, bagels, deli sandwiches, and salads, along with espresso and other coffee favorites. You'll be in good company if you begin your morning here. ◆ Coffeehouse ◆ M-Sa 7AM-5PM; Su 8AM-noon. 106 Keawe St (between Kalakaua St and Waianuenue Ave). 935.0708 &

28 Wild Ginger Inn $ Simple, clean, and inexpensive, this hotel offers 22 rooms and 2 suites, coin-operated washers and dryers, and a complimentary breakfast buffet, but no restaurant, pool, or TVs (except in the suites). It's conveniently located two blocks from downtown Hilo. No smoking is allowed. ◆ 100 Puueo St (between Kou La and Kanoa St). 935.5556, 800/882.1887; fax 969.1225; www.wildgingerinn.com &

29 Dolphin Bay Hotel $ Economical and clean, this 18-unit hotel (including a 2-bedroom suite) is one of Hilo's best-kept secrets. The rooms are plain but inviting, and the grounds feature a dense tropical forest and a profusion of banana trees, orchids, and ginger plants. There are four types of units in the two-story walk-up, most with a full kitchen, an *ofuro*-type bathtub (deep, with a seat), a TV set, and fans. Although there's no air-conditioning or restaurant, and the telephone is in the lobby, you'll love the convenient location, intimate ambience, and friendly banter with owners Margaret, John, and Larry Alexander. ◆ 333 Iliahi St (between Puueo St and Wainaku Ave). 935.1466; fax 935.1523; johnhilo@gte.net; www.dolphinbayhilo.com &

30 Lyman Museum and Mission House Built in 1839 for the Reverend David Lyman and his wife, Sarah, the **Mission House** (pictured below) was among the first wood-frame structures in Hilo. You can see the Lymans' 19th-century furnishings and clothing on guided tours offered seven times daily. The adjoining **Lyman Museum**, completed in 1971, is one of Hawaii's least exhausting museums. One gallery features a *pili*-grass house, *kapa* (bark cloth), and artifacts of Hawaii's ethnic groups; another room displays volcanic and mineral formations; another houses a lava chamber. There's a 15-minute video about the **Mission House.** A 2,000-square-foot, 2-story, $700,000 addition to the main building features an interactive astronomy exhibit that shows visitors how ancient and modern people viewed/see the universe. A 60-foot-long mural depicts Hawaii's environmental zones. ◆ Admission. M-Sa. 276 Haili St (at Kapiolani St). 935.5021 &

Mission House

An Island Gone Nuts

A native of Queensland, Australia, the macadamia was originally known as the "bush nut" and was generally considered more trouble than it was worth to eat (because of its tough shell). The nut was named after Australian chemist John Macadam by his friend Baron Mueller, the botanist who first identified the genus in 1857. The tree that produces the nut was first brought to Hawaii from Australia in the late 1800s. At that time, the trees were valued for their ornamental aspects (many species have spiked leaves, similar to holly, that are used as holiday decorations, and white blossoms). By 1921 the macadamia's commercial potential as a snack food was seen, and the first plantation was established near **Honolulu.** Sixty years later, over 29 million pounds of nuts were being harvested on the islands annually—almost all for export.

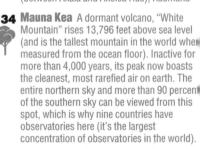

MARK AMMERMAN/NORTH

The macadamia tree, a subtropical evergreen that can grow as tall as 100 feet, is slow to bear fruit. The first harvest appears in 5 years, and the tree reaches its peak of productivity in 15 years, when it yields an average of 25 to 30 pounds of nuts (in the shell) each season.

The meat of a macadamia nut is protected by two layers: a green, oval outer covering lined with a shell so tough it's hard to break without crushing the tender nut. Its long maturation period and limited supply contribute to the macadamia's steep price, but the crisp, white nut holds its own among snack-nut competitors. In recent years it has become an increasingly popular ingredient in candies, cookies, and ice cream.

31 Rainbow Falls Early risers can watch as the sun peeks over the mango trees, forming a rainbow in the mist of the thundering falls that cascade 80 feet into the Wailuku River gorge. With an average discharge of 300 million gallons a day, it's the No. 1 waterfall in the state in terms of sheer water volume. The path to the left of the parking lot leads to a secluded overlook. ♦ Wailuku River State Park, Rainbow Dr (just north of Waianuenue Ave)

32 Boiling Pots The spectacular collection of small waterfalls and pools on the way from Rainbow Falls is worth at least one picture. Take the short (but steep) footpath to the right of the point for a closer look, but resist the temptation to swim—many have drowned here. ♦ Wailuku River State Park, Peepee Falls St (north of Waianuenue Ave)

Nearly half the Big Island's land area is within five miles of the beach.

Lake Waiau, at the top of the Big Island's extinct Mauna Kea Volcano, is the world's only tropical lake fed by permafrost. During the last ice age, Mauna Kea was covered by a 20-square-mile glacier up to 350 feet thick. Though the lake is shallow, ancient Hawaiians believed it was bottomless. With an elevation of 13,020 feet, Waiau is also the state's highest lake.

Between Hilo and Waimea

33 Kaumana Caves In 1881 a huge lava flow from Mauna Loa cooled on the surface and crusted over a flowing tube of molten lava. When the eruption ceased, the lava tube drained and these caves (supposedly radiation-proof) were the result. Seasoned spelunkers will bring flashlights to examine the modern-day petroglyphs, while the timid turn around at the mouth of the caves to gaw at the view looking out. ♦ Kaumana Dr (between Akala and Akolea Rds), Kaumana

34 Mauna Kea A dormant volcano, "White Mountain" rises 13,796 feet above sea level (and is the tallest mountain in the world when measured from the ocean floor). Inactive for more than 4,000 years, its peak now boasts the cleanest, most rarefied air on earth. The entire northern sky and more than 90 percent of the southern sky can be viewed from this spot, which is why nine countries have observatories here (it's the largest concentration of observatories in the world).

The uppermost slopes are generally covered with snow from January through May. Weather permitting, it's quite possible to ski the mountain early in the day and return to your hotel in time for a sunset swim. There's even a **Ski Association of Hawaii** (no phone) whose members you'll recognize by their "Sk

Hawaii" T-shirts. You won't find lift lines here—there are no ski lifts. Instead, skiers drive 20 miles up a paved road through black lava and cinder cones to reach the snow (which generally starts at 11,000 feet) and then continue on foot about a half mile to the start of several trails. Skiers must arrange to have a vehicle meet them at the bottom of one of the three- to five-mile runs, so they can get back up the mountain again.

Mainland skiers note: Not only are there no lifts, there's no snow-covered lodge with après-ski drinking here. The gritty texture of the snow is a lot like sand; locals call it "pineapple powder." The long and fast ski runs are natural, with snow depths generally ranging from five to six feet. Hardly a technical challenge for experienced skiers, but this is not a beginner's mountain either because of the high altitude and unique (sometimes rocky/crusty/steep) terrain. The volcano is skied simply because it's there. **Poi Bowl,** a quarter-mile-wide stretch starting at the summit, is excellent for beginners, while the other runs are steeper and more challenging.

The **Mauna Kea Observatory** offers free tours at the summit on Saturday and Sunday afternoons at 2PM (participants must be at least 16 years of age). Reservations are not required, but you'll need a four-wheel-drive vehicle to get to the observatory. Call **Mauna Kea Support Services** (935.3371) on weekdays for information. If you don't have the requisite vehicle, you can visit the **Onizuka Center for National Astronomy** (961.2180), 9,300 feet up Mauna Kea, Thursday through Tuesday at 7PM for a free lecture and a chance to look through an 11-inch telescope. ♦ North of Saddle Rd

35 Mamalahoa Highway Scenic Drive

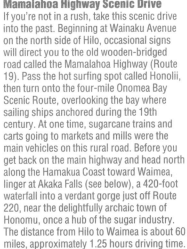

If you're not in a rush, take this scenic drive into the past. Beginning at Wainaku Avenue on the north side of Hilo, occasional signs will direct you to the old wooden-bridged road called the Mamalahoa Highway (Route 19). Pass the hot surfing spot called Honolii, then turn onto the four-mile Onomea Bay Scenic Route, overlooking the bay where sailing ships anchored during the 19th century. At one time, sugarcane trains and carts going to markets and mills were the main vehicles on this rural road. Before you get back on the main highway and head north along the Hamakua Coast toward Waimea, linger at Akaka Falls (see below), a 420-foot waterfall into a verdant gorge just off Route 220, near the delightfully archaic town of Honomu, once a hub of the sugar industry. The distance from Hilo to Waimea is about 60 miles, approximately 1.25 hours driving time.

Along the Onomea Bay Scenic Route:

Hawaii Tropical Botanical Gardens

Some say this 20-acre rain forest and nature preserve is the most beautiful place in Hawaii; take the self-guided walking tour on the 1.25-mile trail to decide for yourself. Daniel J. Lutkenhouse, a retired California trucking executive who had long been charmed by Hilo's rain forests, bought the property, which was a junkyard, and formally opened the gardens to the public in 1984. The tour takes between 1 and 2 hours, with labels providing informative trivia about some of the 2,000 endemic and imported plants; visitors also can simply stroll around the large lily and koi (carp) pond, giant mango trees, pungent guava orchard, or the huge Alexander palms. The exotic plants come from as far away as Fiji, Peru, Madagascar, and Indonesia. Cars are not allowed inside the gardens. Parking and rest rooms are available, but bring mosquito repellent and wear comfortable shoes. ♦ Admission. Daily. 964.5233 &

36 Akaka Falls State Park What sets the

420-foot Akaka Falls and its 100-foot companion, Kahuna Falls, apart from other waterfalls is the lush 65-acre park that surrounds them, an area celebrated in ancient chants and contemporary love songs. Plants and flowers from all over the world—sprays of orchids, groves of bamboo, carpets of moss, bougainvillea bushes, gingers, azaleas, ferns, and countless other exotic plants—create the dense rain forest atmosphere. The moist air and soothing roar of the waterfalls accompany you on the 20-minute walk along the paved circular path. ♦ Rte 220 (west of Mamalahoa Hwy)

37 Kolekole Beach Park Follow the sign on

Route 19 to **Kolekole Beach Park** (turn off on the *mauka,* or mountain, side), and your reward will be a cool (make that cold) fresh-water pond fed by Kolekole Falls. Also on hand are a playing field and two picnic pavilions; camping is allowed, but a permit is required (call 961.8311). ♦ Mamalahoa Hwy (just north of Rte 220)

38 Laupahoehoe Beach Park On this

pleasant, grassy peninsula is a memorial to the 20 students and 4 teachers who lost their lives here in the 1946 tidal wave. The park is on the former site of Laupahoehoe village, which was moved to higher ground overlooking the point. Picnics and camping are allowed but there's no swimming. ♦ Just east of Mamalahoa Hwy

39 Hotel Honokaa Club ★$$ Big Islanders dine at the club (pictured above) when lobsters are in season, since the succulent crustaceans are fresh and inexpensive here. The other fare is just passable—steak, sea food platters—and the decor doesn't get much fancier than vinyl tablecloths and a TV in the corner. This isn't the most chic place (it's strangely lit and generally weird, as is the hotel of the same name), but it's very affordable and loaded with local color. ♦ American ♦ Tu-Su lunch and dinner. 45-3480 Mamane St (northwest of Mamalahoa Hwy), Honokaa. 775.0678

39 Honokaa Trading Company Browse through this 2,200-square-foot emporium of Hawaiiana, and you never know, you may come away with anything from a $4 Kona Bottling Works bottle to a $1,600 set of menus used on the first steamship trips to the islands. ♦ Daily. 45-3490 Mamane St (northwest of Mamalahoa Hwy), Honokaa. 775.0808 &

39 Tex Drive Inn ★$ You'd probably drive right by this place if you didn't know how good the *malasadas* are here. These Portuguese no-hole doughnuts from heaven are best eaten hot, so don't procrastinate—and if you're feeling adventurous, try one with filling. If you're still hungry, try the "local wrap," with *kalua* pig and taro inside. ♦ Country-style ♦ Daily breakfast, lunch, and dinner. Pakalana St (between Mamalahoa Hwy and Mamane St), Honokaa. 775.0598 &

40 Waipio Valley Artworks A showcase for 100 Big Island artists, this shop offers a pleasing mix of paintings, native-wood carvings and bowls, sculpture, furniture, and crafts. The hand-painted T-shirts and other works employ Hawaiian motifs. The adjoining cafe has good local ice cream. ♦ Daily. 240 Old Government Rd (northwest of Rte 240), Kukuihaele. 775.0958, 800/492.4746

41 Waipio Valley The Hamakua Coast ends at the Big Island's largest valley, which has a resident population of about 40. According to oral tradition, this valley was once home to 40,000 Hawaiians. Before Captain Cook arrived, it was the cultural and political hub of the island. Some locals know it as the "Valley of the Kings" or "The Land of Curving Water." Ancient temple sites, stone terraces, waterfalls, and steep valley walls make this an inspiring stop for those with four-wheel-drive vehicles or the tenacity to hike down and back. Make friends with the locals and they may take you to Hiilawe, the awesome waterfall at the back of the valley. The few taro farmers who remain, survivors of the 1946 tsunami, proudly cling to a lifestyle immortalized in the songs and chants of ancient Hawaii. ♦ Waipio

Within Waipio Valley:

Waipio Hotel $ Whether you're a bank executive or a Deadhead, nothing equals the original Waipio Valley hostelry if you like roughing it. Octogenarian Tom Araki's barrackslike "hotel" is a five-room haven without phones, hot water, or even electricity. Bring your own food (there's no restaurant); everything else is provided—gas lamps, taro fields, waterfalls, wild horses, and the pleasure of Tom's company (alone worth the price—$15/day—of your stay). ♦ No credit cards accepted. 775.0368

Waipio Treehouse $$$ Linda Beech's establishment is an exotic lodging option: a one-room cabin suspended 30 feet above ground in a monkeypod tree (pictured above), with one double and one single bed, a refrigerator, hot plates, electricity, and running water . . . all the comforts of a tree house. A waterfall and mountain pool are just down the trail, and a Japanese hot tub bubbles nearby. Standard rental cars can't make it down to the Waipio Valley, but transportation is provided. One warning: For a couple of days every year the cottage is inaccessible because of high river water. If guests are stranded, their accommodations during the delay are complimentary. This is a good base for wagon and horseback-riding tours. There are no TV or telephones. Another unit, a three-bedroom house on the ground, is also available. ♦ 775.7160; fax 775.7160

42 Old Mamalahoa Highway If you have some leisure time, take this little-known scenic drive parallel to Mamalahoa Highway. The extreme diversity of vegetation that can be seen in the 12 miles from east to west provides a splendid overview of the island's plant life.

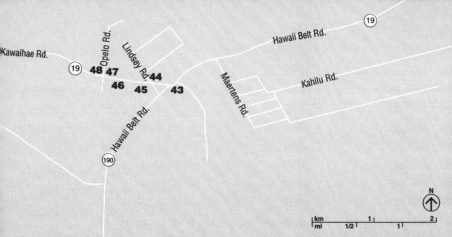

Waimea

Checkered with funky-looking buildings, grazing horses and cattle, and stately homes of landed gentry, Waimea is a friendly town. Its 2,500-foot elevation provides a cool, crisp climate that's refreshing after the hot beaches of **West Hawaii**. **Mauna Kea** looms in the distance, flower and vegetable farms abound, and *paniolos* (cowboys) in boots and hats add a real Western flavor. Volcanic cinder cones long covered by greenery are dotted with livestock. Few people realize that Hawaii's *paniolos* (the word is derived from *"español"*) predate the US West, having come from Spain and Mexico at the request of Kamehameha III in the 1830s to teach Hawaiians how to ride, rope, and herd cattle. Today, Hawaiian cowboys may be Filipino, Portuguese, Chinese, Japanese, or a mixture of some or all of the above.

Waimea is cowboy country thanks to John Parker, a seaman from New England who jumped ship in 1809, settled on the Big Island, and domesticated a herd of wild cattle that belonged to Kamehameha the Great. The king, who gave Parker some land in return, had a granddaughter whom Parker conveniently married and voilà—the **Parker Ranch** dynasty was born. Today the ranch, which is open to visitors, consists of 225,000 acres with more than 55,000 head of cattle.

Note: To avoid confusion with the town of Waimea on Kauai, the post office address for this town is **Kamuela**, Hawaiian for Samuel (after John Parker's grandson Samuel). To get to Waimea from **Kona** take **Route 19** or **Route 190** north for about 40 miles; from **Hilo** take **Mamalahoa Highway** north for about 60 miles.

43 Parker Ranch Visitor Center and Museum A video shows the history of the 225,000-acre **Parker Ranch**, the second-largest ranch in the US, and describes the life of the Hawaiian cowboys. Parker family memorabilia and photographs are on display. You can tour the ranch, visit its original two-acre homestead, or walk through owner Richard Smart's historic 1862 home, **Puuopelu** (pictured on page 24), where his extensive art collection is displayed. ♦ Admission. Daily. Parker Ranch Shopping Center, 67-1185 Mamalahoa Hwy (at Kawaihae Rd). 885.7655 ♦

44 Waimea Country Lodge $ This hostelry—the closest thing to a motor lodge in the islands—has 21 spartan rooms, 5 equipped with kitchenettes. There's no restaurant or pool. ♦ 65-1210 Lindsey Rd (north of Mamalahoa Hwy). 885.4100; fax 885.6711 ♦

45 Edelweiss ★★$$$ Chef/owner Hans-Peter Hager's restaurant is a small place (only 15 tables) in a *paniolo*-style setting of open beams, but on any given night the 14 to 16 house specials range from roast duck to venison to a superb rack of lamb basted in garlic, mustard, and herbs. Also recommended is the Wiener schnitzel. Homemade Bavarian pudding, cheesecake, and fruit pies are worthy finales. ♦ Continental ♦ Tu-Sa lunch and dinner. Reservations recommended. 65-1299 Kawaihae Rd (between Lindsey and Opelo Rds). 885.6800

46 Parker Square Browsing through the shops in this mini-mall without making a purchase is virtually impossible. Start at **Gallery of Great Things** (885.7706), with its wild collection of museum-quality artifacts from Hawaii, Indonesia, Papua New Guinea, and elsewhere in the Pacific, including tribal jade carvings, chopsticks made of exotic woods, Indonesian baskets, koa furniture, coconut-fiber hats, and

Puuopelu, Parker Ranch

MATT MORROW/NORTH MARKET STREET GRAPHICS

handmade jewelry. Work your way toward **Bentleys** (885.5565), a shop that specializes in ceramics and tableware (the Christmas display is unbelievable) but also carries gifts and accessories from around the world. Save some room on your credit card for the **Waimea General Store** (885.4479), which carries patterns for Hawaiian quilts and needlepoint, as well as pillow kits, yarn, and how-to books. ♦ Daily. 65-1279 Kawaihae Rd (between Lindsey and Opelo Rds)

47 Kamuela Inn $ This is definitely the nicer of the two hotels in Waimea and less expensive to boot. Each of the 31 cozy rooms and suites has a private bath and cable TV; some have telephones. The best rooms have full kitchens. Complimentary continental breakfast is served on the hotel's lanai. Although there's no restaurant, the other amenities combine to make this inn a nice place to lay over in Waimea. ♦ 65-1300 Kawaihae Rd (at Opelo Rd). 885.4243, 800/555.8968; fax 885.8857; kaminn@aloha.net; www.hawaii-bnb.com/kamuela.html

Merriman's

48 Merriman's ★★★$$$ The atmosphere here is tropical, with floral-patterned carpet and a banana tree mural. Owner and former chef Peter Merriman pioneered Hawaii's regional cuisine, and his innovative use of seaweed and Big Island–raised beef, lamb, and veal is legendary. The mahimahi and *ono* (wahoo) are in his kitchen soon after they're caught; the goat cheese is made in Puna; and the strawberries and tomatoes are grown down the road. Specialties include wok-charred *ahi* (yellowfin tuna), Kahua lamb, *lokelani* ("rose from heaven") tomato salad, and passion fruit mousse. ♦ Hawaiian ♦ M-F lunch and dinner; Sa-Su dinner. Reservations recommended. Opelo Plaza, Kawaihae and Opelo Rds. 885.6822 &

49 Waimea Gardens Cottage $$ Owner/host Barbara Campbell (who worked for more than 20 years at the **Kona Village Resort**) has perfected the art of hospitality in her lovely bed-and-breakfast establishment overlooking the Waimea hillsides. A longtime resident of Waimea, she has surrounded her two streamside cottages with geraniums, ferns, roses, and day lilies. A graceful willow tree stands in the front yard, and a small henhouse sits across the lawn. There's also a fireplace, Jacuzzi, and full kitchen with a stocked refrigerator. Although not for the budget traveler, this is definitely one of the nicest bed-and-breakfasts on the island. A three-night minimum stay is required. ♦ No credit cards accepted. Kawaihae Rd (between Mamalahoa Hwy and Kohala Mountain Rd). 885.4550, 800/262.9912; fax 885.0559; bestbnb@aloha.net; www.bestbnb.com

50 Kamuela Museum Hawaii's largest privately owned and most unorthodox museum was founded by Big Island native Albert K. Solomon, who claims that when he was eight years old his grandmother predicted he would open a museum. It took several decades, but he proved her right. Opened in 1968 by the former Honolulu policeman and his wife, Harriet, the museum ranks somewhere between an institution and a weekend flea market. Undocumented and unorganized, there's everything from Japanese machine guns to ancient Hawaiian feather money and even an old Model-T tire remover. ♦ Admission. Daily. Kawaihae and Kohala Mountain Rds. 885.4724

North Kohala

Remote and quiet, this small peninsula has the kind of tiny towns with quaint, tumbledown buildings that capture the imagination and give you a sense of how the Big Island once was. This is rain forest country, with plenty of chilly, wet days. But when the sun shines, there's no place finer.

51 Ohana Pizza and Beer Garden $ The highlight here isn't the food, which is okay at best, but the customers. For a real taste of life in Hawi, grab a stool, order a draft and a slice, and watch. ◆ Pizzeria ◆ Daily dinner. Rte 270, Hawi. 889.5888

ʰamboo
Restaurant & Gallery

51 Bamboo Restaurant and Gallery ★★★ $$$ One of those spots the locals won't tell you about, fearing its ruination, this restaurant is an outpost of island ambience not often found in the 50th state. Hawaiian "aunties" make diners feel at home in the wood-paneled, flower-filled restaurant, which shares a storefront with an enticing art gallery. This is a fine dining establishment Hawaiian style, featuring such entrées as blackened *ahi* and Hawaii-Thai *ono* (grilled with coconut sauce, and served with mung bean sprouts, tomato, cilantro, and peanuts). Be sure to have one of the house-specialty passion fruit margaritas that come in a coconut cup. Try to come on a night when a local hula *halau* (school) performs free from 7PM to 8PM. Call ahead for schedule. ◆ Hawaiian Regional ◆ Tu-Sa lunch and dinner; Su brunch. Rtes 270 and 250, Hawi. 889.5555 ᣦ

52 Kohala Irrigation Ditch One of the hot new activities on the Big Island for visitors and residents alike is a trip in a five-person kayak down the Kohala Irrigation Ditch, which has carried water to sugarcane fields for decades. The 1.25-hour kayak adventure through tunnels and over ravines is available twice daily. Intrepid vacationers will be shuttled from **Kohala Mountain Kayak Cruise**'s Kapaau office to the headwaters of the ditch. ◆ Fee. Kohala Mountain Kayak Cruise, Rte 270, Kapaau. 889.6922; fax 889.6944; kmkc@aloha.net; www.kohalakayaks.com

52 Original King Kamehameha I Statue This statue may have a less dazzling setting than the replica across from **Iolani Palace** on Oahu, but its history is much richer. For $10,000, American sculptor Thomas R. Gould was commissioned in 1878 by the Hawaiian legislature to create a statue of the mighty warrior king for the centennial of Captain Cook's arrival in Hawaii. As the model for Kamehameha, Gould used a photograph of Honolulu businessman John Baker, a close friend of King Kalakaua, who posed in loincloth, feather cloak, spear, and helmet.

Gould's clay figure was finished in Florence, Italy; sent to Paris for bronze casting; and eventually shipped to Hawaii. As it neared Cape Horn, the ship burned and sank, carrying the statue to the bottom of the sea. Gould agreed to make another statue for $7,500. This one reached Honolulu intact and was unveiled on 14 February 1883, during Kalakaua's coronation. A few weeks later, the original Kamehameha statue arrived in Honolulu on a British ship whose skipper had bought it for $500 from a salvage yard. The skipper's asking price was $1,500. Since one hand was broken off and the spear was missing, Kalakaua talked him down to $875 and then had the statue repaired and sent to the sleepy town of Kapaau, where Kamehameha was born. The Honolulu statue is more fanciful, but many think the original is a more appropriate homage to the great Kamehameha. ◆ Rte 270, Kapaau

53 Keokea Beach Park Popular on weekends, this picturesque white-sand beach is usually vacant during the week. The surf is good for swimming when the tide is low. There are picnic facilities. ◆ North of Rte 270, Niulii

54 Pololu Valley Lookout and Trail The view is surpassed only by the switchback trail (a 15-minute walk) through tunnels of *pandani* shrubs to a black-sand beach. Good swimmers will love the waves, but there are no lifeguards or facilities. The **Hawaii Trail and Mountain Club** (322.8881; fax 322.8883; www.hawaiiforest.com) has recently begun offering daily three-hour mule rides into Pololu. The route traverses streams, board-walks, guava and java plum forests, and finishes at the black-sand beach, where riders take a half-hour break before heading back to the world as they know it. ◆ Rte 270, Makapala

55 Lapakahi State Historical Park This semirestored fishing village dates back 600 years. Take the self-guided tour among the stone-house sites, canoe sheds, fishing shrines, and stone games. Learn about local legends, fishing customs and techniques, salt gathering, and the prosperous, simple life of Hawaiians centuries ago. ◆ Free. Daily. Rte 270 (between Kawaihae and Hikapoloa)

56 Kawaihae Shopping Center On the way to or from Hawi, this collection of bistros and boutiques makes a great rest stop. Stop by **Tres Hombres Beach Grill** (882.1031) any day at lunch or dinner for a margarita and Mexican appetizers after browsing through the unusual clothing—much of it Indonesian batik—at **Borderlines** (882.1577), and before losing yourself in the paintings and sculpture at the upscale **Kohala Kollection** (882.1510). ◆ Daily. Rte 270 (west of Queen Kaahumanu Hwy), Kawaihae

56 Puukohola Heiau National Historic Site Measuring 224 feet by 100 feet, this fortresslike structure is the largest *heiau* (temple) in Hawaii. It is a marvel of engineering, with waterworn lava rocks and boulders set together without mortar. Built in 1790 by King Kamehameha, it's a powerful reminder of the role of human sacrifice in the ancient Hawaiian religion. A prophecy of the time held that Kamehameha would conquer and unite the islands if he erected a temple to his family war god on the hill at Kawaihae, a prophecy fulfilled after the erection of **Puukohola**. Kamehameha invited his archrival to the temple's dedication ceremony in 1791, and then offered him up as a sacrifice. The *heiau* itself is not accessible, but visitors can walk around the 77-acre site and stop at the visitors' center. ♦ Free. Daily. Rte 270 (west of Queen Kaahumanu Hwy), Kawaihae. 882.7218

Within the Puukohola Heiau National Historic Site:

Samuel M. Spencer Beach Park This white-sand beach offers the best and safest swimming along the North Kohala Coast, as well as good snorkeling and spearfishing. Picnic, camping, and tennis facilities make this a popular spot for families.

Kohala Coast

The northwest edge of the Big Island has something of a split personality. It has the most beautiful white-sand beaches on the island, but there also are barren fields of black lava that come as a surprise to many vacationers, although some come to understand and appreciate their stark beauty. This is also called the "Gold Coast," as numerous tourists flock to the hotels that line the shore.

57 Mauna Kea Beach Hotel $$$$ On his first visit here, Merv Griffin proclaimed, "Now I know where old Republicans come to die." Built in 1965 by Laurance Rockefeller, this property set the standard for super-luxury resorts along the Kohala Coast; a $30-million renovation later upgraded the resort to rival any competitor. The property now has 300 rooms and 10 suites on a whopping 1,839-acre site. Two of the strongest selling points here are nearby Kaunaoa Beach, among the nicest on the island, and the legendary **Mauna Kea Golf Course** (see below). The spacious grounds and court-yards, alive with more than a half-million plants of nearly 200 varieties, are also part of the appeal. There are 6 restaurants and 13 Plexipave tennis courts. ♦ 62-100 Mauna Kea Beach Dr (west Queen Kaahumanu Hwy). 882.7222, 800/882.6060; fax 880.3112; www.maunakeabeachhotel.com ♦

Within the Mauna Kea Beach Hotel:

The 1950 eruption of Mauna Loa spewed 615 million cubic yards of lava, enough to pave a 6-inch-thick highway to the moon.

Mauna Kea Buddha A 1,500-pound pink granite sculpture, this 7th-century Indian Buddha (illustrated above) sits on a solid block of Canadian black granite in the shade of a *bodhi* tree.

The Batik ★★$$$$ Batiks hang from the walls of this cozy, two-tiered dining room, which specializes in European dishes like grilled tenderloin of beef sliced on caper-and-onion mashed potatoes with sauce poivrade and fresh snapper with lobster mushroom ragout. ♦ Continental ♦ Daily dinner. Reservations required; jacket required. 882.7222 ♦

The Pavilion ★★$$$$ Atmosphere and cuisine vie for top honors in this expensive dining room, where floor-to-ceiling windows and a drop-dead ocean view such rival entrées as steamed snapper with shiitake mushrooms, ginger, shoyu, and sesame oil; sautéed mahimahi; and langoustine tails with lobster cream. ♦ Hawaiian ♦ M-Sa lunch buffet and dinner; Su brunch and dinner. Reservations recommended. 882.7222 ♦

Mauna Kea Luau ★★$$ Hawaiian delicacies are served on the grassy oceanside gardens at this very upscale luau held on the hotel's grounds. The feast includes *hulihuli* (spit-roasted) chicken, *kalua* pig on special occasions, poi, *lomilomi* salmon (salted salmon that's been shredded and kneaded with tomatoes and green onions), and baked taro, as well as steak, chicken, ribs, and crab claws. ♦ Luau ♦ Tu 6-9PM. 882.5801 ♦

Mauna Kea Golf Course Designed by Robert Trent Jones Sr., this reclaimed ancient lava flow is widely hailed as Hawaii's toughest course. Though a few refinements cater to fair-weather golfers, the 18-hole course (par 72, 6,737 yards) remains an ego bruiser for even the above-average player. Its beautiful layout has the ocean always in sight. Regularly ranked among America's hundred greatest golf courses and repeatedly designated "Hawaii's finest" by *Golf Digest*, the course hosts two tournaments annually: the **Pro-Am** in July and an **Invitational** in early

December. Hotel guests get preferred starting times and rates. ◆ Expensive greens fees. Daily. 882.5400

58 Hapuna Beach Prince Hotel $$$$ Local residents vehemently (though unsuccessfully) fought the construction of this 32-acre resort because of its location on one of Hawaii's most gorgeous white-sand beaches. This sister hotel to the **Mauna Kea Beach Hotel** has 314 rooms and 36 suites, all with lanais and wide-angle ocean views, three restaurants, and a pool. Its top attractions are the two surrounding 18-hole golf courses (the **Hapuna** and the **Mauna Kea**) and a 13-court tennis center a short shuttle away at the **Mauna Kea Beach Hotel.** The catch is that the property is pretty far from anyplace else. ◆ 62-100 Kaunaoa Dr (west of Queen Kaahumanu Hwy). 880.1111, 800/882.6060; fax 880.3112; www.hapunabeachprincehotel.com

Within the Hapuna Beach Prince Hotel:

The Coast Grille ★★★$$$$ The hotel's circular signature restaurant has an ocean view that won't quit. Dishes include Parker Ranch steak and fresh lobster, clams, oysters, and jumbo shrimp. ◆ Hawaiian Regional ◆ Daily dinner. Reservations recommended. 880.1111

Hapuna Golf Course This 18-hole course (par 70, 6,534 yards) was designed by Arnold Palmer and Ed Seay. The environmentally conscious design uses half the land acreage of a regular 18-hole course and is landscaped with native Hawaiian grasses and trees. Hawaiian birds and waterfowl came gratis. ◆ Expensive greens fees. Daily. 880.3000

58 Hapuna Beach State Park One of the island's nicest white-sand beaches, this is also a primo spot for bodysurfing. But be sure to go out between 9AM and 5PM when the lifeguards are on duty, as currents can be hazardous, particularly when the surf's up. There are also picnic tables perfect for family gatherings. ◆ West of Queen Kaahumanu Hwy

THE ORCHID
AT MAUNA LANI

59 The Orchid at Mauna Lani $$$$ In 1997 this hotel (formerly the **Ritz-Carlton**) was ranked No. 1 among tropical resorts on the island by *Condé Nast Traveler.* The majestic common areas are modeled after luxury plantation homes, with koa furniture, local paintings, and chandeliers. The two six-story wings face the ocean, and 539 large, luxurious rooms have peach and light blue walls and marble bathrooms. An outdoor, 10,000-square-foot swimming pool sits next to an artificial white-sand lagoon; and the 32-acre grounds feature myriad native plants. The **Club** level has its own lounge, tea service, elevator key, and other extras. Tennis buffs can choose from 10 courts, and golfers have special privileges at the **Mauna Lani/Francis H. Ii Brown Golf Course** (see page 29). Other activities include outrigger canoe rides, horseback day trips, and helicopter tours. ◆ 1 N Kaniku Dr (off Puako Beach Dr), Puako. 885.2000, 800/845.9905; fax 885.1064; www.orchid-maunalani.com &

Within The Orchid at Mauna Lani:

The Grill ★★★$$$$ The clubby atmosphere, enhanced by the rich glow of koa

Hapuna Beach Prince Hotel

MATT MORROW/NORTH MARKET STREET GRAPHICS

paneling, suits the continental menu, which features such items as *keawe*-smoked New York sirloin steak, pesto-crusted rack of lamb, and pan-roasted golden trout. A plush private room is available for parties of up to 14 people. ♦ Continental ♦ Tu-Sa dinner. Reservations recommended. 885.2000 ♿

The Orchid Court Restaurant ★★★
$$$$ The fare here features such California dishes as cilantro-crusted steamed *opakapaka* (pink snapper), roasted chicken cannelloni, and barbecued shrimp club sandwiches. The casual dining room features alfresco seating. ♦ California ♦ Daily breakfast and dinner. 885.2000 ♿

Brown's Beach House ★★★$$$$ This
ocean-view dining room set outside features the one-of-a-kind lava-rock lobster taco, pan-seared *ahi* with Asian pesto risotto, and sesame ginger-crusted mahimahi. If you've been stuck in a mainland city during a long winter, this would be the first place to come to unwind. ♦ Hawaiian Regional ♦ Daily dinner. 885.2000 ♿

59 Puako Petroglyph Archaeological Park
Site of one of the largest clusters of petroglyphs in Hawaii, this public park at the north end of The Orchid at Mauna Lani property was officially placed on the Hawaii and National Historic Registers in 1982. The stone carvings (such as the one illustrated on page 43) were created by ancient Hawaiians more than 400 years ago. The park was established to protect the petroglyphs after some were damaged by vandalism, theft, foot traffic, and even bulldozers (cleaning up after fires in the area). A natural trail system posted with signs leads to the petroglyphs, which are within the **Holoholokai Beach Park.** Don't make rubbings from the stone carvings (replica petroglyphs are provided for this purpose) and don't step on them. Damaged petroglyphs are displayed so visitors can see the consequences of mistreating these treasures. ♦ Puako Beach Dr (west of Queen Kaahumanu Hwy), Puako

---

The Big Island is home to 21 of the earth's 22 major climate zones. Arctic tundra is not on the list.

Decades ago, a park ranger introduced the lore that Pele, the volcano goddess, would bring disaster to anyone who removed lava from Hawaii. While this caveat has no basis in historical fact, that doesn't stop repentent visitors from shipping more than 2,000 pounds of rocks a year back to the administrative offices of Hawaii Volcanoes National Park.

Restaurants/Clubs: Red   Hotels: Blue
Shops/♈ Outdoors: Green   Sights/Culture: Black

60 Mauna Lani Bay Hotel and Bungalows
$$$$ This hotel on 29 oceanfront acres has been winning awards for its environmental consciousness, golf course, and overall excellence for some time. A distinctively Hawaiian landmark, it embodies the highest standards of local hospitality: grace, style, architectural excellence, and aloha spirit. In the blue-tile courtyard, a waterfall leads to the **Grand Atrium,** filled with fish ponds and orchids. Rooms (built at a cost of $200,000 each) feature teak and rattan furnishings, color TVs in armoires, roomy baths with twin vanities, and private lanais. Ninety percent of the 350 rooms and suites have ocean views; 29 face the Mauna Kea and Mauna Loa mountains. Guests with deep pockets can opt for one of five 4,000-square-foot bungalows with private pools and 24-hour butler service; families may prefer the luxurious 1-and 2-bedroom ocean villas.

The grounds feature prehistoric fish ponds and a 16th-century lava flow with caves and petroglyphs. Golfers enjoy the nearby 36-hole **Mauna Lani/Francis H. Ii Brown Golf Course,** and there's a pool and a championship 10-court **Tennis Garden.** Activities include windsurfing, racquetball, canoeing, scuba diving, and aqua-aerobics. The hotel has been awarded five diamonds by AAA, and in 1998 *Condé Nast Traveler*'s readers ranked it No. 1 in Hawaii. ♦ 68-1400 Mauna Lani Dr (west of Queen Kaahumanu Hwy). 885.6622, 800/367.2323; fax 885.1483; maunalani@maunalani.com; www.maunalani.com ♿

Within the Mauna Lani Bay Hotel and Bungalows:

The Canoe House ★★★★$$$$ Here
is a rare match of ambience and impressive cuisine. Dine indoors, where a koa canoe hangs from the high ceiling, or outside, where the breaking waves are lit by the setting sun. Specialties include seared peppered *ahi* with crispy slaw and grilled *opakapaka* with chili-garlic–black bean sauce. ♦ Pacific Rim ♦ Daily dinner. Reservations recommended. 885.6622 ♿

Bay Terrace ★★★$$$$ Stop here for
pleasant fare for breakfast or dinner. There are *malasadas* to start the day; candlelight and a three-piece band make for romantic dinners. On Friday and Saturday nights the place really dazzles, with an all-you-can-eat buffet that includes crab legs, made-to-order tempura and pasta, prime rib, and more, presented in

the most elegant manner imaginable.
♦ American/Regional ♦ Daily breakfast
and dinner. Reservations recommended.
885.6622 ♿

The Gallery ★★$$$$ A fairly standard
golf club restaurant at lunch, this place
becomes an intimate, candlelit venue at dusk.
The fare is mostly American, emphasizing
fresh seafood from the Big Island. Daily fish
selections are prepared one of three ways,
including crusted with macadamia nuts and
covered in a lobster brandy sauce. New York
steak and roasted rack of lamb also rank high
on the list. ♦ Steak/Seafood ♦ Tu-Sa lunch
and dinner; M, Su lunch. Reservations
recommended. 885.7777 ♿

**Mauna Lani/Francis H. Ii Brown Golf
Course** Since the course opened in 1981,
these emerald fairways and greens have
received worldwide attention, with *Golf
Magazine* bestowing top honors on them in
1998. Carved out of a 16th-century lava flow,
the **North Course** (18 holes, par 72, 6,913
yards) and the **South Course** (18 holes, par
72, 6,438 yards) flow bright green through the
black *aa* and *pahoehoe* lava fields, sculptured
masterpieces lined by groves of twisted *kiawe*
trees. Ocean views are almost secondary. The
Mauna Lani Beach Club, a popular watering
hole for mai tai lovers, is a shuttle ride from
the pro shop. Hotel guests get preferred
starting times and rates. ♦ Expensive greens
fees. Daily. 68-1310 Mauna Lani Dr. 886.6655

61 Kings Course Designed by Tom Weiskopf
and Jay Morris, this challenging 18-hole, par
72, 7,074-yard course has 6 lakes, 9 acres of
water, 83 sand traps, and a 25,000-square-
foot clubhouse. ♦ Expensive greens fees;
discounts for guests of most Waikoloa hotels.
Daily. 69-600 Waikoloa Beach Dr (west of
Queen Kaahumanu Hwy). 886.4647

61 Beach Course The fairways are adorned
with tropical flowers, while the rough is black
lava at this 18-hole, par 70, 6,566-yard course
created by Robert Trent Jones Jr. A driving
range is on site. ♦ Expensive greens fees;
discounts for guests of most Waikoloa hotels.
Daily. 1020 Keana Pl (west of Queen
Kaahumanu Hwy). 886.6060

61 Royal Waikoloan $$$ Smaller and more
modest than its neighbor, the flamboyant
Hilton Waikoloa Village (see below), this
545-room hotel is for those who favor an
intimate Hawaiian ambience at a more rea-
sonable price. The wide Anaehoomalu Bay is
a key attraction; other special features of this
first-rate resort include the **Royal Cabana
Club,** a 15-room, two-story structure on the
lagoon; Wednesday and Sunday luaus; a
fitness center; six tennis courts; a pool; and
two nearby championship golf courses.
♦ 69-275 Waikoloa Beach Dr (west of Queen
Kaahumanu Hwy). 886.6789, 800/688.7444;

fax 886.7851; reservations@outrigger.com;
www.outrigger.com ♿

61 Hilton Waikoloa Village $$$$ Described
as "Disney-esque" by those who favor more
intimate settings, this 62-acre super resort
has more than a mile of waterways with a
dozen 24-passenger canal boats, a milelong
museum walkway, and an air-conditioned
electric tram. Hardly a potted palm has
changed position since the gargantuan resort
metamorphosed from Hyatt to Hilton in 1993,
though a $24-million renovation included new
high-end oceanfront cabanas, perhaps to keep
pace with the neighboring **Mauna Lani Bay
Hotel and Bungalows.** The $360-million hotel
is more like a small city, with 1,240 rooms,
57 suites, 2,000 employees, 2 main swim-
ming pools, waterfalls, water slides, 24
meeting and banquet rooms, 20,000 square
feet of shopping space, and 8 tennis and
2 racquetball courts. The 25,000-square-foot
spa offers European herbal treatments, mud
wraps, fitness classes, nutrition counseling,
steam rooms, saunas, whirlpools, and
Jacuzzis. The hotel has 6 restaurants and 8
lounges, but the most popular attraction by
far is **Dolphin Quest** (see below), the 2.5-
million-gallon home of 10 Atlantic bottle-
nosed dolphins. Even if you have no intention
of staying at the resort, drop by to gawk at
American excess at its best. ♦ 425 Waikoloa
Beach Dr (west of Queen Kaahumanu Hwy).
886.1234, 800/HILTONS; fax 886.2902;
waikoloa_rooms@hilton.com;
www.hilton.com/hawaii/waikoloa ♿

Within the Hilton Waikoloa Village:

Kamuela Provision Co. ★★★$$$$
This is one of Hawaii's most attractive dining
rooms, with six seating areas (including one
alfresco), dozens of windows overlooking the
sea and pool, and elegant, glass-topped
tables. Diners seeking a languorous evening
should start with a sunset mai tai overlooking
the ocean, progress to the seafood mixed grill,
Keahole lobster, or filet mignon, and finish
with a Kona Sampler—a dish piled with items
like banana-chocolate sandwiches, guava
sorbet, Kona coffee mousse, and Big Island
brulée. ♦ Steak/Seafood ♦ Daily dinner.
Reservations required. 886.1234 ♿

At 4,028 square miles, the Big Island could
hold all the other 131 Hawaiian islands within
its borders.

Go Fish!

Unlike many deep-sea fishing excursions, which take hours to reach prime fishing spots, the action begins minutes after your boat departs the dock at **Kailua-Kona,** since some of the best fishing waters in Hawaii are within a mile or two off the **Kona** coast. On charter trips, no previous experience is necessary, since the captain provides all the equipment, plus expert advice and cheerful assistance for even the most inept of anglers. All you need to bring is food, drink, and sunscreen (fishing licenses aren't necessary). And leave the fish bag at home—the captain has first choice of the catch, and he usually sells it at the market. (What would you do with a hundred-pound tuna?) Half-day charters leave just after sunrise and return by noon; all-day trips are back in time for cocktails. Parties of up to six people can hire charters (with a captain and first mate) for their exclusive use, or you can share boats by paying on a per-person basis.

One excellent service (and the island's oldest) is the **Kona Charter Skippers Association** (75-5663 Palani Rd, at Alii Dr, Kailua-Kona, 329.3600, 800/762.7541; fax 334.0941), which books 30- to 54-foot boats.

Other reliable charter-boat companies include **Kona Activities Center** (329.3171, 800/367.5288; fax 326.7664) and **Charter Locker** (326.2553; fax 329.7590).

Donatoni's ★★★$$$$ One of Hawaii's outstanding Italian restaurants, this is the place to savor Northern Italian favorites: tender *calamari fritti* (fried squid); *linguine al pescatore* (with mussels, scallops, and clams); and *osso buco alla milanese* (veal shanks with vegetables, white wine, and tomatoes). There are four drop-dead-gorgeous dining rooms, three inside and one outside, all featuring inspiring sunset views over the lagoon and the Pacific Ocean. The ambience is all elegance; the service, impeccable. ◆ Northern Italian ◆ Daily dinner. Reservations recommended. 886.1234 &

Dolphin Quest Here's what vacation memories are made of. This is the drill: Pick up dolphin lottery tickets at the hotel's front desk daily by 3:30PM; check back after 5:30PM to see if your number was chosen. Reservations for children and teens must be made two months in advance; otherwise, cross your fingers. Fifteen winners between ages 5 and 12 will spend a half hour in the dolphin pool watching the playful creatures do tricks. The peak experience belongs to teenagers between ages 13 and 19, who act as trainer's helpers and get a firsthand glimpse at how dolphins learn to respond to humans. ◆ Fee; most of the proceeds go toward marine research. Daily 9:30AM, 11AM, 11:45AM, and 4PM for adults; 2PM for teens; 3PM for younger kids. 885.2875 &

61 The Kings' Shops at Waikoloa This upscale collection of shops, located near the Big Island's finest resorts, has some of its best restaurants and lounges. ◆ Waikoloa Beach Dr (west of Queen Kaahumanu Hwy)

Within the Kings' Shops:

Big Island Steak House ★★★$$$$ The filet mignon is unsurpassed here, as are such creative entrées as Maine lobster hatched in Hawaii, but this place's popularity derives from having the closest thing in the county to nightlife. After 10PM on Friday and Saturday, it becomes the Merry Wahine nightclub when the bartender doubles as a disc jockey, spinning techno-pop for an upscale crowd of neighboring hotel guests and local residents. ◆ Steak/Seafood ◆ Daily dinner. 885.8805 &

Noa Noa Stop to admire the unique hand-painted clothing and handbags designed by longtime resident and shop owner Joan Simon and made in Indonesia. ◆ Daily 9:30AM-9:30PM. 885.5449 &

Roy's Waikoloa Bar and Grill ★★★$$$ This trendy bistro is the eleventh in Roy Yamaguchi's string of "in" places. Blackened *ahi*, hibachi-style salmon, and Szechuan baby back ribs are just the beginning. ◆ Pacific Regional ◆ Daily lunch and dinner. Reservations recommended. 885.4321 &

61 Anaehoomalu Bay Ideal for windsurfing, scuba diving, walking, swimming, and sunning, the bay's crescent-shaped white-sand beach fronts the **Royal Waikoloan** (see above). The ancient royal fish ponds behind the beach are preserved by the hotel. Parking and public access are available at the south end of the beach.

62 Waikoloa Village Course At an elevation of 1,200 feet, this 18-holer sometimes has the advantage of being cooler than its oceanfront counterparts. Designed by Robert Trent Jones Jr. and the site of the **Waikoloa Open** every fall, the course (par 72, 6,970 yards) also features spectacular views of the Mauna Kea and Mauna Loa volcanoes. ♦ Expensive greens fees. Daily. Paniolo Ave (just north of Waikoloa Rd), Waikoloa Village. 883.9621

At Waikoloa Village Course:

Roussel's Waikoloa Village ★★★★ $$$ This elegant French/Creole restaurant owned by Herbert Roussel and New Orleans–born Spencer Oliver offers views of all three of Hawaii's active volcanoes. Chef Oliver is a genius with fresh Hawaiian fish, oyster shrimp gumbo, shrimp creole, and soft-shell crab meunière. The Cajun-style blackened fish is legendary. ♦ French/Creole ♦ Su, M lunch; Tu-Sa lunch and dinner. Reservations recommended. 883.9644 &

63 Four Seasons Resort Hualalai $$$$ Each new hotel in Hawaii seems more lavish and resplendent than the last, and the latest addition to the Big Island's repertoire is no exception. The 212 rooms and 31 suites on 35 acres of oceanfront property designed to recall Hawaii in the 19th century will bedazzle most vacationers. Rooms, done in mahogany and muted natural shades, feature petroglyph and banana prints, Jacuzzi tubs—the works. A 16,000-square-foot spa, 4 restaurants, 2 stores, 8 tennis courts, and 18 holes of golf designed by Jack Nicklaus round out the offerings. ♦ 100 Kaupulehu Dr (north of Queen Kaahumanu Hwy). 325.8000, 888/340.5662; fax 325.8100 &

Within the Four Seasons Resort Hualalai:

Pahuia ★★★★$$$$ Bask in opulence, with the breeze coming off the ocean, at this dining spot with walls of koa wood and sight lines to a large aquarium. Enjoy hot herb-roasted, free-range chicken with buttermilk mashed potatoes or thyme-seared salmon with truffle-whipped potatoes and hot buttered corn (there's a low-calorie menu too). ♦ Pacific Rim/International ♦ Daily breakfast, lunch, and dinner. Reservations recommended. 325.8000 &

KonaVillage ᘯᘰ

63 Kona Village Resort $$$$ This is the ultimate "get away from it all" resort, once so remote guests had to be flown in (now they can drive up Route 19). What sets this all-inclusive property apart is what it lacks—telephones, TV sets, radios, and suits and ties. The watchwords are luxury, simplicity, and peace and quiet. Aside from three tennis courts, nothing here even vaguely resembles the standard hotel experience. The 125 individual thatch bungalows, sprawling over 82 acres, are replicas of New Zealand,

Samoan, Tahitian, Hawaiian, and other Polynesian structures. Guests are greeted with flower leis and rum punch, then set free to play with the toys, including kayaks, sailboats, and snorkeling gear; ride in a glass-bottom boat; and attend cocktail parties, luaus, guided petroglyph tours, lei-making classes, and scuba dives. A fitness center is a new addition. Meals are included in the rate. ♦ Kaupulehu Dr (north of Queen Kaahumanu Hwy). 325.5555, 800/367.5290; fax 325.5124; kvr@aloha.net; www.konavillage.com &

Within the Kona Village Resort:

Hale Moana ★★★$$$$ Chef Glen Alos has made this restaurant his creative playground. The luncheon buffet, with elegant samplings of Big Island favorites, is a memorable seaside repast. Dinner selections include fresh *opakapaka* broiled with pineapple salsa; *ono* sautéed with lime-macadamia nut beurre blanc; and jumbo Malaysian prawns stir-fried with garlic, peppers, and Chinese vegetables. Five panels in this high-ceilinged Polynesian *hale* (house) depict Captain Cook's voyages to Hawaii. The panels, entitled *Les Sauvages de la Mer Pacifique*, are made of 18th-century French wallpaper; they were rolled up and stored in a Paris attic for more than a hundred years before an American collector discovered them. ♦ Hawaiian Regional ♦ Daily breakfast, lunch, and dinner. Reservations required for nonguests; no shorts allowed. 325.5555 &

Kona Village Luau ★★★★$$$$ The best luau in Hawaii begins with a tour of the grounds, where you will witness the unveiling of the *imu* (an earthen oven where the pig and sweet potatoes are roasted). It's a dramatic event, with *malo*-clad men chipping away at the *imu* and steam rising from the pit. The feast is as authentic as a commercial luau gets, with *opihi* (limpets, a Hawaiian delicacy), banana pudding, sushi, *laulau* (steamed pork with taro leaves), *poki* (raw fish), and a host of delicacies from Hawaii and the South Pacific. The program, held across a lagoon from the luau pavilion, is fiery and beautifully lit, with chants of Pele, Hawaii's volcano goddess, and ancient and modern dances. Look for Hawaiian artist Herb Kane's brilliant paintings on the back wall of the pavilion. ♦ Hawaiian ♦ F 5:30PM. Reservations required. 325.5555 &

Hale Samoa ★★$$$$ The fancier of the two dining rooms at the **Kona Village Resort** is highly recommended whether you're a guest or not. The menu includes grilled Indonesian lobster tail, tenderloin of buffalo with mushroom leek compote, and fresh *opakapaka* served in a romantic room. ♦ Pacific Rim ♦ M-Tu, Th, Sa-Su dinner. Reservations required for nonguests; guests pay a surcharge to dine here. 325.5555 &

64 Kona Coast State Park A bumpy 1.5-mile drive through an eerie lava field (worth the trip in itself) leads to Kaelehuluhulu Beach, with picnic tables and great snorkeling. Interesting ruins lie in the lava fields behind the 6.5 acres of coarse coral sand. ◆ M-Tu, Th-Su 9AM-8PM. Northwest of Queen Kaahumanu Hwy

65 Natural Energy Laboratory of Hawaii Authority (NEL) Taking advantage of Keahole's unique geographical location, which receives more sunshine than any other US coastal location and has deep water relatively close to shore, the **Natural Energy Lab** pumps up to 28,400 gallons of seawater per minute from depths of 50 feet and 2,000 feet. The temperature difference between the deep and shallow water is used periodically to run heat exchangers, which in turn produce energy (it's something like a reverse refrigerator, making electricity instead of using it). The almost pathogen-free seawater also is used for all sorts of clever aquacultural ideas, including the controlled growth of specialty food products such as Maine lobster and *hirame* (a flounder prized for sashimi); a

Tahitian black pearl research lab; and a *spirulina* (spiral-shaped micro-algae sold in health-food stores) farm. ◆ Free. Lecture: Th 10AM. Self-guided tours. Reservations recommended. 73-4460 Queen Kaahumanu Hwy (between Kaiwi St and Keahole-Kona International Airport). 329.7341; fax 326.3262; nelha@ilhawaii.net; www.bigisland.com/nelha

65 Wawaloli Beach Park (Old Kona Airport) This long stretch of golden sand is a favorite with scuba divers and swimmers. Statistically, this is the sunniest beach in the US. There are bathroom and shower facilities. ◆ West of Queen Kaahumanu Hwy

66 Kona to Hawi Drive Don't miss this drive through cattle country, lava fields, and mountains. Done right, it's an all-day trip—and a magnificent one. From Kona take Mamalahoa Highway (Route 190) north to Waimea. Turn left, and continue northwest on Kohala Mountain Road (Route 250) to Hawi. Take the coastal road (Route 270 and Queen Kaahumanu Highway) back to Kona.

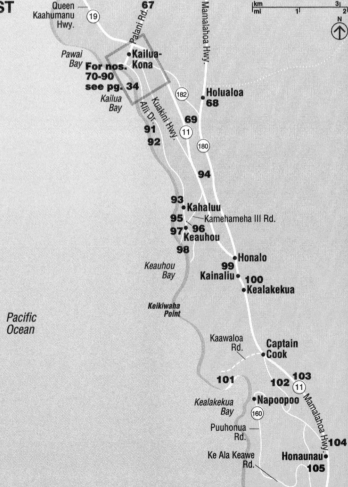

KONA COAST

Queen Kaahumanu Hwy. (19)

Pawai Bay

•Kailua-Kona

For nos. 70-90 see pg. 34

Kailua Bay

Palani Rd.

67

Mamalahoa Hwy.

km mi

N

182

•Holualoa
68

Kuakini Hwy.

Alii Dr.

91
92

69
(11)

180

94

93
•Kahaluu

95 ←Kamehameha III Rd.

97• 96
Keauhou

98

Keauhou Bay

99 **•Honalo**

Kainaliu

100
•Kealakekua

Keikiwaha Point

Pacific Ocean

Kaawaloa Rd.

Captain
•Cook

101

102 103
(11)

Kealakekua Bay

(160)

•Napoopoo

Puuhonua Rd.

Mamalahoa Hwy.

104

Ke Ala Keawe Rd.

Honaunau•
105

Kona Coast

Great beaches, fabulous diving, and almost guaranteed sunshine draw folks to the Kona Coast on the western side of the Big Island. After a day of sand and surf stroll through the tourist town of **Kailua-Kona** (also called either just **Kailua,** or just **Kona**), where there are stores to explore, restaurants to sample, and cocktails to be sipped oceanside while watching the sun swiftly slide below the horizon, ending the day with a fiery glow.

67 Holualoa Drive If you're staying on the Kona Coast, set aside an afternoon for this panoramic drive, easily the best in the area. Start from Palani Road (Route 190) in Kailua-Kona and head north. After four miles, look for a nursery on the right and turn right onto Mamalahoa Highway (Route 180). Take a slow cruise south on Mamalahoa Highway, stopping in quaint Holualoa to browse among the galleries and shops until sunset, then drive a half mile down to the Hualalai Road (Route 182) turnoff. Descending this road at sunset into Kona is what Hawaii is all about.

68 Kona Hotel $ A Holualoa landmark for more than 70 years, this ramshackle pink building attracts a steady stream of artists, hikers, sportfishers, students, and adventurers. Methodically disorganized and undeniably charming, it features the world's most scenic outhouse, 11 spartan rooms without phones or private baths, very inexpensive rates, and locals dozing on the front porch. Even if you don't stay, stop by for a "how's it going?" There's no restaurant. ◆ No credit cards accepted. 76-5908 Mamalahoa Hwy, Holualoa. 324.1155

68 Studio 7 Owned by artists Hiroke and Setsuko Morinoue, this gallery is small and serene, with a quality much like a Zen garden or a tasteful, unpretentious Japanese inn. Morinoue's own paintings and prints share space with the Big Island's best in all media. ◆ Tu-Sa. 76-5920 Mamalahoa Hwy, Holualoa. 324.1335

68 Holualoa Inn $$ One of the finest bed-and-breakfasts on the Big Island, this inn has a spectacular view of the Kona Coast from its immaculate, open-beamed living room. The two suites and four guest rooms have Polynesian- and Asian-inspired decors, with careful attention to detail and artwork; a tiled pool and deck beckon outside. The location—on 40 acres in the quiet, charming town of Holualoa—is another major plus. There's no restaurant. ◆ 76-5932 Mamalahoa Hwy, Holualoa. 324.1121, 800/392.1812; fax 322.2472; inn@aloha.net; www.konaweb.com/hinn

69 Kimura Lauhala Shop Tsuruyo Kimura has been making and selling *lauhala* (items made from woven pandanus) since the days when *hala* trees were abundant in Kona and the Kimuras traveled around the island bartering. The 50-odd–year-old shop is awash in woven fiber goods from Hawaii and the South Pacific—hats, mats, kitchen goods, purses, and wall hangings. Ask for the Kona *lauhala;* it's the best. ◆ M-Sa. 77-9961 Hualalai Rd (at Mamalahoa Hwy). 324.0053

70 Kailua Candy Company Considered by many to make the best chocolate in Hawaii, this small but prolific candy factory uses only fresh ingredients. Grab a handful of free samples and watch the workers do their thing behind the glass windows of the factory, then send 30 pounds of sweets to your dietetic enemies all over the world. ◆ Daily. 74-5563 Kaiwi St (at Pawai Pl), Kailua-Kona. 329.2522, 800/622.2462 ♿

71 Kona Brewing Company ★$$ In recent years microbrew pubs have taken on increasingly high profiles in Hawaii, and this establishment is certainly a popular spot. The pub food served here is one-of-a-kind: Pele's Pizza (Cajun tomato sauce, sausage, rock shrimp, red peppers, and roasted onions) and Kohala Pizza (fresh spinach, red peppers, macadamia nuts, and parmesan sausage), for example. For those less daring, sandwiches and salads are also on the menu. There's a 25-barrel hops processing system visible to diners through a glass wall. Hint: Local wisdom points toward having a Firerock Pale Ale with the meal. ◆ Pub ◆ Daily lunch and dinner. North Kona Shopping Center, 75-5629 Kuakini Hwy (at Palani Rd), Kailua-Kona. 334.1133 ♿

72 Buns In The Sun ★$ Start your day munching on pastries and sipping freshly brewed coffee out on the sunny patio. Order a sandwich to go, and you're set for a picnic lunch at the beach. ◆ Coffeehouse ◆ Daily breakfast and lunch. Lanihau Shopping Center, 75-5595 Palani Rd (between Kuakini and Queen Kaahumanu Hwys), Kailua-Kona. 326.2774 ♿

73 Kona Ranch House $$ The patio bar and homey atmosphere of this plantation-style restaurant make it popular with local families. There are two dining rooms: the country-style **Paniolo Room** inside, and the **Plantation Lanai,** filled with wicker furnishings. The menu focuses on Big Island beef (try the ribs), fresh fish, and local specialties, but the food tends to be pricey. ◆ American ◆ Daily breakfast, lunch, and dinner. 75-5653 Ololi Rd (just east of Kuakini Hwy), Kailua-Kona. 329.7061 ♿

74 Kona Seaside Hotel $ The best choice in town for the budget traveler, this hotel features two swimming pools and 224 rooms with big beds, air-conditioning, cable TV, refrigerators, phones, and private lanais. While the location is ideal for shopaholics, it's not recommended for anyone trying to get away from it all. There are two restaurants on the property, but they're not recommended. ♦ 75-5646 Palani Rd (between Alii Dr and Kuakini Hwy), Kailua-Kona. 329.2455, 800/367.7000; fax 329.6157; konaseaside@juno.com; www.sand-seaside.com/kona.html

74 Quinn's ★$$ A favorite with local restaurant staffers seeking a bite after their evening shifts (it serves dinner until 2AM), this hideaway around the corner from Alii Drive serves salads and sandwiches, vegetarian specialties, fresh fish, and beef in a patio setting. ♦ American ♦ Daily lunch and dinner. 75-5655 Palani Rd (between Alii Dr and Kuakini Hwy), Kailua-Kona. 329.3822 ♿

75 King Kamehameha's Kona Beach Hotel $$ If shopping and sightseeing are more important to you than secluded white-sand beaches, look no further. The "King Kam" is located at the head of Kailua-Kona's main street, Alii Drive, in easy walking distance of **Kailua Pier** (see page 35) and the town's shops, restaurants, and historic sites. The hotel's twin buildings have 451 rooms and suites with lanais, TVs, air-conditioning, phones, and refrigerators. Adjoining the lobby is the Kona Coast's only fully air-conditioned mall, containing 15 shops. The hotel offers guests and nonguests free tours of the grounds. A pool, four tennis courts, and a strand of beach run along Kailua Bay. ♦ 75-5660 Palani Rd (at Alii Dr), Kailua-Kona. 329.2911, 800/367.6060; fax 329.4602; hthcorp@worldnet.att.net; www.konabeachhotel.com ♿

Within King Kamehameha's Kona Beach Hotel:

Kona Beach Restaurant ★$$ The deal here is the prime rib and seafood buffet (Friday and Saturday from 5:30 to 9PM). The daily breakfast buffet and Sunday brunch are also commendable. ♦ American ♦ M-Sa breakfast, lunch, and dinner; Su brunch and dinner. 329.2911 ♿

Island Breeze Luau ★$$$$ The beauty of the historical grounds gives this, your

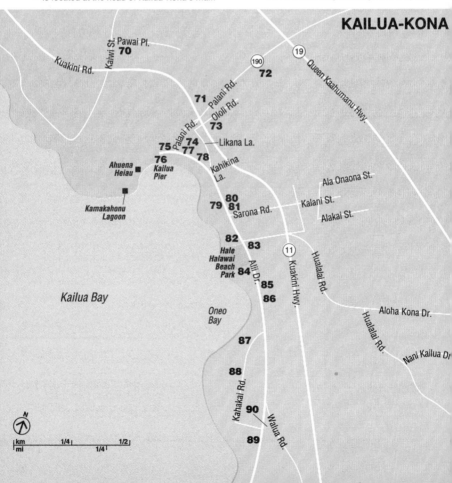

KAILUA-KONA

Ahuena Heiau

average hotel luau, added appeal and atmosphere. ◆ Luau ◆ Tu-Th, Su 5:30PM. Reservations required. 326.4969

Behind King Kamehameha's Kona Beach Hotel:

Ahuena Heiau In his final years, Kamehameha the Great ruled the newly united Hawaiian kingdom from this cove near Kamakahonu ("Eye of the Turtle") Lagoon. Dedicated to Lono, the Hawaiian god of fertility, this was an area of peace and prosperity. Kamehameha died here in 1819, and his body was taken to a secret resting place. Today the remains of royal fishponds and a compound of buildings, including an oracle tower and the historic **Ahuena Heiau** (Ahuena Temple), the king's refuge in his final days, are found at this picturesque historic site, which was restored by the **King Kamehameha's Kona Beach Hotel** under the direction of the **Bishop Museum** of Honolulu. ◆ Free. M, F-Sa 24 hours; closed Tuesday-Thursday, and Sunday 6-10PM; free 45-minute tour M, F-Su 1:30PM

76 Kailua Pier Every water activity in downtown Kona, including sportfishing, **Atlantis** and **Nautilus** rides, parasailing, dinner cruises, day cruises, diving trips, and late-afternoon outrigger **Canoe Club** practices, starts and finishes here. ◆ Alii Dr (just west of Palani Rd), Kailua-Kona

Activities on the Kailua Pier:

Atlantis Submarines The hour-long excursion, from launch craft to sub and back again, is a tightly organized act—though *Honolulu Weekly* recently featured the excursion in its pages as the reader's choice for tackiest tourist attraction. The 48-passenger air-conditioned craft is 65 feet long, 17.5 feet tall, and weighing in at 80 tons, with a silent cruising speed of 1.5 knots. The dives range from 100 feet to 115 feet, depending on the location, and all trips include an on-board commentator. What you see through the 21-inch view-ports depends on where you are; lucky passengers may see sharks, manta rays, dolphins, moray eels, and possibly whales. ◆ Fee. Daily 10AM, 11AM, 12:30PM, 1:30PM, 2:30PM. 326.7939. Also at: Pioneer Inn, 658 Wharf St (between Hotel and Papelekane Sts), Lahaina, Maui. 667.2224; Hilton Hawaiian Village, 2005 Kalia Rd (between Paoa Pl and Ala Moana Blvd), Waikiki, Oahu. 973.9811

Nautilus Semi-Submersible Not to be confused with **Atlantis Submarines** (see above), which dives completely underwater, the **Nautilus Semi-Submersible** remains partially above the surface. The comfortable passenger area, six to eight feet below the water line, has air-conditioning, padded seats, stereo music, and a video monitor. You'll get an up-close view of coral gardens and their denizens from the view-ports. Divers, swimming with the sub, bring up creatures from the bottom, while a knowledgeable commentator answers questions. ◆ Fee. Daily 9:30AM, 10:30AM, 11:30AM, 12:30PM. 326.2003. Also at: Kewalo Basin, Ward Ave (just south of Ala Moana Blvd), Honolulu, Oahu. 591.9199

Captain Beans' Cruise This is basically a floating luau on an orange and brown double-hulled barge owned and operated by **Roberts Hawaii**, a large tour company. Despite the mediocre dinner meal and two hours of touristy entertainment, participants always seem to enjoy themselves. ◆ Fee. Daily 5:15PM. Reservations required. 329.2955, 800/831.5541; fax 329.2631

Body Glove The pseudo-sailboat takes the booby prize for beauty, but it's the best dive

MARK AMMERMAN/NORTH MARKET STREET GRAPHICS

boat out of Kona for beginners. The day trip to **Pawai Bay Marine Preserve** includes breakfast and lunch—and kids will love the 15-foot slide and high dive on the deck. ♦ Fee. Daily 9AM-1:30PM. Reservations required. 326.7122; 800/551.8911; bcruises@gte.net; www.bodyglove@hawaii.com

77 Ocean View Inn ★$ If Kona had a truck stop, this would be it. There's an ocean view (if you look *really* hard through the louvered windows), but since 1935, when dinner cost 50¢, the big attraction at this landmark hotel restaurant has been home cooking at nontourist prices (not, repeat, *not* speedy service). The menu's eclectic mix of Hawaiian, American, Japanese, and Chinese standards has attracted the likes of Lucille Ball, Jimmy Stewart, and Lloyd Bridges. There's even an old soda fountain that looks like it was shipped intact from the "Happy Days" set. ♦ Hawaiian/American/Asian ♦ Tu-Su breakfast, lunch, and dinner; closed in September. No credit cards accepted. 75-5683 Alii Dr (between Likana La and Palani Rd), Kailua-Kona. 329.9998 &

78 Sibu Cafe ★★$ Affordable and well-prepared Indonesian cuisine, served both indoors and outdoors, makes this small cafe an excellent lunch spot. It's casual and pleasant, with a variety of piquant curries, satay dishes with spicy peanut sauces, and barbecued meats and vegetables. The classic *gado gado* (vegetable) salad with peanut and lime dressing has a big following, as do the vegetarian stir-fries. Balinese artifacts adorn this tiny but atmospheric place. ♦ Indonesian ♦ Daily lunch and dinner. No credit cards accepted. Kona Banyan Court, 75-5695 Alii Dr (between Likana La and Palani Rd), Kailua-Kona. 329.1112 &

79 Hulihee Palace Members of the Hawaiian *alii* (royalty) spent their summer vacations at this Victorian-style, coral-and-lava structure built in 1838 by Big Island governor John Adams Kuakini, brother-in-law of King Kamehameha. Operated as a museum by the Daughters of Hawaii since 1924, it is simple but impressive, with a massive koa dining table, Queen Kapiolani's four-poster bed, and fabulous 19th-century cabinetry and mementos. ♦ Admission. Daily. 75-5718 Alii Dr (between Sarona Rd and Kahikina La), Kailua-Kona. 329.1877 &

80 Mokuaikaua Church Built in 1836 by the first missionaries, this is the oldest Christian

church in Hawaii. Its 112-foot steeple is still the tallest structure in town. The lava-rock walls were mortared with a mixture of crushed, burnt coral and *kukui* nut oil. ♦ Alii Dr (between Sarona Rd and Kahikina La), Kailua-Kona

81 Middle Earth Bookshoppe Who would expect a haven for the literati among the tourist shops of Kailua-Kona? This is a bookstore for browsers, with a cornucopia of travel guides, children's books, Hawaiiana, maps, calendars, and art magazines, as well as the standard fiction and nonfiction. Bibliophiles, give yourselves at least an hour. ♦ Kona Plaza, 75-5719 Alii Dr (at Sarona Rd), Kailua-Kona. 329.2123

82 Hula Heaven It's a treasure trove of kitschy Hawaiian collectibles from the 1920s to the 1950s, those halcyon days of raffia-skirted hula dolls, hand-painted neckties, Mundorff prints, and Matson cruise-liner menus. The hula girl lamps, silk aloha shirts, and muumuus can cost hundreds of dollars, but the charm bracelets, salt-and-pepper shakers, and reproductions go for much less. This place is hard to resist. ♦ Kona Inn Shopping Village, 75-5744 Alii Dr (at Hualalai Rd), Kailua-Kona. 329.7885 &

82 Kona Inn Restaurant ★★$$$ The building is fondly remembered as the site of the wonderful old **Kona Inn,** which, unfortunately, was torn down in favor of yet another shopping center. This restaurant got the best of the deal—it overlooks the manicured lawns with a million-dollar ocean view. The proprietors did the site justice by building a beautiful bar, a patio area (great for sunset cocktails), and an open-air dining room with lots of rich koa wood. Less imagination went into the menu, which relies on the unfailingly repetitive catch of the day (expensive here), other seafood dishes such as Kailua prawns and kabobs, plus top sirloin and prime rib. ♦ Steak/Seafood ♦ Daily lunch and dinner. Reservations recommended. Kona Inn Shopping Village, 75-5744 Alii Dr (at Hualalai Rd), Kailua-Kona. 329.4455 &

82 Don Drysdale's Club 53 ★$ The late Los Angeles Dodger pitching great opened this bar and eatery, a local favorite. With indoor and outdoor tables, it's known for its relaxed atmosphere, ocean view, cheap drinks, good service, and 777 cheeseburgers (some say they're Kona's best). This is a lively spot where folks nosh on soups, nachos, and buffalo burgers while watching sports events on TV. ♦ American ♦ Daily lunch and dinner. Kona Inn Shopping Village, 75-5744 Alii Dr (at Hualalai Rd), Kailua-Kona. 329.6651 ♦ Also at: Keauhou Shopping Village, 78-6831 Alii Dr (just north of Kamehameha III Rd), Keauhou. 322.0070 ♦

83 Uncle Billy's Kona Bay Hotel $ This one-time annex to the old **Kona Inn** was converted into a 145-room hotel run by bargain-minded Uncle Billy Kimi (who has 11 kids). The rooms are spartan but clean and air-conditioned, and the property has a pool. Kailua Village's shopping and historic attractions are right outside the front door, and **Kimo's Family Buffet** restaurant offers unspectacular but reasonably priced food. ♦ 75-5739 Alii Dr (at Hualalai Rd), Kailua-Kona. 329.1393, 800/367.5102; fax 329.9210 ♦

84 Waterfront Row A half dozen take-out joints selling everything from coffee to sushi are complemented by three real restaurants here. The lanai dining area on the first floor is a major plus. ♦ 75-5770 Alii Dr (between Kahakai and Hualalai Rds), Kailua-Kona

Within Waterfront Row:

Chart House ★★$$$$ The first Chart House opened in Aspen, Colorado, more than 30 years ago. This ocean-view outpost is No. 66 in the chain and provides selections that mainland Chart Houses lack, like *poki* (raw fish)—a favorite island appetizer—and grilled *ono*. ♦ Steak/Seafood ♦ Daily dinner. Reservations recommended. 329.2451 ♦

Jolly Roger Restaurant ★$$ The best things about this branch of the island-style cafeteria chain are its oceanside location, (relatively) low prices, and Sunday brunch, where the steak and eggs Benedict and orange French toast are standouts. The place also morphs into a mini dance bar on weekend nights; the crowd is young. ♦ Tropical American ♦ M-Sa breakfast, lunch, and dinner; Su brunch and dinner. 329.1344 ♦

Michaelangelo's ★$$ The alfresco oceanfront atmosphere draws folks to this casual dining room, and the all-you-can-eat spaghetti, scampi, and dozens of other choices keep them coming back. ♦ Italian/ Seafood ♦ Daily lunch and dinner. Reservations recommended. 329.4436 ♦

85 Island Lava Java ★$ Order a cup of java and a warm scone at this alfresco cafe (soups, salads, and sandwiches are available too) and enjoy the parade of Hawaii humanity. Local musicians perform here nightly—though the acts are more "Gong Show" than The Back Street Boys. ♦ Coffeehouse ♦ Daily 7AM-10PM. Alii Sunset Plaza, 75-5799 Alii Dr (between Walua and Hualalai Rds), Kailua-Kona. 327.2161 ♦

86 Hard Rock Cafe ★$$ Most diners will have more imagination than to come here for the food—broiled chicken, hamburgers of every description, teriyaki steak, and the like—but this is one of Kona's premier night spots and the main reason to drop in. ♦ American ♦ Daily lunch and dinner. 75-5815 Alii Dr (between Walua and Hualalai Rds), Kailua-Kona. 329.8866 ♦

86 Lulu's ★★$$ This open-air restaurant is a must-do, both for the cuisine (try a crab cake appetizer and a Burrito as Big as Your Head) and the atmosphere (late Hawaiian kitsch). When you take into consideration the fact that Kona is neither a hotbed of social activity nor an outpost of gourmet cuisine, this place ranks high. (Even more so after a "Man vs. Margarita," a 20-ounce cocktail.) ♦ American ♦ Daily 11AM-2AM. 75-5819 Alii Dr (between Walua and Hualalai Rds), Kailua-Kona. 331.2633

86 Durty Jake's ★★$ One of the happening ocean-view eateries in town, this place with alfresco dining serves panfried *ahi* on a bed of rice with baby greens and a mango kiwi salsa that's to die for. Don't forget to have a mango margarita. ♦ Hawaiian ♦ Daily breakfast, lunch, and dinner. 75-5819 Alii Dr (between Walua and Hualalai Rds), Kailua-Kona. 329.7366 ♦

87 Huggo's ★$$$$ This oceanside restaurant is yet another where the setting surpasses the food, though the entrées have improved lately. Fortunately, if you don't like your entrée, you can feed it to the manta rays that play in the floodlights right outside. The lunch fare centers around sandwiches, with prime rib, steak, and seafood (including, when available, fresh lobster and prawns) for dinner. This is also a great place for sunset cocktails. ♦ Steak/Seafood ♦ M-F lunch and dinner; Sa-Su dinner. Reservations recommended. 75-5828 Kahakai Rd (west of Alii Dr), Kailua-Kona. 329.1493 ♦

The first flight from the mainland to Hawaii was in 1925. A 2-engine PN-9 Navy seaplane left San Francisco on 25 August but ran out of gas 300 miles short of Maui and splashed down in the Pacific. The pilots improvised sails and sailed into the harbor at Kauai on 10 September. Two years later, an Army Fokker C2-3 Wright 220 Trimotor made the first nonstop flight from Oakland, California, to Oahu.

Lava Java: The Kona Coffee Story

Kona coffee actually had its beginnings in England: In 1825, King Kamehameha II, and his wife, Queen Kamamalu, both died of measles on a visit to England. The captain of the ship carrying the royal couple back to Hawaii stopped in Rio de Janeiro and purchased several hundred young coffee plants, which he cultivated on **Oahu** until his death in 1827. The coffee fields grew wild until 1842, when cuttings were used to start the first commercial coffee plantation on **Kauai**'s **North Shore.** The 245 pounds of beans exported that year turned out to be the last, however, as the area's weather—warm and wet—was ill-suited to coffee cultivation. (At this time, coffee was sold as unroasted beans. Roasting and grinding was done by the consumer or at the odd coffeehouse. Roasted coffee wasn't packaged until the Civil War, and national distribution only began in 1973.)

Samuel Ruggles, a missionary, brought coffee to the Big Island from **Manoa Valley,** Oahu in 1828. Circa 1875, the phrase "Kona coffee" came into the vernacular, when it was discovered that the **Kona Coast** was the coffee bean's climate of choice—12,000-foot mountains block the tradewinds, porous volcanic soil allows for good root drainage, and the plants thrive on the region's sunny mornings and rain-soaked afternoons. Today there are 650 farms producing Kona coffee on the island's west coast.

Coffee trees usually grow not much taller than a person, and their glossy leaves and white flowers ripen into dark red fruits known as "cherries." These grow in clusters on the branch and must be picked only when they are mature. But the cherries ripen at different intervals; as a result, laborers need to handpick every one, usually returning to each branch about three times over the course of weeks. A machine subsequently removes the pulp from a cherry, with two seeds—or beans—remaining (except the cherry at the end of a branch, which has only one seed and makes a kind of coffee known to consumers as "Peaberry"). The seeds are then dried by sun or machine and covered with parchment, and the pulp discarded. Next, the beans are roasted, a grader separates them by size and weight, and a machine packages them. **Holualoa Kona Coffee** (77-6261 Mamalahoa Hwy, just north of Hualalai Rd, 322.9937) gives a behind-the-scenes look at processing, from bean to box, Monday through Friday from 7:30AM to 4PM. The **Royal Kona Coffee Mill** (83-5427 Mamalahoa Hwy, Honaunau, 328.2511) offers a self-guided tour of its operations and a lava tube. A guide is available if requested a day in advance. It's open daily from 7:45AM to 5PM.

Only a fraction of the world's coffee is made in Kona. Most comes from the continent where Kona coffee has its roots—South America—as well as Africa and elsewhere. Buyer beware: The majority of what is sold today as Kona coffee is in fact a blend, often with precious few Kona beans. For the real thing (which costs more than $18 a pound), make sure the label says "100 Percent Kona Coffee."

The Kona Coffee Festival, a four-day celebration in the name of the crop, is held in Kona each November. A queen is elected and presides over an elaborate parade and series of events aimed at promoting coffee. For more information, call the **Hawaii Visitors' Bureau** in Kona (808/329.7787).

88 Royal Kona Resort $$$ With its landmark saltwater lagoon and lava peninsula, this place manages to be romantic even though it's a somewhat large hotel. The 444 rooms and 8 suites are in 3 towers at the south end of Kona, with private lanais landscaped with bougainvillea looking out at the ocean, mountains, or village. Amenities include four tennis courts (three lighted), a pool, and a small beach nearby. There are two restaurants: **Tropics Cafe,** an open-air dining room with a sweeping view of the Kailua coastline; and the **Windjammer Lounge,** a lunch spot and lounge. The hotel's luau is held oceanside on Monday, Friday, and Saturday from 5:30 to 8:30PM. The close proximity to Kailua Village is another plus. ◆ Kahakai Rd (west of Alii Dr), Kailua-Kona. 329.3111, 800/222.5642; fax 329.9532; cameron@royalkona.com; www.royalkona.com ⌖

89 Kona Reef $$ The big advantage of this condominium resort is its location. It's within easy walking distance of the shops and restaurants, solving the problem of always having to find a parking place. The 58 1-, 2-, and 3-bedroom units come loaded with all the comforts of home (fully equipped kitchens, washer/dryers, air-conditioning, cable TV, telephones), and there's even daily maid service, but no restaurant. ◆ 75-5888 Alii Dr (between Lunapule and Kahakai Rds), Kailua-Kona. 329.2959; 800/367.5004; fax 329.2762 ⌖

90 Tres Hombres ★★$$ Things have been looking up at the former **Tom Bombadil's Food & Drink** since it was remodeled and reopened by Raphael Cifuentes, who has operated the successful restaurant of the same name in the tiny town of Kawaihae since 1991. Pull in for a fish taco or an order of *carnitas* (pork, beans, rice, scallions, and guacamole served with flour tortillas) on the patio. ◆ Mexican ◆ Daily lunch and dinner. 75-5864 Walua Rd (between Lunapule Rd and Alii Dr), Kailua-Kona. 329.2173 ⌖

91 Aston Royal Sea Cliff Resort $$$$ Families who prefer to be self-sufficient will absolutely love the large, attractive units in this condominium complex. The stark, angular white structure stands out along the lava coastline (there's no beach) and includes 150 studios and 1- and 2-bedroom suites with lanais, washer/dryers, cable TV, daily maid service, air-conditioning, and full kitchens with dishwashers and microwaves. There are two pools, a Jacuzzi, a sauna, and a tennis court on the premises, but no restaurant. Five oceanfront villas are also available. ◆ 75-6040 Alii Dr (between Royal Poinciana Dr and Lunapule Rd). 329.8021, 800/922.7866; fax 326.1887 ♿

91 Island Orchard Can't get enough of the beautiful flowers of Hawaii? Stop in here and have bouquets of ginger, orchids, anthuriums, birds of paradise, proteas, and heliconias sent home. The flowers are shipped via Federal Express and are guaranteed fresh on arrival. ◆ M-F; Sa 9AM-2PM. 75-6082 Alii Dr (between Royal Poinciana Dr and Lunapule Rd). 326.2266, 800/622.0230

92 Aston Kona by the Sea $$$$ There's no real beach nearby, but the sea view is spectacular from the 74 1- and 2-bedroom suites. The accommodations in this four-story resort come with kitchens and daily maid service; there's also a pool and Jacuzzi, but no restaurant. ◆ 75-6106 Alii Dr (between Royal Poinciana Dr and Lunapule Rd). 327.2300, 800/922.7866; fax 327.2333; www.aston-hotels.com ♿

93 Jameson's by the Sea ★★$$$ One of the few oceanside restaurants that relies on its food instead of its view (which is quite impressive), this is also one of the only places in town that serves oysters on the half shell. Fresh *opakapaka,* mahimahi, and *ono,* along with scallops, pasta, and an especially delicious scampi, highlight the menu. ◆ Seafood ◆ M-F lunch and dinner; Sa-Su dinner. Reservations recommended. 77-6452 Alii Dr, Kahaluu. 329.3195 ♿

93 White Sands Beach Around November, this beach does a disappearing act, leaving a rocky shoreline (hence its nicknames, "Disappearing Sands Beach" and "Magic Sands Beach"). It's great for swimming when the waves are low, bodysurfing when they're high, and whale sighting during the winter. ◆ Alii Dr, Kahaluu

94 La Bourgogne ★★★$$$ Owner/chef Ron Gallaher proffers Gallic pleasures like rack of lamb with rosemary butter and classically prepared game in an intimate atmosphere of hushed tones and velvet banquettes. There are only 10 tables in this tiny dining spot. ◆ Country French ◆ M-Sa dinner. Reservations recommended. Kuakini Plaza South, 77-6400 Nalani St (at Rte 11). 329.6711

95 Little Blue Church Built in 1889 and officially named **St. Peter's Catholic Church,**

this tiny tabernacle got its nickname from its blue tin roof. ◆ Alii Dr (between Makolea St and Queen Kalama Ave), Kahaluu

95 Kahaluu Beach Park Local fishing enthusiasts have found this a worthwhile spot, and the white-sand beach is great for families and amateur snorkelers, since public bathrooms are available. But stay well within the protective bay; more rescues are made here than on any other beach in Kona. ◆ Alii Dr (between Makolea St and Queen Kalama Ave), Kahaluu

96 Alapaki's The shining gem in an otherwise dull shopping mall, this charming store features handmade items by over 100 local artists and craftspeople, including koa wood jewelry and bowls, handblown glass sculptures, fine original art, and Hawaiian hula instruments. ◆ Daily. Keauhou Shopping Village, 78-6831 Alii Dr (at Kamehameha III Rd), Keauhou. 322.2007 ♿

97 Kona Country Club Golfers staying in the Kona and Keauhou Bay areas will find this 18-hole course (par 72, 6,579 yards) a convenient place to play. Magnificent ocean views and some of Hawaii's most consistently sunny weather make the layout, cut out of black lava rock, a sure bet. Just across the road is the 18-hole **Alii Country Club** course (par 72, 6,470 yards), which is under the same management. ◆ Expensive greens fees. Preferred starting times and rates for **Kona Surf Resort** guests.78-7000 Alii Dr (at Kamehameha III Rd), Keauhou. 322.2595

97 Kanaloa at Kona $$$$ These low-rise villas, with full kitchens and private lanais, rank among the most spacious accommodations in Kona. They're a good value for self-sufficient families or groups who want to share a unit. The resort, slightly off the beaten track, is extremely quiet, comfortable, and well managed, with 80 villas sprawled over 14 acres in a cul-de-sac near Keauhou Bay. Some of the split-level units have great views of the ocean, golf course, or mountains. Ceiling fans compensate for the lack of air-conditioning in some units, and the two- and three-bedroom ocean-view units have Jacuzzis and bathrooms with double vanities and separate showers with double heads. On-site extras include two lighted tennis courts and three pools, as well as a commendable terrace restaurant, **Edward's at Kanaloa,** which overlooks Heeia Bay. ◆ 78-261 Manukai St (west of Kamehameha III Rd), Keauhou. 322.2272, 800/688.7444; fax 322.3818 ♿

98 Kona Surf Resort $$ A striking example of hotel architecture, this resort is all the more impressive because its five four- and six-story wings were erected on rugged lava fields formed centuries ago at the ocean's edge. Unfortunately, the resort looks a little rough around the edges, as it's in need of renovations that are slow in coming. The 530 rooms are large, though, and the lack of a sandy beach is eased by the exquisite ocean view and the manta rays that gather nightly at the point. Amenities include two swimming pools (one of which is saltwater), a massage room, the **Kona Country Club,** three lighted tennis courts, and several shops. ♦ 78-128 Ehukai St (just west of Keleopapa Rd), Keauhou. 322.3411, 800/367.8011; fax 322.3245; konasurf@ilhawaii.net; www.ilhawaii.net/konasurf &

Within the Kona Surf Resort:

Pele's Court Dining Room $$$ The Friday-night prime rib and seafood buffet is the best thing in this marginal dining room, which otherwise features standard preparations of chicken, pasta, steak, and fish. ♦ American ♦ Daily breakfast, lunch, and dinner. 322.3411 &

99 Aloha Theater Cafe ★★$$ This is the kind of cafe you wish you had at home. Big breakfasts of French toast and omelettes with homemade bread and muffins start the day. Huge, healthy sandwiches smothered with bean sprouts and such follow for lunch, and grilled fish and a rotating selection of gourmet specials are on line for dinner. The emphasis is on homegrown freshness. It's definitely worth the drive from Kona, particularly when combined with a show at the **Aloha Performing Arts Center** (322.9924) in the same building. ♦ Cafe ♦ M-Th breakfast and lunch; F-Sa breakfast, lunch, and dinner; Su brunch. Mamalahoa Hwy, Kainaliu. 322.3383 &

100 Bad Ass Coffee Company You'll know by the blue awning and aroma of fresh-brewed joe that you're in the right place. Quality coffee—espresso, cappuccino, and other variations—is ground and brewed on the premises. Drop in for a free sample. ♦ Daily 7AM-8PM. 79-7500 Mamalahoa Hwy, Kealakekua. 322.9196

101 Captain Cook Monument Ancient Hawaiians' first contact with Europeans occurred on 17 January 1779, when the British ships *Resolution* and *Discovery* laid anchor in this bay. Given a royal welcome by the awestruck Hawaiians, Captain James Cook and his crew later suffered tragic consequences over the supposed theft of the *Discovery*'s rowboat. Cook, who unwisely took the local chief hostage, was beaten to death at the water's edge, then burned and dismembered, as was the custom. Four crew members met similar fates. The site is marked by a 27-foot-high white pillar, accessible by boat or arduous hiking trail, but visible from the south shore of Kealakekua Bay, a popular marine preserve. ♦ Kaawaloa Rd (west of the road to Napoopoo)

102 Manago Hotel $ Shabby but clean, this hotel offers lots of character, a great view, and a restaurant that boasts an island-wide following. More than three-quarters of a century old and still going strong, the hostelry is now run by a third generation of Managos. Cheap and quiet, the 42 rooms come with either private or shared baths and without TVs or telephones. ♦ 82-6155 Mamalahoa Hwy, Captain Cook. 323.2642 &

Within the Manago Hotel:

Manago Hotel Dining Room ★$ Locals come from up and down the coast for Mrs. Manago's fresh fish and pork chops. Budget prices and Japanese-style home cooking make this one of West Hawaii's landmarks. ♦ Japanese/American ♦ Tu-Su breakfast, lunch, and dinner. 323.2642 &

103 Bong Brothers The sign in front of this establishment should say "Island Institution." Many visitors pass by this roadside coffee shack. Don't make that mistake. Pull over for a free cup of some of the best Kona coffee the region has to offer; if you're hungry, grab a homemade

The Painted Church

MATT MORROW/NORTH MARKET STREET GRAPHICS

MARK AMMERMANN/NORTH MARKET STREET GRAPHICS

Puuhonua o Honaunau

sandwich or salad to go. ◆ Daily. Mamalahoa Hwy, Captain Cook. 328.9289 &

104 Royal Kona Coffee Mill and Museum
Taste the brew that made Kona famous and take a 15-minute self-guided tour of the old mill and the museum. Old equipment and photographs of past harvests are on display. ◆ Free. Daily. 83-5427 Mamalahoa Hwy, Honaunau. 328.2511 &

105 The Painted Church Officially christened **St. Benedict's Church,** this petite place of worship got its popular name from the biblical scenes that were painted on the walls and ceiling circa 1900. For Hawaiians who couldn't read or write, Father John Berchman Velghe of Belgium illustrated Christianity with images not unlike those in the cathedral of Burgos, Spain. ◆ Painted Church Rd (just north of Ke Ala Keawe Rd), Honaunau

106 Puuhonua o Honaunau (Place of Refuge National Park) When ancient Hawaiians broke *kapu* (sacred law) or were fleeing an enemy in times of war, their only escape was to run and/or swim to the nearest *puuhonua* (place of refuge), where they were exonerated by a *kahuna pule* (priest). Because breaking *kapu* was believed to anger the gods and cause mass death and destruction (lava flows, tsunamis, floods, famine, and the like), offenders were often literally running for their lives, hiding out until things calmed down a bit. This *puuhonua* was the largest in Hawaii, resting on a 20-acre peninsula of lava, and is now part of the 180-acre national historical park. Dominating the site is the **Great Wall,** a massive, mortarless barrier of lava rock—1,000 feet long, 10 feet high, and 17 feet

wide—constructed around two *heiau.* Also here are thatch-roofed huts, wooden idols, royal fish ponds, a trail to cliffs and lava tubes, a visitors' center, picnic area, rest rooms, petroglyphs, and palace grounds. ◆ Admission. Daily 7:30AM-8PM. Ke Ala Keawe and Puuhonua Rds. 328.2326; www.nps.gov/puho

107 Hookena Beach Park Although it's hard to believe when you see it, Hookena was once the main port in South Kona. Now it's a backwater community adjacent to a salt-and-pepper (black and white sand) beach favored by local families. Although the swimming, snorkeling, and bodysurfing here are excellent, the road to the shore is narrow and steep—a trial for those prone to car sickness. Camping is allowed by permit. At press time renovations were in the works that may result in hot showers and other creature comforts. ◆ Hookena

According to the 1990 US Census, 75,000 native Californians are living in Hawaii, and 140,000 Hawaiian-born individuals are living in California.

Hawaii, the southernmost state in the US, is the only island state in the country. It is larger than Rhode Island, Delaware, and Connecticut combined.

Hawaii's first hotel was owned by Don Francisco de Paula Marin, a Spaniard who arrived in Honolulu in 1793 and opened his house to paying guests in 1810. He also controlled the first brewery; the first barrel of beer was made on the hotel site in 1812.

Kau District

The southernmost section of the Big Island and the site of the southernmost point in the United States, the Kau District is a remote and dramatic place. Here green pastureland rolls to a coastline of windswept beaches and striking cliffs that tower above the sea. There are few tourist attractions, and relatively few tourists, but a drive through the region is sure to be memorable. Turn off the main roads to find deserted beaches, incredible views, and a glimpse into the rural lifestyle of the local residents.

108 Ka Lae (South Point) It's only 11 miles from Mamalahoa Highway (Route 11), but it feels like you're driving to the end of the earth. Once barely passable, the road is now paved, making the trip thoroughly enjoyable. Besides being the southernmost point in the US, this area is believed to be where the first Polynesian discoverers of Hawaii landed circa AD 150. Be sure to stop at the **Kamaoa Wind Farm,** a fenced-in field of windmills, and listen to the eerie symphony of 37 Mitsubishi wind turbine generators playing to a captive bovine audience. ♦ South Point Rd (south of Mamalahoa Hwy)

109 Green Sands Beach Volcanic olivine crystals created the color and inspired the name of this secluded beach on Mahana Bay. Accessible only by four-wheel-drive vehicle or by hiking or mountain biking, it's definitely a jaunt for the adventurous at heart. Once you get there, swim only if the water is calm; currents can be treacherous, and the next stop is Antarctica—7,500 miles away! ♦ East of South Point Rd

110 Naalehu There's not a lot to do here except check out the locals at the **Naalehu Fruit Stand** (and be checked out in turn), but you can tell your friends back home you've been to the southernmost community in the US.

111 Colony One at Sea Mountain Resort $$ The key word at this 76-unit condominium complex is seclusion. Halfway between Hilo and Kona, the place is so remote that it often appears vacant, and the neighboring championship 18-hole golf course (par 72, 6,416 yards) is virtually deserted. The 23 studios, 41 1-bedroom units, and 18 2-bedroom units have full kitchens and washers and dryers; the grounds feature a pool, Jacuzzi, and 4 tennis courts, but no restaurant. It's not the fanciest of resorts, but for the price, seclusion, and amenities, it's a deal. ♦ 95-789 Ninole Loop Rd (off Mamalahoa Hwy). 928.6200, 800/344.7675; fax 928.8075; seamount@gte.net; www.vi-great-vacations.com/rentals &

111 Punaluu Black Sand Beach Park One of the Big Island's best-known black-sand beaches, this park offers picnic and camping facilities and a broad bay with concrete

foundations—vestiges of its former days as a significant shipping point for Kau. Palm trees and spring-fed lagoons add to the beauty of the place. The rocky bay is recommended for swimming only when sea conditions permit. ♦ Ninole Loop Rd (off Mamalahoa Hwy)

112 Hawaii Volcanoes National Park Established in 1916, the 358-square-mile park begins at Mauna Loa near the island's center, narrows eastward, then fans south around Kilauea to the coast near the town of Kalapana. Although Mauna Loa is the most obvious landmark, most tourist attractions revolve around Kilauea, the volcano that just won't quit.

Done right, a trip to the park should take all day and part of the night (when the lava glows, an unforgettable sight). Bring binoculars, a flashlight, camera, jacket, sturdy shoes or boots, and a stocked picnic basket. Start your day at the **Kilauea Visitors Center** (985.6000) by watching the 25-minute video of the last major eruption (shown on the hour), then grab a free guide and ask the ranger to point out where the lava flows (if any) are. Continue counterclockwise on the 11-mile Crater Rim Road, making sure to stop at the **Thomas A. Jaggar Museum**; this one-room display of volcano-related things—including Pele's tears and different types of lava—is open daily.

Once you've circumnavigated Kilauea, the park's network of roads leads you to dozens of interesting sites that can be explored on foot. The **Halemaumau Trail** into the Kilauea caldera, leading across fresh lava flows, is for the hardier hiker. The 6.4-mile trek takes 5 hours round-trip, or you can meet a friend with a car at the Halemaumau parking area to avoid the hike back. **Kipuka Puaulu Bird Park** has an easily traveled 1.2-mile unpaved path

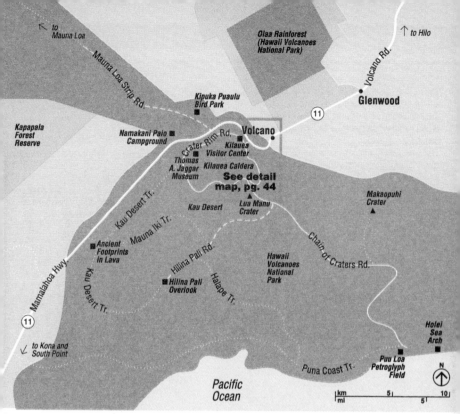

through forest and meadow filled with birds and some of the last indigenous fauna and flora in Hawaii. **Mauna Iki** is a moderate 3.6-mile, 2-hour round-trip (take the **Mauna Iki Trail,** between the 37- and 38-mile markers on Mamalahoa Highway). The paved path over a 400-year-old lava flow passes footprints made by warriors who unsuccessfully attempted to flee Kilauea's eruption of 1790. **Chain of Craters Road,** which used to continue into Hilo, leads toward the famous lava flows that have been oozing from Puu Oo since 1983, ending abruptly 20 miles from Crater Rim Road. The active vent is on park land and off-limits to the public, but people hike here at night anyway to watch the bright red rivers of lava flow into the ocean. (This is extremely dangerous—if you decide to go be very careful and bring a flashlight.) You can also view the vent from the air by helicopter. Worthy stops on the return trip include the **Puu Loa Petroglyph Field,** the **Holei Sea Arch,** and the **Hilina Pali Overlook** (Hilina Pali Rd, 17 miles round-trip from Chain of Craters Rd). Warning: Pele, the volcano goddess, doesn't like visitors taking lava rocks home as souvenirs; the park annually receives returned lava chunks in the mail from thieves besieged with bad luck. ♦ Admission. Kilauea Visitors Center daily 7:45AM-5PM. Crater Rim Dr (off Mamalahoa Hwy). Volcano eruption information 985.6000

Within Hawaii Volcanoes National Park:

Kilauea This volcano's record-breaking eruptive phase has destroyed 181 homes and numerous prominent landmarks since January 1983. A 1977 eruption sent lava less than a half mile from the now devastated Kalapana, while in 1960 the town of Kapoho was destroyed. That eruption added some 500 acres to the island, and Kapoho's lavascape served as a training ground for the astronauts who walked on the moon. Three people have been killed by an eruption in modern times. At press time Kilauea was putting on a show three miles from the end of Chain of Craters Road, but it's a hit-or-miss production.

Thurston Lava Tube Tubes form when a crust of lava hardens and a river of lava continues to flow beneath the surface. A 1975 earthquake temporarily closed this lava tube when a boulder blocked the entrance. It is named for Lorrin A. Thurston, the publisher who pushed for a **Hawaii Volcanoes National Park** and was on the expedition that discovered this tube.

Devastation Trail This eerie landscape looks like a science-fiction film set. Dead ohia trees, burned clean of their leaves by cinders from a 1959 Kilauea eruption, stand like skeletons in a bed of black pumice. A half-mile paved pathway crosses the region, ending at the Devastation parking area.

Volcano Arts Center Built in 1877, this structure served as the **Volcano House Lodge** until the present lodge was completed in

1941. It now houses a variety of locally created artwork—paintings, sculptures, pottery, and photographs—by more than 200 artists. Check out the lavascapes by veteran volcano photographer G. Brad Lewis. ♦ Daily. 967.7511 ♿

Volcano House $$ There have been a succession of **Volcano Houses** since 1846, and all have offered something no other inn in the world can match: the opportunity to eat, drink, and sleep on the rim of an active volcano. Kilauea volcano is the hotel's backyard, best seen with a cocktail in hand at **Uncle George's Lounge** (named for George Lycurgus, who won the inn in a poker game and owned and operated it from 1895 to 1960). The service here has declined, something several changes in management have not been able to remedy, and the 42-room inn and restaurant are eclipsed by the bed-and-breakfasts in the area. The main structure has the feel of a hunting lodge, with a floor-to-ceiling lava rock fireplace whose fire has burned continuously since 1847. ♦ 967.7321; fax 967.8428 ♿

Within the Volcano House:

Ka Ohelo Dining Room $$ The best thing about this restaurant is the view of Halemaumau Crater, a spectacular sight that far outshines the food served daily to mobs of tourists brought in on charter buses. Try breakfast or early dinner to avoid the rush, but don't expect gourmet fare. ♦ American ♦ Daily breakfast buffet, lunch buffet, and dinner. Reservations recommended. 967.7321 ♿

Volcano Golf and Country Club Talk about an unusual location! With the hottest bunker on earth, this high-altitude course (par 72, 18 holes, 6,503 yards) is laid out on the rim of an active volcano—a splendid treat for golfers seeking novel experiences. ♦ Moderate greens fees. Daily. Reservations recommended a week in advance. Piimauna Dr (north of Mamalahoa Hwy). 967.7331

Mauna Loa Sixty miles by thirty miles, "Long Mountain" is taller than Mount Everest and is heavier than the entire Sierra Nevada mountain range. Measured from the seafloor, it is the most massive mountain on earth in total mass (although 117 feet shorter than neighboring Mauna Kea). Having spent two million years of its three-million-year existence reaching the ocean surface, this volcano sleeps for long spells between eruptions, the last of which was in 1984. Fortunately, the chances of being incinerated in a surprise lava flow are slim to none, since it is a shield volcano, not the Mount St. Helens variety that erupts violently without notice. The **Volcano Observatory** keeps a constant watch on the area; metal barricades can be erected to stop motorists within minutes of an alert. Although reaching the summit of the volcano is possible with a three- to four-day hike (take Mauna Loa Strip Rd), the trip exceeds the boundaries of recreational tourism.

Volcano

The tiny village of Volcano has a few places to eat, a lot of bed-and-breakfasts, and an eclectic population of artsy types and adventurous retirees from the mainland that makes for interesting people watching. Thanks to the extremely wet weather, the vegetation is lush and diverse, and on the rare dry day the scenery is gorgeous. Travelers in search of a remote hideaway (with the added bonus of an active volcano nearby) happily vacation here.

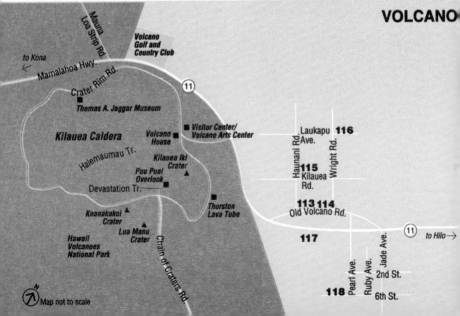

VOLCANO

Map not to scale

to Kona ←
Mamalahoa Hwy.
Mauna Loa Strip Rd.
Volcano Golf and Country Club
Crater Rim Rd.
(11)
Thomas A. Jaggar Museum
Kilauea Caldera
Volcano House
Visitor Center/ Volcano Arts Center
Halemaumau Tr.
Kilauea Iki Crater
Puu Puai Overlook
Devastation Tr.
Keanakakoi Crater
Lua Manu Crater
Hawaii Volcanoes National Park
Chain of Craters Rd.
Thurston Lava Tube
Laukapu Ave. **116**
Haunani Rd.
Wright Rd.
115 Kilauea Rd.
113 114 Old Volcano Rd.
117
(11) to Hilo →
Pearl Ave.
Ruby Ave.
Jade Ave.
2nd St.
118
6th St.

113 Surt's at Volcano Village ★★★$$$
The second-best restaurant in Volcano (after the **Kilauea Lodge Restaurant**) is deceptively ordinary looking, a hole in the wall next to the general store. Don't be fooled. It might not be fancy, but the cuisine is delicately flavored and delicious. Try the green papaya salad followed by an order of sautéed green chili squid with basil. ◆ Continental/Asian ◆ Daily dinner. Old Volcano and Haunani Rds. 967.8511

114 Kilauea Lodge $$ Built in 1938 as a camp lodge for the YMCA, this charming 10-acre estate is, for quality, location, and price, the best deal on the island. All 13 uniquely decorated units, including two cottages (ideal for families) and a suite, have private bathrooms, and some also are furnished with a fireplace and a queen-size bed (be sure to ask). Gravel walkways lead through lush, impeccable landscaping to the best dining spot in the area, the **Kilauea Lodge Restaurant,** which overlooks a large manorial front yard abloom with blue hydrangeas. A full American breakfast is included in the rate. ◆ Old Volcano Rd (between Wright and Haunani Rds). 967.7366; fax 967.7367; stay@kilauea-lodge.com; www.kilauea-lodge.com ♿

Within Kilauea Lodge:

Kilauea Lodge Restaurant ★★★★
$$$$ Easily the best in town, this gourmet continental restaurant offers first-rate cuisine, atmosphere, and service. The large, high-ceilinged dining room was the gathering place of the YMCA, which left its mark in an "International Fireplace of Friendship," built with rocks, coins, and memorabilia from civic and youth groups around the world. Of greater interest, however, are the beef, chicken, and seafood specialties and wonderful soups concocted by owner/chef Albert Jeyte, which attract diners from all over east Hawaii. If you're anywhere in the vicinity (which includes Hilo), stop in for duck à l'orange or seafood Mauna Kea. ◆ Continental ◆ Daily dinner. Reservations recommended. 967.7366 ♿

115 Hale Kilauea $ The four guest rooms here are named after the siblings of owner Morris Thomas, who built this two-story structure on three acres. All the spacious guest rooms face the fern and ohia forests, but the corner room (named **Heidi**) has a balcony and the best view. It's not the nicest bed-and-breakfast in the area (there are no phones or TVs), but what it lacks in character is made up for in price and friendly service. ◆ Kilauea Rd (between Wright and Haunani Rds). 967.7591

116 Chalet Kilauea $$$ One of the most creative and charming bed-and-breakfasts on the island, this two-story cedar-shingle home in the misty Volcano forest is run by Brian and Lisha Crawford, an engaging young couple with exquisite taste in interior decorating. There are five fanciful theme rooms—the **Out of Africa Room**, the **Oriental Jade Room**, the **Continental Lace Suite**, the **Owners' Suite**, and the **Treehouse Suite.** Afternoon tea is served in the large communal living room (stocked with hundreds of CDs), which is surrounded by ohia trees, *hapuu* ferns, and brilliant hydrangeas. Gourmet breakfasts (complimentary for guests) are served on fine china and linen in a cheerful Art Deco dining room, just down the hall from the Jacuzzi. If you seek absolute privacy, the Crawfords also have six vacation homes, all with full kitchens, tasteful furnishings, fireplaces, optional gourmet breakfasts, and interesting settings. Either choice is highly recommended. ◆ Wright Rd and Laukapu Ave. 967.7786, 800/937.7786; fax 967.8660; inkeeper@volcano-hawaii.com; www.volcano-hawaii.com

117 Hale Ohia Cottages $ Bed-and-breakfasts are becoming as plentiful in chilly, rainy, lush Volcano as orchid blossoms, but this retreat, made up of three suites in the main residence and three free-standing cottages, is definitely not of the standard variety. Rooms and cottages offer one-of-a-kind amenities such as lava-rock fireplaces, private gardens, and skylights. There is no restaurant, though several are nearby, and no air-conditioning, though none is needed. ◆ 11-3968 Hale Ohia Rd (at Mamalahoa Hwy). 967.7986, 800/455.3803; fax 967.8610; haleohia@hawaii.net; www.haleohia.com ♿

118 Carson's Volcano Cottage $$ A short path winds through lush foliage to the English cottage and three connected studios that compose this small place. The Victorian decor is enhanced with old Hawaiian photographs, fresh flowers, and large windows looking out to the pine and plum trees. There's a veranda, and hosts Tom and Brenda Carson have equipped the rooms with coffeemakers, small refrigerators, heaters, and goosedown comforters (yes, you may need them). Ask for the room with the Jacuzzi. ♦ Sixth St (west of Pearl Ave). 967.7683, 800/845.LAVA; fax 967.8094; carsons@aloha.net; www.carsonsvolcanocottage.com

Puna District

South of **Hilo,** the Puna towns have a funky, down-at-the-heels rural charm, although some efforts at gentrification can be seen. The effects of the eruptions of the **Kilauea** volcano are far more obvious, however. In the southern section of the district the lush rain forest suddenly gives way to barren lava rock, and lava flowing to the sea has blocked the road along the coast.

119 Akatsuka Orchid Gardens If you like orchids, you'll love this touristy display. All sizes, varieties, colors, and prices can be found, and pre-certified plants and cut flowers can be shipped home immediately. Stop by to use the clean rest room and receive a free orchid. ♦ Free. Mamalahoa Hwy (between Alii Kane Ave and Glenwood Rd). 967.8234

120 Puna Coast Drive Depending on the time of the year, the weather, and just plain luck, this can be one of the most interesting drives on the Big Island. Start at the old mill town of Pahoa, on Route 130, staying just long enough to buy fresh fruit for the trip. Then head down Route 132 through the stunning gauntlet of trees in **Nanawale Forest Reserve,** taking a side trip to **Lava Tree State Park.** Continue on to Cape Kumukahi and see the world's luckiest lighthouse in Kapoho; local lore says it was spared from the volcanic explosion because its kindly keeper was the only one in town to share his food with an old beggar woman (Madame Pele in her favorite disguise). Also on this route you'll have the opportunity to stop at **Isaac Hale Beach Park,** where the kids can swim off the boat ramp and enjoy shave ice; and **Ahala Nui Thermal Warm Ponds** down the road, where the water will relax tight muscles. Head southwest on Route 137 along the *pandani* and palm-lined Puna Coast, keeping an eye out for whales (in season) and dolphins. Stop at the unofficially clothing-optional, old-hippie refuge, **Kehena Beach,** before continuing until the road stops (blocked by lava from several late 1980s eruptions). Take Route 130 back to Pahoa.

Along the Puna Coast Drive:

Lava Tree State Park Fast-flowing lava from the 1790 eruption smothered this ohia

forest, and while moisture from the trees cooled the lava and formed a hard outer shell, their insides burned, leaving this captivating gaggle of ghoulish tree molds. ♦ Daily. Rte 132

120 Paolo's Bistro ★★$$ The town of Pahoa is an odd place to find a high-caliber dining room—crowded as it is with old hippies, New Agers, and the nose-ring contingent—but this bistro is top-notch, serving mouthwatering dishes like cioppino, and pasta with prawns, clams, calamari, and mussels. Stop here for a feast after a drive through Puna—and try for a seat in the gazebo. It's BYOB here. ♦ Italian ♦ Tu-Su dinner. 333 Old Government Rd, Pahoa. 965.7033 &

121 Pamalu—A Hawaiian Country House $ Arguably one of the most restful places to stay in the islands, this country home features a koa-wood staircase, four rooms with queen-size beds and private baths, a hammock, a pool, complimentary breakfasts, access to a poolside barbecue, and the attention of a convivial host. There is no air-conditioning, but ceiling fans do the job. The site also is near Pahoa's thermal ponds, tidepools, and a little-known spot called Green Mountain (a 600-year-old volcanic crater) and Lake. ♦ Rte 132 (east of Rte 130). 965.0830; fax 965.6198

Mauna Loa.
Macadamia Nut Corp.

122 Mauna Loa Macadamia Nut Corporation Owned by C. Brewer & Company of Honolulu, this is the world's largest producer and marketer of the macadamia nut. The visitors' center offers a slide show, viewing stations of the mill's processing and packing machines, and a few free samples. But don't make the mistake of thinking you can save money by buying macadamias from the source; you can usually get the nuts cheaper at a convenience store. ♦ Free. Daily. Macadamia Rd (east of Mamalahoa Hwy). 982.6562

N A N I   M A U
G A R D E N S

123 Nani Mau Gardens If Walt Disney had been a botanist, this would be his park. More than 2,000 varieties of Big Island flowers, shrubs, and trees fill the 20 acres of theme gardens. Take the narrated tram tour or stroll along the paved walkways with a map from the gift shop. It's touristy, but an orchid is an orchid is an orchid. ♦ Admission. Daily. 421 Makalika St (between Railroad Ave and Awa St). 959.3541 &

24 Panaewa Rainforest Zoo Even if you're not a zoo person, you'll like this one. Set deep in the lush rain forest, it's a pseudo-natural environment for its resident birds, plants, and animals, most of which are indigenous to equatorial climates (which eases the inevitable "poor fella" syndrome). In fact, after viewing the tiger playground, you start to wonder who's being fenced in. Come on a weekday, and you'll have the 12-acre zoo to yourself, allowing for private time with the squirrel monkeys, tapirs, giant anteaters, and the zoobiquitous peacock. ♦ Free. Daily. Stainback Hwy (just west of Mamalahoa Hwy). 959.7224 &

Bests

John Alexander
Owner, Dolphin Bay Hotel

Rising at sunrise and watching **Mauna Kea** change colors, then going to the **Hilo Farmers Market** for fresh bread and fruit.

Swimming at **Kolekole Beach Park** and swinging on the rope over the waterfall.

Hiking out to the active lava flow at sunset and watching the color transformation as the sun goes down.

Walking around **Akaka Falls State Park** four times a year to see which orchids are in bloom.

Watching the astronomy show at Mauna Kea base camp Thursday through Sunday from 6 to 10PM (free). Take lots of warm clothing!

Swimming with the turtles at **Punaluu Black Sand Beach Park** down near the southern end of the island.

Jumping off the cliffs at **South Point** for the fantastic snorkeling.

Sig Zane
Owner/Textile Designer, Sig Zane Designs

The bread pudding is served warm, covered with an Amaretto syrup, and topping with whipped cream and a cherry. The pistachio ice cream is pretty good too at the downtown **Hilo** restaurant, **Pescatore.**

Sticky rice, buddha rama with chicken, and garlic shrimp at **Royal Siam** can easily hit the spot when craving Thai flavors. The coconut soup is another one of the usual dishes that we gotta have! Make room for the tapioca made with taro for dessert, even if you're full.

For ambience, **Miyo's** in the **Waiakea Villas** complex can't be beat. Housed in a building that looks like it should be in a Japanese country town, Miyo cooks up great dishes! The all-time favorite is sesame chicken. Look at all the different plates for each serving. Each one is unique!

If you have to get in the water with a boogie board, try surfing at **Honolii**. It's a river mouth break that is usually mellow. Turtles share the waves, and besides, it's really tropical and just like paradise.

Depending on how much rain there's been, the sandbar that forms part of the beach sometimes takes you into the river. It's adventure galore.

If you happen to be in Hilo during Thanksgiving and in the weeks leading up to Christmas, check out the local crafts fairs. They have the most incredible Christmas wreaths made out of the local plants. The choicest ones are made of *liko lehua*, the young bud tips of the island's flower tree, the *ohia lehua*. Many very creative people make these wreaths that dry very well. Lots of them can be shipped to mainland cities—check what plants and ask if they're allowed. These will always bring on the memories of the Big Island!

Randolph A. McCreight
Owner, Pamalu—A Hawaiian Country House

Paolo's Bistro, Pahoa—Enjoy anything on the menu, especially *ahi piccata, pasta puttanesca,* tiramisù. Owner Paolo is an Italian character.

Kapoho Tide Pools—Snorkeling in coral gardens, watching sunset, moonrise.

Ahala Nui Thermal Warm Ponds—Relaxing in lagoon at seaside warmed by volcano-heated springs.

Puna Coast—Watching lava flow into ocean after dark.

Highway 132 (Pahoa to Kapoho)—Driving under canopy of *albiza* trees near **Lava Tree State Park.**

Hilo Farmers Market—Shopping for fresh produce.

Hilo Bay—Watching outrigger canoe races.

Hilo—Attending hula competition just after Easter. Attending Hawaiian music performances, especially slack key guitar.

Peter Merriman
Chef/Owner, Merriman's, the Big Island;
Chef/Partner, Hula Grill, Maui

A breakfast of granola and fresh Hayden mangoes.

Mai tais in the afternoon at the **Mauna Lani Beach Club.**

Kalua pig at the **Ocean View Inn** in **Kailua-Kona.**

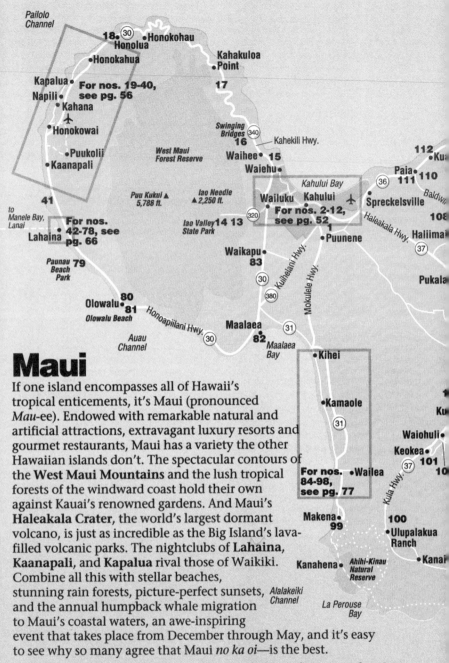

Maui

If one island encompasses all of Hawaii's tropical enticements, it's Maui (pronounced *Mau*-ee). Endowed with remarkable natural and artificial attractions, extravagant luxury resorts and gourmet restaurants, Maui has a variety the other Hawaiian islands don't. The spectacular contours of the **West Maui Mountains** and the lush tropical forests of the windward coast hold their own against Kauai's renowned gardens. And Maui's **Haleakala Crater**, the world's largest dormant volcano, is just as incredible as the Big Island's lava-filled volcanic parks. The nightclubs of **Lahaina**, **Kaanapali**, and **Kapalua** rival those of Waikiki. Combine all this with stellar beaches, stunning rain forests, picture-perfect sunsets, and the annual humpback whale migration to Maui's coastal waters, an awe-inspiring event that takes place from December through May, and it's easy to see why so many agree that Maui *no ka oi*—is the best.

Hawaii's second-largest island can be divided into five general regions: **Central Maui**, the heart of commerce and government, encompassing the towns of **Kahului** and **Wailuku** and the main airport; **West Maui**, containing the glamorous resort communities of Kapalua, Kaanapali, and **Kahana**, the bustling old whaling port of Lahaina, and the highest concentration of tourists; **Southwest Maui**, anchored by the **Kihei** strip of condominiums and the posh, 1,500-acre **Wailea** luxury resort; **Upcountry Maui**, a rustic farming and ranching region on the grassy slopes of

Haleakala, home of Maui's Kula onions as well as Hawaii's only winery; and
the verdant **Hana Coast**, located on Maui's rugged, stunning eastern shores
and accessed by the most scenic drive in all of Hawaii, the **Hana Highway**.
While the majority of resorts line the sunny leeward coasts of West and
Southwest Maui, the most spectacular attractions—the Hana Highway,
Haleakala Crater, and the upcountry—are spread across the island, so
schedule a few days to explore them all.

After landing at **Kahului Airport**, most of Maui's 2.7 million annual visitors
are shuffled off toward the western shoreline, where the weather is consid-
erably better and the beaches more accessible. While Kaanapali—a self-

contained megaresort with a profusion of hotels and condominiums ranging from basic to super-luxurious—accommodates a larger percentage of tourists, the more affluent travelers tend to stay at the exclusive Kapalua and Wailea resorts. Often viewed as a playground for the rich, Maui has a higher percentage of millionaires than the French Riviera or Palm Springs, but even starving college students enjoy the island's natural beauty and easygoing Jimmy Buffett lifestyle.

Of course, Maui is not without its faults. Because of the island's popularity, traffic can be nightmarish and crime is on the rise. Unbridled resort development (Maui's white-collar crime) has turned Kihei into a Condos-R-Us complex and Lahaina into a tropical Knott's Berry Farm; skyrocketing property values mean that local residents (particularly indigenous Hawaiians) can't afford to own homes. Despite these shortcomings, Maui continues to reign as a top all-around destination, with more attractions and tourist activities—from championship golf courses to a historic steam-engine railroad to exciting whale-watching excursions—than any other Hawaiian island. It's no wonder that a significant number of Maui residents are tourists who decided to come back for good.

Area code 808 unless otherwise noted.

Getting to Maui

Airports

Kahului Airport

Kahului Airport (872.3880), two miles east of the center of Kahului, is Maui's major airport, with about 120 flights a day departing from and landing on its windy runway. There's a small, two-story terminal.

Airport Services

Information	872.3893
Lost and Found	872.3821
Parking	871.0610

Airlines

Aloha	244.9071, 800/367.5250
American	244.5522, 800/433.7300
American Trans Air	800/225.2995
Delta	871.0882, 800/221.1212
Hawaiian	800/882.8811
from the mainland	800/367.5320
Island Air, interisland	877.5755, 800/652.6541
from the mainland	800/323.3345
United	800/241.6522

Metal was such a novelty to Hawaiians that when Captain Cook first landed on Kauai he was able to swap a single nail for enough fresh pork, potatoes, and taro to feed his ship's entire crew for a day.

Getting to and from Kahului Airport

By Bus

There is no public transportation system on Maui, but several companies operate shuttles to the resort areas. **Trans-Hawaiian Shuttle** (877.7308, 800/231.6984) transports people between **Kahului Airport** and the Kaanapali resorts daily. The shuttle leaves every half hour; the cost is $13 one way. No reservations are needed for pickups at the airport, but they're recommended for departure from Kaanapali; call to make a reservation at least one day before your flight. **Trans-Hawaiian** also provides transportation to and from the airport and other areas in West Maui; reservations are required. **Speedy Shuttle** (875.8070) takes passengers between the airport and West Maui and Kihei from 5AM to 10PM by reservation. **ABC's Shuttle** (875.6389) uses limousines for fares similar to **Speedy Shuttle;** cars may be reserved between 4AM and 11PM. **Airport Shuttle** (661.6667) operates 24 hours a day, delivering arriving or departing passengers to their resort or airport destination; reservations are required.

By Car

Kahului Airport is about a mile northeast of **Haleakala Highway;** prominent signs point the way both into and out of the airfield. The following car-rental companies have counters at the airport.

Alamo	871.6235, 800/327.9633
Avis	871.7575, 800/331.1212
Budget	871.8811, 800/527.0700
Dollar	877.2731, 800/800.4000
Hertz	877.5167, 800/654.3011
National	871.8851, 800/227.7368
Thrifty	877.2333, 800/367.2277

By Taxi

Cabs wait at the curb across from the baggage-claim area. Otherwise, call **Kihei Taxi** (877.7000). The fare to Kapalua should be under $65; to Kaanapali, under $55; to Wailea, under $35.

Hana Airport

Just minutes north of **Hana, Hana Airport** (248.8208) consists of an airstrip and a one-room terminal building. Two flights a day arrive from Honolulu at this out-of-the-way facility, and two depart.

Airlines

Island Air, interisland 248.8328, 800/652.6541

    from the mainland...........................800/323.3345

Getting to and from Hana Airport

By Bus

There is no public bus system. The **Hotel Hana-Maui** and some bed-and-breakfast establishments provide airport transportation for their guests free of charge. Call your lodging place to make arrangements beforehand.

By Car

Dollar Rent-a-Car (248.8237, 800/800.4000) is the only firm that rents cars in Hana. Anything from convertibles to four-wheel-drive vehicles can be picked up at the airport by prior arrangement.

By Taxi

There are no cabs in this part of Maui.

Kapalua–West Maui Airport

The **Kapalua–West Maui Airport** (669.0623) was built by **Hawaiian Airlines** in 1987 and promptly sold to the state, which now maintains the two-story terminal and 3,000-foot runway. Fourteen flights a day fly in and out of the small, windy airport located between the Kaanapali and Kapalua resorts.

Airlines

Island Air, interisland 669.0255, 800/652.6541

    from the mainland...........................800/323.3345

Getting to and from Kapalua–West Maui Airport

By Bus

Airport Shuttle (667.2605) offers transportation to anywhere on the island between 5AM and 11:30PM.

By Car

The **Kapalua–West Maui Airport** is equidistant from Kapalua and Kaanapali, off **Honoapiilani Highway (Route 30)**. There are no car-rental booths at the airport.

By Taxi

Cabs generally await passengers in front of baggage claim. If you don't see any, call **Alii Cab** (661.3688). The fare to Kapalua is about $10; to Kaanapali, $13; to Wailea, about $45.

Interisland Carriers

Aloha Airlines and **Hawaiian Airlines** make regular hops to **Kahului Airport** from **Hilo International Airport** and **Keahole-Kona International Airport** on the Big Island, **Lihue Airport** on Kauai, **Lanai Airport** on Lanai, **Hoolehua Airport** on Molokai, and **Honolulu International Airport** on Oahu. **Island Air** flies to **Kapalua–West Maui Airport** and **Hana Airport** on Maui from Honolulu.

Ferries

Expeditions (661.3756, 800/695.2624) is a ferry between **Lahaina** on Maui and the island of Lanai. It crosses the channel to Lanai and back five times daily between 6:45AM and 5:45PM. A round-trip excursion is $50 for adults, $40 for children under 12. This is more for fun than transportation, as the round-trip passage takes a couple of hours.

Getting Around Maui

Bicycles and Mopeds

Maui is a good place for two-wheeled travel, although the big hill in the narrow part of the island between West Maui and East Maui is a little tricky to negotiate. Mopeds as well as mountain bikes are available at **A&B Moped Rental** (3481 Lower Honoapiilani Rd, Honokowai, 669.0027). The **Kukui Activity Center** (96 Kio Loop, at S Kihei Rd, Kihei, 875.1151) rents mountain bikes.

Buses

There is no public bus system on Maui, except for the *West Maui Shopping Express* (877.7308), which runs from Lahaina to Kapalua.

Driving

Two things to keep in mind when driving on Maui: **Route 30** from Wailuku to Lahaina can be treacherous during the whale migration season (December through May), when the entire road becomes a parking lot every time someone spots a whale spouting or breaching. Also, many car-rental companies prohibit renters from driving on certain roads (for example, **Route 31** between Hana and Upcountry Maui). Driving on prohibited roads nullifies your car-rental insurance policy, so you're liable for any damage incurred there. Car-rental companies at island airports are listed above.

Hiking

The most popular trek on the island is in the moonlike crater of **Haleakala National Park.** The trail is of medium difficulty, with options to make it longer or shorter, harder or easier. **Hike Maui** (879.5270; hike@hikemaui.com; www.hikemaui.com) is a valuable resource on this trek or any other; the firm offers guided natural history hikes and information on all the Maui wilderness has to offer.

Parking

It's easy to find parking spots on Maui streets; some are metered. If you don't find a space on **Front Street** in Lahaina, you're sure to get one on the side streets.

Taxis

Call **Kihei Taxi** (877.7000). Rates are $1.75 when the flag drops and $1.75 per mile.

Tours

Robert's Hawaii (871.6226) offers a half-day tour of Haleakala Crater and a full-day itinerary that includes the crater, **Iao Valley,** and Lahaina. **Rascal Charters** (874.8633) runs four-, six-, and eight-hour fishing trips from **Maalaea Harbor. Alexair Helicopters** (877.4354) offers breathtaking aerial tours of Hana, the Haleakala Crater, the rain forests, and more. **Blue Hawaiian Helicopters** (871.8844) gives tours that include an hourlong Molokai excursion.

Walking

Perhaps the nicest place to take a walk on Maui is the beach at Kaanapali. It's long and white, and the hotels are set back from the shore. Front Street in Lahaina is pleasant to explore on foot—there are shops to inspect and plenty of people to watch. It's very hot in Lahaina, but there are lots of places to stop for refreshments. The Upcountry towns of **Makawao** and **Paia** are also good strolling spots, with shops in which to poke and browse.

FYI

Shopping

There are five major shopping destinations on Maui. For scrimshaw, head for the old whaling port of Lahaina, where standard souvenirs are also plentiful. **Paia** in Upcountry Maui is the place for ultracool surf stuff—boards, clothing, stickers, photos of Duke Kahanamoku, and other gear. **Makawao,** also in the upcountry, has the best selection of Hawaiian crafts. **Kaahumanu Center** in Kahului has the same upscale shops as your mall back home. And the **Maui Marketplace,** also in Kahului, houses more than 30 outlet stores: nirvana for bargain shoppers, purgatory for everybody else.

Visitors' Information Centers

The **Maui Visitors Bureau** (**MVB;** 1727 Wili Pa Loop, west of Imi Kala St, Wailuku, 244.3530; fax 244.1337; www.visitmaui.com) is open Monday through Friday.

Phone Book

Emergencies

Ambulance/Fire/Police	911
Dental Emergency	879.1944
Hospital (Maui Memorial Hospital)	244.9056
Locksmith (24-hour)	877.0302
Pharmacy	875.4695
Police (nonemergency)	244.6400
Poison Center	800/362.3585

Wailuku/Kahului and Environs

In the past the sister towns of Wailuku and Kahului, on the northern coast of Maui's central valley, have focused on business. Wailuku is the county seat of **Maui County,** and Kahului is a commercial center, site of the island's only jet airport and deepwater seaport. Maui's greatest concentration of population is in or near these towns (40,000 of the 100,000 residents), and it is here that much of the island's work is done.

In recent years the twin towns have also begun to rival the traditional visitor meccas of **West Maui** and **Wailea** as they are now home to a series of trendy shopping malls and activity outlets. As well as shopping, visitors enjoy the historical sites, including the 19th-century **Bailey House** and the **Alexander & Baldwin Sugar Museum.** Also of note to vacationers is the scenic **Iao Valley State Park,** set amidst the majestic **West Maui Mountains** just west of Wailuku.

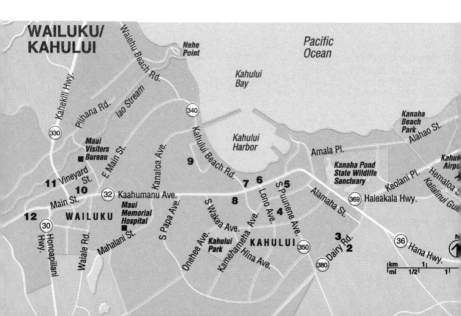

1 Alexander & Baldwin Sugar Museum

Located in a restored plantation manager's house next to a working sugar mill, this small museum documents the history of sugarcane in Hawaii, from its introduction as a crop to its key role in expanding the islands' ethnic diversity with the arrival of workers from Japan, the Philippines, and elsewhere. Photo murals, century-old artifacts, and a working scale model of sugar-factory machinery make this one museum worth checking out.
♦ Admission. M-Sa. 3957 Hansen Rd (at Rte 350), Puunene. 871.8058 ♿

2 Maui Marketplace

Built to resemble Oahu's wildly successful **Waikele Center**, this 300,000-square-foot collection of more than 30 outlet stores includes **Sports Authority** and **Eagle Hardware**. ♦ Daily. 270 Dairy Rd (between S Puunene Ave and Hana Hwy), Kahului. 873.0400 ♿

3 Best of Maui Cassette Tours

If you really want to do the Hana Coast or Haleakala right, stop at the shack with the yellow awning and the flashing light (located just before the Hana Highway turnoff in Kahului) and pick up a tour tape. A worthwhile investment, this high-quality, well-researched package of audio-cassette tours includes a tape, cassette player, Hana Highway guidebook, bird and flower field guides, and a detailed map. The narrator has flawless Hawaiian pronunciation, and the tour is timed perfectly, describing landmarks as you pass them. Highlights include atmospheric music, professional sound quality, pertinent historical background, and tips on where to stop for a snack or picnic. The tapes are also available at **Kmart** (424 Dairy Rd, 871.8553), **Picnics** (30 Baldwin Ave, a half block south of Hana Hwy, Paia, 579.8021), **Sub-Paradise** (395-E Dairy Rd, 877.8779), and **Windriggers Maui** (261 Dairy Rd, 871.7753). ♦ Fee. Daily 6:30AM-1:30PM. 333 Dairy Rd (between S Puunene Ave and Alamaha St), Kahului. 871.1555 ♿

4 Maui Swap Meet

Haggle over new and used handicrafts, clothes, fresh fruit, baked goods, and assorted odds and ends at this down-to-earth flea market. ♦ Nominal admission. Sa 5:30AM-noon. 142 S Puunene Ave (between W Wakea and Kamehameha Aves), Kahului. 877.3100 ♿

5 M.O.M.'s of Maui ★★$

A mecca for java lovers, this coffeehouse offers such healthy fare as breakfast burritos, Kula green salads, and tofu burgers, as well as a wide selection of gourmet coffees ready to be shipped and both tropical and coffee drinks. ♦ Coffeehouse ♦ Daily breakfast and lunch. Maui Mall, 70 E Kamehameha Ave (between Hana Hwy and S Puunene Ave), Kahului. 877.3711. ♿

6 Maui Seaside Hotel $

Businesspeople from other islands frequent this three-story hotel because of its proximity to **Kahului Airport** and to the business hubs of Kahului and Wailuku. (Plus it's cheap.) There are 183 sparse but pleasant air-conditioned rooms, as well as a restaurant, central pool, and small beach. If you're traveling on a tight budget, this is the place to stay. ♦ 100 W Kaahumanu Ave (between N Puunene Ave and Kahului Beach Rd), Kahului. 877.3311, 800/560.5552; fax 877.4618; www.sand-seaside.com ♿

7 Maui Beach Hotel $

Although not likely to win any awards for its architecture or interior design, this 2-story, 147-room hotel is a Maui staple, and with a pool on the property and public tennis courts nearby, it's not a bad place to lay your head. All guest rooms have air-conditioning, TVs, and phones. The two dining rooms serve American and Chinese food, respectively. ♦ 170 Kaahumanu Ave (at Kahului Beach Rd), Kahului. 877.0071, 800/877.0051; fax 871.5797

8 Kaahumanu Center

Maui masses come to this trendy, two-story multimillion-dollar shopping mall to see double, triple, and quadruple features at the sixplex cinema or just to cruise around the upscale shops. ♦ Daily. 275 W Kaahumanu Ave (between Kane St and S Wakea Ave), Kahului. 877.3369 ♿

Within Kaahumanu Center:

Waldenbooks This member of the national chain has more than 30,000 volumes and an extensive Hawaiiana section for those interested in local history, guidebooks, flora, fauna, and other island-related topics. ♦ Daily. 871.6112. ♿ Also at: Kukui Mall, 1819 S Kihei Rd (at Kupuna St), Kihei. 874.3688; Maui Mall, 70 E Kaahumanu Ave (between Hana Hwy and S Puunene Ave), Kahului. 877.0181; Cannery Mall, 1221 Honoapiilani Hwy (at Kapunakea St), Lahaina. 667.6172

Local Motion The statewide chain founded in the 1970s to cater to surfers, now carries surf fashions rather than leashes and sunscreen. If you're a teenager from Duluth, look no further. This is the place to see what your counterparts in Hawaii are wearing and doing. ♦ Daily. 871.7873

Sweet Talk

When the Polynesians first sailed to Hawaii some 1,500 years ago, they used the thick stalks of sugarcane to hold water for the long journey. The rich lava soil and wet climate, coupled with abundant sunshine, proved fertile ground for sugarcane. In 1835, the first commercial sugarcane plantation was established on the island of Kauai, but it wasn't until the end of Hawaii's whaling era in the 1860s that sugar was relied upon as a cash crop. The islands' unrefined sugar was first exported to America during the gold rush, when Northern California's sudden population boom made sugar a profitable commodity.

From 1953 to 1986, Hawaiian fields yielded about a million tons of sugar a year (more than 12 percent of the entire

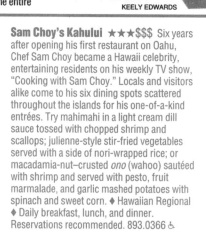

KEELY EDWARDS

country's product) and strengthened Hawaii's economy by $353 million annually. The sugar industry was also primarily responsible for Hawaii's diverse racial mixture. Laborers from China, Japan, Korea, Portugal, South America, and many other lands were brought in to harvest the crop.

But times are changing in Hawaii, and high operational costs and stiff competition have led to the phasing out of the sugar industry on Hawaii (a fate that has also befallen the state's pineapple industry).

Soon Hawaii's economy will be based almost exclusively on military operations and tourism, and the verdant cane fields that for generations symbolized Hawaiian prosperity will be plowed under for good.

Sam Choy's Kahului ★★★$$$ Six years after opening his first restaurant on Oahu, Chef Sam Choy became a Hawaii celebrity, entertaining residents on his weekly TV show, "Cooking with Sam Choy." Locals and visitors alike come to his six dining spots scattered throughout the islands for his one-of-a-kind entrées. Try mahimahi in a light cream dill sauce tossed with chopped shrimp and scallops; julienne-style stir-fried vegetables served with a side of nori-wrapped rice; or macadamia-nut–crusted *ono* (wahoo) sautéed with shrimp and served with pesto, fruit marmalade, and garlic mashed potatoes with spinach and sweet corn. ♦ Hawaiian Regional ♦ Daily breakfast, lunch, and dinner. Reservations recommended. 893.0366 ♿

9 Maui Arts and Cultural Center Maui's $75-million performing arts center opened in 1994. Designed by architect **John Hara,** the large, modern building stands on 10 acres of land and comprises a main and studio theaters, an amphitheater, classrooms, and an art gallery. A variety of groups have taken the stage here, including Santana, the **Moscow Ballet,** and the theater company of the **Maui Academy of Performing Arts.** ♦ Box office M-F; Sa 1PM-5PM. Show times vary. 1 Cameron Way (west of Kahului Beach Rd), Kahului. 242.7469 ♿

10 Chums ★$ A diner atmosphere and local fare make this eatery a Wailuku institution. Early risers will like the hours (it opens at 6:30AM) and budget watchers the prices. Hotcakes, omelettes, and French toast round out the breakfast menu; *saimin* (noodles),

Portuguese bean soup, oxtail soup, teriyaki chicken, and cheeseburgers are offered the rest of the day. No alcohol is served, but feel free to bring your own. ♦ Local/American ♦ M-Tu breakfast and lunch; W-Su breakfast, lunch, and dinner. 1900 Main St (at Central Ave), Wailuku. 244.1000 ♿

11 Siam Thai ★★$ There's nothing fancy about this restaurant, just friendly service and great spicy Thai food like curried shrimp and crispy lobster.

When current owner Phillip Daniells took over he upgraded the interior, which features white brick walls and Thai artifacts, and kept the quality of the food high. ♦ Thai ♦ M-F lunch and dinner; Sa-Su dinner. 123 N Market St (at W Vineyard St), Wailuku. 244.3817 ♿

11 Northshore Inn $ Sequestered in this shabby corner of Wailuku is a clean, cordial, hotel/youth hostel ideal for backpackers, windsurfers, and international budget travelers. There are 18 rooms (with single, double, or bunk beds), clean shared bathrooms, a common kitchen and laundry room, a small TV lounge, and a genial atmosphere, but no restaurant or air-conditioning. The proprietor often takes guests hiking, windsurfing, or to the beach for volleyball and barbecues. "Come as guests, leave as friends" is the motto. ♦ 2080 W Vineyard St (west of N Market St), Wailuku. 242.8999, 800/643.MAUI; fax 244.5004

COURTESY OF MAUI HISTORICAL SOCIETY

12 Bailey House Missionaries Edward and Caroline Bailey came to Maui in 1840 to teach at the **Wailuku Female Seminary,** founded in 1833 by Reverend Jonathan Green. Closed in 1858 due to lack of funding, it was home to the Bailey family for more than 40 years. Upon moving to California in 1885, the family dedicated the building to the display of Hawaiian artifacts. The collection includes quilts, tapa cloth, the island's largest collection of relics from the days before Captain Cook (such as stone and shell implements and an outrigger canoe), and more (don't miss Duke Kahanamoku's redwood surfboard). The Maui Historical Society operates the museum and shop, a worthy stop. ♦ Admission. M-Sa. 2375-A E Main St (between Honoapiilani Hwy and W Alu Rd), Wailuku. 244.3326

13 Kepaniwai Park and Heritage Gardens When the sun's out, you can't beat the drive into this valley setting. The elevated park pays tribute to Maui's various ethnic groups with exhibition pavilions and gardens reflecting the cultures of the Hawaiians, Japanese, Chinese, Filipinos, and Portuguese. Kids love the children's swimming pool and the picnic pavilions. ♦ Pool: daily in summer; Sa-Su the rest of the year. Iao Valley Rd (west of W Alu Rd). 243.7230

13 Hawaii Nature Center A while back, residents founded a nonprofit organization to educate youth on regional environmental issues. Somewhere along the way, dedicated workers realized they needed to find an effective means of supporting their efforts. The result is this center, which offers visitors of all ages the opportunity to walk through the **Interactive Science Arcade,** with its 30 hands-on exhibits on Hawaii's unique plant and animal life; participate in guided hikes; and browse through a multisplendored gift shop. ♦ Fee. Daily. 85 Iao Valley Rd (west of W Alu Rd). 244.6500; fax 244.6505 &

14 Iao Valley State Park A 2,250-foot-high pillar of stone called the **Iao Needle** marks the spot where, in 1790, King Kamehameha the Great conquered the island of Maui in one of the bloodiest battles in Hawaiian history. The dead, legend has it, filled nearby Iao Stream until the water ran red. The Iao Needle is surrounded by sharp cliffs and overlooks lush, verdant Iao Valley, where the ancients buried their *alii* (royalty) in caves to protect the bones—believed to have spiritual powers—from damage or misuse. Iao's beauty is as stunning as its history is haunting; there's a hiking trail and many secluded spots for picnicking. ♦ Iao Valley Rd (west of W Alu Rd). 243.7230

15 Waiehu Municipal Golf Course It's hard to reserve a tee time at this 18-hole course (par 72, 6,330 yards) because it's so reasonably priced. Local golfers and those seeking an alternative to the expensive resorts, where greens fees are four times what they are here, keep the place busy. ♦ Inexpensive greens fees. Daily. Call at least two days in advance for reservations. Lower Waiehu Beach Rd (north of Waiehu Beach Rd), Waiehu. 243.7400

16 Swinging Bridges One of the best and least-known day hikes on Maui is on the windward side of the West Maui Mountains, just beyond the town of Waihee. Here you'll find a moderate trail winding through guava, mango, and passion fruit trees; past bamboo forests, streams, and aqueducts; and across two seemingly perilous (but quite sturdy) swinging bridges. The reward at the end of the 40-minute hike: a first-rate swimming hole fed by an artificial waterfall. Launch yourself off the rope swing and take a dip behind the fall (yes, the water is cold) for a once-in-a-lifetime experience. Warning: Don't attempt this hike if it's raining—flash floods are frequent and sometimes deadly in the area. ♦ Waihee Valley Rd (west of Kahekili Hwy). After you park, turn right at the sign "Private Road, No Parking" and stay on the main trail

17 Route 340 Although the highway is technically for residents only, dozens of adventurous tourists tackle this eroded pass every day in all sorts of cars. The problem used to be that the road wasn't paved; now that's been taken care of, but it's barely one lane wide, so you may find yourself backing up and pulling off the road as much as going forward. From Wailuku to Honokohau it's about a 1.5-hour drive.

In ancient Hawaii, the hula was a religious ritual believed too sacred to be performed by women.

Miffed whalers brought the first mosquitoes to Hawaii, intentionally planting larvae in the freshwater ponds surrounding the home of Reverend Baldwin in Lahaina, Maui. The reverend's unpopularity stemmed from his stand against "philandering" with the local women.

Restaurants/Clubs: Red   Hotels: Blue

Shops/ Outdoors: Green   **Sights/Culture:** Black

WEST MAUI

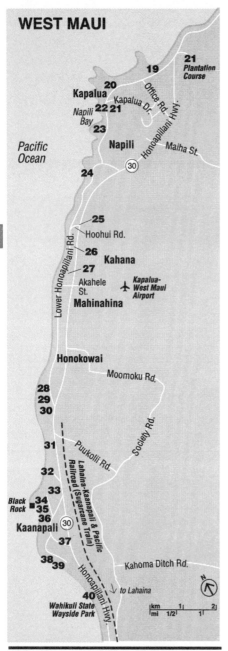

Pacific
Ocean

Kapalua and Environs

In the mid-1970s Colin C. Cameron, a descendant of missionaries who presides over his family's Maui Land & Pineapple Company, commissioned a team of resort specialists to build the consummate luxury destination on a sizable portion of his pineapple empire. He wasn't disappointed. Set against a spectacular backdrop of West Maui hills near one of the region's most extraordinary bays, Kapalua, a 1,500-acre resort community, now boasts three first-rate golf courses, two hotels, and several

restaurants. The 194-room **Kapalua Bay Hotel & Villas** was the development's flagship hotel, although in recent years it has been eclipsed by the **Ritz-Carlton Kapalua.** Access to this sun lovers' Shangri-la has been much easier since the Kapalua–West Maui Airport opened off **Honoapiilani Highway (Route 30)** in 1987.

18 Honolua and Mokuleia Bays Located side by side just north of Kapalua, Mokuleia Bay (known by surfers as "Slaughterhouse") and Honolua Bay together make up the **Marine Life Conservation District,** a legally protected underwater preserve where the fish are fearless. Mokuleia Bay has a gorgeous white-sand beach that's relatively uncrowded, while Honolua Bay attracts snorkelers when the surf's calm. ◆ Honolua. For Honolua Bay, look for the "Marine Life Conservation District" sign and the gaggle of parked rental cars

19 D.T. Fleming Beach Park Named for a manager of the Kapalua Plantation, this popular surfing, bodysurfing, swimming, and snorkeling beach extends from **Kapalua Golf Club**'s 16th hole to the cliffs beyond. Use caution: The steep shoreline is subject to strong riptides. Picnic and public facilities are available. ◆ Honoapiilani Hwy and Lower Honoapiilani Rd, Kapalua

19 Ritz-Carlton Kapalua $$$$ Recently named the No. 3 hotel in Hawaii by *Travel & Leisure* magazine, this member of the Ritz-Carlton family has been bustling since it opened in 1992. Set on 10 acres of gently sloping beachfront, it was designed to allow maximum coastal views with minimal disturbance to the contour of the land. The 490 garden- and ocean-view rooms and 58 suites all feature spacious lanais, twice-daily maid service, and 24-hour room service. Other amenities include a white-sand beach, boutiques, a 10,000-square-foot pool and a whirlpool, 10 tennis courts, a fitness center, a host of noteworthy restaurants, and Kapalua's 3 championship golf courses. As the **Ritz-Carlton Mauna Lani** has done on the Big Island, this stunningly appointed property has raised the competition among Maui's luxury-class accommodations to a new level. ◆ 1 Ritz-Carlton Dr (off Lower Honoapiilani Rd), Kapalua. 669.6200, 800/262.8440; fax 665.0026; www.ritzcarlton.com ✆

Within the Ritz-Carlton Kapalua:

Anuenue Room ★★★$$$$ The **Ritz**'s signature restaurant offers guests a night to remember. As soon as they enter the elegant wood-paneled dining room, with its book-lined walls, subdued lighting, and clubby atmosphere, diners know they're in for something special. The house specialties—herb-crusted *onaga* (red snapper) fillet, caramelized salmon with an orange *shoyu* (soy sauce) glaze, and seared venison chops—are highly recommended.

♦ Pacific Rim ♦ Tu-Sa dinner. Reservations recommended; collared shirt required for men. 669.9200 &

The Terrace ★★$$ The hotel's come-as-you-are eatery overlooks the pool and is accented by marble columns and silk tapestries. The bill of fare features such gourmet entrées as spicy shrimp pizza and Peking duck. Theme buffets are held on most nights. An extravagant breakfast buffet, with such highlights as sweet bread French toast, blintzes, island fruits, and Kona coffee, is served daily. ♦ Pacific Rim/American ♦ Daily breakfast and dinner. Reservations recommended. 669.6200

Kapalua Bay Hotel & Villas

20 Kapalua Bay Hotel $$$$ This Kapalua resort is the venue for several world-renowned sporting and cultural events. The hotel has a spectacular natural setting amid 19th-century pine trees and pineapple fields, with views of the ocean and the West Maui Mountains. The 194 air-conditioned rooms feature such extras as private lanais, TV sets and VCRs, refrigerators, and marble bathrooms with separate showers and tubs, double vanities, and telephones. It's a haven for guests who prefer golf, tennis, or relaxing on the beach or by the pool to wandering in the wilderness. There are 3 award-winning golf courses, 10 Plexipave courts in the **Tennis Garden,** one of the US's best beaches, an excellent scuba program, and 3 restaurants with ocean views. Each summer, this is the site of such international gatherings as the Kapalua Music Festival and the Kapalua Wine Symposium, a noteworthy food-and-wine event. ♦ 1 Bay Dr (off Lower Honoapiilani Rd), Kapalua. 669.5656, 800/367.8000; fax 669.4605; www.kapaluabayhotel.com &

Within the Kapalua Bay Hotel & Villas:

The Bay Club ★★★$$$$ The brief shuttle ride or walk to this restaurant from the **Kapalua Bay Hotel** is especially enjoyable at sunset or on a clear, starry night. The sunset view from a promontory over the ocean is framed by palm trees beyond the veranda and the island of Lanai on the horizon. The dining room's sophisticated ambience blends superbly with soft Maui evenings. Fresh mahimahi, *opakapaka* (pink snapper), and *ahi* (yellowfin tuna) are prepared a half-dozen ways, and the bouillabaisse is excellent. There's also a piano bar. ♦ Hawaiian Regional/Seafood ♦ Daily lunch and dinner. Reservations recommended. 669.8008 &

The Gardenia Court ★★$$$$ Open-air and contemporary, this eatery features a rotating menu, including such items as sugar mill chicken, wild boar wok, and Maui masala, a spicy vegetable curry with chutney and salsa. Or try the restaurant's signature drink, the Kapalua Butterfly. ♦ Pacific Rim ♦ M-Th dinner; F-Sa buffet dinner; Su brunch and dinner. Reservations recommended. 669.8008 &

20 Sansei Seafood Restaurant ★★★★ $$$$ In 1998, this out-of-the-way dining room walked away with the highest rating for cuisine in the state from the *Zagat Survey.* Japanese chef and owner D.K. Kodama prepares such mind-boggling main courses as macadamia-crusted Australian rack of lamb with gorgonzola-and-garlic mashed potatoes with sweet miso sauce, *ahi* sashimi, and rock shrimp cake. Diners are encouraged to sample a series of small plates rather than restrict themselves to a single entrée. A 12-seat sushi bar is so busy it keeps three chefs working. If you're in West Maui at dinnertime, this place is a command performance. ♦ Pacific Rim/Japanese ♦ Daily dinner. 115 Bay Dr (off Lower Honoapiilani Rd), Kapalua. 669.6286 &

20 Kapalua Beach Along with Napili Bay, this is one of the safest swimming beaches in West Maui and a longtime local favorite. Rated No. 1 in the country by University of Maryland's Coastal Research Lab, this place has it all—perfect sand, incredible views, great snorkeling, and a first-rate scuba program (including rentals, introductory dives, and lessons). The beach shack rents snorkel gear and sells assorted sundries, and an adjacent grassy area lined with palm trees is perfect for picnicking. Showers and rest rooms are available, and a bar and cafe are nearby at the **Kapalua Bay Hotel.** ♦ Parking and public access are at the south end of Kapalua (walk toward the rest rooms and through the tunnels to the beach)

21 Kapalua Golf Club These three prestigious layouts—the **Village, Bay,** and **Plantation**— host the **Mercedes Championship.** The Ed Seay and Arnold Palmer–designed **Village Course** (18 holes, par 71, 6,001 yards) and Arnold Palmer and Francis Dwayne **Bay Course** (18 holes, par 72, 6,051 yards) have received numerous awards—*Golf Digest* magazine rated this golf resort among the 10 best in the US. Cut into the base of a 23,000-acre pineapple plantation, these two layouts offer an ocean view from almost every fairway. The **Village Course** presents the greater test; its valleys, ridges, lake, and ironwood and eucalyptus trees make it spectacularly scenic. The newest of the three, the massive 240-acre **Plantation Course** (18 holes, par 73, 6,547 yards), designed by Ben Crenshaw and Bill Coore, includes such natural features as gradual slopes, deep valleys, native grasses, and long, generous fairways, and is also reaping various accolades. One drawback: This site is often windy, and there's a greater chance of mist and rain here than at Kaanapali or Wailea courses. ♦ Expensive greens fees. Daily. Reservations recommended at least four days in advance. Lessons are available. Preferred starting times and fees extended to **Kapalua Bay Hotel & Villas** and **Ritz-Carlton Kapalua** guests.Village and Bay Courses: 300 Kapalua Dr (at Lower Honoapiilani Rd), Kapalua. Plantation Course: 2000 Plantation Club Dr (east of Honoapiilani Hwy), Kapalua. 669.8044

At the Plantation Course:

Plantation House Restaurant ★★★$$$$ Thanks to its elevated setting, open-air lanai seating, regional fare, and stunning vistas, this award-winning restaurant has developed a devoted following. Chef Alex Stanislaw blends island flavors with Euro-Asian and Mediterranean influences; his repertoire includes such entrées as honey-guava scallops and Cajun-seasoned sashimi, along with more traditional New York steak and poultry dishes. Breakfast, besides being surprisingly affordable and served until 3PM, is simply unbeatable, especially when you're seated on the lanai and feasting on fresh pineapple dipped in a light cinnamon–sour cream sauce. ♦ Hawaiian/Mediterranean ♦ Daily breakfast, lunch, and dinner. Reservations recommended. 669.6299 ♿

21 **Jameson's Grill & Bar** ★★$$$ Long popular with residents, this handsome bar and dining room has changed hands and chefs and now is owned by the statewide chain popular on Oahu, but still is serving some of Kapalua's most tempting grinds (Pidgin for "food"). The dining room overlooks the **Kapalua Golf Club** and parts of Napili Bay; the menu includes fresh *opakapaka*, prime rib, and baked artichokes supreme. ♦ Steak/Seafood ♦ Daily breakfast, lunch, and dinner. Reservations recommended. 200 Kapalua Dr (between Office and Lower Honoapiilani Rds), Kapalua. 669.5653 ♿

22 **Napili Kai Beach Club** $$$$ This is the kind of seasoned, classic Hawaiian-style resort that is increasingly rare on the islands, so it's no wonder that up to 60 percent of its clientele are repeat guests. The tastefully landscaped grounds, bordered by a stone pathway fringed with hibiscus and *naupaka*

bushes, adjoin one of Hawaii's finest bays. Decks, barbecue areas, outdoor bars, and complimentary mai tai and coffee parties make this a convivial vacation spot where guests become friends, returning to savor the fabulous sunsets together again and again. The 163 units spread out unobtrusively over 11 acres; the **Lahaina Wing** is closest to the beach. All the units front the ocean and have TVs and phones, most have air-conditioning, and nearly all have full kitchens. Ask the friendly staff about the Napili Kai Foundation, which sponsors a hula and Hawaiian arts program for the children of West Maui; program participants perform here on Friday nights. Other amenities include four pools, a huge Jacuzzi, public access to the Napili Bay and Kapalua beaches, excellent snorkeling, a fitness center, and the **Sea House** restaurant. ♦ 5900 Lower Honoapiilani Rd, Napili. 669.6271, 800/367.5030; fax 669.5740; nkbc@maui.net; www.napilikai.com ♿

22 **Napili Bay** Lined with low-rise hotels and condos and featuring a long, sandy beach between two rocky points, this bay offers excellent swimming, snorkeling, and bodysurfing (watch out for the coral, though). Surfing can be good in the winter, provided the waves are high enough. ♦ Lower Honoapiilani Rd (turn at the Napili Shores sign and park anywhere), Napili

23 **Napili Shores Resort** $$ Choose from 99 roomy, pleasant studios or 1-bedroom condominiums with lanais and kitchens at this 152-unit complex, owned by Outrigger Hotels and Resorts, on 6 acres fronting Napili Bay. Two pools, two restaurants, and a store complete the picture. This is an excellent choice for a quiet, relaxing vacation. ♦ 5315 Lower Honoapiilani Rd, Napili. 669.8061, 800/688.7444; fax 669.5407; www.outrigger.com ♿

Within the Napili Shores Resort:

Orient Express ★$$$ Good Chinese food on Maui is rare, so this restaurant can get away with its high-priced menu of Chinese and Thai cuisine. Signature dishes include coconut chicken soup, spinach duck,

Mandarin fish clay pot, and an eponymous hot beef and seafood dish. The stuffed chicken wings and Thai noodle soup are first-rate. ♦ Chinese/Thai/Sushi ♦ Daily dinner. 669.8077 ♿

24 Coastline between Napili and Kaanapali West Maui's most prominent eyesore is about four miles of shoreline on Lower Honoapiilani Road between Napili and Kaanapali. Overdeveloped with condominiums of garish color and design, this stretch is the antithesis of beauty and serenity. Not surprisingly, accommodations here are cheaper than elsewhere along this coast. Some of the older condominiums are comfortable, but the new high-rises are less appealing.

With very few exceptions, the beaches here range from poor to middling. Although some condominiums advertise their proximity to the water, their beaches may be unsuitable for swimming. In addition, the area is 15 to 20 minutes from West Maui's best restaurants (aside from **Roy's Kahana Bar & Grill, Roy's Nicolina,** and the **Outback Steakhouse**), so you'll have to drive to Kapalua, Kaanapali, or Lahaina to get decent food.

25 Roy's Kahana Bar & Grill ★★★$$$ If you haven't already sampled Euro-Asian cuisine at one of Roy Yamaguchi's 13 other restaurants, you're in for a treat: to the delight of Maui's gastronomes, the celebrity chef has created a copy of his original restaurant in Hawaii Kai on Oahu. Although the shopping-center location lacks a view, and the noise is cacaphonous during the rush hours, the high-ceilinged restaurant is packed with diners who faithfully *ooh* and *aah* at the sight of blackened *ahi,* and every other dish that comes from the signature stainless-steel-and-copper open kitchen. This restaurant easily ranks as one of Maui's finest, awkward location notwithstanding. ♦ Euro-Asian ♦ Daily dinner. Reservations recommended. Kahana Gateway Plaza, Honoapiilani Hwy and Hoohui Rd, Kahana. 669.6999 ♿

25 Roy's Nicolina ★★★$$$ A variation on the Roy's restaurant theme, this fine establishment, named after chef/owner Roy Yamaguchi's daughter Nicole, is a touch more casual than the next-door **Roy's Kahana Bar & Grill** (see above). The kitchen turns out Euro-Asian dishes and such American options as sourdough pizza and grilled Southwestern chicken with smoked tomato sauce and tortillas. ♦ Euro-Asian ♦ Daily dinner. Reservations required. Kahana Gateway Plaza, Honoapiilani Hwy and Hoohui Rd, Kahana. 669.5000 ♿

25 Outback Steakhouse ★★$$$ In 1988, Michael J. "Crocodile" Dundee was a pretty popular figure, and a steakhouse in Tampa,

Florida, with an "Australian cowboy" theme opened its doors. The concept proved so popular that, years after the movie was no longer on the marquee of even the smallest theater, the 500-restaurant chain is flourishing. Specialties here, as at the other outposts, include the 14-ounce New York strip steak and the barbecued-ribs-and-chicken platter—but the real deal is the 22-ounce Big Bloke beer. ♦ Steak house ♦ Daily dinner. Kahana Gateway Plaza, Honoapiilani Hwy and Hoohui Rd, Kahana. 665.1822 ♿

26 Dollies $ If you're on a tight budget or in search of a particular imported beer, this pizzeria is the place for you. There are 30 brands of brew on hand, and no item on the menu is over $10. It has long been the hangout spot for West Maui *kamaaina* (locals), possibly because of the wide variety of drink specials—though a change of ownership may have lost the last traces of class in the translation. But then, who needs class with their pizza and beer? ♦ Pizza ♦ Daily lunch and dinner. 4310 Lower Honoapiilani Rd (south of Hoohui Rd), Kahana. 669.0266 ♿

27 Erik's Seafood Grotto ★$$$$ This rustic, woody dining room offers an enormous selection of fresh island and mainland fish, plus good ocean views. You can choose from 11 fish dishes, several kinds of shellfish, and an award-winning bouillabaisse. If it's available, try the fresh island lobster stuffed with seafood and flame broiled. It's popular with tourists and the early-bird–special crowd. ♦ Seafood ♦ Daily lunch and dinner. Reservations recommended. 4242 Lower Honoapiilani Rd, Mahinahina. 669.4806 ♿

Kaanapali and Environs

In the early 1950s, Amfac Corporation of Honolulu began planning a resort community that would give Waikiki a run for its money. This development, the first master-planned destination resort in Hawaii, was created on a chunk of barren land too dry for sugar cultivation yet lined with three miles of white-sand beaches too inviting to ignore. After Kaanapali's unveiling in 1962, Maui began to attract a volume of business previously seen only by Oahu.

Today Kaanapali is the site of 6 hotels, 4 condominium complexes, 2 golf courses, 37 tennis courts, a shopping center, and 2 whaling museums, all arranged along 3 miles of sandy shore. Kaanapali occupies some 1,200 acres, less than half of which are developed. A free van takes guests around the grounds, or visitors can travel to **Lahaina,** six miles away, aboard a rebuilt sugarcane train or by shuttle bus. The planners of Kaanapali, aware that tourism would grow on Maui, designed a resort that would be secluded from the rest of the island; instead of dispersing the visitors among randomly located hotels and condos, the aim was to encourage staying in a self-contained environment. This plan has worked fairly well, although Kaanapali's proximity to Lahaina has turned that once-sleepy town into a major tourist attraction.

28 Aston at Papakea $$$ Although it won't win any awards, this 13-acre resort offers a perfectly enjoyable family vacation, with all the amenities of the big-name resorts. Located right on the beach, it boasts two pools, two Jacuzzis, two saunas, two putting greens, three tennis courts, and a host of water sports, but no restaurant. All 100 of the 364 studios and 1- and 2-bedroom condo suites rented by Aston Hotels & Resorts have complete kitchens, washers and dryers, telephones, TVs, and daily maid service; the rest are privately owned. ◆ 3543 Lower Honoapiilani Rd (just north of Honoapiilani Hwy), Honokowai. 669.4848, 800/922.7866; fax 665.0662 ♿

29 Aston Kaanapali Shores $$$$ This super-deluxe 464-room beachfront condominium resort has a range of lodging options, from simple studios to 2-bedroom, 2-bath suites with luxurious kitchens, large lanais, and ocean views. The property's **Beach Club** is open daily for breakfast, lunch, and dinner. There are two swimming pools, a fitness center, and kids enjoy **Aston's Camp Kaanapali,** which offers various educational activities. It's in a select location and particularly recommended for families and groups. ◆ 3445 Honoapiilani Hwy (at Lower Honoapiilani Rd), Honokowai. 667.2211, 800/922.7866; fax 661.0836 ♿

30 Embassy Vacation Resorts $$$$ From the highway you can't miss this pink monstrosity, an enormous all-suites Signature Resorts hotel occupying 14 oceanfront acres at the northern edge of Kaanapali Beach. The 413 1- and 2-bedroom luxury suites abound with amenities: A typical 1-bedroom suite occupies 820 square feet and includes a queen-size sofa bed, 35-inch TV, partial kitchen, oversized bath with 2 marble vanities, a lanai, plus views of Lanai and Molokai. Suite rates include full breakfast and a two-hour complimentary cocktail time at sunset. There's a health club, a miniature golf course, and two pools (one of which is an

acre in size and has water slides). The oceanfront restaurant offers fine dining, while the poolside grill and the deli in the lobby offer lighter fare. ◆ 104 Kaanapali Shores La (just west of Lower Honoapiilani Rd), Honokowai. 661.2000, 800/362.2779; fax 667.5821; www.marcresorts.com ♿

30 Mahana at Kaanapali Condominium $$ Managed by Aston Resorts, this beachfront complex has two 12-story towers with 240 units and a good swimming beach a hundred yards away. There are studios and one- and two-bedroom units, all of which face the ocean and feature fully equipped kitchens, TV sets with VCRs, and daily maid service. A pool, poolside grill, and two tennis courts round out the amenities. For families and groups, it's a decent choice, though a three-night minimum stay is required. ◆ 110 Kaanapali Shores La (just west of Lower Honoapiilani Rd), Honokowai. 661.8751, 800/922.7866; fax 661.5510

31 Kahekili Park This white-sand beach is distinguished from all of Kaanapali's others by its ample free parking. The small, grassy expanse and sheltered tables are perfect for picnicking, and there are public facilities. ◆ Aston Maui La (just west of Honoapiilani Hwy), Kaanapali

31 Maui Kaanapali Villas $$$$ About 202 of the 253 huge studios and 1- and 2-bedroom units in this complex, managed by Aston Hotels and Resorts and various independents, are available for vacation rental. The AAA three-diamond resort on 10 acres of prime Kaanapali beachfront has 3 pools and nearby golf and tennis. There's a restaurant where guests can get breakfast, lunch, and dinner. ◆ Aston Maui La (just west of Honoapiilani Hwy), Kaanapali. 667.7791, 800/321.2558; fax 667.0366

The Essence of Kaanapali

32 Royal Lahaina Resort $$$ One of Maui's larger complexes offers 522 rooms and cottages in a variety of sizes, from 2-story seaside cottages to oceanfront suites in the 12-story **Lahaina Kai** tower. The mix of low- and high-rise buildings is enhanced by 27 acres of tropical landscaping, bordered by the ocean, a golf course, and meandering walkways. There is more of everything here: 2 dining rooms and lounges, 3 swimming pools and a whirlpool spa, and 11 tennis courts (including a stadium court). The **Royal Lahaina Luau** (held nightly) is a pleasant outdoor dining affair, with a program bolstered by *kumu hula* (hula teacher) Frank Kawaikapuokalani Hewitt, one of Hawaii's luminaries. All rooms have private lanais and refrigerators, while the suites have full kitchens. ♦ 2780 Kekaa Dr (off Kaanapali Pkwy), Kaanapali. 661.3611, 800/447.6925; fax 661.6150; www.2maui.com &

33 Maui Eldorado Condominiums $$$ These attractive apartments sit on 12 acres between the highway and the beach, alongside a golf course. More than half of the 204 units are available for vacation rentals through the ubiquitous Outrigger Hotels & Resorts and, although not on the water, the resort has its own private beach club within walking distance. Three pools and two golf courses are on the property, but there's no restaurant. ♦ 2661 Kekaa Dr (off Kaanapali Pkwy), Kaanapali. 661.0021, 800/777.1700; fax 667.7039; www.outrigger.com

34 Sheraton Maui $$$$ An exhaustive $170-million renovation turned this Kaanapali institution into one of the area's top hotels. Five wings contain 510 rooms, 80 percent with drop-dead views of the Pacific and of Black Rock promontory, where a cliff diver practices his art nightly at sunset. The 23-acre site has 3 restaurants, a lagoon and a pool, 3 tennis courts, and a health spa. ♦ 2605 Kaanapali Pkwy (north of Nohea Kai Dr), Kaanapali. 661.0031, 800/325.3535; fax 661.0458; www.sheratonhawaii.com &

35 Kaanapali Beach Sort of a mini-Waikiki, this beautiful, mostly uncrowded three-mile stretch of white sand is the perfect spot for swimming, tanning, and people watching. Just about any water-related activity can be found here, from scuba and windsurfing lessons to Hobie Cat rentals, and some great bars are right on the beach. The ocean is generally calm; hotels post red flags when swimming is too dangerous. Still, keep an eye on the kids; the sandy bottom drops off abruptly. Free parking is available, but it usually fills up before noon.

KA'ANAPALI BEACH HOTEL

35 Kaanapali Beach Hotel $$$ Built in the shape of a horseshoe, this hotel features 430 rooms facing a center courtyard that opens to the beach. The whale-shaped pool is only a few yards from the ocean, and nearby is **Whalers Village,** where you'll find an excellent collection of restaurants and shops. All rooms have refrigerators, TVs, phones, and private lanais. A golf course is nearby. ♦ 2525 Kaanapali Pkwy (north of Nohea Kai Dr), Kaanapali. 661.0011, 800/262.8450; fax 667.1963; www.kaanapalibeachhotel.com &

Within the Kaanapali Beach Hotel:

Tiki Terrace $$$ It's still known for its Sunday Champagne brunch, complete with a 24-foot-long pastry table and omelette station, but the seafood and Polynesian cuisine are unspectacular. Dinner specials feature dishes that are unfamiliar to most visitors, like pork *laulau* (wrapped in a banana leaf and steamed), poi, sweet potatoes and long rice; other entrées include fresh fish and teriyaki chicken. There's standard American fare as well. ♦ Pacific Rim/American ♦ M-Sa breakfast and dinner; Su brunch and dinner. Reservations recommended. 661.0011 &

35 Whaler Condominium
$$$$ These twin high-rise towers, 360 units total, sit on an excellent stretch of beach next to **Whalers Village.** It's a simple yet comfortable place, with daily maid service, spacious studios, and the requisite television and telephone. Guests may use the pool, sauna, Jacuzzi, exercise room, and five tennis courts. However, there is no restaurant. 2481 Kaanapali Pkwy (north of Nohea Kai Dr), Kaanapali. 661.4861, 800/367.7052; fax 661.8315; www.ten-io.com/vii

36 Whalers Village Everything from the **Gecko Store** (661.1114) to **Gucci** (661.3315) attracts most visitors at one time or another during their stay to this mix of five dozen restaurants and shops. ♦ 2435 Kaanapali Pkwy (north of Nohea Kai Dr), Kaanapali. 661.4567

Within Whalers Village:

Leilani's on the Beach ★★$$$ When residents want to check out the beach scene and "talk story" with friends, they come here. There's something about a place run by TS Enterprises (which owns **Kimo's, Duke's Canoe Club, Hula Grill,** and other popular restaurants in Hawaii and California) that appeals to everyone. The food is always very good, and the ambience friendly and relaxing—people spend more time here than they mean to. The regular menu has fresh Hawaiian fish, rack of lamb, filet mignon, and smoked ribs and chicken; for smaller appetites, there's a seafood bar called the **Beachside Grill** (&) next to the cocktail lounge on the beach. ♦ Seafood/Steak ♦ Daily lunch and dinner. 661.4495

Restaurants/Clubs: Red   **Hotels:** Blue
Shops/ ⬆ Outdoors: Green   **Sights/Culture:** Black

Seashells by the Seashore

Hawaii is a mecca for serious shell collectors and the island of Maui is their motherlode, for its shores hide some of the world's rarest and most valuable shells, including the prized checkered cowrie. The island is home to ingenious and dedicated treasure hunters who check the daily tide charts in their local newspaper, then scavenge tide pools to study the shells' habitats and camouflages. Many also snorkel or skin-dive to search for their prize.

To the uninitiated, nothing seems simpler than strolling the shores and pocketing the occasional lustrous find. But the amateur sheller should bear in mind that much more is involved than meets the eye. For starters, reefs prevent most shells from reaching the shore wholly intact, making it necessary to search in deeper water, where inexperienced snorkelers may find themselves on the "Tahitian Current Express." To compound the danger, many shelled animals, namely those found in cone shells, have powerful bites or stings that can cause serious illness. Finally, novice shell seekers should keep in mind that a shell is not just another pretty rock, it's the home of a living sea animal better suited to its own ecological circle than to your living-room bookshelf. To avoid depleting the waters of special specimens, leave shells where you find them if the original owner is still inside.

Crenulated Auger *(Terebra crenulata)* These spiny pink or blue shells are commonly found in shallow water. They are carnivores, usually about five inches long, with spiral rings distinguishing them from other island augers.

Fringed Cowrie *(Cypraea fimbriata)* Orange coral is the camouflage in depths of 2 to 60 feet for this orange cowrie.

Golden Yellow Cone *(Conus flavidus)* These 2.5-inch-long shells range from white to greenish yellow. Like other cones, they often have an outer layer of thick *periostracum,* a substance that obscures the shells' fine colors until removed.

Blood-Spotted Triton *(Bursa cruentata)* This lovely, common triton has an inner rim ranging from white to pale violet.

Green-Mouthed Spindle *(Peristernia chlorostome)* More yellow than green, this common one-half- to three-quarter-inch shell is found in coral along the shore.

Brilliant Drupe *(Drupa rubusidaeus)* Long spines and a pinkish mouth distinguish this 1.5-inch-long shell.

Hawaiian Limpet *(Petella sandwichensis)* This exclusively Hawaiian animal is an edible delicacy called *opihi* by locals. It grows up to two inches long and is found in shallow water or on rocks exposed to waves. Many have died in the process of harvesting this delicacy when rogue waves swept them into the sea.

Checkered Cowrie *(Cypraea tessellata)* Native only to Hawaii, this rare and beautiful prize has a tiny three-quarter- to 1.5-inch-long shell and hides in about 50 feet of water.

Horned Helmet *(Cassis cornuta)* Growing as long as a foot, this is among the largest of the Hawaiian shells.

Knobbed Drupe *(Drupa nodus)* A common shell found in shallow water—look for a lavender mouth and black spikes on a white background.

Reticulated Cowrie *(Cypaea maculifera)* This cowrie shell is prized by world collectors. Hawaiians use the shells as jewelry and decoration. The smooth, colorful specimens are found under rocks or on coral near the shore.

Knobby Spindle *(Latirus nodus)* This common pink shell houses a bright red sea creature. Some local divers break the end off this shell to keep others from removing it for their collections.

Rough Periwinkle *(Littorina scabra)* This edible animal lives in shoreline coral.

Snakehead Cowrie *(Cypraea caputserpentis)* Hawaii's most common cowrie is a herbivorous night feeder that grows up to 1.5 inches in length.

Lettered Miter *(Mitra litterata)* These tiny carnivores have a poisonous sting they use to capture worms for dinner. Only one inch long, they hide under loose coral at the water's surface.

Tiger Cowrie *(Cypraea tigris)* This two- to three-inch-long shell is only found in Hawaii and is commonly sold in gift shops with designs carved into its surface.

Marlin Spike Auger *(Terebra maculata)* Found in depths of more than 10 feet, these grow up to 10 inches long and are the largest augers on earth.

Murex *(Murex pele)* These rough, craggy carnivores use their spiky surfaces as spears to capture other mollusks. Found only in Hawaii, they hide in coral at depths of 40 feet.

Tile Miter *(Mitra incompta)* Miters are not generally prized by collectors, since the four-inch-long, rough-textured shells are fairly common. They live among coral beds 30 to 80 feet deep.

Penniform Cone *(Conus Pennaceua)* Inhabitants of these cones fire darts to stun their prey; some species are even dangerous to humans. But the common three-inch-long cones are safe as well as beautiful, with an intricate and varied design. They live buried in sand on the ocean floor.

Pimpled Basket *(Nassarius papillosus)* A scavenger that hops along on a single muscle (or "foot"), its shell grows from 1 inch to 2.25 inches long.

Triton's Trumpet *(Charonia tritonis)* These rare shells, which grow up to 18 inches in length, fasten themselves to coral in deep water.

Hula Grill ★★★$$$ TS Enterprises has managed to create a place that's more Hawaiian than Hawaii itself. Canoes and surfboards are everywhere in this open-air beachside dining room, and the fare too is regional. Peter Merriman, owner and chef at **Merriman's** on the Big Island a fraction of the time, serves up seared *ahi,* mahimahi, and swordfish, as well as Black Angus steak with garlic mashed potatoes and Maui onion strings. Hawaiian entertainment is featured every night, with local musicians and hula shows in the bar. ♦ Hawaiian Regional/Seafood ♦ Daily lunch and dinner. Reservations recommended. 667.6636 ♿

Rusty Harpoon $$$ If you're seriously into fresh fruit daiquiris, this is a great place to get one. The restaurant refers to itself as the "daiquiri capital of the world." The menu includes seafood and steak prepared a thousand different ways—steamed lobster, shrimp scampi, broiled mahimahi, prime rib, New York steak. ♦ Steak/Seafood ♦ Daily breakfast, lunch, and dinner. 661.3123 ♿

THE WESTIN MAUI

36 Westin Maui $$$$ This $155-million resort, owned by Starwood Resorts, is filled with extravagance and possibility. It boasts a fantasy water complex consisting of 5 free-form, multilevel swimming pools, waterfalls, water slides, and meandering streams; a $2.5-million collection of Pacific and Asian art; exotic wildlife; and 8 restaurants and lounges. The 12-acre resort has two 11-story towers containing 741 rooms and suites; the top 2 floors of the **Beach Tower** are reserved for the **Royal Beach Club**—28 ultraelegant rooms and such extras as a private elevator, a breakfast buffet, and reserved poolside seating. ♦ 2365 Kaanapali Pkwy (just north of Nohea Kai Dr), Kaanapali. 667.2525, 800/228.3000; fax 661.5831; www.westinmaui.com ♿

Within the Westin Maui:

Sound of the Falls ★★★$$$$ The high-ceilinged, open-air dining room features distant views of Lanai and Molokai and an elegant setting highlighted by exotic birds gliding along the facing lagoon. The menu has more than 140 items, including Belgian waffles, smoked seafood, and mounds of fresh fruit, and the prix-fixe brunch includes

entertainment. ♦ Continental ♦ Su brunch. Reservations recommended. 667.2525 ♿

Villa Restaurant ★★$$$$ The hotel's sprawling lagoons, gardens, and waterfalls accent this dining spot's casual setting. Seafood is the staple here, and the nightly special is usually outstanding. The crab cakes are superlative, as are the tangled tiger prawns and Kona lobster. ♦ Seafood/Pacific Rim ♦ Daily dinner. Reservations recommended. 667.2525 ♿

Cook's at the Beach ★$$$ This poolside eatery is two cuts above the typical hotel coffee shop, serving such island specialties as *ahi* and shrimp scampi, healthful entrées like "Fruit Fantasy" (fruit salad), and a nightly prime rib buffet (not for the health conscious). A hula show, presented on Monday, Wednesday, and Friday, is free. ♦ Continental/Cafe ♦ Daily breakfast buffet, lunch, and dinner. 667.2525 ♿

37 Kaanapali Golf Course Designed in the 1960s by Robert Trent Jones Sr., the 18-hole **North Course** (par 71, 6,136 yards) offers spectacular views of the West Maui Mountains, the ocean, and the islands of Molokai and Lanai across the channel. It's a good golf test, with numerous water risks. The **South Course** (18 holes, par 71, 6,067 yards), a former executive course extended to championship class, also has ocean views and plays three or four strokes easier than the **North,** advises the resident pro. Kaanapali can be windy, especially in the late afternoon, which is why the greens fees are lower after 2:30PM on the **North Course,** noon on the **South.** Lessons are available. ♦ Expensive greens fees. Daily. Preferred starting times for guests at Kaanapali hotels. Reservations at least four days ahead are required. Kaanapali Pkwy and Honoapiilani Hwy, Kaanapali. 661.3691

38 Maui Marriott $$$$ With its beautiful landscaping, cascading waterfalls, running streams, coconut grove, and trade-wind-touched lobby, this hotel reflects the Marriott chain's attempt to upgrade its image. However, critics say the two 9-story buildings on the 15-acre site look too much like the Marriotts typically found near airports. Nevertheless, the property's swimming pool fronts Kaanapali Beach, and all 720 rooms and suites have private lanais, some of which face the ocean. Amenities include five tennis courts and a resident pro, a children's pool, two Jacuzzis, a championship golf course next door, catamarans, an exercise room, and a whole lot more. ♦ 100 Nohea Kai Dr (off Kaanapali Pkwy), Kaanapali. 667.1200, 800/763.1333; fax 667.8192 ♿

Within the Maui Marriott:

Moana Terrace ★$$ The resort's main dining room opens onto gardens and is terraced to provide maximum ocean views, with alfresco seating the most desirable. It's a nice atmosphere for gorging on chicken Caesar salad, chicken Santa Cruz sandwiches, or grilled sugarcane shrimp on noodles. There's even a kids' corner that features videos. ◆ American ◆ Daily breakfast, lunch, and dinner. 667.1200 ₫

Nikko Steak House ★★$$$$ Marriott's smartest move in Hawaii was opening this Japanese *teppanyaki* (tableside cooking) steak house. It filled a void in West Maui, where exceptional ethnic restaurants are rare. After the house soup, try out the *teppanyaki* selections and the savory sauces, but save room for the fried ice cream (cake filled with ice cream and deep-fried). Tables seat 8, so other diners fill any empty seats, and a 15 percent gratuity is added to the check. ◆ Japanese ◆ Daily dinner. Reservations recommended. 667.1200 ₫

Lokelani Room ★$$$$ The decor in this restaurant (named for Maui's official flower) is nautical, and the menu—featuring stuffed *opakapaka* and grilled *ahi*—matches the theme. ◆ Seafood/Hawaiian Regional ◆ W-Su dinner. 667.1200 ₫

Makai Bar ★★$ Known for its *pupus* (appetizers), this open-air appetizer bar at the southern end of the lobby overlooks the beach from its elevated vantage point. The decor includes six 150-gallon fish tanks and 30 stools along a circular bar. The serious eating begins after 10:30PM, when some dishes, such as sushi, egg rolls, and *poki* (chopped, seasoned raw fish), are half price. No one under 21 is admitted. ◆ Appetizers ◆ Daily 4:30PM-12:30AM. 667.1200 ₫

39 Hyatt Regency Maui $$$$ Developer Chris Hemmeter built this super-deluxe "Disneyland for adults" in 1980 for $80 million. Seven years later, Kokusai Jidosha, a Japanese company, bought it for $319 million (approximately $391,000 per room), throwing in $12 million for renovations in 1990 and another $16 million in 1995. The hotel consists of three 19-story connecting towers on 40 oceanside acres, with 808 rooms and suites. Custom-designed wall coverings, upholstery, and furniture, as well as Italian marble countertops and terra-cotta tile floors, are among luxurious touches added by Kokusai Jidosha. Hemmeter, however, should still be credited for the lavish collection of Asian and Pacific art, including John Young paintings, Hawaiian quilts, Cambodian Buddhas, Ming Dynasty wine pots, and battle shields from Papua New Guinea. Outside, a 154-foot enclosed water slide empties into the 1.5-acre swimming pool. Mexican artists designed the 14-karat-gold tiles that embellish the sprawling pool's mosaic. There's also a swinging rope bridge and a swim-up **Grotto Bar,** set between two waterfalls. Flamingos, swans, penguins, and ducks add to the hotel's flamboyantly exotic flavor. The **Regency Club** offers such extras as concierge service, breakfast, and sunset cocktails and appetizers. ◆ 200 Nohea Kai Dr (off Kaanapali Pkwy), Kaanapali. 661.1234, 800/233.1234; fax 667.4497; www.hyatt.com ₫

Within the Hyatt Regency Maui:

Cascades Sushi Bar & Grill ★★$$$ Paella, filet mignon, and fresh local fish like *ono* and *ahi* are served in a garden setting with nautical touches. ◆ Steak/Seafood ◆ Daily lunch and dinner. 661.1234 ₫

Swan Court ★★★$$$$ The large, elegant dining room of this award-winning restaurant overlooks a lagoon with a flotilla of gliding swans. Hawaiian music enhances the stunning view of the waterfalls and the sun setting between Lanai and Molokai. The fresh fish and roast duckling are excellent choices when they're offered, or try the rack of lamb, chateaubriand, or lobster in puff pastry. The wine list is long—and expensive. In the mornings, a lovely breakfast buffet with pancakes, French toast, and crepes is laid out. Unlike most restaurants, this one encourages cigar smoking. ◆ Pacific Rim ◆ Daily breakfast and dinner. Reservations recommended. 661.1234 ₫

Spats Trattoria ★$$ This place offers a decent selection of dishes such as seafood grill over fettuccine Alfredo and chicken parmigiana. ◆ Italian/Seafood ◆ Daily dinner. Reservations recommended. 661.1234 ₫

Drums of the Pacific ★$$$ An extravagant (if antiseptic) South Seas show accompanies a lavish all-you-can-eat buffet. Main dishes include *kalua* pork (baked in ti leaves), *shoyu* chicken (in soy sauce), and coconut beef. ◆ Luau ◆ Daily dinner. Reservations recommended. 661.1234 ₫

40 Wahikuli State Wayside Park This popular recreation site has picnic pavilions, public facilities, and nearby tennis courts. There's also a beach, but it's very small, usually damp, and covered with debris. ◆ Honoapiilani Hwy (between Front St and Kaanapali Pkwy)

Lahaina

In the course of its history, this waterfront town has had three distinct identities. Under Kamehameha the Great, it was an early political center of the united Hawaiian kingdom. From approximately 1820 to 1860, it served as the most important provisioning stop for America's entire Pacific whaling fleet, and as such was the site of a struggle between sailors dedicated to debauchery and Protestant missionaries trying to save souls. Designated as a National Historic Landmark in 1962, Lahaina has since entered a third incarnation—this town of 14,000 people has become West Maui's main tourist attraction, with attractive shops, fine restaurants, and nightclubs appealing to a young crowd.

The town is only a few blocks deep, and most of the points of interest are on or just off a half-mile stretch of **Front Street.** Sight-seeing should take two to three hours or so (a bit more for dedicated shoppers), but for optimum comfort, plan your excursion for the morning or evening—the town is deserving of its name, *lahaina,* which means "merciless sun."

41 Chart House ★$$$$ The idea behind its high perch at the northern end of Lahaina was to give diners a great sunset and ocean view, which it does. The restaurant's long-standing reputation for good steak and fish holds firm here, but if you're short on cash, the Caesar salad makes a fine meal. ♦ Steak/Seafood ♦ Daily dinner. Reservations recommended. 1450 Front St (at Honoapiilani Hwy). 661.0937. Also at: 100 Wailea Ike Dr (at Wailea Alanui), Wailea. 879.2875 ♿

41 Lahaina Cannery Mall Whatever you need, from beach chairs to Dramamine, you'll find here. The center, a pineapple cannery from 1918 to 1963, has 2 anchor stores (**Longs** and **Safeway**), 50 shops, and a food court, special events such as lei-making and pineapple-slicing demonstrations, and an adorable *keiki* (kids') hula show every Sunday at 1PM. The good news is that the mall underwent a multimillion-dollar face-lift in 1998, making it slick and clean—and air-conditioned (it's the only enclosed mall on Maui that can boast this blissful state). A free shuttle from Lahaina Harbor runs all day. ♦ Daily. 1221 Honoapiilani Hwy (at Kapunakea St). 661.5304 ♿

42 Jodo Mission Lahaina's Buddhist temple, which consists of the Amida Buddha (Great Buddha), temple bell, main temple, and pagoda, was completed in 1970 to commemorate the centennial of the first Japanese immigration to Hawaii, as well as to memorialize loved ones who passed away in the last one hundred years. The Amida

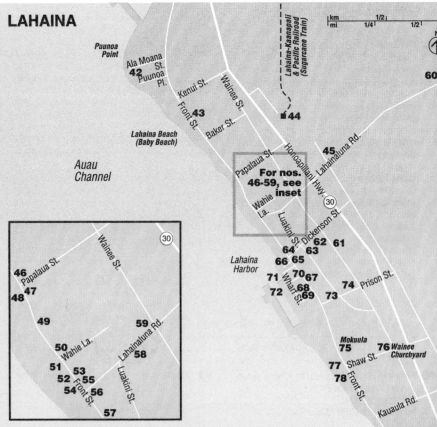

LAHAINA

Buddha, at 12 feet and 3.5 tons, is the largest of its kind outside of Japan. ♦ 12 Ala Moana St (west of Front St). 661.5553

43 Seamen's Hospital During Lahaina's wild whaling days in the mid-1800s, thousands of sailors were left behind on Maui by American and British whaling ships seeking to lighten their loads before embarking on trading trips to Canton. Many of the sailors subsequently died of a "disreputable disease" (venereal disease) at this two-story hospital; in fact, at the time the care of sick sailors in Lahaina and Honolulu used up half the budget appropriated by Congress for the care of all US seamen. Ironically, the place was sold to a group of nuns in 1865 and served as a Catholic school for some 20 years and then as an Episcopalian vicarage for 30 years; it was abandoned in 1908. In 1982, through a unique arrangement between the Lahaina Restoration Foundation and architect **Uwe Schultz**, the deteriorating eyesore was completely restored. The building is currently used as office space. ♦ 1024 Front St (between Baker and Kenui Sts). 661.3262

44 Lahaina-Kaanapali & Pacific Railroad (Sugarcane Train) Children and train buffs will especially enjoy the *Sugarcane Train:* a rebuilt little-train-that-could that chugs six miles between Lahaina and Kaanapali. Puffing beside original narrow-gauge track used by the **Pioneer Sugar Mill** since 1890, this steam locomotive (pictured above) with whistle and open-air passenger cars recalls a bygone era. Buy one-way or round-trip tickets, or choose a package that includes **The Hawaii Experience Dome Theater** movie, a luau, parasailing, a helicopter ride, or a museum tour. A bus (nominal charge) runs between the Lahaina depot and town. There's a boarding platform across the footbridge at the north end of the Kaanapali resort. The narrated trip (about 25 minutes each way) takes passengers past cane fields, mountains, and the shore, and features a singing conductor. ♦ Fee. Five round-trips daily. Three stations: Lahaina Station, Limahana St (east of Honoapiilani Hwy) &; Kaanapali Station, Honoapiilani Hwy (between Halelo St and Puukoli Rd; no parking available); Puukolii Station, Puukolii Rd (just east of Honoapiilani Hwy), Kaanapali. 661.0089

45 Pioneer Sugar Mill Built by sugar magnate James Campbell, the Pioneer Mill Company thrived as others folded and went on to become a kingpin of Maui sugar production,

providing generations of Mauians with employment. The mill's smokestack is as familiar a part of the Lahaina landscape as the cane fields and boat harbors. The building is closed to the public. ♦ Lahainaluna Rd and Mill St

46 Lahaina Center This shopping center has the personality and charm of a refrigerator, but it continues to receive busloads of tourists, and parking is no longer free, so the stores here must be prospering. The major outlets include **Liberty House** department store (661.4451), which sells high-end Hawaiian print fashions, and **Hilo Hattie** (667.7911), which sells low-end Hawaiian print fashions. ♦ Daily. 900 Front St (at Papalaua St). 667.9216 &

Within Lahaina Center:

Hard Rock Cafe ★★$$ It's said that familiarity breeds contempt, but for the Hard Rock chain, all it breeds is success. As usual, the rock music is loud, the walls are adorned with rock and surf memorabilia, and there's always a line to buy T-shirts. The food, if unexceptional and expensive, is good enough to draw even the locals, who come for the six-ounce burgers and Texas-style ribs. Yes, it's predictable and very touristy, but you'd be hard-pressed to have a bad time. ♦ American ♦ Daily lunch and dinner. 667.7400 &

Ruth's Chris Steak House ★★★$$$$ In 1965, a 41-year-old single mother named Ruth bought a joint called Chris' Steak House in the heart of New Orleans, named it Ruth's Chris Steak House, rolled up her sleeves and went to work. Almost 35 years later, the 65th in a nationwide chain of restaurants (the original has since burned to the ground) serves up Hawaiian flipper-tail lobster and US prime filet mignon cooked in an 1,800-degree broiler and served sizzling on 500-degree plates. ♦ Steak house ♦ Daily dinner. Reservations recommended. 661.8815 &

47 Longhi's ★★★$$$ Since it opened in the 1980s, this has been one of the "in" places to dine in Lahaina. Portions are large, so be careful about overordering, especially if you

plan on trying one of the trademark homemade desserts. The cuisine has an Italian flair, with dishes like pasta Lombardi (with snow peas, prosciutto, and cream), lobster Longhi (with pasta, calamari, clams, and mussels in a marinara sauce), filet mignon, and enormous sandwiches. An unusual, if sometimes annoying, feature is the verbal menu, and the restaurant can be loud. However, the meals are delicious as a rule—particularly breakfast!—and there are some stellar bands featured on Friday nights. ♦ Continental/Italian ♦ Daily breakfast, lunch, and dinner. Reservations recommended. 888 Front St (at Papalaua St). 667.2288 &

48 Bubba Gump Shrimp Company ★★$$ If you like the kind of theme restaurant where all the waiters wear roller skates or dress like fairy-tale characters, get thee to this dining room below the massive, 100-year-old monkey pod tree in the center of Lahaina. And flip the two-sided card on your table to "Stop, Bubba, Stop" (the other side reads "Go, Bubba, Go") frequently during the meal, causing one or more of the *Forrest Gump*–inspired restaurant's wait staff to stop in his or her tracks to serve you. If you can get beyond the schtick, the shrimp—served barbecued, fried, in stew, over spaghetti, on sandwiches, in salads, and on and on—is pretty good, and the barbecued ribs aren't bad either. ♦ Seafood ♦ Daily lunch and dinner. 889 Front St (at Papalaua St). 661.3111 &

49 Wo Hing Temple In 1909 Chinese laborers brought here to work in West Maui's sugarcane fields formed the Wo Hing Society, a mid-Pacific chapter of a 17th-century Chinese fraternal organization. Three years later the group built a hall with a separate cookhouse in downtown Lahaina. In 1983 the Lahaina Restoration Foundation turned the building into a museum, preserving a chapter in the history of one of Hawaii's significant ethnic groups. Among the items on display in the cookhouse are Chinese utensils and fire pits once fueled with *kiawe* wood for oversize woks. Films of turn-of-the-century Hawaii made by Thomas Edison are also shown. ♦ Donation. Daily. 858 Front St (between Wahie La and Papalaua St). 661.3262; lrf@maui.net

50 Avalon ★★★$$$$ Some of chef/owner Mark Ellman's imaginative Pacific Rim creations, such as Australian barbecued lamb chop and seared *tiki* salad (a mix of potatoes, salmon, mango, eggplant, greens, and tomato salsa with plum-vinaigrette dressing), are truly exceptional. The setting is comfortable, with wood floors and a brick courtyard. This remains one of the island's finest dining rooms. ♦ Pacific Rim ♦ Daily lunch and dinner. Reservations recommended. Mariner's Alley, 844 Front St (at Wahie La). 667.5559 &

50 Moose McGillycuddy's ★$$ Part of the chain that extends from Oahu to California, this restaurant lacks originality but makes up for it in practicality. By offering a variety of reasonably good food at low prices, it plays a much-needed role in Lahaina. Menu items include prime rib, mahimahi, chicken, steak and lobster, Mexican food (especially the fish tacos), and giant salads. There's also a kids' menu. The breakfasts are huge (all the cops start their day with the $1.99 special), and the bar has nightly specials and live dance music. The cheapest dinners in town are the early-

Wo Hing Temple

致公堂

© RAMSAY

bird specials served from 4 to 7PM (try the prime rib or tequila fettucine). At the other end of the spectrum is the $22.95 all-you-can-eat king crab extravaganza on Monday and Thursday. ♦ American ♦ Daily breakfast, lunch, and dinner. Mariner's Alley, 844 Front St (at Wahie La). 667.7758 ♿

51 Kimo's ★★$$ Two young men who made a fortune with the Rusty Scupper chain on the mainland built this popular oceanfront restaurant and bar on Front Street, with views of Molokai and Lanai from the outside deck. The food isn't anything to write home about, but it's consistently good, including your basic fresh fish, a huge cut of prime rib, steak, and island specials such as *koloa* (plum-sauce–glazed) pork ribs and Polynesian chicken. A Hawaiian singer puts on a show every afternoon, but the best entertainment for locals and visitors alike is the spectacular sunset. ♦ Steak/Seafood ♦ Daily lunch and dinner. 845 Front St (at Wahie La). 661.4811 ♿

52 Lahaina Fish Co. ★★$$$ If you're confused by the names and pronunciations of the fish served in restaurants all over Hawaii, this fish house will set you straight. Comprehensive menus translate the Hawaiian word for each fish, and there's also a wall-mounted guide to island game fish. Although the cuisine isn't particularly memorable, the setting is—an open-air lanai overlooking Lahaina Harbor, Lanai, and Molokai. Prices for the Cajun mahimahi, shrimp Salvador, and the catch of the day are very reasonable, considering the million-dollar sunset that accompanies your meal. If you're not a fan of fish, opt for the popular stir-fry. ♦ Seafood ♦ Daily lunch and dinner. 831 Front St (between Lahainaluna Rd and Wahie La). 661.3472 ♿

53 The Hawaii Experience Dome Theater Admittedly, there's something weird about sitting in a theater watching a film of a volcanic eruption, a school of fish being chased by a bigger fish, or a whale breaching, when that's what you came to Hawaii to see close up (even odder is the film of Alaska shown at 6PM each day). But this 180°, 3-story-high screen gives you a closer view than you'll ever get in real life. ♦ Admission. Daily 10AM-10PM; shows hourly. 824 Front St (between Lahainaluna Rd and Wahie La). 661.7111; het@maui.net ♿

CHEESE BURGER
•I•N• P•A•R•A•D•I•S•E•

54 Cheeseburger In Paradise ★$ Yes, the name comes from the popular Jimmy Buffett tune, which is of the same genre as the continuous background music, live and taped, played at this open-air burger joint. It's cheap, it's pretty good, and it's always jumping. But

no, Jimmy never eats here, though a lively local band does belt out Buffett-style hits on weekend evenings. ♦ Burgers ♦ Daily breakfast, lunch, and dinner. 811 Front St (between Lahainaluna Rd and Wahie La). 661.4855 ♿

Lahaina Inn

55 Lahaina Inn $$ In the 1860s, when Lahaina was the whaling mecca of the world, this hotel housed the whalers who came to port. When the whaling era ended, the hostelry, then called the **Lahainaluna Hotel,** became a gathering place for genteel travelers and local power brokers. The building later served as a general store, and then business offices (destroyed by fire in the mid-1960s). Today it's a 2-story, 12-room inn (including 3 suites) refurbished in old-style grandeur by its current owner, entrepreneur, preservationist, and antiques collector Rick Ralston (of **Crazy Shirts** fame). Luxurious turn-of-the-century touches include beautiful armoires, leaded-glass lamps, floral wall coverings, rocking chairs on the lanais, and lace curtains. No children under 15 are allowed, there are no TVs, and smokers are encouraged to use the lanai. The rooms have air-conditioning and telephones, and continental breakfast is included in the rate. ♦ 127 Lahainaluna Rd (between Wainee and Front Sts). 661.0577, 800/669.3444; fax 667.9480; inntown@lahainainn.com; www.lahainainn.com

Within the Lahaina Inn:

David Paul's Lahaina Grill ★★★$$$$ Once a seedy barroom on the ground floor of the former **Lahainaluna Hotel,** this star on the local culinary scene possesses the same turn-of-the-century ambience as the hotel (and, like the hotel, no longer permits smoking). The large, airy dining room retains the feel of a classy Victorian barroom, with a long wooden bar, ceiling fans, and white tablecloths; it accommodates 122 people and one baby grand piano. The wine list is extensive and the fare, says part-owner and celebrated chef David Paul, features "flavors from around the world perfectly blended with local ingredients." A few examples: tequila shrimp with firecracker rice, Kona coffee–roasted lamb, and *kalua* duck—and triple berry pie for dessert. ♦ International ♦ Daily dinner. Reservations recommended. 667.5117 ♿

Braking Away: Maui by Bike

For those willing to wake up at an ungodly hour, head for the top of a 10,023-foot volcano, risk life and limb getting down to the bottom, and pay $100 for the privilege, a unique vacation experience awaits: biking 38 miles down the slopes of Maui's **Haleakala Crater.**

Before sunrise, a driver will pick you up at your hotel and, after coddling you with coffee and doughnuts, take you to the top of Haleakala, where you will be outfitted with a single-speed, specially designed bicycle (equipped with megabrakes), a windbreaker, gloves, and a helmet.

The chilly but pleasant ride takes about 3.5 hours, cruising through cattle ranches, protea farms, and sugarcane and pineapple fields, with a stop in the picturesque town of **Kula** for lunch. The entire trip ranges from memorable to miserable depending on the unpredictable weather, but one thing is certain: It's downhill all the way.

Bicycle tours from Haleakala are offered daily by **Maui Mountain Cruisers** (871.6014, 800/232.MAUI) and **Maui Downhill** (871.2155, 800/535.BIKE).

KEELY EDWARDS

56 Lahaina Marketplace The impeccable landscaping distinguishes this open-air shopping arcade filled with jewelry and souvenir kiosks. Head toward the back and admire the sentinel-like fan palms, towering hedges, brick patio, and formidable foliage tiki, or to the front, where there's an activity center, to schedule a snorkeling or sailing trip. ♦ Front St and Lahainaluna Rd &

57 Planet Hollywood ★★$$$ Taking the **Hard Rock Cafe** concept (see page 67) and applying it to the world of the silver screen, this chain features movie memorabilia, clips from upcoming films, and other scraps of Hollywood culture (an oxymoron, we know). The food is American—burgers, steak, chicken, ribs, salads, pastas, pizzas, etc. No reservations are taken per se, but there is

priority seating, which means that those who have called in earlier to make the non-reservations would go to the front of any line for fast-track seating. ♦ American ♦ Daily lunch and dinner. 744 Front St (between Dickenson St and Lahainaluna Rd). 667.7877 &

58 Plantation Inn $$$ A group of private investors took over three residential lots in the center of Lahaina and came up with this luxurious, elegant, and surprisingly affordable hotel. In 1998 it was purchased by the owner of the **Kaanapali Beach Hotel;** at press time they had plans to expand. The 19 rooms and suites all have an intimate, plantation-style ambience, with French doors, brass four-poster beds, and other antique furniture, verandas, stained glass, wainscoting and floral wallpaper, and hardwood floors scattered with area rugs. Modern amenities include air-conditioning, TV sets, VCRs, a swimming pool, and a Jacuzzi. A continental breakfast comes gratis. Adjacent to the inn is **Gerard's,** the best French restaurant in Maui (if not Hawaii), and only a block away are the shops and galleries of Lahaina's bustling Front Street. ♦ 174 Lahainaluna Rd (between Wainee and Luakini Sts). 667.9225, 800/433.6815; fax 667.9293; info@theplantationinn.com; www.theplantationinn.com

Adjacent to the Plantation Inn:

Gerard's ★★★★$$$$ An apprentice chef in France at age 14, Gerard Reversade trained with four French culinary masters, acquiring the expertise that makes him one of Hawaii's top chefs. After moving to Hawaii in 1973, Gerard worked in the finest French restaurants in the state and in 1982 established his own place in downtown Lahaina—a small, charmingly unpretentious adjunct to the stately **Plantation Inn.** The decor recalls Provence; the entrées, including rack of lamb and roasted Hawaiian snapper, are impeccably prepared. True to his French roots, Reversade has a policy of using fresh local ingredients. Yes, it's expensive, but it's also the best. (*Wine Spectator* magazine gave the restaurant its top award in 1994, 1995, 1996, and 1997.) Guests of the **Plantation Inn** receive a discount. ◆ French ◆ Daily dinner. Reservations recommended. 661.8939 ஃ

59 West Maui Cycle and Sports For those looking to rent mountain bikes, snorkel sets, boogie boards, surfboards, golf clubs, or baby joggers, this is the place—and the prices are reasonable. ◆ Daily. 193 Lahainaluna Rd (at Wainee St). 661.9005

60 Hale Pai (House of Printing) This structure is the only original building still standing on the **Lahainaluna High School** campus—the first American school established west of the Rocky Mountains. Founded in 1831 by Protestant missionaries as a means of spreading the Christian gospel to the Hawaiian people, the school used a secondhand press to print Hawaii's first newspaper in Hawaiian, *Ka Lama Hawaii* (The Torch of Hawaii), in 1834. The press, brought by the missionaries on their journey around Cape Horn, also turned out translations, history texts, and even Hawaiian currency. The building has been fully restored by the Lahaina Restoration Foundation. ◆ Donation. M-F 10AM-1PM; other times call for appointment. Lahainaluna Rd (east of Mill St). 661.3262 ஃ

ASTON MAUI ISLANDER HOTEL

61 Aston Maui Islander $$ Lush tropical plants and quiet surroundings distinguish this unobtrusive, nine-acre complex of two-story structures. Banana trees, ancient palms, plumeria, papaya, and large torch gingers transform this otherwise plain establishment into a cool oasis in the middle of simmering Lahaina. Its 350 clean but unspectacular rooms and suites have the usual comforts: TVs, telephones, air-conditioning, and lanais for the bedroom suites on the top floor. There's no restaurant, but for the price, location (a short walk from everything), and casual ambience, it's a fairly good choice for lodging in Lahaina. ◆ 660 Wainee St (between Prison and Dickenson Sts). 667.9766,

Hale Pai

800/367.5226; fax 661.3733; www.aston-hotels.com ஃ

62 Lahaina Coolers ★★$$ Very few dining establishments make it onto the locals' favorite-hangout list, but the informal atmosphere and friendly staff make this open-air restaurant and bar *the* place in Lahaina to unwind with a Lahaina cooler cocktail and an "evil jungle" chicken and pasta appetizer. The restaurant offers a host of daily specials in addition to its eclectic menu; it's hard to go wrong with the Molokai sweet bread French toast or a handmade pizza. Free entertainment is usually provided by the resident gecko family, which performs nightly under the neon lights. ◆ American ◆ Daily breakfast, lunch, and dinner. Reservations recommended. Dickenson Square, 180 Dickenson St (at Wainee St). 661.7082 ஃ

63 Kobe Steak House ★★$$$ Lahaina's best sushi bar is located here among the *teppanyaki* (tableside cooking) grills and the human Veg-o-Matics, whose culinary skills are as good as the food. The service is always friendly, the sushi always fresh, and the bill always higher than you think it'll be. For something different and unbelievably good, try the *unagi* (freshwater eel) and *dynamite* (baked scallops), with a Purple Haze (fortified sake) to wash it all down. ◆ Japanese ◆ Daily dinner. 136 Dickenson St (at Luakini St). 667.5555 ஃ

Baldwin Home

64 Take Home Maui The irony of this produce and deli shop is that it's obviously geared toward tourists (with pineapples, coconuts, Maui onions, papayas, macadamia nuts, and other delicacies to send home to loved ones), but it's always filled with locals, who come for the coffee, smoothies, pastries, and deli items. Before you spend the day driving around Maui, grab a table and enjoy a cup of macadamia-nut or chocolate-raspberry Kona coffee, then get a Moon Box lunch—a sandwich, a piece of fruit, a side of pasta or potato salad, and a cookie or chips—to go. Yes, the resident bird talks ("ah*row*ha"), and no, it does not bite (well, not often). ♦ Daily. 121 Dickenson St (at Luakini St). 661.8067 &

65 Village Galleries In a town where marine art is big business, Lynn Shue's gallery offers a refreshing change of genre. It has pieces by Hawaii's finest artists, including George Allan and Pamela Andelin, with works in all media. ♦ Daily. 120 Dickenson St (at Luakini St). 661.4402. Also at: Dickenson Square, 180 Dickenson St (at Wainee St). 661.5559 &; Ritz-Carlton Kapalua, 1 Ritz-Carlton Dr (off Lower Honoapiilani Rd), Kapalua. 669.1800 &

65 Baldwin Home The Reverend Dwight Baldwin, a medical missionary, relocated from the mainland to Lahaina in 1835 for the sake of his own health, then wound up attending to the medical needs of the Hawaiians who gathered daily on his doorstep. In 1853 he singlehandedly fought to save Maui, Molokai, and Lanai from a smallpox epidemic. Until he moved to Honolulu in 1868, the reverend lived with his family in this white two-story house

made of coral, stone, and hand-hewn timbers. He received both royalty and ship captains here, providing them with a seamen's chapel and Christian reading room. The Lahaina Restoration Foundation now operates the house—the oldest standing building in Lahaina—as a museum and also has its administrative offices here. ♦ Admission. Daily. Front St (between Prison and Dickenson Sts). 661.3262 &

66 Sunrise Cafe ★$ A popular hangout for philosophical locals who enjoy deliberating over cappuccino and pastry, this cafe serves light baked goods for breakfast, and sandwiches, quiche, homemade soup, some heartier dishes like mango barbecue chicken, and daily specials for lunch and dinner. If you miss your cafe back home, this will do in a pinch. Open at 6AM, it's also a good wake-up stop to make before an early-morning drive or boat trip. Take note, though: Service is refreshingly slow. ♦ Cafe ♦ Daily breakfast, lunch, and dinner. 693A Front St (at Market St). 661.8558 &

67 Wharf Cinema Center This complex is touristy beyond belief, housing some of

Lahaina's most mediocre shops, and restaurants that aren't much better. But it does have a movie theater and when it gets really hot in Lahaina, a movie offering 90 minutes of air-conditioned comfort can seem like heaven. Nirvana for the 12-and-under set might be a foray into the **Fun Factory** (667.1922) video arcade. ♦ Daily. 658 Front St (between Prison and Dickenson Sts) 661.8748

68 Banyan Tree It's hard to believe that this huge banyan—nearly a block in size including its roots and overhanging branches—stood a mere eight feet tall when it was brought to Lahaina from India. Planted in 1873 by Sheriff William Owen Smith to commemorate the 50th anniversary of Lahaina's first Protestant Christian mission, the venerable tree is now among the oldest and largest in the islands and is listed on the state register of exceptional trees. It reaches up more than 50 feet and stretches outward over a 200-square-foot area, shading two-thirds of an acre in the town's landmark courthouse square. ♦ Banyan Park, Front St (between Canal and Hotel Sts)

68 Lahaina Courthouse The courthouse and palace of King Kamehameha III once stood near the site of this semidilapidated structure, but they were leveled in 1858 by gale-force winds. In 1859 the stones from the destroyed building were used to build the present courthouse, which at one time was the governmental center of Maui County. Now it's the center for the **Lahaina Arts Society,** as well as the **Lahaina Visitors' Center,** the **Old Jail Gallery,** and the **Banyan Tree Gallery.** Both galleries showcase the work of island artists with exhibits that change monthly. ♦ Daily. 649 Wharf St (between Canal and Hotel Sts). 661.0111

69 Waterfront Fort In 1831 a legal battle raged between the whalers, who were accustomed to some immediate R&R with the locals when their ships pulled into harbor, and the missionaries, who regarded the whole affair with disgust. A law was passed prohibiting local women from swimming out to greet the incoming ships, which prompted the rowdy whalers to fire cannons at the missionary complex. At Queen Keopuolani's orders, a one-acre area was then walled off to protect the citizens, with huge coral blocks hacked from the reef fronting the Lahaina shores. The fort was torn down in 1854 and the stones used to build Lahaina's prison. When Lahaina became a historical landmark, a heap of coral blocks was put together to resemble a corner of the fort—and that's about what it looks like today. ♦ Wharf and Canal Sts

70 Best Western Pioneer Inn $$ George Freeland, a member of the Royal Canadian Mounted Police who fell in love with Lahaina after following a criminal to the area, built this inn at the turn of the century. Once weathered and run-down, this funky haunt has been spruced up with a $5-million renovation—though the service is still poor. Thirty-two rooms and two suites with air-conditioning, TVs, lanais, and ceiling fans are located right next to the wharf, making it precisely the place not to get away from it all. There's also a pool. ♦ 658 Wharf St (at Hotel St). 661.3636, 800/457.5457; fax 667.5708

Within the Best Western Pioneer Inn:

Pioneer Inn

The Grill and Bar $$$ If you're going to spend your day in Lahaina, you might as well start it with breakfast in the courtyard of the **Best Western Pioneer Inn**. After breakfast, it's usually too hot to eat or drink here until the late afternoon. Although the food is not memorable (teriyaki chicken burgers, shrimp salad, submarine sandwiches, and the like), the energy level reflects its prime location across from the wharf. ♦ American ♦ Daily breakfast, lunch, and dinner. 661.3636

Pioneer Inn Shops More than a dozen shops are housed in the Front Street side of the hotel, most notably the **Banyan Tree Gallery** (661.4450), which carries all Hawaiian-made gifts, and **Haagen Dazs** (no phone), an oasis at high noon in the town whose name means "merciless sun." ♦ Daily. No phone

71 Brig Carthaginian The original *Carthaginian* left Lahaina for Honolulu in 1972 for dry dock but instead hit a reef and sank. This 93-foot replacement—*Carthaginian II,* the only authentically restored brig in the world—sailed here from Denmark and is operated by the Lahaina Restoration Foundation. Below decks, visitors can inspect a museum of whaling history and watch a program on humpback whales, which migrate to Maui waters every winter. ♦ Admission. Daily. Wharf and Papelekane Sts. 661.8527 &

72 Lahaina Harbor Nearly all Lahaina's water activities start and finish at the harbor. Come here to watch the hustle and bustle of what used to be one of the world's busiest whaling ports. Some activities and recommended companies: sailing with **Scotch Mist** (661.0386); fishing with **Islander II** (667.6625); scuba diving with **Maui Reef Diving** (667.7647); dinner cruises with **Manutea** (661.5309); all-day sailing/snorkeling trips with **Trilogy Excursions** (661.4743); whale watching (in winter) with

Lahaina Princess (661.8397); submarine rides with **Atlantis Adventures** (667.2224); and rides on the **Reef Dancer** semisubmersible (667.2133). ♦ Wharf and Canal Sts

73 Dan's Greenhouse Although it's only a half block off Front Street, this plant and animal emporium is easily bypassed—but shouldn't be. The specialty here is certified bonsai ready to ship home, along with orchids, Maui onion seeds, sprouted coconuts, and other packaged Hawaiian plants. The showstoppers, though, are the tropical birds that love to cuddle and croon. They're also for sale, but before you get too attached, check out the price tags—ol' Prince Eleele, a quixotic and enigmatic black palm cockatoo from way far away, goes for $25,000. ♦ Daily. 133 Prison St (between Luakini and Front Sts). 661.8412 &

74 Hale Paahao Built in 1852 by convicts, this structure was once Lahaina's prison (the name means "the stuck-in-irons house"). Most of the inmates were drunken sailors who failed to return to their ships at sundown, although some were confined for desertion, working on Sunday, or dangerous horseback riding. Ball-and-chain and wall shackles further restrained troublemakers. ♦ Donation. Daily. 180 Prison St (at Wainee St). 661.3262 &

75 Mokuula In 1990, employees of the **Kaanapali Beach Hotel** discovered a sacred island buried underneath **Maluuluolele Park** on Front Street that was used by royalty in the early 19th century. Today the land functions mostly as a baseball field. Right now, there's not much to identify the historic sanctuary beyond one's imagination, but at press time plans were underway to restore the area and construct an interpretive center. ♦ Maluuluolele Park, Front St (between Shaw and Prison Sts). No phone

76 Wainee Churchyard Both prominent and anonymous residents of early Lahaina are buried in this first Christian cemetery in Hawaii, built in 1823. Many of the graves are those of missionaries' children (infant mortality was high then); others belong to Hawaiian royalty, including Queen Keopuolani—wife of King Kamehameha I, mother of Kamehameha II and Kamehameha III, and the first Hawaiian convert to be baptized a Protestant and given a Christian burial; her daughter, Nahienaena; the last king of Kauai, King Kaumualii; high chief Hoapili, Keopuolani's second husband; and

Kekauonohi, one of the five queens of Kamehameha II. To the right of the churchyard is **Waiola Church,** which stands on the site of the first stone church on Maui. The original structure, called **Wainee Church,** was built in 1832 and seated up to 3,000 on the floor. Its history is one bad luck story after another: The church lost its roof in an 1858 whirlwind; was burned down in 1894 by Hawaiians opposed to the overthrow of their monarchy; was rebuilt in 1897, only to be partly destroyed by fire in 1947; and was toppled by another whirlwind in 1951. The present church, erected after the last whirlwind, was given the name "Waiola (living waters)," in hopes of breaking the spell. ♦ Church services: Sunday 8AM, 10AM. 535 Wainee St (at Shaw St). 661.4349

77 **505 Front Street** Designed to resemble a New England whaling village, this small jumble of boutiques, stores, and restaurants actually offers more than some of the larger malls lining Front Street. It's within easy walking distance of the town's famous banyan tree. ♦ Daily. At Shaw St. 667.2514

Within 505 Front Street:

Pacifico Restaurant ★★$$$$ This place is a favorite with local residents. Try the local fish wrapped and grilled in a banana leaf, or the rack of lamb roasted with macadamia nuts. The polished wood bar, with its friendly staff and laid-back ambience, is perfect for an afternoon cocktail or three. Alternatively, drop by for live jazz on Thursday, Friday, and Saturday nights. Another reason to come here is the outside dining area with a view of the island of Lanai and some of the most beautiful sunsets on the planet. ♦ Pacific Rim ♦ Daily lunch and dinner. Reservations recommended. 667.4341 &

Village Pizzeria ★★$$ There's no ocean view, no live music, but no question that this pizzeria serves the best pie to be found in Lahaina: clam and garlic pizza—the halitosis house special. ♦ Pizza ♦ Daily lunch and dinner. 661.8112 &

78 **Lahaina Shores Beach Resort** $$$ What makes this place unique is that it's the only hotel in town that's right on the beach, with a comfortable pool and a grassy sunbathing area bordering the sand. Once a rambling, plantation-style mansion, the building has been converted into a 199-room hotel with studios and one-bedrooms, and eight 1,400-

square-foot penthouse suites, all with full kitchens, daily maid service, and reasonable rates. Over a complimentary continental breakfast on their first morning, new arrivals are briefed by knowledgeable staff members on the activities and sight-seeing possibilities nearby. There's no restaurant, but considering the location, price, hospitality, and spacious accommodations, even the pickiest of travelers won't be disappointed. ♦ 475 Front St (between Kauaula Rd and Shaw St). 661.4835, 800/628.6699; fax 661.4696; info@classicresorts.com; www.lahaina-shores.com

79 **Paunau Beach Park** Small and unspectacular, the closest beach park to Lahaina offers fair swimming, summer surfing, and picnic facilities. The water is fairly shallow, with a rock and sand ocean floor. ♦ Honoapiilani Hwy (south of Front St)

Cruising the Upcountry

The cattle and farming land on the fertile slopes of **Haleakala** is Maui's "upcountry," extending from the 10,023-foot summit to the island's isthmus and resting at the foot of the **West Maui Mountains.**

A drive to these parts offers a chance to explore another side of Maui—where people, including island residents, go to escape the crowded beach scene. The verdant rolling hills and cool, fresh air seem to miraculously erase tension and worry. In fact, it's common for smitten tourists to make the upcountry their new home.

The best route to the upcountry is along **Baldwin Avenue,** which begins in **Paia** east of **Kahului Airport.** The gently ascending road is bordered by fragrant eucalyptus trees, cactus plants, brightly flowering jacarandas, and green hillsides where cattle graze among brilliant flowers. The air grows much cooler as you reach the top, so bring a jacket. And on your way, take the time to stop in Paia, once the hub of Maui's commercial scene and now just a pleasant shopping and snacking stop on everyone's way to somewhere else; **Makawao,** an artsy little town with great shops and restaurants; and the area of **Kula,** where the scenery alone is worth the excursion.

MARK AMMERMAN/NORTH MARKET STREET GRAPHICS

Between Lahaina and Kihei

80 Olowalu A nearby cliff face covered with petroglyphs indicates that the impenetrable West Maui Mountains were once traversable via an ancient trail connecting Olowalu to Iao Valley. But historians know this seaside village as the site of the 1790 Olowalu Massacre, when Captain Simon Metcalfe, seeking revenge for the loss of a sailor and a boat (presumably at the hands of local thieves), invited a group of Hawaiians to visit his American ship under the pretense of trading goods. Once the Hawaiians had gathered on the starboard side of the *Eleanora,* Metcalfe ordered the gunwales uncovered. He and his men fired down on the startled, defenseless islanders, killing more than one hundred and seriously wounding many more.

Within Olowalu:

Chez Paul ★★$$$$ This dining landmark in West Maui dates back more than 20 years, when a Boston couple opened this upscale French place with private dining rooms in the middle of nowhere. The unusual operation was in a shabby building that had a certain cachet, especially when juxtaposed with the ultrachic Kaanapali establishments. Today, an overpriced menu, featuring items like duck Tahitian and *opakapaka* beurre blanc, and outdated decor make this restaurant, now run by Lucien Charbonnier, less desirable. ♦ French ♦ Daily dinner. Reservations required. 661.3843

Olowalu General Store An example of a classic Hawaiian phenomenon is this old-fashioned general store (originally a plantation store owned by the **Pioneer Sugar Mill**), which sells a little of everything you'll ever need on an island. If you're going to spend the day at Olowalu Beach, stop here first and pick up some *onolicious* (delicious) homemade local grinds, all packaged and ready to go. But watch out for the treacherous turnoff—locals don't slow down. ♦ Daily. 820 Honoapiilani Hwy. 661.3774 ♿

81 Olowalu Beach It remains a Maui mystery why so many tourists are smitten with this beach. Yes, the snorkeling is usually good, especially for beginners, but the stretch of gray sand is tiny, damp, and right off a busy highway. And there are no facilities. ♦ Honoapiilani Hwy (Mile 14)

82 Maalaea Harbor The only reasons to come to Maalaea used to be either to take a boat trip or to have supper at Buzz's Wharf restaurant, but the opening of the aquarium (see **Maui Ocean Center,** below) now provides another incentive for stopping here. ♦ Maalaea Rd, Maalaea

At Maalaea Harbor:

MAUI OCEAN CENTER

Maui Ocean Center This is a modern marine park, featuring a 750,000-gallon saltwater tank stocked with 2,000 fish, sharks, and other sea creatures; a computerized arcade of interactive learning stations centering around the humpback whales; and an authentic reef display. The supreme irony, of course, is that the real thing is just a few hundred yards away, but nevertheless, the center offers children and adults the chance to see and understand a great deal about Hawaii's marine life without getting their feet wet. A restaurant serves breakfast, lunch, and dinner. ♦ Fee. Daily. 192 Maalaea Rd. 270.7000; www.coralworld.com/moc ♿

83 Maui Tropical Plantation and Country **Store** Sugarcane, pineapples, bananas, papayas, coffee beans, macadamia nuts, exotic flowers, and other crops can be found in this 60-acre showcase for Hawaii agriculture. The park was developed by Australians Bill and Lynn Taylor on land owned by the C. Brewer Corporation. More than a dozen fields fan out from the restaurant and market area; the 40-minute narrated tram tours take visitors through 40 acres of the plantation, with stops for walking around to take a closer look at the products. The *kapu* (Keep Out) signs posted in most agricultural areas on the islands are nowhere in sight here.

Orchids, hibiscus, and other greenhouse plants in the nursery can be shipped home, and the store sells produce grown on the property, including fruit that's been inspected and approved for shipment from the island. The **Tropical Restaurant** (244.7643) serves fresh fruit creations—try the *lilikoi* (passion fruit) and ginger parfaits; from 10:30AM until 2PM daily there's a tropical luncheon buffet. ♦ Daily. Reservations required for the barbecue. 1670 Honoapiilani Hwy (between Kuihelani Hwy and Waiko Rd). 244.7643; 800/451.6805 ♿

Kihei and Environs

The town of Kihei is a prime example of what happens when there's no central planning for urban development. Shamefully overbuilt and crowded and utterly lacking any cohesive form or design, this stretch of coast has just two selling points apart from the consistently sunny weather: less expensive accommodations than in Lahaina, and above-average beaches (unfortunately, most are hidden behind a ragtag assortment of hotels and condos, and they're also notoriously windy; by early afternoon, you'll give up trying to keep your beach towel in place). For information about condominium rentals in Kihei, call **Condominium Rentals Hawaii** (879.2778), and be sure to specify if you want a room on the beach.

84 Mai Poina Oe Lau Beach Park This is a good swimming beach with a few rocks on the sandy ocean bottom, but it's still known as "the windsurfing beach" because of the blow that often picks up in the afternoon. You can still see what's left of the old **Kihei Landing** at the shoreline. Picnic and public facilities are provided. ♦ S Kihei and Ohukai Rds, Kihei

85 Kalepolepo Beach Remains of a fishpond create a nice wading pool for children, but ocean swimming is trickier because of the rocky bottom. This area was once a Hawaiian village complete with taro patches, coconut groves, shoreline fishponds, churches, and a small whaling station. Picnic and barbecue facilities are available. ♦ S Kihei Rd (between Kulanihakoi and Kaonoulu Sts), Kihei

86 A Pacific Cafe Maui ★★★$$$$ Jean-Marie Josselin's fourth restaurant in the islands presents diners with impossible decisions, like whether to order the delicious signature mahimahi, pan-seared with a garlic-sesame crust and lime ginger sauce, or the roasted half Island chicken with grilled Japanese eggplant and garlic mashed potatoes. The kitchen is open and the bar set in the center of this establishment that attracts patrons from the far reaches of the island. ♦ Hawaiian Regional ♦ Daily dinner. Reservations recommended. Azeka Place Shopping Center, 1279 S Kihei Rd (between W Lipoa and Nohokai Sts), Kihei. 879.0069 ⅙ Also at: 3350 Lower Honoapiilani Rd (at Honoapiilani Hwy), Honokawai. 669.2724 ⅙

87 Kalama Beach Park This 36-acre park is more for sports enthusiasts than beachgoers: the prime attractions being soccer and baseball fields; volleyball, basketball, and tennis courts; and a children's playground. ♦ S Kihei Rd and Halelani Pl, Kihei

88 Kamaole Beaches All three beach parks (marked I, II, and III) have great sand, good swimming, lifeguards, and picnic and public facilities. Kamaole III also has a playground, and the reef area between II and III is good for snorkeling. ♦ S Kihei Rd, Kamaole

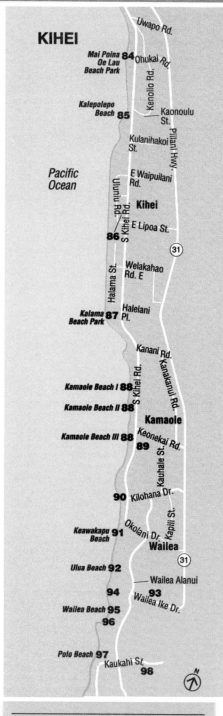

Each summer, the slopes of the 10,023-foot Haleakala Crater are the site of a race—"The Run to the Sun"—during which a field of runners storm the nearly 40 miles from base to summit.

89 Kamaole Sands $$ One of the best deals on Maui, especially for families, the 440 well-managed, roomy, freshly renovated condos sit on 15 acres across the street from Kamaole Beach III, and many of the suites look out across the ocean to the islands of Molokini and Lanai. Fully equipped kitchens include dishwashers, and there are also washer/dryers and daily maid service. There's a swimming and a wading pool, two Jacuzzis, a restaurant and barbecue area, and four tennis courts. A two-night stay is required. ♦ 2695 S Kihei Rd (between Kilohana Dr and Keonekai Rd), Kamaole. 874.8700, 800/367.5004; fax 879.3273; www.castleresorts.com &

90 Carrelli's on the Beach ★★$$$$ One of the few highly commendable restaurants in the area is ideally situated right on the beach. Gourmet Italian cuisine is served in an open-air setting. Menu selections include homemade pizzas, fresh seared *ahi sorrentine,* and the *specialità della casa* (specialty of the house)—*zuppa di mare cioppino,* a tempting assortment of clams, mussels, scallops, prawns, lobster, squid, and crab in a spicy tomato sauce. Factor in Maui's stunning sunsets, and it's hard not to enjoy the evening. ♦ Italian ♦ Daily dinner. Reservations recommended. 2980 S Kihei Rd (at Kilohana Dr), Kamaole. 875.0001 &

Wailea and Environs

In 1973 no one imagined that this 1,500-acre stretch of coastline dotted with patches of scraggly *kiawe* and *wiliwili* trees would become a deluxe resort area, but Wailea had two important things going for it: great weather and white-sand beaches. Located on the dry, leeward side of **Haleakala,** the area has an average yearly rainfall of 11 inches and an average temperature of 75.15 degrees Fahrenheit. Not only is the volcano a beautiful backdrop, but it acts as a natural buffer, protecting Wailea from rain and wind. Each of Wailea's five beaches has a smooth, sandy bottom protected by coral reefs, excellent for swimming and snorkeling.

Built in 1976, the **Aston Wailea** was the first Wailea resort hotel, followed two years later by the **Renaissance Wailea Beach Resort.** In 1990 the **Four Seasons Resort** opened, followed by the **Grand Wailea Resort** in 1991 and then the unusual **Kea Lani Hotel.** Wailea is now considered a luxury resort area on par with the Big Island's Kohala Coast. Within the region you'll find 54 holes of golf, one of the largest tennis complexes on the islands, the **Wailea Shopping Village,** and several first-rate restaurants.

91 Keawakapu Beach South Kihei Road dead-ends at the parking lot of this charming beach with excellent swimming (thanks to a sandy bottom) and fair snorkeling. There are no public rest rooms but there are showers. ♦ S Kihei Rd and Okolani Dr, Wailea

92 Renaissance Wailea Beach Resort $$$$ A luxury resort for the traveler who likes to get away from it all, but not be too far away from room service or a world-class restaurant, this property is on a secluded, small (15.5 acres), and intimate site. The landscaping is dense and lush, with bridges and pathways that lend themselves to romance, lingering, and the occasional wedding. Many of the 345 rooms have ocean views, and all are the same size—small but very pleasant, with spacious lanais. The **Mokapu Beach Club,** a separate wing with 26 suites on the beach, offers VIP perks and services. The peaceful beach is ideal for swimming, sunning, snorkeling, or windsurfing. A pool, three Jacuzzis, and two tennis courts complete the list of amenities; there's a shuttle bus to **Wailea Golf Club.** ♦ 3550 Wailea Alanui (between Wailea Ike and Okolani Drs), Wailea. 879.4900, 800/992.4532; fax 874.9421 &

Within the Renaissance Wailea Beach Resort:

Palm Court ★★★ $$$$ This restaurant is the stuff dreams are made of when stuck in traffic during a winter afternoon in Minneapolis. It overlooks a waterfall and is open and airy, with foliage abounding. Entrée selections include half-seafood risotto with clams, scallops, shrimp, and fresh Hawaiian fish.  ♦ Pacific Rim ♦ Daily breakfast and dinner. Reservations recommended. 879.4900 &

92 Ulua Beach Located behind the **Renaissance Wailea Beach Resort,** this well-maintained stretch of white sand is the most popular of the Wailea beach quintet, and the best for bodysurfing. On calm days snorkeling is excellent because of the exceptionally clear water. Showers are available but not rest rooms. ♦ Wailea Alanui (between Wailea Ike and Okolani Drs), Wailea

93 Joe's Bar and Grill ★★★$$$$ Here's how the story goes: Bev and Joe Gannon had the successful **Haliimaile General Store** in

Upcountry Maui. Bev cooked; Joe made suggestions. Until one day Bev made a suggestion: "Joe," she said, "let's get you a restaurant of your own." Thus was born this popular burgundy and green venue, with sliding glass doors open on three sides and views of the golf course. Favorite menu items are grilled pork chops with Molokai sweet potatoes, Port wine and dried fruit compote; lobster seafood potpie; and *farfalle* (butterfly-shaped pasta) with blackened *ahi* in a white-wine butter sauce. ♦ New American ♦ Daily dinner. Reservations recommended. 131 Wailea Ike Pl (north of Wailea Ike Dr), Wailea. 875.7767 &

94 Aston Wailea Resort $$$$ Flanked by crescents of white sand, this AAA four-diamond hotel has an elaborate porte cochere and a Hawaiian roofline based on the architecture of **C.W. Dickey.** It occupies 22 acres of oceanfront, with 516 rooms and suites in 7 low-rise buildings and an 8-story tower. There are 3 swimming pools and 14 tennis courts (3 grass and 11 hard courts) across the street, and guests enjoy privileges at the **Wailea Golf Club** and the small putting green alongside it. ♦ 3700 Wailea Alanui (between Wailea Ike and Okolani Drs), Wailea. 879.1922, 800/367.2960; fax 875.4878; awrmaui@gte.net &

Within the Aston Wailea Resort:

Hula Moons ★★★$$$$ One of the area's most popular casual eateries, this comfortable, Hawaiian-style dining room serves interesting dishes, including pork loin chop with peppered pineapple compote, Maui onion tomato relish, fig and tamarind marmalade, and *poha* (a local berry) and cranberry chutney. Other favorite features are a hula dancer and copious *pupus* nightly between 5:30 and 6:30PM. ♦ Hawaiian Regional ♦ Daily lunch and dinner. Reservations recommended. Central pool. 879.1922 &

95 Grand Wailea Resort, Hotel and Spa $$$$ This Disneyesque creation, which cost a whopping $600 million, features 761 rooms and suites with all the extras and 40 acres of impeccably maintained landscape and attractions, including a $15-million water playground; $30 million in museum-quality artwork from around the world, including Colombian sculptor Fernando Botero's buxom bronzes and works by Jan Fisher, Fernand Léger, and others; a 300,000-square-foot floor of stone quarried from around the world; 12 lounges and 5 restaurants—including the celebrated **Cafe Kula** (see below); **Camp Grande,** a phenomenal kids' program; a 50,000-square-foot health spa; and various recreational activities, including golf, tennis, scuba diving, sailing, windsurfing, and deep-sea fishing. With rates starting at $380 and topping out at $10,000 per night, this resort obviously caters to an exclusive clientele, but nonguests are more than welcome to ogle and observe what unlimited funds and a prodigal imagination can accomplish. ♦ 3850 Wailea Alanui (between Kaukahi St and Wailea Ike Dr), Wailea. 875.1234, 800/888.6100; fax 874.2442; info@grandwailea.com; www.grandwailea.com &

Within the Grand Wailea Resort, Hotel and Spa:

Humuhumunukunukuapuaa ★★★$$$$ First off, just call this dining spot "humu" (*who*-moo); everyone will know what you mean. And no, you don't *have* to handpick your lobster dinner from the 4,000-gallon saltwater lagoon on which this thatch-roofed Polynesian-style building is perched (although you *can*). With those things out of the way, you're free to enjoy your meal—lobster *pulehu* (grilled local style with Hawaiian salt and garlic) or wok-fried with vegetables and black-bean sauce, or a whole sizzling *opakapaka* with stir-fried vegetables and pineapple-vinegar sauce—in peace. ♦ Polynesian ♦ Daily dinner. Reservations recommended. 875.1234 &

Cafe Kula ★★★$ This cafe offers a fine balance between health-consciousness and palate appeal; dishes such as grilled vegetables on inch-thick bread leave diners feeling both full and fit. The very casual, open-air eatery has counter service and a view of the gardens. ♦ Health food ♦ Daily breakfast and lunch. 875.1234 &

95 Wailea Beach Maui's longest crescent beach is popular with swimmers and snorkelers and offers both rest rooms and showers. ♦ Wailea Alanui (between Kaukahi St and Wailea Ike Dr), Wailea

---

Before discovering they could sell the juice of the pineapple, producers of the fruit flushed it into the sea as a waste product.

At press time, the average US visitor spent $133.79 a day on vacation in Hawaii; the typical Japanese traveler $340.88.

Catch of the Bay

Whether you're peering through your diving mask or admiring the entrée on your plate, you will encounter a mind-boggling variety of fish in Hawaii. To make things even more confusing, each fish can have several names, including a Hawaiian name (for instance, broadbill swordfish are also called marlin and *au*). Here's a brief illustrated guide to the fish you'll find on many of Hawaii's menus (usually deepwater fish) as well as those cruising the local reefs:

Fish to Eat

Au (broadbill swordfish or marlin) An expensive delicacy that, once on the hook, puts up a legendary fight. The meat is most commonly consumed as jerky.

Ahi (yellowfin tuna) A favorite of deep-sea sportfishers for its fighting spirit, *ahi* weighs up to 300 pounds (the average is 80 pounds). It makes excellent sashimi and plays an important role in Hawaii's tuna industry.

Ahipalaha/Tombo Ahi (albacore) The world's premium tuna, usually destined for mainland canneries, is a small predator that averages 40 to 80 pounds. It migrates extensively throughout the north Pacific, far away from Hawaii, and is occasionally substituted for *ahi* and *aku* in raw fish preparations.

Aku (skipjack tuna) Although the flesh of this smaller (10 to 20 pounds) tuna is less firm than that of *ahi,* it is still common on Hawaiian tables.

Mahimahi (dorado or dolphinfish) *Not* the same animal as the beloved "Flipper," the mahimahi/dorado/dolphinfish has beautiful jeweled scales of iridescent blues, lavenders, and greens that turn to dull gray as the fish dies. A playful swimmer weighing up to 25 pounds, it is often seen chasing flying fish through the waves. Mahimahi is a favorite local food most of the year, although availability peaks from March through May and September through November. Frozen fillets from Taiwan and Japan have made this fish available to budget-conscious diners, while fresh mahimahi is a coveted item on continental menus.

Onaga (red snapper) A popular bottom fish served in upscale restaurants, *onaga* ranges from 1 to 18 pounds in Hawaiian waters. Availability peaks in December.

Ono (wahoo) *Ono* is Hawaiian for "the best"—an apt name for this fish. Its flaky white meat is served in everything from grilled sandwiches to sophisticated continental preparations. The best times to look for *ono* are summer and fall. In Hawaii it typically weighs 8 to 30 pounds, but it can grow up to a hundred pounds.

Opah (moonfish) One of the most colorful commercial fish species in Hawaii, with crimson fins and large, gold-encircled eyes, *opah* range from 60 to 200 pounds. They are well liked for their moist, extremely flaky texture.

Opakapaka (pink snapper) Hawaii's premium table snapper is usually caught in deep water. A bottom fish, weighing 18 pounds on average, it appears on island menus year-round, although availability peaks from October through February.

Uku (gray snapper) One of Hawaii's 3 most popular deepwater snappers, *uku* usually weigh 4 to 18 pounds. They are most abundant from May through July.

Ulua (jackfish) Ranging from 15 to 100 pounds, this sport fish is a favorite among deepwater spearfishers. Its white flesh with a meaty texture is popular year-round.

Fish to Meet

Humuhumunukunukuapuaa (triggerfish) The fame of this fairly common fish, Hawaii's state fish, comes from its long name. *Humuhumu* means "to fit pieces together," and *nukunukuapuaa* is Hawaiian for "nose like a pig." The triggerfish is equipped with two protective devices: its eyes can rotate independently, enabling it to see in two directions at once, and when frightened it dives for its nest and locks itself in place with its dorsal fin.

Kihikihi (Moorish idol) The breathtaking beauty and fragility of the *kihikihi* places it in a class by itself. It's usually found in small schools, using its long snout to probe for food in the crevices of reefs.

Lauwiliwili (crochet or lemon butterfly fish) The *lauwiliwili* (shown above) is found in abundance throughout Hawaii but so far has been seen nowhere else. You can identify this fish, which grows up to 6 inches long, by the 11 vertical rows of spots on either side of its body.

Oiliuwiuwi (fan-tailed filefish) Yellow with black dots, the fan-tailed filefish makes grunting and squealing noises when removed from the water (*oiliuwiuwi* means squealing filefish). Early Hawaiians used them as fuel to cook tastier fish since they were too scrawny to eat.

Uhu (parrot fish) Often found in the waters of **Hanauma Bay** off **Oahu,** this fascinating fish scrapes algae off the coral with its jagged beak. By day, *uhu* flash their one- to four-foot-long gaudy bodies covered with blue-green, gray, and rust-colored scales. While sleeping at night, they cover themselves in a secretion that forms a protective bubble. Remarkably, *uhu* can change sex; those born as males eventually turn into females. The omnivores also create sand: They eat coral, crustaceans, and mollusks, which are excreted as grains of sand.

FOUR SEASONS RESORT
Maui at Wailea

96 Four Seasons Resort $$$$ Billing itself as an island of tranquillity within an island, this 8-story, 380-room hotel offers comfortable rooms and super-deluxe, mansionlike suites on 15 acres at Wailea Beach. The specially commissioned works of art in the public areas are scaled to the architecture—understated yet impressive. The rooms are large and luxurious, and each has a lanai with teak interior walls, potted orchids, and thick-cushioned rattan furniture. The enormous bathrooms are all marble and mirrors, each with a deep bathtub, separate glass shower, and an eight-foot marble counter with double vanities. Most of the rooms have ocean views, and all have TVs and VCRs, fully stocked mini-bars, and twice-daily maid service. The hotel prides itself on its personal services: Attendants on the pool terrace will bring you towels and chilled Evian spritzers, gratis; your shoes can be shined while you sleep; and the general manager trots out the silver coffee urns and croissants at 5:30AM for jet-lagged tourists. There's an extensive fitness center and weight room. A kids' program focuses on Hawaiian culture and nature. ♦ 3900 Wailea Alanui (between Kaukahi St and Wailea Ike Dr), Wailea. 874.8000, 800/334.6284; fax 874.2222; www.fourseasons.com ♿

Within the Four Seasons Resort:

Seasons ★★★★$$$$ This open-air dining room has a piano, a small dance floor, and an unforgettable menu. You can't help noticing the effort to use island ingredients in particularly innovative ways. There's salmon and *opakapaka* carpaccio, *onaga* with a Hawaiian salt crust, and lobster with couscous—to name a few of the mindbending menu items. The extraordinary dining experience is enhanced by the crisp, cordial service. Be sure to try the scrumptious desserts (ask about the cream cheese with fruit compote) and vintage Port, then end the evening by dancing cheek-to-cheek. ♦ Pacific Regional ♦ Tu-Sa dinner. Reservations recommended; jackets recommended. 874.8000 ♿

97 Kea Lani Hotel $$$$ If you can get past the garish Arabian architecture (a torrent of whitewashed domes, arches, and tents), you'll find 413 of the largest suites in Hawaii (and 37 two- and three-bedroom villas). At a minimum of 840 square feet, every unit of this luxury resort is twice the size of an average hotel room and impeccably furnished, with a marble European bathroom containing an oversize "love-tub"; an entertainment center with VCR, CD player, and wide-screen TV; a mini-fridge; and a huge bedroom with a king-size bed. Amenities include three restaurants, three pools, and white-sand beach that's excellent for snorkeling and swimming, as well as complimentary transportation to the nearby championship golf courses and tennis courts and extensive meeting space. For honeymooners who don't plan on getting out much, this is the place to stay. ♦ 4100 Wailea Alanui (at Kaukahi St), Wailea. 875.4100, 800/659.4100; fax 875.1200 ♿

Within the Kea Lani Hotel:

Nick's Fishmarket ★★★★$$$$ The original Nick's on Oahu was one of the most popular of the elegant dining rooms in the 1980s, largely due to the weekly patronage of Tom Selleck during his extended stays in Hawaii for the filming of "Magnum, P.I." The decor is all about low lighting and padded booths, the menu about elaborate seafood concoctions like Chicago-style abalone (with asparagus, shiitake mushrooms and rock shrimp) and *opaka katina* (pink snapper fillet sautéed with rock shrimp and served with lemon butter and capers). ♦ Seafood/Mediterranean ♦ Daily dinner. Reservations recommended. 879.7224 ♿

97 Polo Beach Club $$$$ If the **Grand Wailea Resort, Hotel and Spa** is exactly the type of place you want to avoid, you'd probably prefer this subdued condo resort. Hidden behind the **Kea Lani Hotel,** the complex has 30 well-appointed 2-bedroom, 2-bathroom ocean-view apartments set on a white-sand beach and available for short-term rental. The property offers a pool, spa, and sundeck, with easy access to Wailea's golf and tennis clubs, but no restaurant. ♦ 20 Makena Rd (at Kaukahi St), Wailea. 879.1595, 800/367.5246; fax 874.3554

97 Polo Beach Because of its somewhat remote location, this white-sand beach was uncrowded until the **Kea Lani Hotel** was built right in front of it. There's still public access (by law), and a parking lot in front of the **Polo Beach Club.** The sandy bottom and rock outcroppings make it a great swimming and snorkeling beach. Public facilities are provided. ♦ Makena Rd and Kaukahi St, Wailea

---

More than 30 percent of the people on Maui at any one time are tourists.

When the Eagles sing "Jesus is Coming" in their song, "The Last Resort," they're referring to a large sign that was posted for decades outside a Lahaina church.

98 Wailea Golf Club One of Wailea's main attractions is a trio of carefully manicured, bone-dry golf courses on the leeward slopes of Haleakala Crater. The **Blue Course** (18 holes, par 72, 6,758 yards) is visually pleasing but less exciting (read: also less challenging) than the longer **Gold Course** (18 holes, par 72, 7,078 yards), which has more hills and trees, and even ancient stone walls. The newer **Emerald Course** (18 holes, par 72, 6,825 yards) has tropical vegetation and stunning scenery. Be prepared for strong afternoon winds. ♦ Expensive greens fees. Preferred starting times for Wailea hotel guests. Reservations required. Kaukahi St (east of Wailea Alanui), Wailea. 879.2966

At Wailea Golf Club:

SeaWatch Restaurant ★★$$$$ With such dishes as Pacific crab cakes in a spicy ginger remoulade with scallion butter and beef tenderloin with a sweet Maui onion confit, gastronomes will be assured that they're not in Kansas anymore. Chef Richard Matsumoto and his staff of culinary pranksters delight diners in this out-of-the-way location, distin-guished by high ceilings and indoor/outdoor seating that invites lingering. ♦ International ♦ Daily breakfast, lunch, and dinner. Reservations recommended. 875.8080 &

99 Maui Prince Hotel $$$$
Somewhat controversial when it opened owing to its spare, Japanese-influenced architecture and decor, this hotel has matured into a beautiful resort that many former critics have grown to appreciate. The 291 rooms and 19 suites have unobstructed ocean views encompassing the islands of Molokini and Kahoolawe. The central courtyard, with waterfalls, rock gardens, fishponds, and footpaths, is a lush, pleasing space. On arrival, guests are greeted with hot, almond-scented towels (the traditional *oshibori* service) to refresh them after their journey to this rather isolated location at the western end of the island. Compared to the nearby resorts, this hotel leans toward the unpretentious, capitalizing on its secluded location to attract a clientele that prefers anonymity. The resort also contains the **Makena Golf Course,** a fitness center, jogging trails, an award-winning tennis facility with six courts, and two pools. A children's program keeps youngsters happily entertained. A shuttle service transports guests throughout the resort and surrounding area. ♦ 5400 Makena Alanui, Makena. 874.1111, 800/321.6284; fax 879.0082 &

At the Maui Prince Hotel:

Hakone ★★★$$$$ The wood interior, slate floors, and refined ambience are well suited to the fine food and professional service. Multicourse *kaiseki* dinners consist of dainty samplings of soup, salad, appetizers and fish—raw, boiled, grilled, or fried. The sushi is excellent, the *chawanmushi* (a light steamed custard) otherworldly, and more ordinary dishes such as tempura and noodles are cooked to perfection. ♦ Traditional Japanese ♦ Tu-Sa dinner. Reservations recommended. 874.1111 &

Prince Court ★★★★$$$$ At this place, listed in *Who's Who in American Restaurants,* even the appetizers—notably steamed fresh vanilla clams and mussels—are gustatory adventures. The world-class fare—such as roasted lamb with mushroom and onion bread, catch of the day in avocado butter and macadamia-nut oil, swordfish and filet mignon with three lobster claws—is complemented by the elegant setting and sunset views. The Sunday brunch, with free-flowing Champagne and hundreds of international dishes, shouldn't be missed. ♦ Mediterranean/Asian ♦ M-Sa dinner; Su brunch and dinner. Reservations recommended. 874.1111 &

Makena Golf Course Robert Trent Jones Jr. designed this layout, which has mountain and ocean views, tight fairways, huge greens, and enough sand for a beach. Named one of the top 10 courses in Hawaii by *Golf Digest,* it was expanded to 36 holes (the original course was divided and nine new holes were added to each half). The **North Course** is par 72, 6,914 yards; the **South Course** par 72, 7,017 yards. The 15th and 16th holes of the **South Course** (part of the original back nine) skirt the ocean, and throughout you can spot quail, panini plants, hibiscus, and the rolling hills of Ulupalakua. ♦ Expensive greens fees. Daily. Reservations required. 5415 Makena Alanui. 879.3344

99 Makena Beach (Big Beach) More than a mile long, this is the beach of choice for Maui's *kamaaina,* who have been coming here with their families and their coolers for generations. This glorious, golden stretch is commonly called Big Beach by islanders; over a hill to the right is Little Beach. Both are excellent swimming spots but must be approached with caution because of occasional steep shore breaks and riptides. Though this is unofficially thought of as a nude beach, nude sunbathing is prohibited by Hawaii state law (some visitors learn this the hard way when arrested during one of the twice-yearly raids). ◆ Makena Rd (off Makena Alanui), Makena

Upcountry

The western slopes of **Haleakala**, known as Upcountry, are in a quiet rural region whose land is devoted to sugarcane, pineapple, protea flowers, and pastureland. Thanks to the higher elevation, it's always cooler here than elsewhere on the island, with average daytime temperatures in the low 70s. Upcountry is remarkably scenic—green and hilly, with a plethora of panoramic views.

The uplands are ranch country, and Maui's largest ranch, **Ulupalakua,** with 20,000 acres and about 5,000 head of Hereford and Angus cattle and 250 head of elk, is located here. Also here is the **Kula District,** the center of vegetable, fruit, and flower farming on Maui. In recent years, this cool and quiet rural area has captured the imagination of folks from elsewhere on Hawaii and from the mainland, resulting in an influx of artists and entrepreneurs. The newcomers have changed the nature of some upcountry towns. The farming community of **Kula,** for example, now has a number of restaurants and bed-and-breakfasts, and **Makawao,** once a sleepy *paniolo* (cowboy) town, now boasts cafes, trendy shops, and art galleries.

100 Tedeschi Vineyards The rich volcanic soil of Ulupalakua has proved fertile ground for Hawaii's first and only commercial vineyard. The 25-acre enterprise produces a variety of wines, including Pineapple Blanc, Maui Splash, Maui Brut Champagne Blanc de Noir, Rose Ranch Cuvee, Ulupalakua Red, Plantation Red, Pineapple Sparkling Wine, and Maui Blush (similar to White Zinfandel). It all began in 1974, when vintner Emil Tedeschi (Te-*des*-ki) and Pardee Erdman, owner of the surrounding 20,000-acre **Ulupalakua Ranch,** experimented with numerous varieties of grapes to determine which would best adapt to the 2,000-foot elevation. They eventually chose the Carnelian grape, a cross developed at the University of California at Davis, and it seems they were right. Visitors can tour the winery, where Hawaiian royalty and visiting dignitaries used to gather for lavish parties when the property was a cattle ranch and sugar mill. Wine connoisseurs and anyone else driving through Maui's beautiful upcountry will find this an interesting side trip. ◆ Free. Guided tours: daily 9:30AM-2:30PM on the half hour; tasting room: daily. Kula Hwy, Ulupalakua Ranch. 878.6058 &

101 Silver Cloud Ranch $$ Maui isn't all white-sand beaches and multimillion-dollar resorts, and here to prove it is a bed-and-breakfast establishment at 3,000 feet in the upcountry village of Keokea. The six guest rooms in the old ranch house are all individually decorated (one features white lace, another bamboo, another black lacquer, and so on). There are also six modern studio apartments with kitchenettes. Some have TVs; none have phones. Horseback riding is available on the property. ◆ 201 Thompson Rd (between Kamaole Rd and Kula Hwy), Keokea. 878.6101, 800/532.1111; fax 878.2132; slvrcld@maui.net; www.maui.net/~slvrcld &

101 Grandma's Coffeehouse ★★$ While he was growing up, Alfred Franco's grandmother showed him how to harvest and roast coffee from the trees on her land. She taught him well; for years Franco has been doing just that in the upcountry town of Keokea, using Grandma's more-than-a-century-old roaster to process his lovingly tended beans. His homespun restaurant sells not only coffee, but homemade soups, sandwiches, and pastries. Try a cup of java and an I-Am-Hungry sandwich, which comes piled high with turkey, avocado, cheese, and ham. Takeout is available. ◆ Coffee shop ◆ Daily breakfast and lunch. 153 Kula Hwy, Keokea. 878.2140 &

102 Bloom Cottage $$ Situated high on the western slopes of Haleakala overlooking Maui's picturesque leeward coast, this bed-and-breakfast is one of the nicest on the island. Herb and Lynne Horner's secluded guest cottage, which would be perfectly at home in the English countryside, features a four-poster bed, a fireplace, twig curtain rods, wood floors, handmade quilts, Victorian prints, and an aromatic display of fresh herbs picked from the garden. Also included in the surprisingly reasonable price is a fully stocked kitchen, an alcove with a single bed, and complete privacy. Located just off the Kula Highway, this bright, cheerful hostelry is highly recommended. ◆ No credit cards accepted. Maukanani Rd (just southeast of Kula Hwy). 878.1425

103 Halemanu $ The lack of hotels and resorts in Kula and the town's growing popularity have spawned some terrific bed-and-breakfast operations in the area. This rural retreat is one of the best. *Halemanu* means "perch" or "bird-house," and that's exactly what it is—an elevated, 3,600-foot aerie with a spectacular view. Maui native and newspaper columnist Carol Austin's inn is filled with collectibles from all over the world. The one guest room has a queen-size bed, private bath, and a deck with a spectacular view. If you don't mind the 20-minute drive to the beach, this is an excellent choice for a memorable vacation. ♦ 221 Kawehi Pl (south of Waipoli Rd), Kula. 878.2729; fax 878.2729; carolaus@maui.net

104 Haleakala National Park The world's largest dormant volcano, Haleakala—the name means "House of the Sun"—is the showpiece of this 28,655-acre national park. High above the ubiquitous cloud layer is Haleakala's huge, moonlike crater—21 miles in circumference and 3,000 feet deep, with almost 30 miles of interior trails winding around nine cinder cones. Peaking at 10,023 feet above sea level, it is Maui's highest elevation—ideal for a gorgeous sunrise or spectacular view.

Hawaiian legends flourish around this giant landmark, and modern-day spiritualists come here for inner renewal (even US Air Force research indicates that this is the strongest natural power point in America). The drive to the summit (open 24 hours daily) takes about 90 minutes from Kahului; it's a good idea to bring something warm to wear or wrap up in. If you're going to see the sunrise, bring something very warm, because it's at least 30 degrees cooler here than in the flatlands. A flashlight will also help you make your way from the parking lot up to the unattended observatory at the summit lookout. Be sure to call park information (871.5054) the night before for sunrise time and viewing conditions.

If the idea of rolling out of bed at 4AM doesn't appeal to you, there's plenty to see and do here during the day; stop at the headquarters near the park entrance for maps, information, or camping and hiking permits. En route to the summit, which is 11 miles from the entrance, are 2 overlooks and a **Visitors' Center.** Park rangers conduct scheduled tours from the summit building. Drivers should make sure to use the lower gears when descending. For an unforgettable experience, see if you can score one of the three very inexpensive cabins in the crater. (Reserved by monthly lottery; cabin requests must be made at least 90 days in advance. Send requests with preferred and alternate days to **Haleakala National Park,** PO Box 369, Makawao, HI 96768, 572.4400.) Like the Grand Canyon or Niagara Falls, this volcano is something that must be seen at least once in your life. ♦ Admission per car. Park Headquarters/Visitors' Center: daily 7:30AM-4PM; Haleakala Visitors' Center: daily sunrise-3PM. Haleakala Crater Rd (east of Kekaulike Ave). 572.4400; www.nps.gov/hale

105 Kula Lodge $$ When the residents of Maui need a mini-vacation or a weekend of romance, they come here. Located high upon the cool grassy slopes of Maui's upcountry, this lodge is a switch from the typical Hawaiian resort: There's no sand, no program of activities, and no tropical ambience, and the temperature at 3,200 feet rarely rises above cool. The five individual chalets are small but cozy, with private lanais overlooking incredible vistas. Two of the chalets have fireplaces (romantic and practical), and four have lofts especially suitable for children. The adjoining **Kula Lodge Restaurant** (&) has the best panorama in Maui, although the cuisine and service could stand a little improvement (fortunately, excellent restaurants are only a short drive away). Spending the day at nearby Makena Beach—one of Maui's best—and the evening by the fire watching the sun set is about as good as it gets. ♦ Haleakala Hwy and Kimo Dr. 878.1535, 800/233.1535; fax 878.2518

106 Olinda Drive From Kula, follow Kula Highway (Route 37) north to Pukalani, then take Makawao Avenue (Route 365) to Makawao and turn right onto Route 390, a pleasant five-mile stretch of scenic vistas, small forests, and enviable homesteads. Take Piiholo Road (Route 394) back to the main highway just below Makawao.

107 Casanova Italian Restaurant & Deli ★★★$$$ Regularly voted "Best Italian Restaurant" by readers of *The Maui News,* what started as a chic deli that sold squid-ink pasta to upscale hotels has now come of age as an extremely popular restaurant and nightclub housed in a storefront on Makawao's main street. Inside the restaurant are koa tables and bar, and an Italian pizza station. Put together a picnic of pasta salads, cheeses, and desserts from the petite but bountiful deli, or go next door and dine on classic Italian cuisine. Fresh fish, Big Island beef, wood-oven–fired pizza, and lobster pasta are only a few of the items on the extensive menu. There's also music and dancing Wednesday through Saturday. Part-time area resident Willie Nelson occasionally puts in an appearance. Watch the alcohol consumption; it's a long drive home to almost anywhere. ♦ Italian ♦ M-Sa lunch and dinner; Su dinner. 1188 Makawao Ave (at Baldwin Ave), Makawao. 572.0220 &

107 Komoda's Store This sparse yet charming half-century-old Makawao landmark is a combination old-fashioned general store and bakery that's famous throughout the islands for its monumental cream puffs. The *azuki* bean pie is popular too. ♦ M-F 7AM-5PM; Sa

7AM-2PM. 3674 Baldwin Ave (at Makawao Ave), Makawao. 572.7261

107 Viewpoints Gallery This fine arts collective is a cooperative venture dreamed up, designed, and run by two dozen Maui artists. A wide range of interesting and unusual artwork is represented, including oil paintings, sculpture, pottery, watercolors, and etchings printed on Hawaiian fiber paper. ♦ Daily. 3620 Baldwin Ave (at Nakui St), Makawao. 572.5979 ♿

107 Makawao Steak House ★★★$$$ The simple menu at Dickie and Judy Furtado's upcountry establishment, which lists the basic beef, lamb, poultry, fish, and salads, gives little hint of what's in store for diners here. The straightforward bill of fare doesn't do justice to the consistently excellent dishes, which include such mouthwatering specialities as slow-cooked prime rib and stuffed chicken breast baked in wine sauce. Add top-notch service and a soothing environment of flickering fireplaces, dim lighting, and polished woodwork, and you've got the best steak house on the island. ♦ Steak ♦ Daily dinner. Reservations recommended. 3612 Baldwin Ave (between Nakui and Ukiu Sts), Makawao. 572.8711 ♿

108 Haliimaile General Store ★★★★$$$$ Bev and Joe Gannon converted an old plantation store in the middle of the pineapple fields into an oasis of fine dining. High ceilings, hardwood floors, two dining rooms, and works by noted Maui artists provide the ambience, while the kitchen produces some of the best cuisine on Maui. Gastronomes from all over the island drive to the 1,200-foot elevation for the brie-and-grape quesadilla, Bev's boboli (similar to pizza crust) with crab dip, barbecued Szechuan salmon, coconut seafood curry, and the Hunan-style rack of lamb (simply unbelievable). The wine list is outstanding, as is the chocolate–macadamia-nut pie. The owners' showbiz background (Joe has produced concerts for Julio Iglesias, Alice Cooper, and Ringo Starr; Bev was once

the road manager for Liza Minnelli and Joey Heatherton) makes this a celebrity haunt too. You just never know who might show up. ♦ Pacific Rim ♦ M-Sa lunch and dinner; Su brunch and dinner. 900 Haliimaile Rd, Haliimaile. 572.2666 ♿

109 Hui Noeau Visual Arts Center Noted architect **C.W. Dickey** designed this 1917 stucco mansion (pictured above) ensconced in a manorial five-acre setting. Vestiges of one of the island's first sugar mills mark the tree-lined entrance. Originally built for prominent longtime residents Harry and Ethel Baldwin, the estate was turned into an arts center by their grandson, Colin Cameron, in the late 1970s. Today it offers ongoing exhibits, and regular classes in line drawing, printmaking, and other arts. The new children's studio might be a good place for your youngster to spend the afternoon painting or making paper with others his or her own age. The gift shop features earrings, paintings, ceramics, and handmade paper. ♦ Donation. M-Sa. 2841 Baldwin Ave (between Makawao Ave and Kaluanui Rd). 572.6560 ♿

110 The Vegan Restaurant ★★$ This small eatery is persuading more and more people around the island that pure vegetarian cuisine is not only wholesome and good for you, but also can be quite delicious. Bovine-free dishes include *tofucci* (lasagna without meat or dairy products), grilled basil polenta, and *banini* (banana shakes without milk or sugar). A favorite choice is the tasty vegan burger, a clever combination of wheat gluten, tempeh, and grains. ♦ Vegetarian ♦ Daily lunch and dinner. 115 Baldwin Ave (south of Hana Hwy), Paia. 579.9144 ♿

111 Picnics ★$ If you're going to make the trip to Hana, be sure to stop here and stock up on edibles. Basically a take-out counter serving hot and cold sandwiches, salads, burgers (the spinach-nut burger has fans around the world), and complete box lunches ranging from spartan to exotic, this eatery also serves espresso and cappuccino—a godsend for hungover Hana-bound drivers. The huge newsprint menu is a boon, too: on the flip side is a guide to Hana, a map of Maui, a list of the state and county parks, and a chart of distances to Hana (it even lists Hana's 56 bridges). A tablecloth, ice chest, and ice are provided for a fee. ♦ Cafe/Takeout ♦ Daily 7AM-7PM. 30 Baldwin Ave (just south of Hana Hwy), Paia. 579.8021 ♿

112 Mama's Fish House ★★★
$$$$ Despite its remote location in a converted beach house, this has been Maui's best-known fish house for over 30 years. Located just past Paia, it features such one-of-a-kind delicacies as *Pua Me Hua Hana*—fresh fish sautéed with bananas, coconut milk, and lime juice, served with Maui sweet potatoes. The landscaped grounds, ocean view, and rustic Polynesian decor are memorable. For dessert, try the Oreo and macadamia-nut crust filled with caramel and Hawaiian chocolate mousse. ♦ Seafood ♦ Daily lunch and dinner. Reservations recommended. 799 Poho Pl (off Hana Hwy), Kuau. 579.8488 ⟨♿⟩

112 Mama's Vacation Rentals $$$ For over 20 years, the owners of **Mama's Fish House** (see above) invested in property around their restaurant on Kuau Bay. They now rent the units—four two-bedroom oceanfront homes and two one-bedroom apartments—to families, couples, and groups. Each of the oceanfront units sleeps six, which makes them a bargain for those traveling in numbers. They also have TVs, phones, full kitchens, ceiling fans, CD players, VCRs, and Weber barbecue grills. There's a housekeeping surcharge for stays of fewer than three nights. ♦ 799 Poho Pl (off Hana Hwy), Kuau. 579.9764, 800/860.HULA; fax 579.8594; mamas@maui.net; www.maui.net/~mamas

113 Pauwela Cafe ★★$ Had enough of the same old thing? Pull into this former cannery in the middle of (apologies to friendly owners Chris and Becky Speere) nowhere for a sandwich of *kalua* turkey (smoked, shredded turkey baked in ti leaves) with green chili pesto and fresh cilantro on a French roll. Local residents are already muttering that the cavernous cannery is starting to seem a bit small. ♦ Cafe ♦ Daily breakfast and lunch. 375 W Kuiaha Rd (between Haiku Rd and Hana Hwy). 575.9242 ⟨♿⟩

Hana Coast

A small, remote village on Maui's eastern coast, Hana consists of little more than a post office, a couple of restaurants, and one exclusive, exceptional resort, the **Hotel Hana-Maui**. But people don't travel to Hana for a glitzy resort scene or lively nightlife—they come for the countryside, which is rural, isolated, undeveloped, tranquil, and beautiful. Thanks to more than 70 inches of rainfall annually, the region is part dense, luxuriant rain forest laced with waterfalls, and part green and open countryside. The entire district is home to only some 2,500 people, many of them pure or part Hawaiian. A number of outsiders, including many celebrities and entertainers, have homes in Hana, but they have come for the peace, quiet, and privacy, and they haven't changed Hana one bit.

This region's splendid isolation is due, more than anything, to the narrow, pitted, potholed winding country road called the **Hana Highway.** Those who want their Maui vacation to be a simple interlude in the country, with the added attraction of a few beaches (though not the best on the island), and with no nightlife and no TV, will choose to stay in Hana. For everyone else, the road to Hana itself, and the scenery along it, is the attraction.

114 Hana Highway With its 54 miles of horseshoe turns, one-lane bridges, and narrow shoulders, this highway offers one of Hawaii's most demanding yet popular drives. It should be undertaken at a very leisurely pace; if you plan to make the entire trip in a day, try to start early (although driving back at night is actually faster). Those prone to car sickness should take Dramamine first, and picnickers should bring insect repellent. Start with a full tank of gas, as there are no stations between Paia and Hana (and gas may not be available in Hana after dark). Packing a lunch is also wise, even if you choose not to picnic among the waterfalls and jungle foliage; food service along Hana Highway can be limited to what's growing on the trees. But don't let all this intimidate you—the Hana Highway deserves to be ranked among the wonders of the world and shouldn't be missed.

The drive begins near the **Kahului Airport**, where you'll see the sign: "Hana 54 miles." In fact, the road seems *much* longer—it curves, twists, curls, and pirouettes through 617 hairpin turns, passes over 56 miniature bridges, and is so narrow it's often impossible for two cars to pass unless one pulls over. The road took several years to build with pick and shovel, and several more to pave, using convict labor. Before it was paved, the road often washed out; drivers blocked from passing by mud slides were known to swap cars and continue on their respective ways, later meeting back at the same mud slide to switch cars again for the return trip. The now-defunct **Keanae Chinese Store** provided free overnight beds for these stranded motorists.

Of course, the infamous road itself is not the only reason the drive to Hana takes so long. After all, it would be a travesty not to make an occasional stop to explore the myriad waterfalls, gardens, beaches, freshwater caves, and swimming holes. The roadside harbors a living catalog of Hawaiian plant life, with ferns and flowers vying for space among trees hung with breadfruit, mango, and guava. Picturesque rest stops include the **Waikamoi Ridge Trail** (leading to a forest perfect for picnicking), Puohokamoa Falls (where you can swim in a natural pool), Keanae Lookout, and the Waianapanapa Black Sand Beach. About 10 miles beyond Hana are the **Seven**

Sacred Pools, part of **Haleakala National Park.** Stop in at the visitors' center to get maps and directions to the four miles of trails to waterfalls and natural habitat. Since it's impossible to see everything in one day, try to keep to some sort of schedule (but not too rigidly) and remember to save some energy for the trip back.

The Piilani Highway (Route 31), which starts at Hana and continues around Haleakala toward Kihei, is supposedly off-limits to rental cars because of the somewhat rugged terrain, but tourists drive it all the time anyway (although if your rental car breaks down here, your insurance may not cover it). While much of the highway was paved years ago, it's still punctured with potholes further deepened by the tour buses that careen down it regularly. Although this way back to civilization is longer and much more energy-sapping than retracing your steps on the Hana Highway, it's worth it just to witness the dichotomy of terrain within a matter of miles, from lush jungle growth to barren deserts of lava rock.

Along Hana Highway:

Huelo Point Flower Farm $$ This parcel of paradise belonged to spiritual teacher and author Shakti Gawain before the current owners, Guy Fisher and Doug Self, stumbled onto it in the mid-1980s. There's one three-bedroom house, two two-bedroom houses, and a cottage for two, but wherever you stay, you'll spend a lot of time wandering from the pool to the cliffside hot tubs to the private waterfall across the driveway and through the woods. This place is not recommended for socialites. There's no restaurant and there's a two-night minimum stay. ♦ No credit cards accepted. Huelo. 572.1850; fax 572.1850; huelopt@maui.net; www.maui.net/~huelopt ♿

 Waikamoi Ridge Trail Because it is unmarked and relatively unknown, this trail, which leads to one of the most isolated and beautiful picnic areas in Hawaii, makes for an ideal all-day excursion. Starting at the sign "QUIET—TREES AT WORK," hike for about 15 minutes up the ridge to a sun-filled oasis with a manicured lawn and a picnic table with a barbecue grill. After lunch, continue to explore the significantly narrower trail that leads through bamboo forests and passes numerous pools and waterfalls. Bring mosquito repellent. ♦ Look for a small dirt turnoff between the 9- and 10-mile markers; a metal gate and a green post mark the trailhead

Keanae Arboretum Don't miss this spectacular collection of native and introduced plant life that includes trees from around the world, notably a stunning collection of towering eucalyptuses. Past the taro patches irrigated by the Piinaau Stream is a small trail that leads to a pleasant forest. ♦ Free. Daily

Waianapanapa State Park Try not to leave Hana before exploring the rugged volcanic shoreline of Waianapanapa (which means "glistening water" and refers to the cold, crystal-clear freshwater pool in a cave in the park). You can hike along an ancient three-mile trail to Hana, sunbathe at the black-sand cove (although swimming there can be treacherous), and look for turtles and seabirds from the elevated trail over the lava rock outcroppings. There are cabins and picnic facilities, and camping is available by permit (984.8109).

115 Hotel Hana-Maui
$$$$ With its secluded location, soothing atmosphere, and cordial staff, this top-notch property has attracted celebrities, VIPs, and respite-seeking world travelers for more than 40 years (it has a repeat-visitor rate of 80 percent). Just a few of its many awards: Most Romantic Resort in the World *(Romantic Hideaways);* Top 10 Resorts in the US *(Harper's Hideaway Report);* Top 10 Tropical Resorts in the US *(Condé Nast Traveler* magazine); and Best Small Hotel in Hawaii *(Aloha* magazine). Although the property has changed management four times since the mid-1980s (it's now run independently by former staff), there's been no hint of decline. The 66-acre site houses 74 rooms and 19 large, luxurious suites in one-story cottages spread out across the property. Forty charming **Sea Ranch Cottages**—stained dark green like old plantation homes—skirt the shoreline with stone pillars, pitched corrugated-iron roofs, and borders of lava rock. The decor recalls an elegant Hawaiian beach cottage, with bleached hardwood floors, quilts, tiled baths that open onto private gardens, and lots of rattan, bamboo, fresh orchids, and greenery. There are many special touches (our favorite: fresh Kona coffee beans and a coffeemaker in every room), but the greatest luxuries are the four-poster bamboo beds and the huge decks with Jacuzzis and ocean views. The leisurely pace and various recreational activities give visitors ample opportunity to enjoy the natural surroundings. The **Hana Health and Fitness Retreat** offers nature walks and hikes, aerobics, yoga, and exercise and diet programs. Guests can also ride bicycles or horses, attend cookouts and picnics, and participate in outings to the historic **Piilanihale Heiau** (a nearby stone temple) and the adjacent **Kahanu Botanical Garden.** The restored **Plantation House,** formerly the plantation manager's home on a hill away from the beach, is used for weddings, meetings, and groups of up to 25. Although the drive to the hotel from **Kahului Airport** is pleasant, most guests fly into the nearby **Hana Airport.** As

expected, the rates are astronomically high, but that's the price of perfection. ♦ Hana Hwy and Hauoli St, Hana. 248.8211, 800/321.4262; fax 248.7202 ♿

Within the Hotel Hana-Maui:

Hotel Hana-Maui Main Dining Room
★★★$$$$ If you want to do Hana in style, you won't pass up the chance to dine at the finest restaurant in town. In an open-beamed room best described as "Old Hawaii elegant," with polished wood floors and views of the verdant courtyard, you can enjoy meals that reflect Pacific Island, American, and Asian influences. Seared scallops and angel-hair pasta, and flame-broiled *ahi* sautéed with spinach-papaya puree are among the delicacies to savor. Dishes incorporate wonderful local touches—even at breakfast, the menu features macadamia-nut waffles with guava, *lilikoi*, and coconut syrup. The kitchen also prepares fabulous picnic baskets. ♦ Pacific/American/Asian ♦ Daily breakfast, lunch, and dinner. Reservations required for nonguests; recommended for guests. 248.8211 ♿

Hana Coast Gallery All of the artists (about 60) whose work is displayed here live in Hawaii. The gallery serves as a showcase of original art and master crafts reflecting the beauty and heritage of the islands and their people. Pieces range from bronzes of the volcano goddess Pele and rare paintings by Herb Kane to Todd Campbell's turned-wood bowls and the lush landscape paintings of James Peter Cost. The owners are Gary Koeppel, producer of the annual **Maui Marine Art Expo,** and Carl Lindquist, a longtime prominent Hana citizen and former manager of the **Hotel Hana-Maui.** ♦ Daily. 248.8636 ♿

Hana Ranch Stables Although the stables are part of the **Hotel Hana-Maui's** activities program, nonguests are welcome to partic-ipate in the hourlong horseback rides along the scenic Hana coast (available daily at 8:30AM, 10:30AM, and 1:30PM). Also possible is a two-hour Tuesday-only luau ride that goes up into the hills and back down to Hamoa Beach for the luau. Make arrangements through the **Hotel Hana-Maui's** activities desk. ♦ Fee. Daily. Reservations required. 248.8268

115 Hana Cultural Center Located on the grounds of the old courthouse and jail, the center has ever-changing exhibits culled from the more than 4,000 items in its archives. Also

called **Hale Waiwai,** the center has more than 200 members who collect and display photographs, shells, quilts, and other objects and artifacts. The courthouse was built in 1878, and the adjoining jail was in use from 1871 to 1878. (Everyone in town knew when the jail held an inmate because, with grounds-keeping a required prisoner task, the lawn would suddenly be mowed.) ♦ Nominal fee; seniors free. Daily. Ua Kea Rd and Keawa Pl, Hana. 248.8622

115 Hana Beach Park Grab the kids and head to the safest swimming area in town. This has been a surfing spot for centuries, with the best breakers occurring in the middle of the bay. There's a pier to one side and an island, Puukii, beyond it. Picnic and public facilities are available. ♦ Ua Kea Rd and Keawa Pl, Hana

At Hana Beach Park:

Tutu's at Hana Bay $ This small take-out stand on Hana Bay hawks sandwiches, burgers, and plate lunches (called *bentos* by those in the know), but is best known for its Maui-made *haupia* (coconut pudding) ice cream. ♦ Takeout/Ice cream ♦ Daily. No credit cards accepted. 248.8224 ♿

115 Hasegawa General Store More than just a shop, this is one of Hana's main attractions, both a gathering place and a purveyor of everything from appliances to food and fishing supplies. A song has even been written about it. The Hasegawa family has created an institution by piling their store from floor to ceiling with an assortment of goods no one can live without (particularly useful is their latest addition—an automatic teller machine). The place doesn't have quite the character it did before a fire gutted it and forced the proprietors to move down the road to this building, but if you need something, chances are the Hasegawas have it (you just have to figure out where they've hidden it). ♦ Daily. 5165 Hana Hwy (just south of Haouli St), Hana. 248.8231

116 Hana Ranch Restaurant ★$$ Eggs, ham, French toast, and bacon for breakfast; burgers, hot dogs, and teriyaki sandwiches for lunch are the offerings at this down-home, ranch-style restaurant. Dinner is served in the dining room three nights a week; take-out suppers are available the other four nights. Wednesday is pizza night. ♦ American ♦ Daily breakfast, lunch, and dinner. Reservations recommended. 360 Hana Hwy (just south of Mill Pl), Hana. 248.8255 ♿

117 Pools at Kipahulu (Seven Sacred Pools) As a promotional scheme, an activities director at a Hana hotel nicknamed the pools at Kipahulu the "Seven Sacred Pools," which soon became a misnomer of staggering popularity (much to the dismay of Hawaiians, many of whom will sardonically respond "The seven what?" when asked about the pools). Although the pools are inspiring and beautiful, they are neither "sacred" nor do they number seven. There are more like 24 pools, but who's counting? The long series of freshwater pools cascades down to the sea, creating a perfect setting for swimming, picnicking, and camping. A road bridge passes between the fourth and fifth pools; slightly beyond the bridge you can leave your car and either walk the trail down to the lower pools near the ocean or take the pleasant 30-minute hike to the higher pools, which are much more entertaining.

If you choose to venture upward, you'll be rewarded by the Makahiku and Waimoku Waterfalls, a bamboo forest, and a series of interconnecting pools. Note: Before trekking uphill, it's a good idea to ask the park ranger about the anticipated weather conditions. Also, get out of the pools immediately if the water suddenly rises: On at least five occasions, when streams rose rapidly due to flash flooding, ranger Pu Bednorse has risked his life to save people from drowning—receiving a presidential citation for his heroism. (For details on **Haleakala National Park,** see page 84.) ♦ Piilani Hwy, Haleakala National Park

Bests

Robin Curry
Concierge, Kapalua Bay Hotel

Hawaii's Natural Wonders

Hiking through the forest or in a dormant volcano. Hawaii has no snakes or poison ivy.

Rope swinging in a mountain stream pool, like you see in your dreams.

Whale watching, peaking in February.

Jumping off **Black Rock** at **Kaanapali.**

Photo-worthy rainbows.

Frequent "pull-over-and-snorkel" opportunities.

Haleakala Crater at sunrise.

On Maui, I wouldn't miss:

Enjoying the charm of **Lahaina** on a sunset sail.

Catching the sunset with a mai tai on your lanai and *really* relaxing.

Great Values on Maui

Eating at the bar at **Avalon** after 5PM. Discreet and affordable—a hidden gem.

Playing golf at **Waiehu Municipal Golf Course.** It's the only place where fivesomes and walking are okay.

Renting a condo instead of a hotel room. More space, less money, best for families.

Monday Night Football by satellite during Happy Hour at **Dollies** in **Kahana.**

Maui Film Festival at the **Maui Arts and Cultural Center.** Original versions on the biggest screen. Classy.

Playing two rounds of golf in a day at any of the big resorts. The second round is so inexpensive that just nine holes extra even makes sense, and you can play a different course.

Hawaiian Lifestyle

"Dressing up" means wearing a collared shirt.

You never wear shoes in someone's home.

Riding a bike or hitchhiking to work is very common.

Whales and dolphins come to your boat and check *you* out.

You miss the trade winds if they aren't blowing.

It's nice to have a gecko around the house.

You are part of a vibrant, East meets West, multi-cultural society, unlike anywhere on the mainland!

Mazie K. Hirono
Lieutenant Governor, State of Hawaii

The Aloha Spirit—A feeling of love, warmth, and hospitality communicated by word and action by the people of Hawaii.

S. Matsumoto Shave Ice Store—Cold and sweet in colorful **Haleiwa** town on **Oahu's North Shore**.

Merrie Monarch Festival—The premier competition for native Hawaiian dance is held on the **Big Island.** It draws hula *halau* (groups) from across the world.

Bishop Museum—Learn about the deepness and richness of Hawaii's native Hawaiian culture.

Honolulu Academy of Arts—An oasis of art from around the world in a gem of a building.

Prince Lot Hula Festival—Historic **Moanalua Gardens** in **Honolulu** is the lush backdrop of the pageantry of Hawaiian dance.

The Contemporary Museum—For lunch with art in a garden setting up in **Makiki Heights** in Honolulu.

Hawaii Volcanoes National Park—Madame Pele shows her splendor on the Big Island. See a lava flow up close and personal.

Swim at **Ala Moana Beach Park.** Lots of families here on weekends. It's fun and it's free.

Gerard Reversade
Owner/Chef, Gerard's

Bike down **Haleakala Crater.**

Survive the **Hana Highway** with over fifty bridges.

Go to **Makawao** and see the *paniolos* (cowboys).

Check out **Tedeschi Vineyards** for Champagne tasting.

Go to **Makena Beach.**

Kahoolawe

Although dry and uninhabited, Kahoolawe (Kah-*ho*-oh-*law*-vay) is one of Hawaii's most controversial islands. Located about seven miles off the southwest coast of Maui and easily visible from both Maui and Lanai, for decades Kahoolawe had the dubious honor of being the most heavily bombed place in the Pacific. It was used as a practice range by the US Navy until 1990, and to date this 45-square-mile booby trap remains littered with unexploded bombs. Finally, in September 1998, the government began a $400-million project to rid the island of the mines. The navy and its contractor, Parsons-UXB Joint Venture, have until 2003 to conduct the cleanup of 100 percent of Kahoolawe surface and 30 percent of the island's subsurface.

The smallest of Hawaii's eight major islands, for centuries Kahoolawe was a sacred place inhabited by ancient Hawaiians. Today evidence of that occupation is now scattered, bombed remains of ancient temples, fishing shrines, and villages. Abandoned possibly because of an unfavorable shift in climate, the island wasn't inhabited by people again until 1839, when it served unsuccessfully as an Alcatraz of sorts for convicted criminals. In 1858 the first of several attempts was made to turn the island into a large cattle ranch, and after a long period of trial and error, the inhabitants of Kahoolawe managed to sustain horses, cattle, fowl, and an assortment of trees and grasses. But in 1939 the ranchers made the grave error of leasing the southern end of the island to the Navy for target practice. After the attack at Pearl Harbor in 1941, the Navy unceremoniously booted the ranchers and their stock off Kahoolawe and turned the entire island into a gunnery range, providing an occasional pyrotechnical display for the citizens of Maui as huge battleships blasted the extinct volcano with their 16-inch guns.

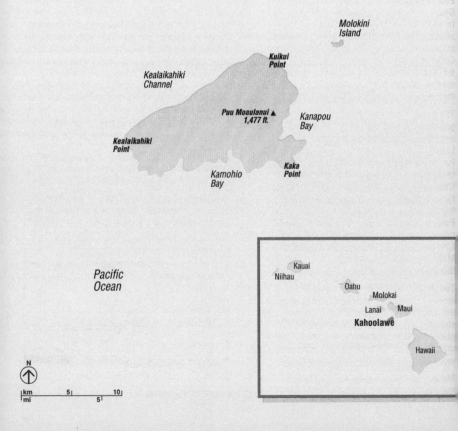

In 1976, Protect Kahoolawe Ohana (PKO; *ohana* means "family" in Hawaiian), a Hawaiian activist group, initiated both a series of occupations of the island and statewide protests to stop the bombing. Two members of PKO were killed and lost at sea during this period. The same year, PKO filed a lawsuit, claiming that the island was home to 600 archaeological sites and 2,000 sacred natural features. By 1977, a federal court had ordered the Navy to conduct an environmental impact survey and to protect the natural historic sites of the island. PKO was granted stewardship of the island the same year.

In 1994, after three years of hearings, the US government returned the island to its rightful owner, the state of Hawaii. Under state law, the island is held in trust for eventual transfer to its owner: a sovereign Hawaiian entity. In addition, commercial use of the **Kahoolawe Island Reserve** (which includes a two-mile ocean buffer) is prohibited.

Since 1977, the PKO has brought more than 8,000 visitors to the island to participate in religious and cultural ceremonies, to begin revegetating Kahoolawe, to rededicate shrines and temples, and to establish a permanent base camp on the northeast side of the island. Ancient Hawaiians had dedicated Kahoolawe to Kanaloa, Hawaiian god of the ocean and navigation, and today the island is respected by Native Hawaiians as a body form of Kanaloa. Traditionally, the science of wayfinding by the constellations and nature was studied and taught on the island.

Currently Kahoolawe is off-limits to the public, except for PKO members who are allowed access to the island four days every month, ten months a year, for religious, cultural, educational, and scientific activities.

Hawaiian Lands in Hawaiian Hands?

Ever since Hawaii became the 50th of the United States in 1959, there's been a growing movement to return the islands to Hawaiian rule. That activity accelerated in 1993 on the centennial of the overthrow of the monarchy, when President Bill Clinton signed a Congressional Resolution apologizing to Hawaiians for US interference in the islands' governance. This act gave new hope to Hawaiians that their demands for independence might be heard.

The quest for self-rule dates back to 1893, when a group of American expatriates orchestrated an overthrow of the Hawaiian monarchy, unbeknownst to the US government (communications from the Pacific Rim to the East Coast were not what they are today). Queen Liliuokalani, a ruler beloved by the Hawaiian people and critical of the US presence in Hawaii, was deposed in a bloodless battle and imprisoned for months in her residence, the **Iolani Palace** in **Honolulu.** President Grover Cleveland refused to annex the islands at the time; five years later the United States (under President William McKinley) officially took this action. Five weeks after this the Hawaiian islands became a US territory.

Today about 50 groups are involved in an increasingly visible but factionalized sovereignty movement (their emblem is the upside-down flag shown at right). One of these groups, Ha Hawaii, plans to hold a convention in November 1999 to draft a constitution for Hawaiian government, which would coalesce native demands for self-rule.

The greatest challenge to the independence movement is the lack of agreement on what sovereignty

means or how it would play out in a place whose local landscape and culture has been irrevocably altered by 100 years of foreign government. Even more problematic is a lack of understanding of just who is Hawaiian: a blood-quantum definition established by the Hawaiian Homelands Trust in 1921 states that to qualify for native status, a person must have at least 50 percent Hawaiian blood. Many believe today that a Hawaiian is someone with Hawaiian ancestry, regardless of the intervening effects of intermarriage. Still others defend the rights of all Aloha State residents to step forward at the time of succession and claim Hawaiian citizenship while relinquishing ties to their country.

At press time Hawaii Senator Daniel Inouye had expressed willingness to introduce a sovereignty bill in Congress when Hawaiians are in agreement on the makeup of such a statute. Clearly, sovereignty is a complex issue, and not one that is expected to be resolved quickly.

Lanai

For nearly a century the entire island community of Lanai (Lah-nah-*ee*) worked under a single employer to harvest what was once the largest pineapple plantation in the world. But in October 1993, Castle & Cooke Properties, a subsidiary of Dole Foods, shut down the pineapple operation because of high labor costs, shifting the bulk of its operations to Thailand and the Philippines. Faced not only with immediate unemployment but with an end to a way of life, Lanai's 2,800 residents were determined to retain their strong ties to the land and the community. Hands callused from harvesting pineapples were retrained to drive shuttle buses and tend gardens as Lanai's luxury resorts, the **Manele Bay Hotel** and the **Lodge at Koele**, opened the doors to tourism on an island that had been uninhabited for hundreds of years for fear of the ghosts of the *alii* (Hawaiian royalty) buried here.

When visiting Lanai, you will immediately sense an esprit de corps among the islanders. The majority of residents live in Lanai's only town, **Lanai City**—a cool, sleepy mountain community 1,700 feet above the sea. Lightly coated with a fine, iron-rich dust and lined with majestic Norfolk and Cook Island pines, Lanai City consists mainly of multicolored tin-roofed plantation houses that reflect a bygone era. James Dole first laid out the town in 1924 after purchasing the entire island for $1.1 million, and most of Lanai City's buildings date from those early years. Residents often gather to "talk story" (Hawaiian for gossiping) while roasting local mouflon sheep or axis deer on someone's porch, perhaps sharing a case of beer brought over from Maui. It's a close-knit community, proud of its hardworking lineage and unscathed by its narrow escape from extinction—for if tourism hadn't replaced the pineapple industry, Lanai would have been returned to the restless spirits.

Three main roads trisect the 140-square-mile island, but dozens of unpaved roads lead to remote beaches, well-preserved *heiaus* (temples) and petroglyphs, misty mountaintops, and various other natural wonders, so renting a four-wheel-drive vehicle is mandatory if you want to truly explore Lanai. The 13-mile-wide, 18-mile-long island is also ideal for camping, hunting, hiking, and mountain-bike riding, and the exquisite beach at **Hulopoe Bay** (a popular playground for spinner dolphins) makes for a pleasant day trip from Maui via the *Expeditions* ferry. Whether arriving by plane or boat, make sure you've arranged to be picked up by your hotel or **Lanai City Service**, the island's only taxi/car-rental agency, as there's no public transportation from the harbor or the airport. Tourists who can't foot the $300-plus per night bill at either resort hotel will most likely be content staying at the island's only other hostelry, the **Hotel Lanai.** Once James Dole's clubhouse, it's now a cozy, unpretentious, and moderately priced inn in the heart of Lanai City. Wherever you stay, it is impossible to spend any amount of time on Lanai and not fall under the spell of the island and its people.

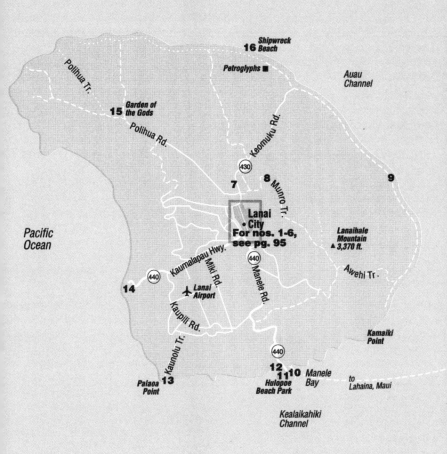

Kalohi
Channel

Polihua Tr.

Garden of
the Gods

15

Polihua Rd.

Shipwreck
Beach

16

Petroglyphs ■

Auau
Channel

Keomuku Rd.

430

7   **8**   Munro Tr.   **9**

Pacific
Ocean

Lanai
• City
**For nos. 1-6,
see pg. 95**

Lanaihale
Mountain
▲ 3,370 ft.

Kaumalapau Hwy.

Miki Rd.

440

Manele Rd.

440

Lanai
Airport

Kaupili Rd.

Awehi Tr.

Kamaiki
Point

Kaunolu Tr.

Palaoa
Point

13

12 **11****10** Manele
Bay

Hulopoe
Beach Park

to
Lahaina, Maui

14

Kealaikahiki
Channel

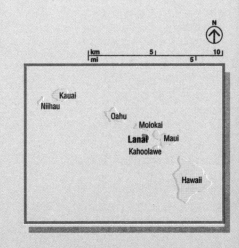

N

km
mi

5   10

5

Kauai

Niihau

Oahu

Molokai

Lanai   Maui

Kahoolawe

Hawaii

Area code 808 unless otherwise noted.

Getting to Lanai

Airports

Lanai Airport

Four miles southwest of Lanai City, **Lanai Airport** (565.6757) is a runway and a one-room terminal in what used to be pineapple fields. The building is open only when flights (interisland only) are scheduled.

Airlines

Hawaiian 800/882.8811
   from the mainland..........................800/367.5320

Island Air, interisland 565.6744, 800/652.6541
   from the mainland..........................800/323.3345

Getting to and from Lanai Airport

By Bus

No public buses serve the small airport, but the **Lodge at Koele** and the **Manele Bay Hotel** provide shuttle buses for their guests.

By Car

There are no car-rental booths at the airport.

By Taxi

Lanai City Service (565.7227) provides limited taxi service, but must be called. There are no taxi stands at the airport.

Interisland Carriers

Hawaiian Airlines flies to **Lanai Airport** direct from Honolulu and Molokai. **Island Air** flies direct from Honolulu and from **Kahului Airport** on Maui.

Ferries

Expeditions (661.3756, 800/695.2624) is the island's only ferry. The boat makes the trip from Lahaina, Maui to **Manele Bay** on Lanai and back five times daily; passage takes about an hour and can be choppy. The first ferry departs Lanai at 8AM; the last one leaves the island at 6:45PM. A round-trip excursion is $50 for adults, $40 for children under 12.

Getting Around Lanai

Bicycles

Mountain bikes are a good way to travel on the island's many unpaved roads. The **Lodge at Koele** (565.7300) provides them for its guests for a fee. **Lanai City Service** (1036 Lanai Ave, between 11th and 10th Sts, Lanai City, 565.7227) also rents bikes.

Buses

There is no public bus system on Lanai.

Driving

The streets of Lanai City are on a grid system. Almost everything is on **Lanai Avenue,** which intersects streets from **Kaumalapau Highway** to **Third.** Only two "main" roads—**Route 430 (Keomuku Road)** and **Route 440 (Kaumalapau Highway** and **Manele Road)**—cross the rest of the island; off these branch

numerous unpaved four-wheel-drive roads. There's also a network of dirt roads through pineapple fields, but visitors can easily get lost in these paths. **Lanai City Service** (see above) rents compact cars and four-wheel-drive vehicles.

Hiking

The most popular trek on Lanai is the **Munro Trail,** named for George Munro, who imported Norfolk pines from his New Zealand homeland. The hike to the top of 3,370-foot **Lanaihale Mountain** and back takes 6 hours. To reach the trailhead, drive north from Lanai City on Route 430 and take the first major gravel road to the right a mile-and-a-half out of town stick to the roads most traveled.

Parking

To say that parking is not a problem on Lanai would be a gross understatement. Park anywhere—there are no meters, and unless you block entry to one of the larger hotels, you won't be ticketed or towed.

Taxis

Call **Lanai City Service** (see above) with any transportation needs; they're the only game in town.

Tours

The **Lodge at Koele** (565.7300) offers a half-day tour of the island in a small bus that includes lunch. Be sure to reserve 24 hours in advance. The **Lodge** also has one- to two-hour plantation rides on horseback.

Walking

Lanai City can be covered on foot in an hour or two. Points of interest outside the city are far-flung, so you'll also need another mode of transportation.

FYI

Shopping

It's interesting to stroll by the rustic stores on Lanai Avenue in Lanai City, but unless you're in the market for a plastic comb, you probably won't need your wallet. There are more souvenir possibilities in the gift shops at the **Lodge at Koele** and the **Manele Bay Hotel,** but you're better off buying your alohawear and koa wood bowls on one of the other islands, where the prices are lower and the selection wider.

Visitors' Information Centers

Destination Lanai (730 Lanai Ave, at Eighth St, Lanai City, 565.7600) is open by whim or appointment. The staff is very knowledgeable about the island.

Phone Book

Emergencies

Ambulance/Fire/Police 911

Hospital (Lanai Community Hospital)........565.6411

Pharmacy..565.6423

Poison Control 800/362.3585

Police (nonemergency) 565.6428

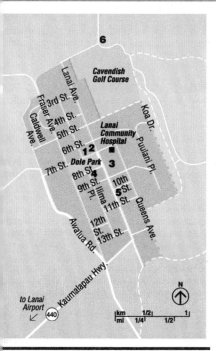

Lanai City

The only town on the island is a 10-minute drive from the airport and a 25-minute drive from **Manele Bay.** The **Hotel Lanai** is located here, as are a few very small galleries, boutiques, stores, and cafes that line the edges of a small, grassy square called **Dole Park.** The **Lodge at Koele** is on the outskirts of the tiny town.

1 Blue Ginger Cafe ★$ A great place to meet friendly locals, this restaurant is also known for its delicious, low-priced local coffee selections. The cafe doubles as a bakery, serving croissant sandwiches, along with omelettes, hamburgers, and pizza. ♦ Cafe ♦ Daily breakfast, lunch, and dinner. 409 Seventh St (between Lanai Ave and Ilima Pl). 565.6363

1 Tanigawa's $ Lanai City's version of a short-order diner serves island-style meals and snacks at a counter with swivel stools. The shakes are by far the best choice, made at an old-fashioned soda fountain that ranks as one of Lanai's favorite attractions. ♦ Diner ♦ M-Tu, Th-Su breakfast and lunch. 419 Seventh St (between Lanai Ave and Ilima Pl). 565.6537

2 Lanai Playhouse Looking for after-dark entertainment on laid-back Lanai? This is about the only choice the island offers. The movies aren't exactly first-run, but if you're lucky, you can catch up on something you missed. ♦ Nominal admission. Hours vary; call for schedule. 456 Seventh St (at Lanai Ave). 565.7500

HÔTEL LANAI

3 Hotel Lanai $$ If you don't mind staying miles from the nearest beach, this hotel is an excellent choice. Built in 1923 to house guests and serve as an entertainment center for James Dole's executives, for decades it was the only hotel on the island. Now dwarfed by two super-luxury resorts, the property continues to fill a niche in Lanai's tourist industry, providing reasonably priced accommodations and casual dining. The 10 rooms are small but tastefully decorated (a 2-room cottage is available for those who would like more space and privacy), and the staff is friendly to a fault. There's a shaded veranda, a rustic dining room (where the complimentary continental breakfast is served), and acres of cool green lawns under Norfolk pines. All the accommodations have telephones, but not TV or air-conditioning. Two golf courses are nearby. ♦ 828 Lanai Ave (between Ninth and Eighth Sts). 565.7211, 800/795.7211; fax 565.6450; hotellanai@aloha.net; www.onlanai.com

Within the Hotel Lanai:

Henry Clay's Rotisserie ★★$$$ The cozy fireplace, large wood tables, paintings and photographs by island artists, and the friendly staff lend a pleasant ambience to this dining spot. The kitchen serves such items as rotisserie chicken; oven-baked rabbit with Cognac, pancetta, and a tomato-flavored brown sauce; as well as gourmet pizza. ♦ American Country ♦ Daily dinner. 565.7211 ᏸ

4 Akamai Trading and Gifts Locally grown Norfolk pines are used to create the one-of-a-kind bowls that make this small store and espresso bar a highly recommended stop on a town tour. ♦ Daily. 408 Eighth St (between Lanai Ave and Ilima Pl). 565.6587 ᏸ

5 Lanai City Service Don't try shopping around for a better deal, because this is the only car-rental agency, cab company, and gas station on the island. It also does a brisk business renting Jeeps, so make reservations as far in advance as possible. ♦ Daily. 1036 Lanai Ave (between 11th and 10th Sts). 565.7227

The average cost of living for a family of four is $15,000 higher in Hawaii than the national average of $45,000.

Exploring Eden: A Beginner's Guide to Hiking Hawaii

The Hawaiian islands are lush with life—flowers, trees, plants, birds, animals, insects, and reptiles flourish throughout. Add to this such natural features as beaches, volcanoes, waterfalls, tide pools, deserts, thermal ponds, cliffs, valleys, mountain ridges and peaks, freshwater streams, and rain forests, and you've got an instant recipe for a hiker's paradise.

Amazingly, although hundreds of square miles in the islands have been transformed into parking lots, office buildings, megaresorts, megamalls, outlet stores, fast-food restaurants, golf courses, condominium complexes, and other "unnatural resources," just fractions of a mile from the pavement the intrepid can discover untouched idylls that look like they've been lifted piecemeal from the set of *Fantasia*.

Note: Some things to watch out for: If it's raining heavily, don't go on treks involving waterfalls or streams; flash flooding is common and can occur without warning. Don't try your hand at rock climbing anywhere in the islands; Hawaii's volcanic rock faces are porous and unreliable. (Ditto for grabbing onto trees and plants as you ascend a hill, lest you find yourself plummeting, vegetation in hand.) Bring fresh water wherever you go. Apply sunscreen liberally and often. Beware of centipedes, which sting viciously and unexpectedly, particularly in the woods. And finally, don't drink from streams or pools, because they are often home to the parasite giardia or the bacteria leptospirosis, which can cause serious illness.

A brief summary of some of the top treks in the 50th state follows. Robert Smith's guides to hiking in the islands, particularly *Hawaii's Best Hiking Trails* (Hawaiian Outdoor Adventures Publications, 1997) are also good sources. For more detailed information and whether permits are necessary, call the **Department of Land and Natural Resources, Division of State Parks** (587.0300) or the **County Parks and Recreation Department** (523.4525).

Diamond Head Crater, Oahu
To get to the trailhead: Drive to the intersection of Diamond Head Road and 18th Avenue on the northeast side of the crater; the road into the crater begins just west of the intersection. Follow the road through the tunnel to the parking lot.

This crater on the outskirts of **Waikiki** houses an elaborate fortress that was used in both world wars to command the artillery defense of leeward Oahu. Extensive fortifications and tunnels are built into the crater's walls. These can be seen on the less-than-a-mile, 1.5-hour round-trip journey to the 750-foot-high extinct crater's rim. En route to the summit, the trail passes through an angular tunnel and winds upwards on a mountainside, ridge, and over 273 steps. This is a fairly easy excursion. Be sure to bring a flashlight.

Green Sands Beach, Big Island
To get to the trailhead: Take Mamalahoa Highway south to South Point Road just west of the town of Waiohinu and drive to the boat ramp at the end of the road. The trailhead is directly to your left.

Not only is this one of the few places where you can sink your toes into green sand (olivine crystals), it's also at the southernmost point in the United States. The 45-minute hike delivers you to a bluff overlooking a remote, romantic bay where you can settle back against a sand dune and contemplate the horizon virtually uninterrupted. Leave at least three-quarters of a day to fully enjoy this journey, and bring a picnic.

Hawaii Volcanoes National Park, Big Island
To get to the trailhead: Take Saddle Road (Route 200) west from Hilo. A wooden sign marks the trailhead, which is on the left (south) side of the road just under a half mile beyond the 22-mile marker.

Hiking trails abound in **Hawaii Volcanoes National Park,** but the hike on the **Puu Oo Trail** when conditions are right can offer an unparalleled view of fresh lava. In addition, the trail crosses flows from

Kalalau Valley

MARK AMMERMANN/NORTH MARKET STREET GRAPHICS

1855, 1881, and 1935, among others, which give good examples of both *aa* (sharp) and *pahoehoe* (smooth) lava. Some parts of the 7.5-mile round-trip trail may be hard to follow; keep an eye out for *ahu* (stone cairns) that mark the way. As few people take this trail and ohelo berries abound, the bird watching is usually good. It will take at least four hours to do this hike in its entirety.

Kalalau Trail, Kauai

To get to the trailhead: Take Kuhio Highway (Route 36) north to its end at Kee Beach. The trail begins at a sign-in stand on the left side of the parking lot.

This 11-mile trail along the **Na Pali Coast** has been walked by characters ranging from Koolau the leper, running from his would-be captors and hiding out in lush **Kalalau Valley,** to scores of trust-fund babies fleeing convention in the 1960s. It's a magical place—the area gets more than 200 inches of rain a year and is usually a luxuriant green as a result. Novice hikers may choose to camp at **Hanakapiai Beach** two miles in (or simply to make it a day hike), while the hardy will go all the way to **Kalalau Beach** (a white-sand beach with a waterfall where clothing is unofficially optional) in a day.

King's Highway, Maui

To get to the trailhead: Take Hana Highway (Route 360) two-thirds of a mile past Hana Airport to Waianapanapa Campground. The trail runs between the parking lot and the ocean.

Water-worn stepping stones placed on the jagged lava to guide travelers mark this ancient trail, used by kings and their retainers to collect taxes from residents of the island's many districts. Not far from the trailhead at **Waianapanapa State Park** is an ancient *heiau* (temple). The trail, which can be followed for days in each direction, parallels the sea along small lava cliffs and is bounded by a forest of *hala* trees. Camping is possible in cabins at the park, and at many places along the trail, though most will choose to do this as a day hike.

Munro Trail, Lanai

To get to the trailhead: Take Keomuku Road (Route 430) north from Lanai City for 1.5 miles and turn right onto a paved road that leads to a cemetery where the hike begins.

Named for George Munro, who planted the Norfolk pines that carpet the 5.5-mile trail, this path follows the remains of the rim of Lanai's ancient caldera. Hikers climb to **Lanaihale Mountain,** the highest point on the island at 3,370 feet, where there are good views of **Molokai, Kahoolawe,** Maui, the Big Island, and Oahu. Save a day to make the trip, which is suited to novice and intermediate hikers. Call the **Lanai Company** (565.3000) before venturing onto the trail.

6 Lodge at Koele $$$$ Once the site of Lanai's ranching operations (a big business before the pineapple industry took over), the 20-acre grounds here now combine the elegance of an English manor with the rustic comfort of Old Hawaii. The riding stables, bowling lawn, croquet course, swimming pool, three tennis courts, reflecting pool, and acres of meticulously maintained lawns impart the atmosphere of a handsome English estate. This ambience attracts a large number of European guests and is a refreshing alternative to the muumuus-and-mai-tais mood of many Hawaiian resorts. The chilly upland air is equally invigorating. The aptly named **Great Hall,** with 35-foot-high ceilings and immense stone fireplaces, is an ideal place to linger with a book and a glass of Port. The 102 rooms and suites are decorated in old plantation style, with hand-carved four-poster beds and oil paintings and artifacts from around the world. There's a library, tearoom, gameroom, and even a music room for listening to the classical selection of the day. Guests may choose from a full range of activities, from horseback riding to tennis, boating, hiking, and croquet. The 18-hole championship golf course, designed by Greg Norman and Ted Robinson, is a draw for many. ♦ Keomuku Rd (north of Third St). 565.7300, 800/321.4666; fax 565.4561; reservation@lanai-resorts.com; www.lanai-resorts.com ♿

Within the Lodge at Koele:

Dining Room at the Lodge at Koele
★★★★$$$$ Inventive gourmet dishes are served in an elegant octagonal dining room looking out over the English gardens and pools. The cuisine is New American and the menu changes regularly, but includes such legendary dishes as local axis deer and seafood caught that day and served steamed, poached, smoked, raw, or however else you like. Although the competition is slim to none, this is unquestionably the best restaurant on the island—and one of the finest in the state. ♦ New American ♦ Daily dinner. Reservations required; jackets required. 565.7300 ♿

The Terrace at the Lodge at Koele ★★
$$$ Guests at this casual spot can request a table at the edge of the gardens and dine on lamb shank with a side of tiger prawn coleslaw as the sun sets, all the while pitying their friends back home. ♦ Hawaiian Regional ♦ Daily breakfast, lunch, and dinner. 565.7300 ♿

Elsewhere on Lanai

7 Lanai Pine Sporting Clays The only resort sporting clay (skeet shooting) course in the Pacific, this 15-acre facility is located a few miles north of the **Lodge at Koele.** It offers a 14-station course, including 6 fully automated competition high towers, and compact sporting, skeet, and Olympic trap clays.
♦ Fee. Daily. Keomuku Rd. 565.7300

8 Munro Trail This winding dirt road extends the length of 3,370-foot Lanaihale Mountain, to the east of Lanai City. New Zealander George Munro, Lanai's answer to Johnny Appleseed, scattered seeds and plants from his homeland along this ridge in the early 1900s. His Norfolk pine trees were so successful at trapping moisture on the mountain that more were planted in Lanai City, helping to keep it cooler. Take heed, though—this is not an easy trail for the hiker, mountain biker, or Jeep, especially when it's wet.

9 Keomuku An extreme example of what happens to a town when a nearby sugar plantation fails, Keomuku was abandoned at the turn of the century when the local commercial sugar venture collapsed. Almost all of the buildings have vanished except for the **Ka Lanakila o Ka Malamalama Church.** Built in 1903, the restored church stands as a testament to the deserted village, once home to nearly 2,000 people. ♦ Southeast of Keomuku Rd

10 Manele Bay Like nearby Hulopoe Bay, this was once the site of an ancient Hawaiian village. The only public harbor on the island, Manele Bay is now part of the **Marine Life Conservation District.** Swimming is unsafe here because of heavy boat traffic, so don't bother to bring your flippers. ♦ Manele Rd

11 Hulopoe Bay The usually calm waters of the bay make this by far the nicest beach on the island for swimming and snorkeling. You can also watch spinner dolphins frolic while you sunbathe or search for the interesting marine creatures that often turn up in the tide pools. The beach is equipped with public rest rooms as well. There's a sad legend associated with Puupehe, the rock islet just to the south of the bay. According to island lore, a woman named Pehe was so beautiful that her jealous husband, Makakehau, hid her in a sea cave on the isle, where she drowned during a storm. With the help of the gods, Makakehau scaled the cliff with Pehe's body and buried her at the islet's summit, now known as the Hill of Pehe. ♦ Southwest of Manele Rd

On an ordinary day in Hawaii, 170,000 people go to the beach.

12 Manele Bay Hotel $$$$ In direct contrast to the **Lodge at Koele,** this hotel has operated on the basic tropical resort principle since its opening; it offers the requisite expansive white-sand beach, central pool with dozens of deck chairs, and numerous water activities (sailing, fishing, snorkeling, and swimming). The decor reflects Mediterranean and Asian influences, and the grounds are lined with Hawaiian, Japanese, and Chinese gardens. There are 250 luxury villas and suites (including 13 suites attended by a staff of traditionally trained butlers) with private verandas and ocean views in the hills behind striking Hulopoe Bay. A Jack Nicklaus–designed 18-hole golf course is nearby and the on-site deluxe **Spa at Manele Bay** offers personal fitness training, and evaluation, massage, and beauty treatments. ♦ West of Manele Rd. 565.7700, 800/321.4666; fax 565.2483 ♿

Within the Manele Bay Hotel:

Ihilani Dining Room ★★$$$$ The best thing about this fine dining room is its unbelievable ocean view. Next best is either the roasted prime Colorado lamb loin or the panfried *opakapaka* (pink snapper)—both prepared with fresh ingredients. The decor is elegant and somewhat Asian, with Chinese vases, sculptures, paintings, and screens. ♦ French/Mediterranean ♦ Daily dinner. Reservations required. 565.7700 ♿

Hulopoe Court ★★★$$$$ Most of the produce served at this Mediterranean-themed dining room comes from Lanai's soil. More important, though, is what it goes into: such mouthwatering dishes as Szechuan-glazed beef short ribs with rock salt–crusted red potatoes and steamed baby carrots or skillet blackened big eye *ahi* (yellowfin tuna) steak served with ratatouille. The restaurant offers both indoor and outdoor seating, with walls and upholstery done in a sultry maroon floral pattern. ♦ Mediterranean ♦ Daily breakfast and dinner. Reservations recommended. 565.7700 ♿

13 Kaunolu The fishing grounds of this well-preserved ancient Hawaiian village were Kamehameha the Great's favorite. Archaeologists have found 86 house sites, 35 stone shelters, and numerous grave markings here. The road leading to the site is difficult to find and even harder to negotiate (a four-wheel-drive vehicle is a must), but the shoreline at road's end is perfect for sunbathing and snorkeling. ♦ Kaunolu Tr

14 Kaumalapau Harbor The harbor was completed in 1926 by the Hawaiian Pineapple Company (later the Dole Company) to ship pineapples from Lanai to a cannery in Honolulu. From 1968 to the mid-1970s, when operations were in high gear during the summer months, more than a million pineapples a day were transferred from trucks to barges for the journey. It's still the principal seaport for Lanai (tourist operations use Manele Harbor), with good shore fishing. ♦ Kaumalapau Hwy

15 Garden of the Gods The scattered assemblage of huge rocks and unusual lava formations here has the appearance of having dropped in from outer space. At sunrise and sunset, the eerie moonlike shapes are in every shade of purple, pink, and sienna. The stacked rocks signify absolutely nothing (they're stacked by tourists). The fenced-in area just before this site is a project by the Nature Conservancy of Hawaii aimed at maintaining Lanai's native dryland forest, one of the fastest-disappearing ecosystems in the world; the fence is to keep the axis deer out. Extremely rare species of plants, including a dryland gardenia tree, are able to survive here. ♦ Polihua Tr (off Polihua Rd)

16 Shipwreck Beach The hull of a World War II Liberty ship offshore marks the spot where many vessels from West Maui end up when they break their moorings. A spectacular collection of Hawaiian petroglyphs is located a few hundred feet inland from the end of the dirt road. This is a nice beach for wading and beachcombing. ♦ Northwest of Keomuku Rd

Tall Tales and Matters of Fact

Scour them six months before your trip or page through them between catnaps on the beach; either way, you're sure to find something of interest in each of the following books about the Hawaiian Islands:

The Atlas of Hawaii (University of Hawaii Press, 1983) The authors of this book must know everything about Hawaii. Their book is crammed full of fun facts like what plants grow where on what islands and how long it takes to drive from place to place on each isle.

The Happy Isles of Oceania, Paddling the Pacific by Paul Theroux (Fawcett, 1998) This travelogue and memoir about kayaking around the Pacific Ocean has a chapter dedicated to Hawaii. Theroux's pull-no-punches perspective will interest skippers and landlubbers alike.

Hawaii to Da Max! by Douglas Simonson, Ken Sakata, and Pat Sasaki (Bess Press, 1992) The subtitle—"Everything You Always Wanted to Know about Hawaii, But Didn't Have a Local Friend to Tell You"—says it all. Written half in English, half in Pidgin, this casual, chatty guide gives visitors a behind-the-scenes look at their vacation paradise.

Hawaiian Hiking Trails by Craig Chisholm (Fernglen Press, 1994) This useful book includes photos, basic maps, and tips on hiking some of Hawaii's better-known trails, from **Maui**'s 45-minute **Waikamoi Ridge Trail** to a four-day trek into the **Kalalau Valley** on **Kauai**.

Hawaii by James Michener (Random House, 1959) Published the year Hawaii became a state, this epic novel is hard to put down—and easy to forget that it's only fiction.

Letters from Hawaii by Mark Twain (University of Hawaii Press, 1975) Mark Twain was one of three well-known 19th-century authors (the others: Robert Louis Stevenson and Jack London) to take a turn at immortalizing the island chain in print. This book is fairly hard going, but it gives readers an idea of daily life in what was to Twain a foreign country.

The Many Splendored Fishes of Hawaii by Gar Goodson (Stanford University Press, 1985) If you plan to snorkel, take this paperback along. If you don't plan to snorkel, this overview of the islands' marine life might change your mind.

Maui's Hana Highway: A Visitor's Guide by Angela Kay Kepler (Mutual Publishing of Honolulu, 1987) Pick up this book before you drive to **Hana;** it will lead you down side roads that you'd drive right by otherwise. (And side roads are the heart and soul of the Hana adventure.)

Shoal of Time by Gavan Daws (University of Hawaii Press, 1968) This is one of the most definitive—and most readable—books on Hawaiian history in print.

Stories of Hawaii by Jack London (University of Hawaii Press, 1965) John Griffith London (1876-1916) sailed his self-designed ketch, *Snark,* from San Francisco to **Honolulu** in 1907 and spent five months touring the islands. He learned to surf, met with the deposed Queen Liliuokalani, checked out dormant **Haleakala Crater** and active **Kilauea Volcano,** and chronicled his adventures and misadventures in this easy-to-read volume.

Travels in Hawaii by Robert Louis Stevenson (University of Hawaii Press, 1973) The writer and his family arrived in Hawaii on the chartered yacht *Casco* in 1889 and stayed five months. These are stories of Stevenson's adventures on the **Big Island** and **Molokai**, with a handful of poems included.

Wild Meat and Bully Burgers by Lois-Ann Yamanaka (Farrar, Straus & Giroux, 1995) Born in **Hilo**, Yamanaka has achieved national critical acclaim for her fiction and poetry in recent years. This novel incorporates her trademark local dialogue, making readers feel—once they get used to it—as if they're listening in on a long series of pidgin conversations in the heart of small-town Hawaii.

Molokai

Compared to its neighboring islands, Molokai (Moh-loh-*kah-ee*), is in a world of its own. For hundreds of years Molokai was home to powerful *kahuna* (priests) who were feared throughout the island chain, and the island was given a wide berth by warring chiefs who called it "The Lonely Isle." When victims of leprosy were unceremoniously dumped on the island in the late 1800s, that reputation was sealed (**Kalaupapa**, the infamous exile colony for victims of leprosy—now called Hansen's disease—is now home to fewer than 70 people, all over the age of 55, and the site of various tours). In an attempt to convalesce from the historical drubbing, the state's fifth-largest island retitled itself "The Friendly Isle," which, when islanders are treated with due respect, is unquestionably accurate. Other than Niihau, Molokai is the only major Hawaiian island where most of the 7,000 residents are of native descent.

Molokai is a late–20th-century hybrid. It's a cross between a sleepy rural island with striking natural features—the world's highest sea cliffs (reaching 3,000 feet) on the north shore and Hawaii's longest white-sand beach in the west—and the vision that the multibillion-dollar Molokai Ranch Development Corporation (which owns about a third of the island) has for Molokai. At press time, the company's dream was well underway to turn Molokai into the Pacific hub of ecotourism. The company had sunk almost $100 million into remodeling the tranquil town of **Maunaloa**, and at press time was looking to do the same with the sleepier port of **Hale o Lono**. The centerpiece of the Maunaloa project, the **Molokai Ranch Outfitters Center**, provides "ecotourists" with opportunities for platform tent camping and such adventures as cliff-climbing and mountain biking. The latest addition to Molokai Ranch Development Corporation's (MRDC) complement of attractions is **The Lodge at Molokai Ranch**, a recently opened high-end resort that is expected to make its closest competition, **Kaluakoi Hotel and Golf Club**, look like primitive digs. Second-, third-, and fourth-generation islanders are understandably resistant to the company's plans, although avoidance, rather than outright opposition, has characterized their approach to the encroaching development.

There is only one main road on the island, running from one end to the other, and, unlike those on Lanai, most of the sights worth seeing don't require a four-wheel-drive vehicle. Although there are tour companies that will shuttle you around, Molokai is best traveled by car so you can set your own pace (it's impossible to get lost here, even without a map).

Pacific Ocean

Kalaupapa
Airport

Kalaupapa
Peninsula

Kalaupapa
Harbor

Kalaupapa

St. Philomena's
Church

Haupu Bay

Kalaupapa
National
Historic
Park

Waikolu
Lookout

*Molokai
Forest
Reserve*

▲ Kamakou
Mountain
4,970 ft.

'uukapele Ave.

Hoolehua

rington Ave.

21

omomi Ave.

Hoolehua
Airport

Maunaloa Hwy

19

16 18

15 17

•**Kalae**

Kualapuu

(470)

Maunahui Rd.

*Halawa Valley
County Park*

1

*Halawa
Bay*

Halawa

•**Waialua**

•**Pauwalu**

•**Pukoo**

(460)

Kapuaiwa
Coconut Grove

14

**For nos. 9-13,
see pg. 104**

Kaunakakai

8

7

•**Kamiloloa**

Kaluaaha 3

2

Kawela

(450)

Kamehameha V Hwy

Kamalo

5

6

4 **Ualapue**

*Kalohi
Channel*

*Pailolo
Channel*

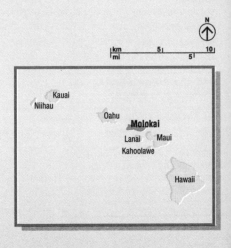

N

| km | 5 | 10 |
| mi | 5 | |

Kauai

Niihau

Oahu

Molokai

Lanai

Maui

Kahoolawe

Hawaii

Area code 808 unless otherwise noted.

Getting to Molokai

Airports

Hoolehua Airport

Seven miles northwest of the island's main town of **Kaunakakai, Hoolehua Airport** (567.6140) is open daily from 5:30AM to 7:30PM. The single terminal is tended by just a few employees.

Airlines

Island Air, interisland 567.6115, 800/652.6541
   from the mainland............................800/323.3345

Hawaiian 800/882.8811
   from the mainland............................800/367.5320

Molokai Air Shuttle......................................545.4988

Pacific Wings 567.6844, 888/575.4546

Getting to and from
Hoolehua Airport

By Bus

The only bus serving **Hoolehua Airport** is the shuttle to and from the **Kaluakoi** resort. The service is for resort guests only (552.2555). The shuttle operates during business hours.

By Car

Two car-rental companies have booths at the airport: **Budget** (567.6877, 800/BUD.GET7) and **Dollar** (567.6156, 800/342.7398 interisland, 800/342.7398 mainland).

By Taxi

There are usually cabs at the airport to meet arriving travelers.

Kalaupapa Airport

Two round-trip flights per day land on the tiny airstrip at Kalaupapa (567.6331). The airport here has no facilities except rest rooms, but travelers won't need any; they'll be whisked aboard a van that will have them in the center of town in a matter of minutes.

Airlines

Island Air, interisland 567.6115, 800/652.6541
   from the mainland............................800/323.3345

Molokai Air Shuttle......................................545.4988

Pacific Wings 567.6844, 888/575.4546

Getting to and from
Kalaupapa Airport

Those who fly to Kalaupapa must take the van tour run by **Damien Tours** (567.6171); there is no other way to visit the historic town.

Boats The *Maui Princess* (661.8397, 800/275.6969) goes from Lahaina, Maui to Kaunakakai on Tuesday and Thursday at 6:30AM (return boat leaves Molokai at 2PM). The cost ranges from $69 to $129, depending on whether a guided tour or rented car is desired.

Getting Around Molokai

Bicycles Bicycles can be rented at **Molokai Bicycle** (553.3931, 800/709.BIKE) in Kaunakakai.

Buses There is no public bus system on the island.

Driving Most roads on Molokai are paved and easy to travel. Four-wheel-drive vehicles are usually not necessary. Car-rental companies at **Hoolehua Airport** are listed above.

Hiking The island's best-known excursion is to **Halawa Valley** at the eastern end. At press time, the only way to hike here was with a tour operator; try **Maa Hawaii** (558.8184). Check at **Molokai Ranch Outfitters Center** (552.2791) for expeditions, both guided and unguided, to other sites.

Parking You can park pretty much anywhere on Molokai. The only place on the island with meters is **Hoolehua Airport.**

Taxis Two cab companies share the Molokai business—**Kukui Tours and Limousines** (553.5133) and **Molokai Off-Road Tours and Taxi** (553.3369), both based in Kaunakakai.

Tours **Damien Tours** (567.6171) is the only operator that offers excursions to Kalaupapa, site of the historic leper colony. **Kukui Tours and Limousines** (553.5133) runs a half-day tour that covers the town of Maunaloa, a macadamia-nut farm, coffee fields, the **Kalaupapa Peninsula** overlook, and Kaunakakai. **Kukui**'s full-day tour stops at all of the above, plus fishponds, a church built by Father Damien, and Halawa Valley. **Molokai Off-Road Tours** (553.3369) has day trips to **Waikolu Lookout.**

Walking Stroll down the wide main street of Kaunakakai, stopping to shop and snack along the way; the excursion will take about an hour if you walk slowly. The sugar town of Maunaloa is also a nice place for leisurely on-foot explorations.

FYI

Shopping Kaunakakai is the place to buy T-shirts and other souvenirs. The town of Maunaloa has a farmers' market, a kite shop, and gift shops.

Visitors' Information Centers The **Molokai Visitors' Association** (PO Box 960, Kaunakakai, HI 96748, 553.3876; fax 553.5288; www.visitmolokai.com) will answer questions and provide information over the phone. It is open to travelers during the week at **Milepost 0** on **Kamehameha V Highway.** Call ahead to receive an extensive packet of information in the mail.

Phone Book

Emergencies

Ambulance/Fire/Police 911

Hospital (Molokai General Hospital) 553.5331

Pharmacy..553.5790

Police (nonemergency) 553.5355

East Molokai

1 Halawa Valley County Park The valley begins at the eastern tip of the island, where Kamehameha V Highway (Route 450) ends. Hundreds of families once occupied the valley, but a tidal wave in 1946 prompted their evacuation, and only a few families returned. Remains of the once-thriving taro patches and old irrigation ditches can still be seen. Intrepid hikers can get to the waterfalls at the back of the valley, but as a result of a liability suit trekkers must now go with a tour company (**Maa Hawaii,** 558.8184, for example). The black-sand beach at the trailhead is gorgeous in its own right. ♦ Kamehameha V Hwy, Halawa

2 Molokai Horse & Wagon Ride If you can't find a luau on the island, this will suffice nicely. Owner Junior Rawlins drives passengers from a beachside hut up into a 50-acre mango patch and straight up the mountain to a turn-of-the-century stone temple. You'll cross a stream (on the wagon), smell the wild guavas and flowers, and return to the beach, where you'll be greeted with a laid-back, Hawaiian-style barbecue. The whole deal takes about two hours. ♦ Fee. M-Sa 10:30AM. Kamehameha V Hwy (between Miles 16 and 15). 558.8380

3 Our Lady of Seven Sorrows Church Father Damien built this white wooden structure in 1874. A statue of the priest, the island's most famous former resident, stands in the church pavilion. ♦ Kamehameha V Hwy, Kaluaaha

4 Wavecrest Resort $$ All 10 rental units in these Marc Resorts–owned wooden buildings front the ocean, which makes the condominiums a pretty fair bargain, although they're far from everything but the ocean. All the units have full kitchens, and a few have TV sets; none is air-conditioned. There's a pool and a general store on the premises. Solitude seekers, look no further. ♦ Kamehameha V Hwy, Ualapue. 558.8103, 800/535.0085; fax 558.8206 ♿

5 The Neighborhood Store ★$ Both counter and take-out service are available at this tiny place that's vintage Hawaii. Pick up a *bento* (Japanese-style boxed lunch) or settle in for a plate of sautéed mahimahi and "talk story" with the locals. ♦ Lunch counter ♦ M-Tu, Th-Su breakfast and lunch. No credit cards accepted. Kamehameha V Hwy (Mile 12). 558.8498

6 St. Joseph Church This small, white, wood-frame church was the last one built (in 1876) by Father Damien before his death. ♦ Kamehameha V Hwy (between Miles 11 and 10)

7 Hotel Molokai $$ The 56 rustic A-frame bungalows that stood on this site for decades have been given a face-lift by new owners Castle Hotels & Resorts, and include TVs, telephones, quilted Hawaiian bedspreads, woven bamboo wall coverings, and large lanais complete with swinging love seats. There's also a restaurant and pool. ♦ Kamehameha V Hwy, Kamiloloa. 553.5347, 800/367.5004; fax 553.5047; www.castle-group.com ♿

8 Molokai Shores $$ A set of 101 individually owned condominiums (though only 26 are rented to visitors), this complex has long been a haven for residents of other islands. The rental units have ocean views, but the coastline is rocky and there's no beach for swimming. The accommodations have kitchens and cable TV, but no phones or air-conditioning. A pool and a shuffleboard court are on the grounds. There's no restaurant. ♦ Kamehameha V Hwy, Kamiloloa. 553.5954, 800/535.0085; fax 553.5954 ♿

St. Joseph Church

MARK AMMERMAN/NORTH MARKET STREET GRAPHICS

KAUNAKAKAI

Molokai General Hospital

Makaena Pl.

Kaunakakai Gulch

Rock Wall

Home Olu Pl.

Hotel La.

Ilio Rd. Kikipua St.

Kokio St.

460 Maunaloa Hwy.

Manila Rd.

11 12 13 Ala Malama Ave.

Kamoi St.

Kolapa Pl.

10

Alloa St.

Kaunakakai Pl.

Mohala Pl.

Oki Pl.

450 Kamehameha V Hwy.

Kamiloloa Gulch

Beach Pl.

9

Seaside Pl.

Kapaakea Loop

Kaunakakai Harbor

Kaunakakai Landing

Kalohi Channel

N

| km | 1/2 | 1
| mi | 1/4 | 1/2

Kaunakakai

This town inspired the song "The Cock-Eyed Mayor of Kaunakakai," although, truth be told, Kaunakakai has no official mayor (Molokai is technically a part of Maui County). The town's two biggest attractions are its main street, **Ala Malama Avenue,** which looks like a Hollywood Western set in the 1920s, and the three-quarter-mile-long wharf, where local teens cruise up and down in their cars. The pace is blissfully slow.

9 **Pau Hana Inn** $ With lots of down-home charm and a fabulous view of the ocean, this cottage-style inn on the fringe of Kaunakakai features 39 budget-priced rooms, including poolside studios with kitchenettes. The open-air **Pau Hana Inn Restaurant** now offers breakfast to guests only (previously it was a daytime gathering place and the hub of the island's nightlife), and the pool is nice enough—but this place isn't the repeat-visitor destination it used to be as new lodging options have recently emerged in Molokai. There are no phones, TVs, or air-conditioning. ◆ Seaside Pl (just west of Oki Pl). 553.5342, 877/728.4262; fax 553.3928

10 **Molokai Drive Inn** A Molokaian McDonald's of sorts, this take-out counter is a rarity. Try the fresh mahimahi, a perfect complement to the french fries. The hamburgers are also popular, as is the *bento*. ◆ Daily. Kamoi St (between Kamehameha V Hwy and Ala Malama Ave). 553.5655

11 **Outpost Natural Foods** A great stop for a healthy take-out snack, hot or cold, this juice bar is known for its Mexican food, smoothies, and sandwiches. The organically grown produce is mostly fresh from Molokai. ◆ M-F, Su. 70 Makaena Pl (just northwest of Ala Malama Ave). 553.3377

12 Molokai Fish & Dive The island's only sporting goods store is also the home of the "original Molokai T-Shirts & Caps," two items you just can't be without. Snorkeling gear, boogie boards, and fishing poles are available for rent here. Stop in to see the goods and to chat with part-owner Jim Brocker, author of *A Portrait of Molokai,* and a repository of island facts. ♦ Daily. 61 Ala Malama Ave (between Manako La and Makaena Pl). 553.5926 &

12 Molokai Island Creations Swimwear, T-shirts, fragrances, soaps, Hawaiian note cards, original Molokai glassware and coral jewelry, and other Molokai miscellanea are offered at this pleasant country boutique. ♦ Daily. 63 Ala Malama Ave (between Manako La and Makaena Pl). 553.5926 &

13 Kanemitsu Bakery Open since 1925, this bakery is a Molokai legend, with bread that appears on menus all over the island. When other islanders visit here, they inevitably take home some of the famous Molokai bread, a round white loaf that's simply delectable. You'll also find Molokai raisin-nut, onion-cheese, and wheat bread, along with doughnuts, pies, cakes, cinnamon crisps, and a first-rate *haupia* (jelly roll). Try to get here early—everything tends to go fast. ♦ M, W-Su. 73 Ala Malama Ave (between Home Olu Pl and Hotel La). 553.5855

Vest of Kaunakakai

14 Kapuaiwa Coconut Grove Kamehameha V planted a thousand palm trees here in the 1860s when he was only a prince, and several hundred of them can still be seen in one of Hawaii's last surviving royal groves. There's a shoreside park nearby for picnicking. ♦ Maunaloa Hwy (south of Maunahui Rd)

15 Kualapuu Reservoir Molokai residents are very proud of this rubber-lined reservoir. The world's largest, it contains 1.4 billion gallons of water. ♦ Just southwest of Farrington Ave, Kualapuu

16 Kualapuu Cookhouse ★$ A tiny converted plantation house with an old-fashioned diner decor—complete with Formica tables—this restaurant serves enormous omelettes, chili, saimin (noodles and spices), salads, chicken sandwiches, and quarter-pound burgers. But the real specialties are the plate lunches and homemade chocolate macadamia-nut pie. ♦ Diner ♦ Daily breakfast, lunch, and dinner. No credit cards accepted. Farrington Ave (north of Kalae Hwy), Kualapuu. 567.6185

17 Coffees of Hawaii The only coffee grown commercially in Molokai is sold by Malulani Estates from their plantation store, which also displays an oddball assortment of crafts created by local artisans. ♦ Daily. Kalae Hwy (east of Farrington Ave). 567.9023 &

18 Ironwood Hills Golf Course The 1,500-foot elevation and majestic eucalyptus and ironwood trees make this a distinctive and enjoyable course. Play the nine championship holes twice for a full round (par 68, 6,176 yards). ♦ Inexpensive greens fees. Daily. Ahe Pl (north of Kalae Hwy). 567.6000

19 Molokai Mule Ride The popular mule ride down into the leprosy colony at Kalaupapa is a highlight of a Molokai visit; as many as 20 riders a day can saddle up and take the 6-hour tour, which includes 3 hours of rugged riding, a 2-hour tour of the settlement, and lunch. Riders must be over 15 years old, in good physical condition, and weigh less than 250 pounds. Overnight and other packages also are available. ♦ M-Sa, 8AM check-in. Reservations required. Kalae Hwy (Mile 5). 567.6088, 800/567.7550; fax 567.6244; muleman@muleride.com; www.muleride.com

19 Palaau State Park One of Molokai's few designated recreation areas, this 234-acre park forms part of the **Molokai Forest Reserve** on the north side of the island. Camping and picnic facilities are available in this forested mountain area. ♦ Kalae Hwy (just north of Mile 5)

Within Palaau State Park:

Kalaupapa Lookout The exquisite view of Kalaupapa from this 1,500-foot-high lookout is considered one of the finest sights in Hawaii. A series of displays tells the story of the settlement below.

What do Tom Selleck, Jack Lord, Dolly Parton, Tom Cruise, Charo, Steven Spielberg, Jim Nabors, Kenny Rogers, Huey Lewis, George Benson, Dionne Warwick, and Wally "Famous" Amos all have in common? They've each held ownership in a Hawaii business.

Restaurants/Clubs: Red   **Hotels:** Blue
Shops/ Outdoors: Green   **Sights/Culture:** Black

The Hawaii of Old

There are two kinds of Hawaiiana: the real thing and kitsch. An illustration of the former is a stone instrument used by a person in ancient times to pound the root of a taro plant into food. An example of the latter is a ceramic mug made to look as though it's crafted from a hollowed-out coconut. Both varieties of antiques are available in stores throughout the islands.

If the idea of antiquing intrigues you, get a copy of *Hawaiiana* by Martha Blackburn (Shiffer Publishing, 1996), which will not only whet your appetite further, but provide elaborate details on what to look for and how to proceed.

Here are some tips on how to be sure that the piece you're purchasing is authentic:

1. Read up on antiques in general and Hawaiiana in particular.

2. Get a guarantee in writing.

3. Check to see if the store is affiliated with the Better Business Bureau, the Small Business Assocation, or has a certified appraiser on the premises.

The following shops have longstanding reputations: **Anchor House Antiques** in Honolulu, Oahu (471 Kapahulu Ave, at Kanaina Ave, 732.3884); **Islander Trading Company** in the Kapaa area of Kauai (Coconut Marketplace, 484 Kuhio Hwy, at Papaloa Rd, 822.3333); and **South Seas Trading Post** in Lahaina, Maui (780 Front St, at Lahainaluna Rd, 661.3168).

Artifacts

Calabashes—First made in the early 1800s, these often sizable bowls were commonly carved from the wood of kaimani or kou trees and turned using a coral or stone adze. Production took months. The current value is $5,000 and up, depending on size, condition, detail, and other factors. An excellent read on the subject is *Hawaiian Calabash* by W. Jenkins (Booklines Hawaii, 1994).

Kukui Oil Lamps—The kukui tree produces nuts, which in turn produce oil burned by ancient Hawaiians for light in crudely carved stone containers. The current value is $500 and up, depending on size, condition, and detail.

Poi Pounders—These stone implements were used to pound taro roots into the Hawaiian staple poi. The current value is $500 and up, depending on size, condition, and detail.

Collectibles

Aloha Furniture—Made in the 1950s by prisoners on Maui, these thick, chunky home furnishings made from the now pricey koa wood were offloaded in garage sales and even trundled to the dump before coming into vogue in the late 1970s. The current value is $5,000 and up for a full set (sofa, two armchairs, two end tables, and a coffee table), depending on style and condition.

Aloha Shirts—That's right, the ubiquitous aloha shirt—the vintage kind, that is, produced in the 1930s and 1940s—has come into its own. The current value is $125 to several thousand dollars, depending on style and rarity.

Bottles—Soda bottles are some of the most coveted finds in this category, with milk bottles some of the most common. The current value is $5 to hundreds, depending on style, condition, and rarity.

Ceramics—Examples include those coconut mugs, and "hula nodders," the porcelain figures whose loosely connected body parts simulate hip swiveling or head nodding. The current value is $25 to $500, depending on style and rarity.

Fishing Floats—Just a couple of decades ago, these pale blue and amber glass floats were commonly used by Japanese fishing fleets in place of plastic. They went unnoticed until a severed sphere washed up on a local beach. Now the floats are prized possessions; the most coveted are those with stamps on them. The current value is $5 to $125, depending on size, style and color (the amber ones ar rarer and more valuable).

Hula Lamps—Made of pot metal, these were given out a prizes in the Hawaii State Fair in the 1930s. The hardest to find are the ones with the hula girl's arms down at her sides The current value is $500 to $1,100. Reproductions, whic have lately become popular, are selling for upwards of $350.

Matson Menus and Other Memorabilia—The Matson Corporation, now exclusively a cargo shipping line, operated passenger service to faraway Hawaii in the early 1900s. A menu from the earliest days of cruise-ship service is highly prized. The current value is about $125, depending on condition

POGs—Many will remember the bottle-cap craze tha swept the nation in the mid-1990s. The fad originate in Hawaii, where the round, cardboard tops of bottle bearing a range of imprints have been collected and traded by local schoolchildren like marbles for decades. The current value is small change to a couple of dollars, post-craze. During the craze, the most valued caps were bought and sold for over $5

Phallic Rock If you think Mother Nature lacks a sense of humor, check out this large and rather provocative stone, which has given rise to various legends, including the tale that childless women who spend the night at its base soon become pregnant. Bring the camera for this one.

20 Kalaupapa This little town on the flat, isolated Kalaupapa Peninsula on the northern coast of Molokai figures poignantly and tragically in the history of the island. In 1866 the Hawaiian monarchy began banishing people with Hansen's disease (leprosy) to this area, separating them from families and loved ones. Lacking decent food and shelter, they lived here in great misery until their deaths. After arriving in 1873, a Belgian priest named Damien de Veuster chose to live in isolation with these people, selflessly providing them with spiritual and physical aid. Father Damien contracted the disease in 1884 and died five years later, shortly after the completion of his **St. Philomena's Church.**

After his death, Father Damien became known as the "martyr of Molokai" for his heroic dedication to the leprosy victims. When sulfone drugs brought the disease under control in the 1940s, the patients still living here were free to go. They chose to stay, however, as Kalaupapa had been their home since childhood. Today, fewer than 70 residents remain.

A steep, zigzagging trail leads down the 1,600-foot slopes overlooking Kalaupapa, but only those with permits may hike down it, and only those on tours may visit the settlement. (For information on permits and tours contact **Damien Tours,** 567.6171.) Visitors may also fly to Kalaupapa from **Hoolehua Airport** or from Maui (contact the **Activity Information Center,** 800/624.7771). The tours, led by a resident, include a stop at Father Damien's church, a visit to the guide's home, and a picnic lunch.

21 Purdy's All-Natural Macadamia Nut Farm With heavy emphasis on the "all natural" part, friendly and vivacious Tuddie

Purdy will teach you everything you ever wanted to know about macadamia nuts. You'll learn how to crack the hard inner shell of the nut without breaking your nails, how long it takes for a nut to mature (nine months), and how long macadamias have been in Hawaii (more than a hundred years). Purdy will also assure you that macadamia nuts roasted without oil have few calories and no saturated fats or cholesterol (let your conscience be your guide). You'll also learn how to open a coconut and then dip its flesh into honey. Best of all, Purdy will tell you all this just because he thinks you should know, never pressuring visitors to buy his nuts (you will anyway out of guilt). Purdy's nut farm is one of Molokai's top attractions. ♦ M-F 9:30AM-3:30PM; Sa 10AM-2PM. Lihi Pali Ave (between Kulea St and Puukapele Ave), Hoolehua. 567.6601 days, 567.6495 evenings Ꮣ

22 Paniolo Hale Condominiums $$$ Some of the 25 rental units at this 6-acre property on Kepuhi Beach feature private hot tubs on the lanais; all have telephones, full kitchens, and washers and dryers. There's also a pool, and golf at the nearby **Kaluakoi** course (but no restaurant). Choose from studios and one- and two-bedroom suites. ♦ Kakaako Rd (north of Kaluakoi Rd). 552.2731, 800/367.2984; fax 552.2288; paniolo@lava.net; www.lava.net/paniolo

22 Kaluakoi Villas $$ Each of the 74 villas in this Castle Resorts & Hotels property features an ocean view, island-style decor with rattan furnishings, ceiling fans, TV, kitchenette, and private lanai. Guests can use the **Kaluakoi Hotel and Golf Club**'s facilities (see below). ♦ 1131 Kaluakoi Rd (north of Maunaloa Hwy). 552.2721, 800/367.5004; fax 552.2201; www.castle-group.com Ꮣ

22 Ke Nani Kai $$ This Marc Resort property offers 39 large 1- and 2-bedroom suites that are well managed, clean, and set in clusters of wooden buildings. This isn't exactly a deluxe hotel, and there's no restaurant, but it's comfortable, with ocean and mountain views, large kitchens, a pool, TVs, phones, and lanais. It's a five-minute walk to the beach. ♦ Kaluakoi Rd (north of Maunaloa Hwy). 552.2761, 800/552.2761; fax 552.0045

22 Kaluakoi Hotel and Golf Club $$ Molokai's destination resort is an oasis for the traveler who truly wants to get away from it all. The property consists of two-story redwood and ohia structures overlooking a wide stretch of Kepuhi Beach. There are 122 rooms with lanais, high, beamed ceilings, and fans to augment the ocean breezes. A championship golf course, 15-kilometer (9-mile) jogging path, and a pool are for sports enthusiasts. ♦ Kaluakoi Rd (north of Maunaloa Hwy). 552.2555, 800/435.7208; fax 552.2821 ♿

Within the Kaluakoi Hotel and Golf Club:

Ohia Lodge ★$$$ This tiered dining room gives every table a panoramic view of the beach and of Oahu in the distance. At breakfast, Molokai bread makes a splendid French toast. The dinner menu includes Hunan duck, Indonesian herbal chicken, and rack of lamb. ♦ Continental ♦ Daily breakfast and dinner. 552.2555 ♿

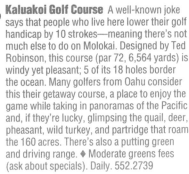

Kaluakoi Hotel & Golf Club

Kaluakoi Golf Course A well-known joke says that people who live here lower their golf handicap by 10 strokes—meaning there's not much else to do on Molokai. Designed by Ted Robinson, this course (par 72, 6,564 yards) is windy yet pleasant; 5 of its 18 holes border the ocean. Many golfers from Oahu consider this their getaway course, a place to enjoy the game while taking in panoramas of the Pacific and, if they're lucky, glimpsing the quail, deer, pheasant, wild turkey, and partridge that roam the 160 acres. There's also a putting green and driving range. ♦ Moderate greens fees (ask about specials). Daily. 552.2739

23 Papohaku Beach If you continue on Kaluakoi Road past the **Kaluakoi Hotel and Golf Club,** you'll see the sign for Papohaku, Hawaii's longest natural white-sand beach. The three-mile stretch is ideal for beachcombing, sunning, and swimming during the calm summer months. ♦ Just northwest of Kaluakoi Rd

24 The Lodge at Molokai Ranch $$$ The Molokai Ranch Development Corporation sunk $11 million into this exclusive 22-unit property with the feel of Old Hawaii to make it the island's high-end lodging of choice. The 6 suites and 16 duplex cottages are decorated in old plantation style, and feature TVs, phones, and air-conditioning. A pool, free shuttle to the beach, and of course, ample activities provided by the **Molokai Ranch Outfitters Center** (see below), are additional highlights of this recently opened resort. There's no restaurant. ♦ 1 Maunaloa Hwy (west of Kaluakoi Rd). 552.2741, 877/PANIOLO; fax 552.2908; www.molokai-ranch.com ♿

MOLOKAI RANCH

H A W A I I

24 Molokai Ranch Outfitters Center "What's there to do on Molokai?" once was the refrain of vacationers considering an interisland hop to this laid-back isle. These days, since the advent of the Molokai Ranch Development Corporation and its well-funded drive to make Molokai an ecotourism center, the question is, "How much can I possibly fit into one vacation?"

Much of what is offered here, though, can only be booked by guests at one of the company-operated lodgings (see **The Lodge at Molokai Ranch**, and **Paniolo Campsite**, below). On-site adventurers can partake in everything from cowherding to backpacking, kayaking to cliff-climbing. Other visitors will have to be satisfied with a mountain-biking tour or whale watching excursion in season. ♦ Daily. 5 Maunaloa Hwy (west of Kaluakoi Rd). 552.2791, 800/254.8871; fax 552.2773

24 Maunaloa Cinemas This modern triplex cinema, owned and operated by the Molokai Ranch Development Corporation, shows first run movies. ♦ Daily. 10 Maunaloa Hwy (west of Kaluakoi Rd). 552.2707 ♿

25 Maunaloa General Store It's the only store within miles of Maunaloa, an old plantation town, and since Molokai Ranch Development Corporation took over its management, the store is a little more modern than in former years. ♦ Daily. 200 Maunaloa Hwy, Maunaloa. 552.2346

25 The Village Grill ★★$$$ The fare at this restaurant gives new meaning to the words "ranch style." Pistol Pete's Prime Rib and Cactus Charlie's Big Catch of the Day are the two most popular menu items come suppertime and the decor continues the theme, with bits hanging from the ceiling and pictures of ranching operations in Hawaii's history hanging on the walls. ♦ American ♦ Daily lunch and dinner. 200 Maunaloa Hwy, Maunaloa. 552.0012 ♿

25 Big Wind Kite Factory and Plantation Gallery It took a windy town like Maunaloa to spawn Hawaii's only kite factory. Jonathan and Daphne Socher design and make kites with images of Diamond Head, tropical fish, giraffes, whales' tails, and other colorful Hawaiian motifs. Adjoining the kite shop is their gallery of local and Indonesian crafts—clothing, handbags, T-shirts, native wood bowls, Balinese carvings, and the like. ♦ M-Sa; Su 10AM-2PM. 120 Maunaloa Hwy, Maunaloa. 552.2364 ♿

26 Paniolo Campsite $$$ This is Molokai Ranch Development Corporation's answer to the baby boomer market, which, they feel, likes the benefits of camping without the liabilities.

A night in a platform tent for two, including round-trip transportation from the airport, three gourmet meals a day, and two activities arranged through the **Molokai Ranch Outfitters Center** (see above), is $185. Hot and cold running water come gratis, but there are no phones or TVs. ♦ South of Maunaloa Hwy. 552.2791, 800/254.8871; fax 552.2773; www.molokai-ranch.com ♿

27 Hale o Lono Harbor The best times to come here are either during Hawaii's annual Aloha Week in September or for the grueling 42-mile international Bankoh Molokai Hoe (Bank of Hawaii Molokai Paddle) canoe race from Molokai to Oahu on the second Sunday in October. Founded in 1952, the race is celebrated as the world's first and foremost long-distance, open-ocean canoeing competition. It begins at southwest Molokai's little Hale o Lono Harbor, crosses the treacherous Kaiwi Channel, and ends at Fort DeRussy Beach in Waikiki. The women's race takes place two weeks earlier.

Lava Lore

Say "volcano" to most people and they envision an eruption that spews miles into the air and takes numerous lives and villages—on the order of Mount St. Helens or Mount Vesuvius—in its wake. The volcanoes, however, that gave birth to the Hawaiian Islands are called "shield" volcanoes, because lava moves just a few miles an hour down the volcano's slope, rather than covering everything in its path in an explosive burst.

Shield volcanoes are formed by a series of undersea eruptions that build until the peak of the accumulated lava nears the ocean's surface. The blasts then mix with air and become more explosive for a while. Once above water, however, the growing land mass sinks into itself, sealing off its vent and forcing the lava to move horizontally under the surface, rather than vertically above it. Lava tubes—some of which have aboveground entrances (such as the **Thurston Lava Tube** in **Hawaii Volcanoes National Park** on the **Big Island**), form when rivers of lava magma crust over while the molten material is still flowing.

Eventually the tube that carried lava inside the earth to the surface folds in on itself, becoming a caldera, or crater. Wind- and water-carved lava forge craggy peaks and smooth valleys. *Aa*—rough, crumbly lava—and *pahoehoe*—smoother, ropey-looking lava—are scattered at random across the landscape. (The chemical makeup of lava—silica, iron oxide, magnesia, and lime—is the same, regardless of its appearance. The difference is in the amount of gas remaining when the lava hardens.)

Hawaiians, however, don't see the nature of volcanoes in such practical terms. To them, the *aina* (land) is sacred, integral to human spiritual life, and volcanoes are inhabited by Pele, a goddess worshiped by the people for her power to create and destroy Hawaii's land at will. "Pele's hair" and "Pele's tears" are used to describe volcanic glass that forms thin strands (in the former term) and hardened lava drops (in the latter), rather than the scientific nomenclatures. And each time a lava flow spares a home or town, as when one missed **Hilo** in 1942 when the lava stopped just 12 miles short of urban boundaries, Pele is praised.

While examples of *aa* and *pahoehoe* are prevalent in many parts of the Big Island—the state's youngest island—and visible at **Diamond Head, Koko Head, Hanauma Bay,** and **Punchbowl Crater** on **Oahu,** and **La Perouse Bay** and **Haleakala** on **Maui,** Hawaii's only currently active volcano is **Kilauea,** located at the center of **Hawaii Volcanoes National Park.** Known as the world's only "drive-up" volcano, Kilauea has been erupting nearly continuously since 1983, making it the world's most active volcano. Output there has been estimated at 650,000 cubic yards a day, about 55,000 truckloads of cement—enough to submerge each of 38 football fields under a mile of lava.

Because there is time to get out of the path of a shield volcano, only one life has been taken by lava in Hawaii in modern times—that of a photographer named Prem Nagar who was instantly killed by 2,200-degree magma in **Hawaii Volcanoes National Park** when a newly cooled shelf of land on which he stood collapsed into the ocean.

Hawaii's dormant and inactive volcanoes (the former may erupt at any time—even though the last explosion was centuries ago—and the latter are believed to have stopped erupting permanently) include **Mauna Kea** and **Mauna Loa,** also on the Big Island, as well as Haleakala on Maui. Diamond Head on Oahu has been dormant for more than 150,000 years. **Kauai,** the oldest Hawaiian island, has not had any active or dormant volcanoes for five million years.

In recent years, geologists have discovered a new volcano 1,000 yards underwater 30 miles southeast of the Big Island. Named **Loihi,** it's expected to breach the surface within 10,000 years.

KEELY EDWARDS

Oahu

With its avenues of avarice, high-rise hotels, legendary beaches, historical battleships, and banzai surfers, Oahu (O-*ah*-hoo) is the nucleus of Hawaii, the island that has it all and then some. Although smaller than Maui and only slightly larger than Kauai, Oahu is where the majority of Hawaii's citizens choose to live— 900,000 people, a whopping 75 percent of the state's entire population. Consequently, Oahu has more problems than any other island. It's one of the greatest ironies of tourism in Oahu that the J.O.J. (just off the jet) tourists come to Hawaii expecting to get away from it all, only to find themselves stuck in **Honolulu's** rush-hour traffic and hopelessly lost (the one-way street system in Honolulu is comical at best). And developers continue to build mammoth creations, including a new convention center in **Waikiki** and the $3-billion **Koolina Resort** in **Kapolei** (touted as the isle's Second City) on the **Waianae Coast.** Fortunately, Oahu's undaunted aloha spirit compensates for these excesses. Even in the major metropolis of Honolulu, this remains a friendly island whose people take great pride in their homeland. Cars here still slow down for yellow lights, warm smiles greet you at the hotels and restaurants, and there is plenty of prime beachfront space for relaxing.

In addition to having some of the most exclusive hotels (the **Royal Hawaiian,** the **Halekulani,** the **Sheraton Moana Surfrider,** the **Kahala Mandarin Oriental**), famous attractions (**Pearl Harbor,** the **Polynesian Cultural Center**), finest restaurants (**Roy's, La Mer**), and largest shopping malls (**Ala Moana, Royal Hawaiian**) in the state, Oahu also has **TheBus,** the only serious public transportation system in Hawaii. These seemingly ubiquitous brown-and-yellow behemoths will, for only a buck, take you anywhere on the island—the **Greater Honolulu** area, which includes Pearl Harbor, Waikiki, and the **Diamond Head** and **Koko Head** volcanoes; the scenic windward side, from **Kahaluu** to **Makapuu Point,** site of the popular **Sea Life Park;** the **North Shore,** home of fabled **Sunset Beach,** monster waves, and insane surfers; and the Waianae Coast on the western side of the island. All of these areas warrant exploring. The North Shore in particular makes for a pleasant day trip (not to be missed when the voluminous surfing waves come in), while the stunning views across the **Pali Highway** and

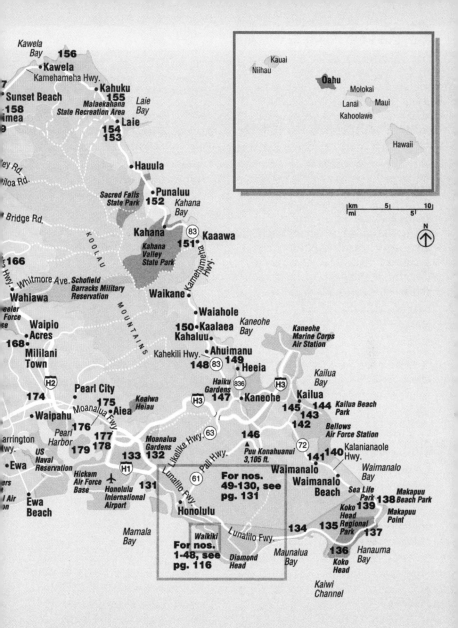

For nos. 49–130, see pg. 131

For nos. 1–48, see pg. 116

round the southeastern tip of the island offer a more close-at-hand break
rom the cityscape.

asically, two types of tourists come to Oahu: the first-timers, who are at the
nercy of their travel agents' advice; and the frequent flyers, who know
xactly where to go and what to do. The former usually end up in Waikiki,
/hich is paradise to some and a bumper-to-bumper nightmare to most
thers. Waikiki suffers from overabundance; there is simply too much of
verything in too small a space, overcrowded with coupon-laden tourists
urchasing cheap souvenirs and dining at overrated, overpriced restaurants.
ut "vacationing" is a relative term, and what some would consider as much
un as watching paint dry is a great time for others. That's the key to Oahu—
here *is* something for everyone: you just have to know where to look.

Area code 808 unless otherwise noted.

Getting to Oahu

Airport

Honolulu International Airport (HNL)

Hawaii's main airport has two bi-level terminals, one for domestic flights, the other for international; more than a thousand flights take off and land on its runways each day. The airport is nine miles northwest of Waikiki.

Airport Services

Airport Emergencies	711 on courtesy phones
Information	836.6413
Lost and Found	836.6547
Parking	861.1260
Police	836.6606

Airlines

Aloha	484.1111, 800/367.5250
American	833.7600, 800/433.7300
Canada 3000	888/226.3000
Canadian	839.2244
from the mainland	800/426.7000
Continental	523.0000, 800/525.0280
Delta	800/221.1212
Hawaiian	838.1555, 800/367.5320
Island Air, interisland	484.2222, 800/652.6541
from the mainland	800/323.3345
Northwest, interisland	955.2255, 800/225.2525
from the mainland	800/441.1818
Qantas	800/227.4500
in Australia	13/13/13
TWA	800/221.2000
United	831.5225, 800/241.6522

Getting to and from Honolulu International Airport

By Bus

Oahu's efficient bus system, aptly named **TheBus** (848.5555), pulls up at the curb near the baggage-claim area regularly, with connections to such far-flung locations as the North Shore, Waikiki, **Windward Oahu** (the towns of **Kailua** and **Kaneohe**), Honolulu, and just about everywhere else. The fare for a ride anywhere **TheBus** goes is only a dollar (50¢ for students).

In addition, a program called the "Oahu Discovery Passport" enables visitors to purchase a 4-day pass at any one of 30 **ABC** stores for only $10. The problem is that no luggage is permitted on board

(taxi companies lobbied for and got this proviso so that the bus company wouldn't nab their business). Wheedling and choking back the occasional sob ma get you on with a small knapsack at an off hour, but you have the usual amount of luggage forget it.

Some Waikiki hotels offer airport shuttle service; be sure to ask when you're booking your room.

By Car

You can reach downtown Honolulu on **Interstate H1** Interstate signs are easy to follow between the city and the airport. On the return trip, stay to the right o H1 and watch for the airport sign or you'll end up at Pearl Harbor.

The airport is usually a 20-minute drive from Honolulu, although the trip may take an hour during rush hours (Monday through Friday 7 to 8:30AM an 4 to 6PM). On Friday afternoon traffic is even slower you may as well stay in the airport lounge until after dinnertime. Long- and short-term parking lots are within easy walking distance of the main terminal.

The following car-rental companies have 24-hour counters at the airport:

Alamo	833.4585, 800/327.9633
Avis	834.5564, 800/331.1212
Budget	836.1700, 800/527.0700
Dollar	831.2331, 800/800.4000
Hertz	831.3500, 800/CAR.RENT
National	831.3800, 800/227.7368

By Limousine

A ride between the airport and downtown Honolulu via limousine costs about $40. A reputable local company is **Charley's Taxi and Tours** (531.2333).

By Taxi

Taxi stands are outside the baggage-claim area. Loc for an attendant holding a radio; he will call for a cab if there isn't one waiting. A ride from the airport into Honolulu will cost about $20.

Interisland Carriers

Aloha Airlines flies to Honolulu from **Keahole-Kona International** and **Hilo International Airports** on the Big Island, **Lihue Airport** on Kauai, and **Kahului Airport** on Maui. **Hawaiian Airlines** has flights to Honolulu from those airports as well as from **Lanai Airport** on Lanai and **Hoolehua Airport** on Molokai. **Aloha Island Air** flies to Honolulu from the **Kahului, Kapalua–West Maui,** and **Hana Airports** on Maui; from both the **Molokai** and **Kalaupapa Airports** on Molokai; and from **Lanai Airport** on Lanai.

Getting Around Oahu

Bicycles, Mopeds, and Motorcycles

Although parts of the island are too overdeveloped for slow-moving creatures on wheels, places like Waikiki and the North Shore are tailor-made for bicycle, moped, and motorcycle riding. The folks at **Blue Sky Rentals** (1920 Ala Moana Blvd, between

Kalakaua Ave and Ena Rd, Waikiki, 947.0101) can provide you with a rented bicycle or moped. You'll need a valid driver's license to rent a moped. **Ferrari Rentals** (942.8725) rents everything from Ninjas to Harleys to licensed bike hounds.

Buses

Oahu's very efficient bus system, **TheBus** (848.5555), covers the entire island every day for one dollar one way. It's one of the best deals in Hawaii. It's also accessible to people with disabilities.

Driving

The good news is that driving on Oahu is much the same as driving elsewhere in the US. The bad news is that the island has the heaviest traffic in the state, and progress can be "slow" to "no" within a 10-mile radius of Honolulu Monday through Friday between 7 and 8:30AM and 4 and 6PM—and driving on Friday afternoons is a thoroughly hopeless proposition.

A single road, known as **Farrington Highway,** H1, **Route 93, Kalanianaole Highway, Route 72, Route 83, Kahekili Highway,** and **Kamehameha Highway,** depending on which portion you're on, skirts the coast. Sightseers can't drive completely around the island, since the northwestern tip, **Kaena Point,** is accessible by four-wheel-drive vehicle only. Another highway, called **Route 99,** Kamehameha Highway, and **Interstate H2** at various points, bisects the island, meandering between Honolulu and the North Shore. A new highway, **Interstate H3,** goes from Kaneohe to Honolulu.

The main thoroughfares in Waikiki are **Kalakaua** and **Kuhio Avenues;** traffic on Kalakaua runs east toward Diamond Head, while cars on Kuhio move west toward Honolulu. In Honolulu, cars driving east on **King Street** arrive in Waikiki; while those moving west on **Beretania Street** wind up in **Chinatown.** Many downtown streets are one way, and there are only two ways around the **Ala Wai Canal** into Waikiki—take Kalakaua Avenue from Honolulu or **Kapahulu Avenue** from the **University of Hawaii** area.

Hiking

Some of the most popular half- and full-day hikes are to the top of **Diamond Head,** to the waterfall at the end of the **Sacred Falls Trail** on the North Shore, and along one of the lush loops off **Tantalus Drive** in the hills overlooking Honolulu. For more information, contact the Hawaii chapter of the **Sierra Club** (PO Box 2877, Honolulu, HI 96803, 538.6616).

Limousines

This isn't a big industry on Oahu, but several companies will arrange transportation and tours in luxurious stretch limos, complete with televisions and bars. One such company is **Charley's Taxi and Tours** (see above), which operates 24 hours a day.

Parking

Finding a parking place in Honolulu and Waikiki can be challenging, particularly during business hours for the former and nightclub hours for the latter. In Waikiki, try the second-level garage at the **Royal Hawaiian Shopping Center** (2201 Kalakaua Ave, at

Lewers St); parking is free with validation at one of the center stores (no purchase necessary). In Honolulu, try the **Bishop Square Parking Garage** (1001 Bishop St, at S King St, 536.0127). There are also metered spaces on the street. A caveat: If you park on Beretania or King Streets on a weekday, check the signs for "No Parking" hours. All parked cars will be towed from the streets at those times. If you forget, expect to pay about $75.

Taxis

Don't wait for a cab to drive past (especially if you're not right in Honolulu or Waikiki)—call **Charley's Taxi and Tours** (see above) or **The Cab** (422.2222). Both serve the entire island.

Tours

The top tour operators here are **Robert's Hawaii** (539.9400) and **Trans-Hawaiian Services** (566.7420). Both offer half- and full-day trips by bus or van to Diamond Head, Pearl Harbor, the **National Cemetery of the Pacific, Hanauma Bay,** and other attractions.

Specialized tours are offered by dive companies (**Aaron's Dive Shops,** 262.2333), sailing charter firms (**Honolulu Sailing Company,** 239.3900), ecotourism businesses (**Oahu Nature Tours,** 924.2473, 800/861.6018), helicopter operators (**Rainbow Pacific Helicopters,** 834.1111), and others. One of the most appealing packages is offered by **Atlantis Adventures** (973.9811) and includes admission to **Waimea Valley Adventure Park; Sea Life Park;** a submarine tour; and either a kayak tour, horseback-riding excursion, or mountain-bike ride.

Honolulu Time Walks (2634 S King St, between Waialae and University Aves, No. 3, 943.0371) offers a variety of inexpensive, entertaining three-hour tours: living-history, crime-beat, ghost, wartime Honolulu, children's tour, Chinatown . . . the list goes on. Other walking tours of Chinatown are offered by the **Hawaii Heritage Center** (1128 Smith St, between N Pauahi and N Hotel Sts, 521.2749) and the **Chinese Chamber of Commerce** (42 N King St, between Nuuanu Ave and Smith St, 533.3181).

Trolleys

The Waikiki Trolley (596.2199) offers narrated tours of Waikiki and Honolulu daily from 8:30AM to 11PM. The two-hour "Old Town Honolulu" tours depart every 15 minutes from the **Royal Hawaiian Shopping Center** for the **Bishop Museum;** the route includes **Iolani Palace,** Honolulu's historic waterfront, and other sights. Passengers can ride all day for one price, getting off and on at will. The trolley also shuttles between central Waikiki hotels and the **Aloha Tower Marketplace** daily from 9AM to 2PM.

Walking

You can't see everything in a day (or a week, for that matter), but Waikiki and Honolulu are both good places for long, meandering walks. Both areas are organized on a grid pattern and are easy to explore. Kalakaua and Kuhio Avenues are the main arteries in Waikiki; King and Beretania Streets are the main thoroughfares in Honolulu.

FYI

Shopping

Hyper-commercial Waikiki is heaven for some shoppers, hell for others. Good buys are aloha shirts, muumuus, marine art, Hawaiian calendars, macadamia-nut candy, coconut syrup, Hawaiian-print fabric, grass skirts, coconut hats, fruit jelly, Kona coffee, Hawaiian music, surf paraphernalia, T-shirts, tiki torches, and koa wood bowls.

To get a sense of your souvenir options, start by window-shopping, with Waikiki as your first target. Most stores don't close until 11PM, so take it slowly. After walking Kalakaua Avenue end to end, turn around and do Kuhio Avenue and the side streets.

Other favorite shopping stops are: the **Ala Moana Shopping Center** (1450 Ala Moana Blvd, between Atkinson Dr and Piikoi St, Honolulu, 946.2811), home of 200 stores including **Neiman-Marcus** and **Nordstrom;** the alfresco **International Marketplace** (2330 Kalakaua Ave, between Kaiulani Ave and Duke's La, Waikiki); the two-story **Ward Warehouse** (1050 Ala Moana Blvd, between Kamakee St and Ward Ave, Honolulu, 591.8411); and the neighboring **Ward Centre** (1200 Ala Moana Blvd, between Queen and Kamakee Sts, Honolulu, 591.8411).

Tickets

Looking for tickets to a cultural, musical, or athletic event? Check with the **Blaisdell Center Box Office** (777 Ward Ave, between Kapiolani Blvd and S King St, Honolulu, 591.2211) or **The Connection** (phone orders only, 545.4000).

Visitors' Information Centers

The central office of the **Hawaii Visitors and Convention Bureau** (**HVCB**; 2270 Kalakaua Ave, No. 801, Honolulu, HI 96815, 923.1811; fax 924.0290; www.gohawaii.com) is open Monday through Friday.

Phone Book

Emergencies

Ambulance/Fire/Police	911
AAA Emergency Road Service	800/222.4357
Dental Emergency	845.0686
Hospital (Queen's Medical Center)	538.9011
Locksmith (24-hour)	946.1011
Pharmacy	737.1777
Poison Center	941.4411
Police (nonemergency)	529.3111

Visitors' Information

Better Business Bureau	536.6936
Handicapped Visitors' Information	586.8121
Hosteling International	946.0591
TheBus	848.5555
Time	983.3211

Waikiki

Waikiki, with its long stretch of sand set against the romantic **Koolau Mountains,** has long been a favorite vacation spot. Oahu's *alii* (nobility) came here to surf and swim long before Kamehameha conquered the island, and hotels have catered to mainland tourists since the swampy area was drained early in this century. It was the great building boom of the 1950s, however, that made Waikiki a bustling urban resort area. Bounded by the **Ala Wai Canal** and **Diamond Head,** Waikiki is two miles long, a half-mile wide, and chock-full of hotels, condominiums, restaurants, and stores. There's no denying that it's commercial and crowded. But Waikiki retains its natural attractions—the mountains and Diamond Head Crater, frequent rainbows, spectacular sunsets, and of course, great beaches. Add an array of sports and activities, first-class restaurants, high-quality entertainment, and a few cultural attractions, and you will see why vacationers continue to flock to Waikiki.

1 Hawaii Prince $$$$ Created in a meant-to-be-noticed style best described as "international opulence," this luxurious hotel boasts English slate, Spanish glass, Italian marble (some say there is too much marble), Japanese tile, and French accessories. All 521 rooms, including 57 1- and 2-bedroom suites, have floor-to-ceiling windows overlooking the yacht harbor. A pool and whirlpool are on the premises as well.

Although the hotel is within walking distance of **Ala Moana Beach Park** and **Ala Moana Shopping Center,** a free shuttle service takes guests to both places and to most other attractions in Waikiki, including 2 nearby tennis courts and a 27-hole golf course. ♦ 100 Holomoana St (north of Hobron La). 956.1111, 800/321.6248; fax 800/946.0811; www.westin.com &

Within the Hawaii Prince:

Prince Court ★★★$$$$ The menu changes monthly at this dining spot, but it might include *kiawe*-roasted pork chops; sautéed catch of the day over angel-hair pasta; and deep-sea prawns stuffed with blue-crab hash with black bean, tomato, and fennel sauces. The decor is chic and modern, with a central fountain and works of fine art, including a painting by Marc Chagall. The view of the harbor is cheerful by day and romantic at night. ♦ Hawaiian Regional ♦ M-Sa breakfast, lunch, and dinner; Su brunch and dinner. Reservations recommended. 956.1111 &

Hakone ★★★$$$$ The dishes served here are both traditional and exquisite: *kaiseki* (prix-fixe dinners of soup, pickles, sashimi, broiled fish, and other Japanese favorites), sukiyaki, noodles, tempura, and assorted sashimi. When in season, the Kona crab is cooked to perfection. The dining room is elegant in its simplicity, with delicate Japanese paintings and carved wood furniture from Japan. ♦ Japanese ♦ Tu-F lunch and dinner; Sa dinner. Reservations recommended. 956.1111 &

2 Red Lobster ★★$$$ A **Red Lobster** is a **Red Lobster** is a **Red Lobster.** The advantage to dining here is that you know what you're getting (which can also be the disadvantage to dining here). The all-you-can-eat deals on Alaskan king crab legs, steak and lobster, and shrimp can't be beaten. The airy interior is filled with plants, wood, and bamboo. ♦ Seafood ♦ Daily lunch and dinner. 1765 Ala Moana Blvd (at Hobron La). 955.5656

3 Ilikai Hotel $$$$ Located on the outer fringe of Waikiki overlooking the **Ala Wai Yacht Harbor,** this 780-room high-rise offers a compromise for people who want to be near the action but not consumed by it. Although dramatically eclipsed by the **Hawaii Prince** hotel next door, this property still reigns as Waikiki's acknowledged tennis center, with two courts (including a lighted court with artificial grass) and a resident tennis pro. In addition there are two pools, a fitness center, and three restaurants. Nearby you'll find a placid beachfront lagoon and **Ala Moana Beach Park;** the **Ala Moana Shopping Center,** a mecca for shopping enthusiasts, is only a five-minute walk away. Many of the large guest rooms include full kitchens. ♦ 1777 Ala Moana Blvd (between Kalia Rd and Hobron La). 949.3811, 800/245.4524; fax 946.1523; wilisales@lava.net; www.nokko.com &

Within the Ilikai Hotel:

Canoes at the Ilikai ★★$$$ The cuisine at this high-end eatery runs to such Pacific Rim dishes as rotisserie chicken, teriyaki chicken (an island favorite), and local fish prepared Polynesian style. There's a nice view of the harbor from the terrace and split-level dining room, and live entertainment in the lounge on Tuesday, Thursday, Saturday, and Sunday. ♦ Pacific Rim ♦ Daily breakfast, lunch, and dinner. 949.3811 &

Paddles Bar The deal here is the all-you-can-eat *pupu* (appetizer) menu, available Monday through Friday from 5:30 to 7:30PM for $10 (give the teriyaki skewers a try). Hawaiian entertainment is featured here on Monday, Wednesday, and Friday evenings. ♦ Daily 10AM-11PM. 949.3811 &

4 Hilton Hawaiian Village $$$$ With a total room count of 2,545 in 2 towers, this is the largest hotel in the state—and it's going to get even larger with the addition of a third tower, slated to be constructed at press time.

Just short of a self-contained village, it has more than a hundred shops, 20 restaurants and lounges, 3 pools (one has 2 tiers), beautifully landscaped gardens, banquet and convention facilities for up to 2,400 people, a 6-story parking garage, and a boat dock. Those seeking an even more upscale stay should check into the **Alii Tower,** an exclusive hotel within the hotel, with its own separate guest reception area, concierge, private pool, and exercise room. The garish 16,000-tile rainbow mural on the **Rainbow Tower**'s exterior is the tallest mosaic mural in the world, according to *Guinness.* A big plus is the choice location on Kahanamoku Beach, with catamaran sailing, Pearl Harbor cruises, and other outdoor activities. ♦ 2005 Kalia Rd (between Paoa Pl and Ala Moana Blvd). 949.4321, 800/445.8667; fax 947.7815; www.hilton.com &

Within the Hilton Hawaiian Village:

Benihana of Tokyo ★$$$ Not only is everything here cooked (making it a perfect choice for those who avoid raw fish), cooking is the main attraction. Chefs perform at the *teppanyaki* grills set in the middle of tables of eight, slashing at beef, lobster, chicken, shrimp, and vegetables with blinding speed. ♦ Japanese ♦ Daily lunch and dinner. Reservations recommended. Rainbow Bazaar. 955.5955 &

GOLDEN DRAGON

Golden Dragon ★★★$$$$ A festive atmosphere prevails when Chef Steve Chiang serves up Imperial beggar's chicken (spiced and cooked for most of a day; 24-hour advance notice required) and Peking duck, the signature dishes of this vermilion and black Chinese restaurant. The extensive menu also includes such traditional Cantonese dishes as lemon chicken, smoked duck, and lobster in curry sauce. ♦ Chinese ♦ Tu-Su dinner. Reservations recommended. Rainbow Tower. 946.5336 &

Bali by the Sea ★★$$$$ With spectacular views of Waikiki Beach and Diamond Head, this restaurant lives up to its name. A distinguished roster of visiting chefs specializes in fresh seafood and imaginative sauces—*opakapaka* (pink snapper) with basil sauce, tiger prawns on linguine, and herb-crusted rack of lamb. ♦ Continental ♦ M-Sa breakfast, lunch, and dinner. Reservations recommended. Rainbow Tower. 941.2254 &

Atlantis Submarines Two submarines (48- and 64-passenger), fitted with viewing ports, have been providing 2-hour excursions off Waikiki Beach for years, letting visitors in on a world they might not otherwise see. Those who dive or even snorkel will most likely not enjoy this as much as those who have no other way to see eels, parrot fish, sharks, and dozens of other undersea inhabitants. ♦ Fee. Daily. Hotel pier. 973.9811; fax 973.9840

5 Wailana Coffee House $ This Honolulu institution offers typical coffeehouse fare. Nothing special here, but it's very popular among residents and tourists. (Parking is a nightmare, so use the garage in the same building and validate your ticket.) ♦ Coffeehouse ♦ Daily 24 hours. 1860 Ala Moana Blvd (at Ena Rd). 955.1764 &

6 California Pizza Kitchen ★★$$ The immensely popular pizza-and-pasta chain has successfully invaded Honolulu, serving oven-fired pizzas with an eclectic choice of toppings, including rosemary chicken and potato, Peking duck, and Thai chicken. The ingredients are fresh and the crusts are just perfect (try the honey-wheat dough). Even the pasta dishes stand out. If you can't decide what to order, the Sante Fe chicken pizza is a sure thing. An extra bonus: There's validated parking for two hours. ♦ Pizza/Italian ♦ Daily lunch and dinner. 1910 Ala Moana Blvd (between Kalakaua Ave and Ena Rd). 955.5161 & Also at: Kahala Mall, 4211 Waialae Ave (at Kilauea Ave), Honolulu. 737.9446 &

DOUBLETREE ALANA WAIKIKI HOTEL

7 Doubletree Alana Waikiki $$$$ This 19-story property is marketed mostly in Japan and is often crowded. The 313 guest rooms are decorated in a modern yet subdued manner, with meticulous attention to detail. Amenities include a pool, fitness center, business center, and conference facilities; room service is provided by the hotel's **Padovani's Bistro & Grill,** a restaurant operated by Philippe Padovani, the former chef at Lanai's **Manele Bay Hotel.** ♦ 1956 Ala Moana Blvd (between Kalakaua Ave and Ena Rd). 941.7275, 800/367.6070; fax 949.0996; www.doubletreehotels.com &

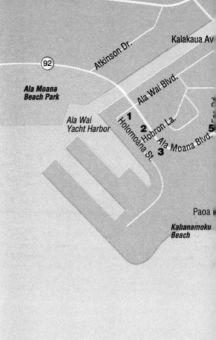

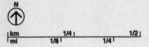

8 Wave Waikiki For Waikiki (and all of Hawaii), this is as wild as the nightlife gets. (The islands' trendy clubs are tame by mainland standards.) Strictly for the young and tireless, this hot spot features live music until late into the night and DJ-spun dance music until much, much later. ♦ Cover. Daily 9PM-4AM. 1877 Kalakaua Ave (between Ena Rd and Ala Wai Blvd). 941.0424 &

9 Eggs 'n Things ★$ An institution for insomniacs, late-night party fiends, and workers getting off the graveyard shift, this is the place to come for a midnight snack or early breakfast. Try a spinach, bacon, and cheese omelette; lemon crepes; or pancakes with macadamia nuts, chocolate chips, pecans, raisins, or bananas. Fresh mahimahi, cajun swordfish, and *ono* (wahoo) straight from the owner's fishing boat are favorites, too. There's validated parking at the Hawaiian Monarch hotel for a small fee. ♦ American ♦ Daily 11PM-2PM. 1911B Kalakaua Ave (between Ala Moana Blvd and Ena Rd). 949.0820

10 Keo's ★★$ First, there was Honolulu's **Mekong** restaurant. Then that popular Thai hideaway expanded to an orchid-drenched

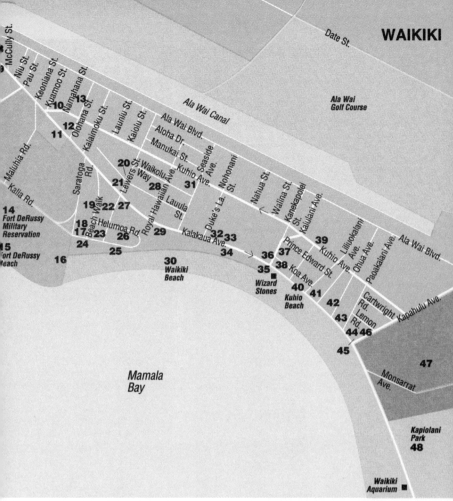

dining room, called **Keo's** after the patriarch of the family business, Keo Sananikone. After that, several branch restaurants opened, and now the top-rated main location has moved from the outskirts of Waikiki to the center of the action—and cut its prices by almost two-thirds. Orchids still abound, and intimate dining is still possible in this larger space. The menu is still enormous. Highlights include Evil Jungle Prince (a blend of chicken, lemongrass, coconut milk, Chinese cabbage, and red chilies), green papaya salad, prawns in a sweet peanut sauce, and delicious spring rolls. Sananikone grows his own herbs, bananas, and produce on the North Shore. ◆ Thai ◆ Daily breakfast, lunch and dinner. Reservations recommended. 2028 Kuhio Ave (between Namahana and Kuamoo Sts). 951.9355. Also at: Ward Centre, 1200 Ala Moana Blvd (between Queen and Kamakee Sts), Honolulu. 956.0020 &

11 Kyo-ya ★★★$$$$ An ultracontemporary but very Japanese structure, this restaurant is a statement in minimalist elegance—marble, glass, granite, and concrete abound. A corner of the restaurant is devoted to soba noodles

and the main dining room is downstairs. The breathtaking private tatami rooms are upstairs amid tasteful Zen gardens. The food is first-rate; the sashimi is always fresh, the *kaiseki* de rigueur, and the fish *misoyaki* (fish soaked in a savory soybean by-product) superb. ◆ Japanese ◆ M-Sa lunch and dinner; Su dinner. 2057 Kalakaua Ave (between Saratoga and Maluhia Rds). 947.3911 &

12 Nick's Fishmarket ★★★$$$$ Nick Nickolas opened the first of his seafood palaces here, and it has since been a home away from home for many a discriminating diner, Tom Selleck notably among them. The luxurious black booths and classic seafood selections such as sautéed *opakapaka* and sautéed *ahi* (yellowfin tuna) make for a

117

pleasant dining experience at this, one of Honolulu's premier seafood restaurants. Valet parking is available. ◆ Seafood ◆ Daily dinner. Waikiki Gateway Hotel, 2070 Kalakaua Ave (at Olohana St). 955.6333 &

13 The Royal Garden at Waikiki $$ The bad news is that the 220-room hotel isn't on the beach. The good news is that this cozy property is one of Waikiki's best-kept secrets. Splurge on a suite and lounge by the pool. Rooms are equipped with phones and TVs, and there are two restaurants. ◆ 440 Olohana St (between Kuhio Ave and Ala Wai Blvd). 943.0202, 800/367.5666; fax 946.8777; www.royalgardens.com &

Within The Royal Garden at Waikiki:

Cascada ★★★$$$ Named for the cascading waterfall at its periphery, this dining spot evokes serenity from the moment you enter. High ceilings, chandeliers, and alfresco dining beside the pool are a perfect match for the excellent food. Grilled *ahi,* angel-hair pasta primavera, and chicken and vegetable linguine are the top draws at this relatively unknown Waikiki establishment. ◆ Mediterranean/Pacific Rim ◆ M-F breakfast, lunch, and diner; Sa-Su breakfast and dinner. Reservations recommended. 945.0270 &

14 Hale Koa Hotel $ The centerpiece of the Army's **Fort DeRussy** property—73 acres of prime Waikiki real estate—this military-owned, twin-tower high-rise is a sweet deal for military personnel and retired officers (nonmilitary folks need not apply). Located next to one of the best beaches in Waikiki, the renovated 12-story hotel has 817 units, 3 restaurants, a fitness center, and 2 pools. ◆ 2055 Kalia Rd (just southeast of Paoa Pl). 955.0555, 800/367.6027; fax 800/HALE.FAX; reservations@halekoa.com; www.halekoa.com &

15 Fort DeRussy Beach This oasis is a favorite of residents and the military, with military personnel serving as lifeguards (talk about a cushy assignment). Picnic facilities, volleyball courts, and a snack bar complete

the picture. ◆ Fort DeRussy Military Reservation, Kalia Rd (southeast of Paoa Pl)

16 US Army Museum of Hawaii Wartime artifacts and memorabilia are displayed inside a 1911 bunker with 22-foot-thick walls built so solidly that the army turned it into a museum to avoid having to tear it down. Exhibits include ancient Hawaiian weapons, as well as memorabilia from World War II and the Korean and Vietnam Wars. Uniforms and tanks, coastal defense artillery, and articles and photos relating to the army in Hawaii have also been preserved. ◆ Donation. Tu-Su. Guided tours must be booked in advance. Fort DeRussy Military Reservation, Kalia Rd (southeast of Paoa Pl), Bldg 32. 438.2822 &

17 Outrigger Royal Islander Hotel $$ Within walking distance of Waikiki Beach, this nicely decorated hotel is ideal for the budget-minded. There are 94 rooms and 7 suites; one-third of the rooms overlook the beach, and the rest have views of the neighboring park or the city. All accommodations have air-conditioning, TVs, phones, and refrigerators. There's no pool on site, though guests have full privileges at any of the other Outrigger hotels nearby. There's a **McDonald's** on the property. ◆ 2164 Kalia Rd (at Saratoga Rd). 922.1961, 800/688.7444; fax 923.4632; reservations@outrigger.com; www.outrigger.com &

18 Malihini Hotel $ Okay, so it's not (repeat, not) the Waldorf. There's no restaurant or pool, and only partial air-conditioning, and it's not even on the water (though it's near the beach). But for the price, this is a steal. The 28 rooms are spartan but clean, with kitchenettes, TVs, ceiling fans, and daily maid service. This low-budget hotel is very popular, so make reservations well in advance. ◆ No credit cards accepted. 217 Saratoga Rd (between Kalia Rd and Kalakaua Ave). 923.9644

19 The Breakers $$ Those who want to be close to the beach without paying the price of a big-name hotel should check out this two-story lodge hidden among the high-rises. It's reasonably priced, with 50 air-conditioned rooms (with kitchenettes) and 14 suites in a setting complete with the requisite palm trees and tropical plants. There's a pool, snack shop, and bar; daily maid service is provided. ◆ 250 Beach Walk (between Kalia Rd and Kalakaua Ave). 923.3181, 800/426.0494; fax 923.7174; breakers@aloha.net; www.breakers-hawaii.com &

19 Hawaiiana Hotel $ Another refreshingly unpretentious low-rise located a half block from Waikiki Beach and close to Fort DeRussy Beach, this 3-story hotel has 95 rooms complete with kitchenettes, air-conditioning, and connecting rooms for families. It's a good deal for Waikiki, and the mostly Hawaiian staff is unforgettable. There are two pools and complimentary Kona coffee, but no restaurant. ♦ 260 Beach Walk (between Kalia Rd and Kalakaua Ave). 923.3811, 800/367.5122; fax 926.5728; www.hawaiianahotel.com ♿

20 Aston Waikiki Joy Hotel $$ On a small, noisy side street off the beach, this hotel has a curious charm despite the absence of views from its 2 towers, one with 11 floors and the other with 8. With a total of 50 rooms and 44 suites, the property is petite, but it's big on extras like Jacuzzis and state-of-the-art stereo speakers. It caters to business travelers, offering such nice touches as the Corporate Program, with special rates for business travelers; valet parking; complimentary newspapers, breakfast, and local calls; and many business services. A pool and restaurant round out the deal. ♦ 320 Lewers St (at Lauula St). 923.2300, 800/922.7866; fax 924.4010; www.aston-hotels.com

21 Moose McGillycuddy's ★★$$ Part of a chain, this is a yuppie-holiday kind of place, with daily drink specials, cheap breakfasts, and a popular early-bird dinner menu (try the rib-eye steak). Rock music plays every night upstairs, and sporting events are shown via satellite. ♦ American ♦ Daily breakfast, lunch, and dinner. 310 Lewers St (between Kalakaua Ave and Lauula St). 923.0751 ♿

22 House of Hong ★$$$ Run by the Hong family, this place features large glittery dining rooms decorated with ancient art objects. The huge Cantonese menu includes such standard choices as Mongolian beef and Hong Kong shrimp. ♦ Chinese ♦ M-F lunch and dinner; Sa-Su dinner. 260-A Lewers St (between Helumoa Rd and Kalakaua Ave). 923.0202 ♿

23 Trattoria ★★$$$ A longtime favorite located in the **Outrigger Edgewater Hotel,** this dining spots serves lasagna, fettuccine Alfredo, and other Northern Italian classics. This is one of Waikiki's perennial, reliable restaurants—even locals eat here. There's valet parking. ♦ Northern Italian ♦ Daily dinner. 2168 Kalia Rd (at Beach Walk). 923.8415 ♿

24 Outrigger Reef on the Beach $$$ Located on Waikiki Beach, this is one of the

nicest (and most expensive) hotels of the Outrigger chain. The 838 air-conditioned rooms (some with kitchenettes) and 47 suites on 17 floors encompass a wide price range. Fort DeRussy Beach, with its volleyball courts and water activities, is nearby, and there's a pool and two restaurants. Rates are more reasonable than at most beachfront hotels. ♦ 2169 Kalia Rd (southeast of Paoa Pl). 923.3111, 800/688.7444; fax 924.4957; reservations@outrigger.com; www.outriggers.com ♿

Halekulani

25 Halekulani $$$$ *Halekulani* means "the house befitting heaven," and this hotel combines the standards of a first-class establishment with the gracious atmosphere of Old Hawaii. When Robert Lewers opened for business in 1907, the property consisted of quaint cottages with overhanging eaves nestled in a coconut grove. In 1981 the hotel was sold to the Halekulani Corporation, which razed the aging cottages but restored the main building and the **House Without a Key** lounge (leaving untouched an impressive beachside *kiawe* tree). Most of the 456 rooms and suites look out at the beach, each thoughtfully decorated to the smallest detail, like bathrobes and a complimentary morning paper. Another luxury is the in-room check-in service. Several restaurants and bars and a pool are on the premises. If you can afford the steep rates, this is the place to stay. ♦ 2199 Kalia Rd (southeast of Paoa Pl). 923.2311, 800/367.2343; fax 926.8004; www.halekulani.com ♿

Within the Halekulani:

Orchids ★★★$$$$ With a terraced open-air dining room overlooking Diamond Head and the Pacific, this casually elegant dining establishment has one of Hawaii's nicest restaurant settings. The innovative entrées range from smoked mahimahi to steamed *onaga* (red snapper) Oriental style. Sunday brunch is the most popular production, though you may have to abuse the credit card a bit to attend. ♦ International/Seafood ♦ M-Sa breakfast, lunch, and dinner; Su brunch and dinner. Reservations recommended. 923.2311 ♿

La Mer ★★★$$$$ Serious connoisseurs dub this restaurant the finest in Hawaii. The view from the elegant dining room is incomparable, with palm trees silhouetted against the darkening ocean at sunset. The menu matches this picture-perfect setting. The signature here is fresh seafood prepared a number of imaginative ways—such as *onaga* poached with three-caviar sauce, and *kumu* (goatfish) *en papillote,* with seaweed and shiitake mushrooms—and a carefully gleaned selection of meat and fowl. Leave room for dessert—the fruit tulip with passion fruit *coulis* is amazing. Yes, it's a very expensive meal, especially if you have to buy a jacket in order to get in, but at least you can say you've dined at the best restaurant in Hawaii. ♦ French ♦ Daily dinner. Reservations required; jackets required. 923.2311 &

House Without a Key ★★$$ A key would actually be useless, as this is an open-air restaurant and cocktail bar. A full breakfast buffet, sandwiches on whole wheat bread, and hamburgers, as well as such local favorites as sashimi and saimin (noodles in broth), are served with a view of the ocean and Diamond Head. A romantic hula show under the old *kiawe* tree may inspire you to dance under the stars after knocking back a few mai tais. ♦ American ♦ Daily breakfast, lunch, and dinner. 923.2311 &

Lewers Lounge Plush with leather and teak, this cocktail spot is perfect for couples and conferring businesspeople. It's quiet except for the tinkling of the ivories at the piano bar and the voices of the fine jazz singers who perform here after 9PM. ♦ Tu-Sa 8:30PM-1AM. 923.2311

26 Waikiki Parc $$$$ The Halekulani Corporation built this 23-story hotel as a less expensive alternative to the **Halekulani** just across the street. If you can live with the limited ocean view and the 30-second walk to the beach, it makes sense to stay here. All 298 rooms have private lanais or balconies, fully stocked refrigerators, and mini-bars. There's also a pool and Laundromat. ♦ 2233 Helumoa Rd (east of Lewers St). 921.7272, 800/422.0450; fax 923.1336; www.waikikiparc.com &

Garbage collectors in Honolulu have a clause in their contract that allows them to go fishing as soon as they're done with their route, which is usually just before dawn. This is part of what Hawaiians used to call the *"ukapau"* ("go fast and be done") system of receiving payment for work done instead of time spent.

Within the Waikiki Parc:

Parc Cafe ★★★$$$ The casual dining room here has high ceilings, tile floors, and plants abundant. The buffet is appealing in terms of price and selection, though it's not as big as those at the fancier hotels. The continental and American dishes are prepared with an island flair, and the dinner buffet is one of Honolulu's best values, with a variety of fresh fish; stir-fried vegetables; duck, leg of lamb, or chicken carved to order; and a fabulous salad bar, with everything from Peking duck salad to Kula tomatoes and charbroiled eggplant. ♦ Continental/American ♦ M-Sa breakfast, lunch, and dinner; Su brunch and dinner. 921.7272 &

KACHO

Kacho ★★$$$$ Sushi is the specialty in this small but stunning restaurant highlighted by a long granite sushi bar. The more adventurous might try the *kaiseki* dinner or the traditional Japanese breakfast, which includes miso soup, grilled fish, steamed rice, and a raw egg. ♦ Japanese ♦ Daily breakfast, lunch, and dinner. 924.3535 &

27 Royal Hawaiian Shopping Center This 4-level, 150-store complex has the biggest names in international fashion: **Chanel** (923.0255), **Hermès** (922.5780), **Lancel** (971.2000), **Gianni Versace** (922.5337), and more, as well as a liberal selection of restaurants. ♦ Daily. 2201 Kalakaua Ave (at Lewers St). 922.0588

Within the Royal Hawaiian Shopping Center:

Restaurant Suntory ★★$$$$ Suntory Ltd., the Japanese liquor producer that has built restaurants all over the world, reportedly spent more than $2 million on this one. Elegance abounds, from the handsome cocktail lounge to the separate dining rooms, each devoted to a special style of Japanese cuisine: *shabu-shabu* (cook-it-yourself soup), *teppanyaki* (tableside cooking), sushi, and so on. There's also a traditional Japanese room with tatami seating (sunken areas accommodate extended legs). ♦ Japanese ♦ M-Sa lunch and dinner; Su dinner. Reservations recommended. Orchid Court, Third floor. 922.5511

Paradiso Seafood & Grill $$$ New York steak and fresh local seafood top the menu at this oddly located coffee shop, closely followed by pizza. The outdoor seating makes it a nice place to take a break from shopping. ♦ American ♦ Daily breakfast, lunch, and dinner. Orchid Court, Ground floor. 926.2000 ♿

28 Duty Free Shops If you have an airline ticket for a destination outside the US, you can visit a duty-free shop at the **Honolulu International Airport** or here in Waikiki. Japanese tourists like duty-free shops because the merchandise is often less expensive than at home, but there aren't many bargains for Americans. ♦ Daily 9AM-11PM. 330 Royal Hawaiian Ave (between Lauula St and Waikolu Way). 931.2700

29 Sheraton-Waikiki $$$$ The hotel is larger than a football stadium, with 1,835 rooms and suites and more than 45,000 square feet of meeting space. The lofty ocean views remain the best feature of this monstrosity, the largest resort in the world when it opened in 1971 (**Hilton Hawaiian Village** has since surpassed it). A recent $20-million renovation upgraded the rooms and lobby. Don't blink or you'll miss the actual beachfront, which seems tiny compared to the size of the building. The *honu* (sea turtle) figures big in the room decor, reproduced in paintings, on bedspreads, and on wallpaper in pastels throughout the hotel. There are two pools and a fitness center. ♦ 2255 Kalakaua Ave (between Kaiulani Ave and Lewers St). 922.4422, 800/325.3535; fax 923.8785; www.sheratonhawaiii.com ♿

Within the Sheraton-Waikiki:

Hanohano Room ★★$$$$ Take the glass elevator up 30 floors for a panoramic view and unmatched black-tie service. Your best bets here are breakfast and sunset cocktails, but there's continental cuisine at dinner (garlic prawns and lobster medaillons with Pernod sauce are good) and dancing afterwards. ♦ Continental ♦ M-Sa breakfast and dinner; Su brunch and dinner. Reservations required. 922.4422 ♿

THE ROYAL HAWAIIAN

29 Royal Hawaiian Hotel $$$$ Despite high-rise neighbors, this hotel clings to its glory days as the "Pink Palace of the Pacific." The original Spanish-Moorish design, by **Warren**

& Wetmore, had cost the Matson Navigation Company a cool $4 million by the time the hotel opened in 1927 (Matson built it to provide world-class accommodations for passengers on their luxury liners). Before World War II, the hotel was the playground of the wealthy and famous. Such Hollywood celebrities as Mary Pickford and Douglas Fairbanks vacationed here, as did honeymooners Nelson Rockefeller and Henry Ford II (with their brides, that is). The halcyon days ended during World War II, when the hotel was leased to the Navy as an R&R spot for sailors from the Pacific fleet.

Sheraton bought the hotel in 1959 and added the 16-story **Royal Tower.** It's now owned by a company called Kyo-Ya (though Sheraton continues to operate it). The ornate porte cochere is impressive; chandeliered walkways leading from the spacious lobby are wide and richly carpeted. A green lawn framed by lush foliage and banyan trees leads to Waikiki Beach, where hotel guests enjoy a private stretch of sand. There's also a pool on the grounds. Though the **Royal Tower** offers modern levels of comfort, nostalgic guests will prefer to stay in the original stucco structure, still regularly repainted its traditional pink color. There are 526 rooms on the 10-acre property, all with air-conditioning, refrigerators, and pink telephones. ♦ 2259 Kalakaua Ave (between Kaiulani Ave and Lewers St). 923.7311, 800/325.3535; fax 924.7098; www.royal-hawaiian.com ♿

Within the Royal Hawaiian Hotel:

Mai Tai Bar Watch the action on Waikiki Beach from this open-air, beachside bar. True to its name, it serves excellent (and expensive) mai tais. There's also live Hawaiian entertainment. ♦ Tu-Su 5:30PM-1AM. 923.7311 ♿

Surf Room ★★$$$$ Suitors searching for the perfect place to pop the question need look no further than this open-air, oceanside dining room. The pink tablecloths match the glow of the exquisite sunsets seen here. The roasted rack of lamb with mushroom risotto and Japanese eggplant ratatouille are recommended, as is the swordfish broiled with Champagne-brined pineapple relish, and broiled marinated shiitake mushroom steak. ♦ Continental/Pacific Rim ♦ M-Sa breakfast, lunch, and dinner; Su brunch and dinner. 923.7311

In 1900, three buildings in Chinatown were slated to be burned by the Department of Health to stop the spread of bubonic plague. Unfortunately, strong winds fanned flames that devoured a 40-acre section of town, leaving more than 4,000 people homeless.

Royal Hawaiian Luau $$$$ If you want to experience the classic hotel luau, you might as well go all out and do it here. There's no *imu* (Hawaiian oven dug into the ground) for pig roasting, however, and on the whole, the authenticity of the proceeding is questionable. ♦ Luau ♦ M 6-8:30PM Reservations recommended. 931.7194 &

30 Waikiki Beach The mother of all Hawaii beaches stretches in broken segments from Fort DeRussy to Diamond Head, absorbing the tourists and hotel facades that encroach upon its golden grains. Despite what hotel markers claim, the beach is public property up to the high-water mark (and plenty of the public takes advantage of it). Parts of the beach were widened in the mid-1980s to ease traffic, but congestion is still a problem. Swimming is safe, even for beginners, and surfboards, boogie boards, umbrellas, beach mats, snorkel gear, and more can be rented from concession stands along the beach. You can even take up surfing; several places offer lessons, including **Leahi Beach Services** (Reef Hotel; no phone). An hour of instruction, equipment included, costs about $15, and they guarantee you'll stand on the board (they don't say for how long).

Along Waikiki Beach:

Wizard Stones A modest outcropping in front of a bronze statue of champion Hawaiian surfer/swimmer Duke Kahanamoku, these stones look like ordinary rocks, but, like the memorial, add a quiet majesty to the spot. Hawaiian lore has it that four Tahitian *kahuna* (priests) who journeyed here in the 16th century gave their *mana* (healing powers) to the stones and then vanished.

Kuhio Beach Swarming with people, this section of Waikiki Beach doesn't boast the clearest water in the world, but it's still great for strolling. Use caution while wading, though; large underwater holes pose an invisible danger. ♦ Kalakaua and Liliuokalani Aves

Sans Souci Beach Park Local families often picnic here, but this crescent of sand, also called "Queen's Beach," is best known as the spot where gay men come to cruise and be cruised. ♦ Kalakaua Ave (between Paki and Monsarrat Aves)

The original plans for the Hilton Hawaiian Village hotel were drawn on placemats at the Tropics restaurant, where the Ala Moana Hotel now stands. This "in" cafe was a home away from home for a celebrity lineup that included John Wayne, Henry Fonda, James Cagney, Bing Crosby, Jane Russell, Mickey Rooney, and Henry Kaiser—who built the Hilton Hawaiian Village.

31 Matteo's ★★$$$$ Well-known restaurateur Fred Livingston, who also owns **Trattoria** (see page 119), as well as the **Crouching Lion** on the North Shore, uses high-backed booths, soft lighting, and amber tones to create an intimate ambience. The osso buco, live Maine lobsters, and New York steaks are all popular with the lawyers, yuppies, and showbiz types who frequent this place. Valet parking is available. ♦ Italian/Continental ♦ Daily dinner. Reservations recommended. 364 Seaside Ave (at Kuhio Ave). 922.5551 &

32 Waikiki Beachcomber $$$ Set in the very heart of congested Waikiki, this property offers 496 air-conditioned rooms (and 4 suites) with balconies. There's also a pool, Hawaiian entertainment nightly in the **Don Ho Showroom,** and dining in the **Hibiscus Cafe.** Easy access to the shopping malls and Waikiki Beach is another plus. ♦ 2300 Kalakaua Ave (at Duke's La). 922.4646, 800/622.4646; fax 926.9973; beach@dps.net; www.waikikibeachcomber.com &

Within the Waikiki Beachcomber:

The Magic of Polynesia Showroom This 2.5-hour dinner/show combination featuring magician-cum-musician John Hirokawa is one of Waikiki's best show deals. The $7.3-million showroom sports a lava-tube entranceway, a replica of a volcanic island, and tiered seating. The dinner, however, is nothing special. ♦ Admission. Dinner seating: 5PM; cocktail seating: 6, 8PM; shows: 6:30, 8:45PM. Fourth floor. 971.4321

33 International Marketplace The fancy name belies the mostly worthless merchandise scattered among 150 carts. Located across from the **Sheraton Moana Surfrider Hotel,** the open-air grounds are shaded by a huge banyan tree. The only thing remotely international about the place is the bargaining system—you can pick up souvenirs for a song if you're not afraid to haggle. ♦ Daily 9AM-11PM. 2330 Kalakaua Ave (between Kaiulani Ave and Duke's La). 923.9871 &

34 Outrigger Waikiki on the Beach $$$$ A cornerstone of the ever-expanding Outrigger chain, this hotel has an underground freshwater stream that empties into the ocean directly in front of the property. The waterway prevents the growth of coral, thus affording easy swimming along the stretch of beach in front of the hotel. The 494 rooms are

36 suites in this sprawling property have the standard amenities, including air-conditioning, TVs, phones, and refrigerators. For a treat, take a room on **Floors 14** through **16,** dubbed the **Voyager's Club**—it boasts the maximum in accommodations and services. There's a fitness center, pool, and three restaurants, including the popular **Duke's Canoe Club** (see below). ♦ 2335 Kalakaua Ave (between Kaiulani and Lewers St). 923.0741, 800/688.7444; fax 921.9741; www.outrigger.com ら

Within the Outrigger Waikiki on the Beach:

Duke's Canoe Club ★★$$$ The namesake of this popular eatery was one of the best and best-loved surfers of all time; his koa-wood surfboard hangs from the ceiling and pictures of him surrounded by Hawaii's royalty cover the walls. In addition to being a memorial, the restaurant holds its own in the culinary department—if evidence is required, go with a plate of *panko opa* (breadcrumb- and herb-crusted moonfish), sautéed *au* (swordfish), or Big Island pork ribs with mango barbecue sauce and *hulihuli* (rotisserie-roasted) chicken. ♦ Hawaiian Regional ♦ Daily breakfast, lunch and dinner. Reservations recommended. 922.2268 ら

35 Sheraton Moana Surfrider $$$$ This venerable landmark was the first hotel on Waikiki Beach. It opened in 1901, a time when Hawaiian beachboys hung out at the 300-foot Moana pier, greeting tourists with music as the sun set. Luxuries included a ballroom, saloon, billiard room, pool, roof-garden observatory, and the area's first electric elevator. Subsequent expansions, changes in ownership, and a $50-million renovation produced today's impressive property. Restored to its original design and listed in the National Register of Historic Places, the hotel is furnished with indigenous woods, four-poster beds with bamboo headboards, marble-top tables, a grand staircase, Victorian-style lamps, colonial verandas and millwork, and memorabilia. It's rumored that Robert Louis Stevenson may have penned some of his prose under the banyan tree in the courtyard. Planted in 1885, the famous tree now towers more than 75 feet, with a 150-foot span. The **Banyan Court** and **Banyan Veranda** feature sunset performances of great Hawaiian music. The 791 rooms (including 44 suites) in 3 towers have all the modern amenities, including air-conditioning, refrigerators, TVs, and 24-hour room service. ♦ 2365 Kalakaua Ave (between Kaiulani Ave and Lewers St). 922.3111, 800/325.3535; fax 923.5984; www.sheratonhawaii.com ら

Within the Sheraton Moana Surfrider:

Banyan Veranda ★★★$$$ The Hawaiian music program at this restaurant has become a top beach attraction. Nightly performances by a variety of Hawaiian musicians, such as the Puuhonua Trio and the Banyan Serenaders, give a glimpse of the elusive "real Hawaii." The nightly buffet features intriguing fare including stir-fried shrimp, scallops, and mussels; and roasted marinated beef flank steak. Casual breakfast, afternoon snacks and cordials, and Sunday brunch are patronized by both hotel guests and Waikiki residents. The setting is unbeatable: rattan chairs sheltered by a banyan tree, and a view of the **Banyan Court** and the Pacific. Drinks, be warned, are hideously expensive. ♦ Continental/ International ♦ M-Sa breakfast, afternoon tea, and sunset buffet; Su brunch, afternoon tea, and sunset buffet. 922.3111 ら

Ship's Tavern ★★$$$$ This "tavern" is the hotel's most formal dining room, with an oceanside setting. The menu features steak and seafood such as fresh Maine lobster, poached *onaga*, sautéed scallops, and Kahuku prawns. ♦ Steak/Seafood ♦ Daily dinner. Reservations recommended. 922.3111 ら

36 Princess Kaiulani Hotel $$$ This Sheraton hotel has expanded significantly since 1955, when the 11-story main building opened. The addition of a 29-story tower and 3 wings brought the total number of rooms to 1,150. Located across from the **Kings Village** shopping center, it's only one block from Waikiki Beach. There are air-conditioned rooms in several price categories, dictated by ocean, city, or mountain views; note, however, that this is not an oceanfront hotel. A pool and several restaurants and bars are on the premises. ♦ 120 Kaiulani Ave (between Kalakaua and Kuhio Aves). 922.5811, 800/325.3535; fax 931.4526 ら

37 Odoriko ★$$$$ Tanks of lobsters, prawns, crabs, and oysters add living color to this authentically furnished Japanese seafood and steak house. The specialties include boiled lobster and crab platters; there's also a sushi bar. For something different, try the Japanese-style breakfast. ♦ Japanese ♦ Daily breakfast, lunch, and dinner. Kings Village, 2400 Koa Ave (at Kaiulani Ave). 923.7368 ら

Honolulu has the smallest temperature range of any major US city, with an average low of 57 and high of 88.

Hyatt Regency Waikiki

38 Hyatt Regency Waikiki $$$ Designed by **Wimberly, Allison, Tong and Goo** in association with **Lawton & Taylor,** the hotel (pictured above) was built in 1976 for $100 million and sold in 1987 for $300 million. Forty-story twin towers rise on both sides of the landscaped atrium lobby. There are 1,230 rooms, 19 suites, several restaurants and bars, an indoor pool, more than 70 boutiques, and a 2-story waterfall. The rooms, with Asian furnishings, have private lanais and air-conditioning. Although impressive, this isn't a place to get away from it all, since it's located in the busiest part of Waikiki. ♦ 2424 Kalakaua Ave (between Uluniu and Kaiulani Aves). 923.1234, 800/233.1234; fax 923.7839; info@hyattwaikiki.com; www.hyattwaikiki.com ♿

Within the Hyatt Regency Waikiki:

Musashi ★$$$$ As much attention is paid to drama and theater as to food in this Japanese restaurant, named after famous samurai Miyamoto Musashi. (His classic study of the warrior code, *A Book of Five Rings,* is the bible in Japanese business schools.) Servers dress in kimonos, chefs in samurai garb, and buspeople in traditional street-acrobat wear. Try the *shokado* (sashimi, tempura, and beef teriyaki presented on one dish) or the *sakani shioyaki* (broiled catch of the day). Diners may sit at the sushi bar, *teppanyaki* grills, or tables. ♦ Japanese ♦ Daily dinner. Reservations recommended. 923.1234 ♿

Furusato ★★$$$$ This dining spot predates the hotel; it was a restaurant in the **Biltmore,** which was razed to make room for the current hotel. It's remarkably good, very authentic, extremely expensive, and caters to Japanese tourists. Order *ishiyaki* steak, which is cooked on hot rocks, or sukiyaki with beef and vegetables. ♦ Japanese ♦ Daily breakfast, lunch, and dinner. Reservations recommended 922.4991 ♿

39 Hy's Steak House ★★$$$$ If this plush bar/dining room makes you feel you're in a baron's wood-paneled library, that's because the interior actually came from a private estate in the eastern US. The dining room features a stunning gazebo, Tiffany-style glass ceiling panels, chandeliers, and a glassed-in *kiawe* broiler. The menu includes rack of lamb and beef Wellington, but steak Neptune (grilled over *kiawe* charcoal and topped with béarnaise sauce) is the best choice. There's valet parking. ♦ Steak house ♦ Daily dinner. 2440 Kuhio Ave (between Liliuokalani and Kaiulani Aves). 922.5555

40 Aston Waikiki Beachside Hotel $$$$ you want to be right in the middle of the action but feel as though you're in a different world, this European-style Aston hotel is the place to call. It's tiny, with 79 rooms (also tiny but well-appointed) in a narrow 12-floor tower drenched in travertine marble. André and Jan

---

Restaurants/Clubs: Red   Hotels: Blue
Shops/♥ Outdoors: Green   **Sights/Culture: Black**

Tatibouet made this their dream project, decorating it lavishly with careful attention to detail. The entrance looks like Tiffany's, with moldings galore, Oriental art and furnishings, and expensive wall coverings. Three of the eight rooms on each floor have ocean views over bustling Kalakaua Avenue, and all feature Chinese lacquered furniture, Oriental screens, and black-chrome-and-gold shower heads that cost more than a room for the night. There are none of the traditional resort accoutrements like restaurants, room service, pools, or tennis courts. Ask about the specials on room rates. ♦ 2452 Kalakaua Ave (between Liliuokalani and Uluniu Aves). 931.2100, 800/922.7866; fax 931.2129; www.aston-hotels.com &

41 Pacific Beach Hotel $$$$ The 38-story **Ocean Tower** and 17-story **Beach Tower,** across from Kuhio Beach, have 837 rooms and 8 suites with ocean, city, and mountain views. Each room has a private lanai, air-conditioning, and refrigerator. Other amenities include 2 tennis courts, a swimming pool, 24-hour fitness center, and Jacuzzi. ♦ 2490 Kalakaua Ave (between Kealohilani and Liliuokalani Aves). 922.1233, 800/367.6060; fax 922.8061; whcorp@worldnet.att.net; www.pacificbeachhotel.com &

Within the Pacific Beach Hotel:

Oceanarium Restaurant ★$$$ The big attraction here is dining alongside what is claimed to be Hawaii's largest indoor oceanarium—3 stories of glass holding 280,000 gallons of water and a profusion of colorful sea creatures. Otherwise, it's your basic, unexciting American menu, featuring steak and seafood. Go for Sunday brunch, which offers more unusual items, including *poke* (raw fish), Portuguese sausages, and sashimi. ♦ Continental ♦ M-Sa breakfast, lunch, and dinner; Su brunch and dinner. Reservations recommended. 922.1233 &

Neptune Gardens ★★★$$$$ Even trendier than **Oceanarium,** and also with a view of the town's biggest fish tank, this restaurant is a logical place for a dinner meeting or romantic soiree. The live Maine lobster is pulled directly from the tank—or if you'd rather not see your dinner mobile before it turns up on your plate, try the Szechuan rack of lamb. ♦ Seafood/Steak ♦ Daily dinner. Reservations recommended. 921.6112 &

Shogun ★$$$ This Japanese restaurant is popular among seafood lovers. Sample the shrimp tempura and the *nigiri* (raw fish rolled in sushi), or try the sukiyaki in which simple ingredients (meat, broth, vegetables, noodles, eggs) yield surprising results. The trade-off is its pedestrian environment on the third floor of the hotel, with a view of a concrete building. ♦ Japanese ♦ Daily breakfast, lunch, and dinner. Reservations recommended. 922.1233 &

42 Damien Museum Granted the museum is a dive, but it still houses some interesting pictures, artifacts, and other possessions of Father Damien. The Belgian priest dedicated his life to the physical and spiritual needs of patients with Hansen's disease (leprosy) who were confined to a colony on the island of Molokai. The museum is run by the Sacred Heart Society, an organization Damien founded. Even if you aren't interested in the displays, it's a great place to park your car for nothing. ♦ Donation. M-F 9AM-3PM. 130 Ohua Ave (between Kalakaua and Kuhio Aves). 923.2690

R

hawaiian regent
at Waikiki Beach

43 Hawaiian Regent Hotel $$$ A decent but hardly dazzling hotel, except for the impressive lobby and courtyard, this property, which is managed by Otaka Hotels and Resorts, is a sister to the nearby **Hawaiian Waikiki Beach Hotel.** There are 1,346 rooms, many with ocean views, in 2 towers on more than 5 acres. Request an oceanside room; the view is spectacular. There are six restaurants, two pools, a tennis court, a nightclub, and a shopping arcade. ♦ 2552 Kalakaua Ave (between Paoakalani and Ohua Aves). 922.6611, 800/367.5370; fax 921.5222; sales@hawaiianregent.com; www.hawaiianregent.com &

44 Hawaiian Waikiki Beach Hotel $$ For the price and location (near the **Honolulu Zoo, Kapiolani Park,** and the **Waikiki Aquarium**), this is one of the better deals in town, with 675 rooms and 40 suites in 2 towers. After you've visited the nearby attractions, relax in the hotel's pool or take a break in the coffee shop. Rooms are clean but offer only the standard amenities and decor—TVs, phones, air-conditioning, wicker furniture. ♦ 2570 Kalakaua Ave (at Paoakalani Ave). 922.2511, 800/877.7666; fax 923.3656 &

45 Park Shore Hotel $$ Smack dab on a busy corner, with Kuhio Beach across one street and **Kapiolani Park** across the other, this hotel offers 227 guest rooms, some with kitchenettes and all with private lanais and views of Diamond Head, the park, or the ocean. There's also a small pool, two Japanese restaurants, and a **Denny's.** ♦ 2586 Kalakaua Ave (at Kapahulu Ave). 923.0411, 800/367.2377; fax 923.0311; www.westcoasthotels.com/parkshore/

46 Waikiki Grand Hotel $$ Taking into consideration the rooms (which have a pleasant tropical decor), the location, and the affordable price, this hotel is a bargain if you can live with the noises from the nearby **Honolulu Zoo.** It's relatively small (173 rooms), with a rooftop sundeck, pool, and a **Jack in the Box** on the premises. ♦ 134 Kapahulu Ave (between Lemon Rd and Kalakaua Ave). 923.1511, 800/535.0085; fax 923.4708

47 Honolulu Zoo Building a zoo in Waikiki is like taking coals to Newcastle, but there's one here nonetheless. The usual animals peer out through cages that are covered with vegetation for a tropical jungle effect. The **Children's Zoo** lets kids play with goats, llamas, chickens, and the like. Tykes also have a chance to feed Mari, the zoo's only elephant, under the supervision of zookeepers. The **Education Pavilion** stages puppet shows at noon on the first and third Saturday of the month. Ask about the monthly moonlight walks. The main attraction during summer months is the weekly "Wildest Show in Town," featuring the best local entertainers, including Hookena and the Pandanus Club. The show is immensely popular and, even

better, it's free. ♦ Admission; children age 5 and under free when accompanied by an adult. Daily. Summer show: W 6PM. 151 Kapahulu Ave (between Paki and Kalakaua Aves). 971.7171 &

At the Honolulu Zoo:

Art Mart Twice a week, local artists with varying degrees of expertise set up card tables and prop their wares against the zoo's fence. The predictable ocean sunsets and palm-fringed beaches cover most canvases, although there is the occasional snowy New England scene. It's a pleasant outing, with souvenir potential. ♦ Free. Sa-Su. Monsarrat Ave (between Paki and Kalakaua Aves) &

48 Kapiolani Park Hawaii's first public park has been popular since it opened in 1877, a gift from King Kalakaua to the people of Honolulu (in return, he asked that it be named after his wife, Queen Kapiolani). Sprawled across 220 acres in Diamond Head's shadow, it's conveniently close to Waikiki yet away from the roar of the crowd, drawing joggers, softball games, barbecues, and picnics. It also encompasses the **Waikiki Aquarium** and the **Waikiki Shell** amphitheater. In mid-December it's the site of the finish line of the annual Honolulu Marathon, one of the world's largest foot races. ♦ Kalakaua Ave (between Paki and Monsarrat Aves)

Within Kapiolani Park:

Waikiki Shell Although a variety of performances are staged here, this modern, outdoor theater is best known as the home of the Kodak Hula Show. A Waikiki institution, the show premiered in 1937, and some of its original dancers, now in their eighties, still perform. Three mornings a week, nearly 3,000 people wait in line an hour or more for the

Waikiki Shell

MATT MORROW
NORTH MARKET STREET GRAPHIC

chance to plop down on bleachers and watch a revue they've probably already seen a dozen times on TV: Hawaiians in G-rated native garb dancing to ukuleles played by *tutus* (grandmothers) wearing bright muumuus and floppy hats. Spectators who volunteer to dance with the performers inevitably provide the most entertainment. ♦ Free. Tu-Th 10AM-11:15AM. 2805 Monsarrat Ave (between Paki and Kalakaua Aves). 591.2211 &

Waikiki Aquarium This 2.3-acre marine museum features a 35,000-gallon shark tank; a theater showing two 10-minute video programs; exhibits on monk seals and Hawaiian jellyfish; and **Corals Are Alive,** a multimedia interpretive exhibit on living coral. Also here is a mahimahi hatchery, a working aquaculture research center where visitors can observe mahimahi bred on-site. Other tanks display stingrays, butterfly fish, turtles, octopi, live coral, lionfish, a seahorse, and a giant clam—a total of 350 marine species. In 1990 the aquarium became the first in the US (and second in the world) to successfully hatch a chambered nautilus. The **Nautilus Nursery** tank opened that year and furthered the aquarium's renown as a national resource on the rare mollusk. There's a wide range of children's activities, summer reef explorations, music festivals, field trips, workshops, and many other programs. ♦ Admission. Daily. 2777 Kalakaua Ave. 923.9741

49 New Otani Kaimana Beach Hotel $$ A favorite among many repeat visitors, this modest high-rise is in the best part of Waikiki—on historic Sans Souci Beach, where Robert Louis Stevenson sunned himself in the 1890s. The small stretch of white sand offers a refreshing alternative to Waikiki congestion. Hikers and joggers have easy access to **Kapiolani Park** and to the road around the base of Diamond Head, where a lookout offers views of the surfers and windsurfers below. **Kaimana** manager Steve Boyle founded the popular Diamond Head Climbers Hui, a club for hikers who've made it to the top of the crater. There are 104 guest rooms and 20 beautiful suites. Some rooms are quite small, but they all have air-conditioning and refrigerators; corner suites

have the best views. ♦ 2863 Kalakaua Ave (between Paki and Monsarrat Aves). 921.7017, 800/356.8264; fax 922.9404; kaimana@pixi.com; www.kaimana.com &

Within the New Otani Kaimana Beach Hotel:

Hau Tree Lanai ★★$$$$ A giant 100-year-old *hau* tree serves as a canopy for this open-air dining room. Set right on the ocean's edge, it commands an extraordinary view of the Pacific—come at sunset when the seascape is exceptionally beautiful; Saturday and Sunday from 6 to 9PM a guitarist serenades diners. Items worth trying include New York steak crusted with blue cheese and served with shiitake mushrooms, and fresh *opakapaka* Chinese style. ♦ Pacific Rim ♦ Daily breakfast, lunch, and dinner. Reservations recommended. 923.1555 &

Miyako ★★$$$$ Fine food is served in a pleasant setting, with family-style seating on tatami mats at low tables. The menu includes *shabu-shabu,* good tempura, *teppanyaki,* and a wide variety of other Japanese favorites. ♦ Japanese ♦ Daily dinner. Reservations recommended. 923.1555 &

49 Colony Surf Hotel $$$$ Indonesia-meets-Western-civilization is the feel of the hotel that emerged resplendent from its recent multimillion-dollar renovation. Each of the 50 rooms on this property at the edge of Waikiki Beach features Balinese furniture, bedspreads, and wall hangings; a CD player; and a private lanai with views of Diamond Head and the Pacific. In a separate building, there are also 19 condominium units that are a little more expensive. There's no pool but a second-rate strip of sand is a short walk from the lobby. A free continental breakfast is served each morning, and two of the town's best dining establishments are on the premises. ♦ 2885 Kalakaua Ave (between Poni Moi Rd and Monsarrat Ave). 924.3111, 888/924.7873; fax 923.2249; www.colonysurf.com &

The average age of enlisted men killed aboard the *USS Arizona* in 1941 was 19.

An average of 88,000 tourists bump elbows daily in Waikiki, Oahu.

In the hills overlooking Honolulu lives a family of wallabies, descendants of a pair of the animals that escaped from the Honolulu Zoo in 1916.

Hollywood and Hawaii: A Love Story

Hollywood's infatuation with the Hawaiian Islands started in 1913 with Universal Pictures' *Hawaiian Love* and *The Shark God,* came of age in 1953 with *From Here to Eternity,* and reached new heights in the 1990s, when on-location filming brought $70 million to state coffers and celebrities like Bo Derek and Steven Spielberg to local shores. You may be surprised at how many Hollywood stars have smiled for the cameras here . . . perhaps right where you spread your beach towel yesterday. The following are some favorite Hawaiian flicks filmed in the Aloha State:

The Black Camel (1931) Honolulu police detective Charlie Chan is called in to solve the murder of a movie star stabbed in **Waikiki.** This mystery, starring Bela Lugosi and Robert Young, was filmed in Waikiki and **Kailua** on **Oahu.**

Black Widow (1985) A female investigator with the federal Justice Department (Debra Winger) becomes obsessed with apprehending a woman who marries men, then kills them. Her search leads to the **Big Island.**

Blue Hawaii (1961) Guy meets girl; guy woos girl on the beach; guy sings "Can't Help Falling in Love"; guy gets girl. Elvis Presley stars in this **Kauai**-based classic.

Curly Top (1935) Based on Jean Webster's book *Daddy Long Legs,* the film, shot on Oahu, features Shirley Temple singing "Animal Crackers in My Soup."

From Here to Eternity (1953) This Oscar winner, shot on Oahu, adapted James Jones's novel of Army life in Hawaii just before the attack on **Pearl Harbor.** It stars Montgomery Clift, Frank Sinatra, Burt Lancaster, Deborah Kerr, and Donna Reed.

Gidget Goes Hawaiian (1961) When a beach-loving teen from California goes on a tropical vacation with her parents, anything can—and does—happen. Shot on Oahu; with Deborah Walley and James Darren.

Hawaiian Love and *The Shark God* (1913) These pre-missionary short films were shot at **Liliuokalani Park** on Oahu. In the first, a chief's daughter has a love affair; in the second, a Hawaiian girl is wooed by a sea captain.

Hook (1991) The legendary Peter Pan (Robin Williams), now grown up and a corporate lawyer, returns to Never Never Land when Captain Hook (Dustin Hoffman) kidnaps his children. Julia Roberts is Tinkerbell; Kauai is Never Never Land.

Islands in the Stream (1977) An adaptation of the Hemingway novel, the story of an island-dwelling sculptor (George C. Scott) and his three sons was filmed on Kauai.

Jurassic Park (1992) In this movie based on the book by best-selling author Michael Crichton, Kauai reprises its role as a remote island, this time one turned into a dinosaur theme park. Jeff Goldblum, Laura Dern, and Sam Neill star in this special-effects blockbuster.

Karate Kid II (1985) The sequel sees Pat Morita and Ralph Macchio traveling to Japan from Oahu to face Morita's long-standing archenemy.

King Kong (1976) Jessica Lange debuted in the remake of this 1933 classic, with scenes on the **Na Pali Coast** of Kauai.

Lord of the Flies (1989) This remake is based on William Golding's novel about schoolboys who become savage on a remote island (played by Kauai). Balthazar Getty stars.

The Old Man and the Sea (1958) The movie version of Ernest Hemingway's tale about an aging fisherman's daily battle with the elements stars Spencer Tracy and is set on the **Big Island.**

Outbreak (1994) Kauai is the stand-in for yet another remote island in this thriller about the spread of a deadly virus. Dustin Hoffman stars.

Papillon (1973) An action-packed, pathos-infused film based on Henri Charriere's novel about two escapees from Devil's Island, it features Dustin Hoffman, Steve McQueen, and **Molokai.**

Point Break (1990) A maverick FBI agent (Keanu Reeves) goes undercover into Southern California's surfing community to investigate a series of bank robberies. Patrick Swayze plays the leader of the gang and his prime suspect. The dramatic California surfing scenes were filmed on Oahu's North Shore.

Raiders of the Lost Ark (1980) An archaeologist/adventurer (Harrison Ford) searches the world for a unique religious artifact, finding hair-raising danger at every turn. Scenes shot on Kauai.

Six Days, Seven Nights (1998) Filmed on Kauai, this movie features a washed-out helicopter pilot (Harrison Ford) and a yuppie ad executive (Anne Heche) who fall in love after they find themselves stranded on a deserted South Pacific island.

South Pacific (1958) Mitzi Gaynor stars in a story of life, love, and music on the Pacific Isles during World War II. The Rodgers and Hammerstein favorite was filmed on Kauai's North Shore.

10 (1979) Dudley Moore plays a middle-aged songwriter smitten with scantily clad Bo Derek; shot on Oahu and Kauai.

Throw Momma from the Train (1987) Danny DeVito and Billy Crystal make an agreement to kill each other's mother and wife, respectively, in this comedy filmed on Kauai.

Waterworld (1994) Shot on the Big Island, Kevin Costner's futuristic flick about an artificial island world was one of the most expensive films to produce in filmmaking history.

Within the Colony Surf Hotel:

Michel's ★★★$$$$ Owned by restaurateur Andy Anderson, who owns the renowned **John Dominis** restaurant (see page 138), this place was featured on "Lifestyles of the Rich and Famous." The dining room has a setting few restaurants can match. Literally on the beach, the oceanside halves of the three large dining rooms are kept completely open except during storms, and diners lucky enough to secure the best tables are within a linen napkin's toss of the beach. The decor is lavish, with candlelight, crystal, and chandeliers. The front-row views of the sunset and Waikiki's glittering lights can prove mesmerizing. The cuisine is supposed to be French, but the menu actually emphasizes local seafood and a legendary rack of lamb. ♦ French/Continental ♦ Daily dinner. Reservations recommended. 923.6552 ♿

David Paul's Diamond Head Grill ★★★★$$$$ Since its 1998 opening, this top-of-the-line restaurant has been the end of the line for many seeking the sort of culinary experience one speaks of into old age. Designed by Steve Jones, who outfitted several of Wolfgang Puck's restaurants, the place boasts a serpentine martini bar, appetizer bar, baby grand piano, and an elegant "Chef's Table," seating 10. The cuisine is unparalleled—some examples include Kona coffee–roasted lamb, miso salmon, and pepper-crusted veal loin. At lunch, the most popular items are the whole Kona lobster salad and portobello sandwich. ♦ Hawaiian Regional ♦ Daily lunch and dinner. Reservations recommended. 922.DPDH ♿

50 **Diamond Head Beach Hotel** $$$ A small European-style establishment with 26 suites and 31 luxury rooms, this hotel features fully equipped kitchens (there's no restaurant), complimentary continental breakfast, and lanais overlooking the Pacific. It's a charming hostelry on a minuscule wedge of white sand on Diamond Head Beach. Guests can jog, play tennis and soccer, or fly kites in **Kapiolani Park** just across the street. Ask about the special 50-percent discount. ♦ 2947 Kalakaua Ave (between Poni Moi Rd and Monsarrat Ave). 922.1928, 800/367.2317; fax 924.8980; www.diamondheadbeach.com

51 **Diamond Head Beach Park** A narrow, rocky two-acre beach along Diamond Head Road, this beach is dangerous for swimming and surfing and is best used for meditating or fishing. Check out the view from the overlook. The trail leads to tide pools. Although there's unlimited access, parking is tricky. ♦ Diamond Head and Beach Rds

52 **Diamond Head** If you fly into Hawaii, chances are the first thing you'll see (at least if you're seated on the right side of the plane) is this landmark, a volcanic crater that's been dormant for an estimated 150,000 years. Early Hawaiians called it "Leahi" (referring to the forehead of an *ahi* tuna) because its lines resemble the profile of a fish. But when sailors found diamondlike crystals here in the 1800s, they nicknamed it "Diamond Head" (the crystals turned out to be calcite). The crater's walls are 760 feet high; a 40- to 60-minute climb (roughly 1 mile) up the inside slopes to the top is rewarded by a stunning view of Honolulu. ♦ Daily 6AM-6PM; bring flashlights for the climb, which goes through a tunnel. Diamond Head Rd (between 22nd Ave and Trousseau St)

53 **Queen Kapiolani Hibiscus Garden** Pathways meander around dozens of varieties of hibiscus, free for the looking but not for picking. This showcase garden thrives on conscientious care from its curator and manure from the nearby **Honolulu Zoo.** ♦ Free. Daily. Paki Ave (between Monsarrat and Kapahulu Aves) ♿

Honolulu

The Honolulu beyond the tourist paradise of **Waikiki** is a modern metropolis, a center of commerce between the Far East and Australia and the United States, and the legislative and executive capital of the 50th state. This is a working city, but it has much of interest to the traveler, such as **Iolani Palace,** the only royal palace in the United States. The historic harbor area, once a seedy sailors' port and now revamped and restored, has a marketplace filled with shops and restaurants, new piers to accommodate giant cruise ships, and a narrated boat tour. There are art and historical museums, cultural centers, parks, botanical gardens, numerous places to shop (including **Ala Moana Shopping Center,** the largest in the state, and the upscale **Aloha Tower Marketplace**), and lots of fine places to eat and drink (such as **Restaurant Row,** a collection of trendy eateries near the waterfront).

There's also **Chinatown,** which preserves the traditions of one of the city's major ethnic groups. Centered on **Maunakea Street,** Chinatown's multiracial population actually includes Chinese, Filipinos, Hawaiians, and, more recently, Vietnamese and Laotian immigrants. Urban renewal has provided a face-lift, and the seedy bars, pool halls, and rooming houses are now outnumbered by noodle factories, open-air markets, herb shops, bakeries, clothing and jewelry stores, art galleries, and restaurants.

A tour through Honolulu gives visitors a greater understanding of Hawaii's history, its diverse cultures, and its place in the world today.

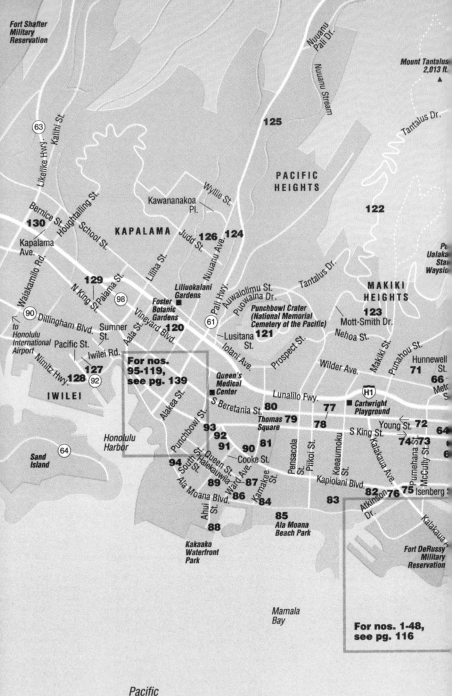
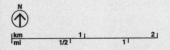

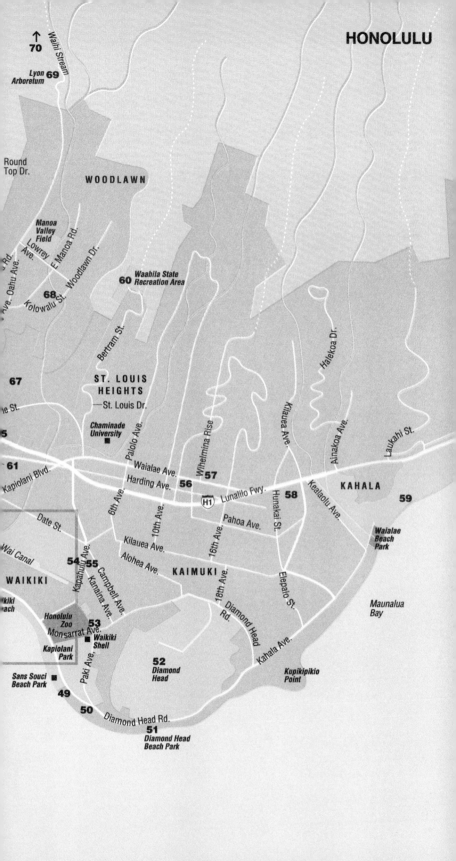

↑ **70**
Waihi Stream

Lyon **69**
Arboretum

Round
Top Dr.

WOODLAWN

Manoa
Valley
Field
Lowrey Ave.
E. Manoa Rd.
Ave., Oahu Ave.
Rd.
Woodlawn Dr.

68
Kolowalu St.

60 Waahila State
Recreation Area

Bertram St.

Halekoa Dr.

67

**ST. LOUIS
HEIGHTS**
—St. Louis Dr.

e St.

Chaminade
University

Palolo Ave.

Wilhelmina Rise

Kilauea Ave.

Ainakoa Ave.

Laukahi St.

5

61
Kapiolani Blvd.

Waialae Ave.

Harding Ave.   **56** **57**

H1 Lunalilo Fwy.

58

Kealaolu Ave.

KAHALA

59

Date St.

6th Ave.

10th Ave.

Pahoa Ave.

Hunakai St.

Waialae
Beach
Park

Wai Canal

54 55
Kapahulu Ave.

Kilauea Ave.

16th Ave.

Alohea Ave.

Campbell Ave.

Kanaina Ave.

KAIMUKI

18th Ave.

Elepaio St.

Maunalua
Bay

WAIKIKI

kiki
each

Honolulu
Zoo
Monsarrat Ave. **53**
Waikiki
Shell

Paki Ave.

Kapiolani
Park

Diamond Head
Rd.

Kahala Ave.

Kupikipikio
Point

Sans Souci
Beach Park

49

50

52
Diamond
Head

Diamond Head Rd.

51
Diamond Head
Beach Park

54 Ala Wai Golf Course The greens fees here are relatively low, so this flat, moderately interesting 18-hole course (par 70, 6,065 yards) bordering the murky Ala Wai Canal is crowded with local players. Getting a tee time can be difficult; make reservations a minimum of one week in advance. ◆ Inexpensive greens fees. Daily. 404 Kapahulu Ave (between Ala Wai Blvd and Date St). 733.7387

55 Bailey's Antiques and Aloha Shirts Pre-statehood aloha shirts and other clothing combine with antique bottles and local memorabilia to make this a must stop on any souvenir-shopping itinerary. ◆ Daily. 517 Kapahulu Ave (between Kanaina Ave and Herbert St). 734.7628

56 Hale Vietnam ★★$ The specialty here is *pho*, a steamy Vietnamese soup prepared in nearly two dozen ways—and consistently voted the best in town by *Honolulu Magazine*. *Pho* lovers come here from all over the island to linger over hot bowls of soup or light, piquant spring rolls. ◆ Vietnamese ◆ Daily lunch and dinner. Reservations recommended. 1140 12th Ave (at Waialae Ave). 735.7581

57 3660 On The Rise ★★$$$ Following on the heels of other successful trendy establishments, this small yet elegant restaurant specializes in "Euro-Island" cuisine. Its patrons are for the most part wealthy locals who come for the well-rounded menu of uniquely prepared veal, steak, lamb, and seafood, including farm-raised catfish tempura with *ponzu* sauce (a citrusy soy sauce) and steamed *opakapaka* with black bean sauce. The location is somewhat removed from the tourist scene, but it's certainly worth the short drive for lunch or dinner. ◆ Pacific Rim ◆ Tu-Su dinner. 3660 Waialae Ave (at Wilhelmina Rise). 737.1177 &

KAHALA
MANDARIN ORIENTAL
HAWAII

58 Kahala Mall The **Ala Moana Shopping Center** may be larger, but this shopping center has more character. Located in Oahu's wealthiest neighborhood, the mall houses standard merchandisers—**Liberty House, The Gap,** and **Banana Republic**—as well as many unique specialty shops that warrant serious browsing by visitors and residents alike. ◆ Daily. 4211 Waialae Ave (at Kilauea Ave). 732.7736

Within Kahala Mall:

California Pizza Kitchen ★★$$ It serves up exactly the same fare as the Waikiki restaurant, and likewise packs 'em in with pizza and pasta specials. ◆ Pizza/Pasta ◆ Daily lunch and dinner. 737.9446 & Also at: 1910 Ala Moana Blvd (between Kalakaua Ave and Ena Rd), Waikiki. 955.5161; Pearlridge Center, 98-1005 Moanalua Rd (at Kaonohi St), Aiea. 487.1771

Yen King ★$ The specialty is Szechuan cuisine, with nearly a hundred items on the menu, most of which are reasonably priced. If you like spicy dishes, try the garlic chicken, lemon beef, or sizzling rice shrimp. ◆ Chinese ◆ Daily lunch and dinner. 732.5505 &

59 Waialae Country Club One of Hawaii's most exclusive and private country clubs is home to the **Sony Hawaiian Open** golf tournament, held every February. Built in 1927 in a then-remote part of Oahu, the flat 18-hole course (par 72, 6,651 yards) borders the ocean and offers vicious doglegs, deep bunkers, and nearly 2,000 palm trees—many of them centuries old—to challenge even the most skilled golfers. ◆ Daily. Members and guests only. 4997 Kahala Ave (northeast of Kainapau Pl). 732.1457

59 Kahala Mandarin Oriental Hotel $$$$ Designed by **Edward Killingsworth**, this high-end of high-end Hawaiian resorts has 371 rooms and suites, some at the edge of a lagoon filled with large sea turtles, tropical fish, and cavorting bottle-nosed dolphins (lagoon units must be booked far in advance). Set on 6.5 acres well removed from the congestion of Waikiki, it also offers a wide private beach (excellent for swimming) surrounded on 3 sides by the greenery of the **Waialae Country Club**, a pool, and lush landscaping. Quiet pathways wind through tropical foliage, passing tiny streams, miniature waterfalls, and flowering gardens. Amenities include a fitness center with Jacuzzi, sauna, weights, and massage therapists for ultimate indulgence. Many of the guests are Hollywood stars, producers, agents, and writers who appreciate the privacy here. The staff keeps a record of repeat guests and their preferences. ◆ 5000 Kahala Ave (northeast of Kealaolu Ave). 734.2211, 800/367.2525; fax 739.8800; www.mandarin-oriental.com &

Within the Kahala Mandarin Oriental Hotel:

Hoku ★★$$$$ Dramatic is the word for this Asian restaurant, which features a spectacular ocean view and such interesting menu selections as wok-seared Hawaiian prawns on Asian vegetables with a basket of tomato goat-cheese pesto bread. An open kitchen and sushi and oyster bar add an element of fun, as does a pianist playing jazz during the dinner hour. ♦ Euro-Asian ♦ M-Sa lunch and dinner; Su brunch and dinner. Reservations recommended. 734.2211 ♿

60 Waahila State Recreation Area
Residents who want to escape the heat drive to this cool, elevated retreat at the top of residential St. Louis Heights. Picnic facilities (including barbecue grills) are available under the Norfolk pines and ironwoods, and there's a great strawberry guava grove that's open to all pickers when the fruit is in season. ♦ Bertram St (northeast of St. Louis Dr)

61 Down to Earth Natural Foods Store
Everything from fresh organic produce to "Tom's of Maine" toothpaste is stocked in this natural foods store, including a fine selection of vitamins, pasta, Indian chutney, grains, nuts, greeting cards, health-conscious cosmetics, cheese, and other products sold in bulk. Within the store is the **Down to Earth Deli,** a vegetarian mecca dispensing healthful salads, chili, tabbouleh, pastries, and pastas. It's de rigueur to bring your own bag for groceries. ♦ Daily 8AM-10PM. 2525 S King St (between Kapaakea La and Hausten St). 947.7678 ♿

62 Maple Garden ★★$ A longtime favorite for spicy Mandarin and Szechuan cuisine, this establishment is usually crowded and noisy with chatter and platter-clatter. Specialties include smoked Szechuan duck and eggplant with spicy garlic sauce. ♦ Chinese ♦ Daily lunch and dinner. Reservations recommended. 909 Isenberg St (between Date and S King Sts). 941.6641 ♿

63 Chiang Mai Northern Thai Restaurant
★★★$$ If you didn't know about this Honolulu find, you'd never notice it among the other glitzier options. Don't let the storefront exterior deceive you—inside all is simple and serene. Stop in for papaya salad, Cornish game hen, or a plate of curried local fish, and find out why many locals are having their mail forwarded here. ♦ Thai ♦ M-F lunch and dinner; Sa-Su dinner. Reservations recommended. 2239 S King St (between Isenberg St and Makahiki Way). 941.1151 ♿

64 Quilts Hawaii Hawaiian quilts are the specialty here, most of them in the four-digit

price range. There's also a smattering of other Hawaiiana, including fine koa furniture and bowls, handbags, jewelry, pillows, and quilt kits. ♦ M-Sa. 2338 S King St (between Isenberg St and Hoawa La). 942.3195 ♿

65 Anna Bannana's ★$ During the day you'll still see the occasional Harley-Davidson motorcycle parked in front of this unpretentious social pub. In the 1960s and 1970s, it was the hangout for beer-guzzling students from the nearby university campus. Now, it's better known for serious dartboard tournaments, satellite TV, pool tables, and substantial and colorfully named sandwiches like the Rick Nelson (roast beef with melted cheese, Dijon mustard, cream cheese, and bean sprouts) and Gary's Superturkey (sliced turkey with bacon bits, cheese, and salad dressing). Reggae bands play to a crowded house Friday and Saturday nights, and there's live blues and rock music on Thursday and Sunday evenings. It's also a great place to use the rest room (you'll see). ♦ American ♦ Cover after 9PM. Daily 11AM-2AM. 2440 S Beretania St (between Kaialiu and Isenberg Sts). 946.5190

66 Manoa Valley Inn $$ Under the direction of T-shirt magnate Rick Ralston (owner of the local Crazy Shirts chain), this two-story 1920s structure survived impending destruction and was designated a historical home. Ralston furnished the inn, which consists of seven bedrooms and a cottage, from his extensive collection of antiques and period furnishings, including brass beds. Marc Resorts took over the inn in 1994; while not up to its former splendor in terms of service and comfort, it continues to offer guests continental breakfast; afternoon cheese, wine, and fruit; and other amenities—though there's no restaurant. It's precariously close to the bustling university, there's no pool, and not all rooms have TVs and phones. Still, the inn is a good choice for the price and the ambience. ♦ 2001 Vancouver Dr (at Hunnewell St). 947.6019, 800/634.5115; fax 946.6168

67 University of Hawaii (UH) Probably the ugliest collection of unrelated architectural styles in Hawaii is on the university's 300-acre campus, although the extensive landscaping provides some relief. The center for higher education opened in 1908 with 12 teachers and 5 full-time students. Now 20,000 full-time students attend the Manoa campus, with another 30,000 enrolled at the Hilo campus and in the university's statewide community college system. The university earned its reputation with strong international studies, marine biology, tropical agriculture, and oceanography programs, along with specialized programs in the travel industry and hotel management. It's also in the forefront of astronomy research and the world search for alternative energy sources. ♦ 2444 Dole St (just east of University Ave). 956.8111

Within the University of Hawaii:

East-West Center In 1960 this institution and the surrounding 21 acres were dedicated by Congress to promote better relations, both cultural and technical, between the US and the countries of Asia and the Pacific. Funded by various nations and private companies, the center contains several artistic treasures from the Far East, including murals, paintings, and sculptures from China, Korea, Thailand, and Japan in the exhibition hall. **Friends of the East-West Center** offer hourlong tours by appointment, or you're welcome to browse solo. Be sure to stroll through the landscaped grounds; look for the Japanese garden. ♦ Free. M-F. 1601 East-West Dr (south of Dole St). 944.7111 &

68 Coffee Manoa ★$ A popular gathering place for university students, this small cafe sells dozens of varieties of coffee beans. Or, if you prefer, you can take home a bag of your favorite gourmet blend ground on the premises. Banana poi and ginger pumpkin muffins are available, as well as other breads, scones, and assorted pastries. ♦ Cafe ♦ Daily breakfast, lunch, and dinner. Manoa Marketplace, 2752 Woodlawn Dr (between Lowrey Ave and Kolowalu St). 988.5113 &

69 Lyon Arboretum Taro, orchids, bromeliads, ferns, cinnamon, coco, koa, kava, palms, coffee, yams, bananas, and hundreds of other plant species can be found in these lush botanical gardens, only a short drive from downtown Honolulu. The arboretum is closely associated with Beatrice Krauss, an ethno-botanist who has taught here for decades. Crafts, gardening, and cooking workshops; plant sales; special outings; and many other activities are offered here, and mosquito repellent is provided. Also on the property are a bookstore and gift shop. One-hour guided tours are offered on the first Friday and third Wednesday of the month at 1PM. ♦ Donation. M-Sa 9AM-3PM. Reservations required for guided tours. 3860 Manoa Rd (northeast of Oahu Ave). 988.7378

Shirley Temple danced the hula in one of her early films on the second floor of what is now the Burger King building at Kalakaua Avenue and Lewers Street.

Dr. Sun Yat-sen, founder of the Republic of China, lived and studied in Hawaii as a young man; a statue in Chinatown immortalizes him.

70 Manoa Falls Tired of the Waikiki hustle? Escape to this cool, quiet forest fragrant with ginger and tropical blooms. It's the perfect place for a long picnic followed by a swim in the freshwater pool underneath the falls. To get here, take the trail that begins at the end of Manoa Road (look for the brown trail marker and park just past it). It's about a 30-minute hike (1 mile) to the falls. ♦ Manoa Falls Tr (north of Manoa Rd)

71 Punahou School Hawaii's most famous private school opened in 1841 for children whose parents were Congregationalist missionaries and Hawaiian *alii*. The grounds were donated by Queen Kaahumanu, Kamehameha I's favorite wife and one of the mission's noteworthy converts. The alumni list reads like a *Who's Who of Hawaii*, and new generations of missionary descendants, joined by Honolulu's nouveau riche, perpetuate the exclusivity of the kindergarten-through–high-school enrollment. ♦ 1601 Punahou St (at Wilder Ave). 944.5711

72 King Tsin ★★$$ The Joseph Wang family oversees the kitchen, which specializes in remarkably creative Szechuan dishes. Try the beggar's chicken baked in clay pots—a half-day advance notice is required—or if you're not planning that far ahead, the spare ribs in orange-honey sauce. ♦ Chinese ♦ Daily lunch and dinner. 1110 McCully St (between Young and S Beretania Sts). 946.3273 &

73 Chef Mavro Restaurant ★★★★$$$$ George Mavrothalassitis, who put in a stint as senior executive chef at the **Four Seasons Resort** on Maui, has returned to Honolulu and opened his first restaurant on US soil (he originally apprenticed with three-Michelin-star chefs in Paris). Diners can choose from such à la carte dishes as grilled *ahi* with black bean, corn, and tomato salsa, or blackened *ono* served with a lime and macadamia-nut beurre blanc, or pull out all the stops and order from the small prix-fixe menu. The outstanding fare complements the sophisticated setting of marble walls decorated with Hawaiian paintings. Be sure to reserve far in advance as there's room for only 60 people. ♦ Hawaiian Regional ♦ Daily dinner. Reservations recommended. 1951 S King St (at McCully St). 944.4717 &

74 Alan Wong's ★★★★$$$$ The *opihi* shooters (liqueur of your choice with a limpet at the bottom) at one of the most successful of Honolulu's restaurants have gotten substantial press; less well known are the honey–macadamia-nut lamb chops and ginger-crusted *onaga*. Alan Wong is a world-renowned chef who worked at a number of fine-dining establishments in Hawaii before opening his own restaurant just outside Waikiki. The small room, featuring high beams strung with white lights and koa-wood tables, gives a sensual, out-of-the-ordinary feel. ♦ Hawaiian Regional ♦ Daily dinner. Reservations recommended. 1857 S King St (at Pumehana St). 949.2526 ♿

75 Hard Rock Cafe ★★$$ It's all here—loud music, central bar, wood and brass decor—but Hawaiian icons (surfboards) are mixed in with the rock 'n' roll memorabilia (including John Lennon's Starfire 12 guitar). The all-American fare—Texas-style ribs, barbecued chicken, chili, burgers, and steaks—is served carhop style. Don't bother looking for free parking; it's not worth the trouble. ♦ American ♦ Daily lunch and dinner. 1837 Kapiolani Blvd (between McCully St and Kalakaua Ave). 955.7383 ♿

76 Hawaii Convention Center At the site of the former **Aloha Motors** dealership is this recently constructed $200-million, million-square-foot convention center. Designed by prominent local architects **Wimberly, Allison, Tong and Goo,** in tandem with a Seattle firm, the center has an exhibit hall, ballroom, theaters, alfresco courtyards, and dozens of meeting spaces. ♦ Kapiolani Blvd and Kalakaua Ave

77 Mekong I ★★★$ The first of a now well-established family-run chain, this tiny restaurant offers a long list of Thai specialties. Those who come here are strictly interested in the menu, which includes curries, spring rolls, ginger fish, satays, and Evil Jungle Prince. Alcohol isn't served, but you're welcome to bring beer or wine. ♦ Thai ♦ M-F lunch and dinner; Sa-Su dinner. 1295 S Beretania St (between Keeaumoku and Piikoi Sts). 591.8841 ♿

78 Wisteria ★$$ A longtime local favorite, this is one of those word-of-mouth places you'd never discover on your own. The cuisine is Japanese (sushi, shrimp tempura), with some American selections (spaghetti, barbecued chicken). Don't try to get in on a Friday night without reservations. ♦ Japanese/American ♦ Daily breakfast, lunch, and dinner. Reservations recommended. 1206 S King St (at Piikoi St). 596.0976 ♿

79 Auntie Pasto's ★$$$ If you're in the mood for a quiet, relaxing dinner, keep looking. But if you want decent Italian food at very reasonable prices and are willing to endure some noise, this is the place. Start with an order of basil bread, then try the eggplant Parmesan or fish

stew. Save room for the delicious mud pie. ♦ Italian ♦ M-F lunch and dinner; Sa-Su dinner. 1099 S Beretania St (at Pensacola St). 523.8855 ♿

80 Honolulu Academy of Arts The 30 galleries here display world-renowned European and American masterpieces, a permanent Oriental collection, and the best of Hawaii's art. The handsome, tile-roofed building, which opened as a museum in 1927, encloses landscaped courtyards filled with plants and sculptures. The academy was founded by avid art collector Mrs. Charles Montague Cooke, whose family home had been on this site. New York architect **Bertram Goodhue** designed the structure, a blend of Hawaiian, Oriental, and Western styles. ♦ Donation requested. Tu-Sa; Su 1-5PM. Tours: Tu-Sa 11AM; Su 1:15PM. 900 S Beretania St (at Ward Ave). 532.8700; fax 532.8787 ♿

Within the Honolulu Academy of Arts:

Garden Cafe ★$ This canopied cafe serves commendable but modestly sized salads, sandwiches, and bowls of soup for lunch, but since it's a fund-raising venture for the academy, operated mostly by volunteers, who would dare complain about quantity, especially in such a pleasant garden setting, surrounded by sculptures and hanging plants? (A bonus: the volunteers often share family recipes with the cafe; try the warm goat-cheese sandwich, for example.) ♦ Cafe ♦ Tu-Sa lunch. Reservations recommended. 532.8734 ♿

81 Neal S. Blaisdell Center (NBC) Formerly the **Honolulu International Center (HIC),** this $12.5-million complex was renamed in the 1970s for a popular Honolulu mayor who served from 1955 to 1968. The 8,000-capacity arena plays host to basketball, boxing, and sumo wrestling, as well as conventions, rock concerts, circuses, ballet performances, and major theatrical productions. ♦ 777 Ward Ave (between Kapiolani Blvd and S King St). 591.2211 ♿

ALA MOANA HOTEL

82 Ala Moana Hotel $$$ At 36 stories high, this 1,169-room hotel is the tallest building in the state. Better yet, it's linked by a footbridge to the **Ala Moana Shopping Center** (see below). The rooms on the concierge floors feature such nice extras as Jacuzzis, lanais, and Japanese robes; the others are standard 500-square-foot

Ala Moana Hotel

rooms. There's also a pool, sundeck, and business center. ♦ 410 Atkinson Dr (at Mahukona St). 955.4811, 800/367.6025; fax 947.7388; martyamh@gte.net; www.alamoanahotel.com &

Within the Ala Moana Hotel:

Royal Garden ★★$$ Traditional Chinese fare (try the lobster with garlic sauce, the Peking duck, or the shark's fin soup) is served until very late at night in this eatery, a favorite among local Chinese-Americans. For lunch, the waitresses cart dim sum from table to table. ♦ Chinese ♦ Daily lunch and dinner. Third floor. 942.7788 &

Nicholas Nickolas ★★$$$$ Enjoy fabulous views of Waikiki while dining on steak or seafood. Fish lovers should consider the *opakapaka* with lemon butter and capers or the *ahi* with eggplant and goat-cheese crust. This is among the most popular places for sophisticated after-dinner dancing, nightly until 3AM. ♦ Continental/American ♦ Daily dinner. Reservations recommended. 36th floor. 955.4466

83 Ala Moana Shopping Center The granddaddy of all malls, this is the largest shopping complex in the state, with more than 200 stores and restaurants and 4 levels of open-air walkways alongside carp-filled ponds. When it opened in 1959, it was the biggest shopping center in the world. **Palm Boulevard,** on the upper level, is its snobby subsection, a mini-version of Beverly Hills' Rodeo Drive, with **Chanel, Gucci, Dior, Tiffany & Co.,** and **Cartier.** Other stores include **The Nature Company, Sharper Image, Ralph Lauren,** and **Crazy Shirts,** a locally owned chain of T-shirt shops. **Liberty House,** the major local department store, and **Sears** are the anchors. Among the interesting gift and crafts shops are **Hawaiian Island Creations** and **Irene's Hawaiian Gifts.** The center is under what seems like eternal renovation; a new wing, anchored by **Nordstrom,** has been added, as well as more space for parking (which is free). More than 60 million shoppers come here every year, and state residents pile in from the outer islands to shop, but if you live in a big city, you may find it no more interesting than your local mall. ♦ Daily. 1450 Ala Moana Blvd (between Atkinson Dr and Piikoi St). 946.2811 &

Within the Ala Moana Shopping Center:

Makai Market $ If hunger strikes while you're shopping, stop at this carnival of fast-food establishments. Among the tasty choices are pizzas at **Sbarro's,** Korean plate lunches at **Yummy's,** Cantonese cuisine at **Patti's Chinese Kitchen,** Szechuan favorites at **Panda's,** and much more, including Japanese and Thai food to go, hot dogs, hamburgers, deli items, baked potatoes, and salads. ♦ Fast food ♦ Daily. Street level

84 Ward Centre Located on the Diamond Head side of **Ward Warehouse** (see below), this trendy mall has restaurants and fast-food establishments upstairs and two dozen shops downstairs. ♦ Daily. 1200 Ala Moana Blvd (between Queen and Kamakee Sts). 591.8411 ♿

Within Ward Centre:

Keo's Thai Cuisine ★★$ Another offshoot of Keo Sananikone's restaurant dynasty, this establishment offers patrons a choice of dining in an air-conditioned room or in the open-air courtyard amid orchids and Thai art. The menu includes Keo's command-performance Evil Jungle Prince, spring rolls, and Danang seafood curry. ♦ Thai ♦ M-Sa lunch and dinner; Su dinner. First level. 596.0020 ♿

Honolulu Chocolate Company The owners fill their largest shop with toys (including stuffed animals they make themselves), gift boxes, preserves, teas, and sinful sweets. Indulge in the apricots or ginger dipped in dark chocolate, truffles, liqueur-flavored candies, macadamia turtles, and more. ♦ Daily. First level. 591.2997 ♿ Also at: Restaurant Row, 500 Ala Moana Blvd (at Punchbowl). 528.4033 ♿

Borders Books & Music More than 150,000 books and 50,000 CDs and cassettes line the shelves at this branch of the national chain; there's even a coffeehouse upstairs where friends and family members can go for refuge while the book buyer browses, and an open stage for readings and performances. ♦ M-Th 9AM-11PM; F-Sa 9AM-midnight; Su 9AM-10PM. First level. 591.8995

Mocha Java Espresso & Fountain ★$ With its wide selection of gourmet blends and pastries, this is the best coffeehouse in the area. The espresso milk shakes are great for an afternoon boost. In addition, the expanded menu includes treats like Dijon chicken crepes and whole wheat tortillas with beans, garlic, eggs, cheese, potatoes, green peppers, and onions. ♦ Coffeehouse ♦ M-Sa breakfast, lunch, and dinner; Su breakfast and lunch. First level. 597.8121 ♿

A Pacific Cafe Oahu ★★★$$$ Jean-Marie Josselin's first eatery, on Kauai, was such a runaway hit that he and wife Sophie, who designed the restaurant, have expanded to three islands. The ceiling of this uptown eatery is curved and colored to resemble a wave, the furnishings are bamboo, and the overall ambience is one of sophisticated languor. Signature dishes include tower of lamb loin with pine-nut–and-watercress crust, and grilled portobello mushroom and roasted baby vegetable risotto with smoky tomato broth at dinner; Hawaiian fish, and tempura shrimp for lunch; and firecracker salmon rolls and hot-and-sour dip *pupus.* Much of the produce used in Josselin's culinary creations comes from his organic garden on Kauai. ♦ Hawaiian Regional ♦ M-F lunch and dinner; Sa-Su dinner. Reservations recommended. Second level. 593.0035 ♿

Compadres Mexican Bar and Grill ★$$ Enjoy a pitcher of margaritas with compl-imentary tortilla chips and salsa. A few fish and American entrées have slipped onto the basically Mexican menu, and you can't go wrong ordering the all-American burger or the *pollo* burger (broiled chicken sandwich), which come with a huge pile of curly fries. Specialties include baby back ribs and *pollo borracho* (literally "drunk chicken"—chicken cured in Tequila, rock salt, and herbs for 24 hours and grilled to a crisp). Live music is featured on Friday night. ♦ Mexican ♦ Daily lunch and dinner. Second level. 591.8307 ♿

Ryan's Bar & Grill ★$$ Extremely popular for the affordable menu, which includes sandwiches (try the Thai chicken variety), fish, salads, pastas (opt for *rigatoni basilica,* with sweet peppers, sausage, and seasoned ricotta), and *pupus,* this restaurant is also a well-known singles bar, with a wide selection of beer and fresh oyster shooters. ♦ American ♦ M-Sa lunch and dinner; Su brunch and dinner. Reservations recommended. Second level. 591.9132 ♿

85 Ala Moana Beach Park Protected by an offshore reef, this beach is safe for swimming year-round, with lifeguards on duty during peak hours. It's also equipped with picnic facilities, public bathrooms, a snack stand, and tennis courts. ♦ Ala Moana Park Dr (just south of Ala Moana Blvd)

86 Ward Warehouse A variety of family restaurants (everything from pizza and sandwiches to seafood), boutiques, and specialty stores are found in this two-story mall. ♦ M-Sa 10AM-9PM; Su. 1050 Ala Moana Blvd (between Kamakee St and Ward Ave). 591.8411 ♿

Within Ward Warehouse:

Native Books & Beautiful Things Owner Maile Mayer, a local small-press publisher, founded this business in 1990 as a mail-order company after becoming aware of how many inauthentic items were being sold to visitors seeking Hawaiian goods. She opened her first store in Honolulu in 1995. This, the third—and largest—outlet, at 4,000 square feet, carries 1,300 titles and handicrafts by a two-dozen-member collective . . . and all very authentic. ◆ Daily. First level. 596.8885 ♿ Also at: 222 Merchant St (between Richards and Alakea Sts). 599.5511; Bishop Museum, 1525 Bernice St (between Kapalama Ave and Likelike Hwy). 848.4119

NOHEA GALLERY

Nohea Gallery This eclectic gallery features crafts by Hawaiian artists. You'll find paintings, lithographs, ceramics, sculpture, woodwork, glasswork, prints, and jewelry. ◆ Daily. First level. 596.0074 ♿

The Old Spaghetti Factory ★$ Part of the popular mainland chain, this is the perfect place for feasting on inexpensive carbohydrates. ◆ Italian ◆ Daily lunch and dinner. Second level. 591.2513 ♿

Kincaid's Fish, Chop and Steak House ★★$$$$ Locals come here for lunch meetings and to fraternize after work, visitors go—and rightly so—for the rock salt–roasted prime rib or the New York steak with garlic-pepper crust. A distant tie for second on the list are the drop-dead harbor view and rich koa-wood interior. Third place? The marinated pork chops on the sunset menu. ◆ Seafood/Steak ◆ Daily lunch and dinner. Second level. 591.2005 ♿

87 Dixie Grill ★★$ Nothing at this popular indoor-outdoor dining room is endemic to Hawaii. Straight out of the South, it offers plates filled with smoked pulled pork, skillet-fried chicken, coconut shrimp, and steamed crab, as well as singing waiters, popular streetside eating, and an enormous basin front and center for washing up after the meal. ◆ Southern ◆ Daily lunch and dinner. 404 Ward Ave (at Halekauwila St). 596.8359 ♿

Aiea, Oahu is the only city in the United States whose name is composed exclusively of vowels.

The islands are home to 80 poisonous plants.

At the height of the most recent real estate boom in 1990, a Japanese corporation paid $75 million for all 58 of Hawaii's 7-Eleven stores.

JOHN DOMINIS

88 John Dominis ★★$$$$ Named after an early governor of Oahu, this oceanside restaurant beckons from a spectacular point in Kewalo Basin; floor-to-ceiling windows showcase the exceptional view (if you can stop gawking at the indoor lagoon filled with stingrays and manta rays). Favorites include the fish-and-prawns dish and the macadamia nut cream pie. This restaurant is also a fabulous, albeit high-priced, choice for Sunday brunch, with omelettes, pasta, or waffles prepared to order at different food bars. ◆ Continental ◆ M-Sa dinner; Su brunch and dinner. Reservations recommended. 43 Ahui St (south of Ala Moana Blvd). 523.0955 ♿

89 Hawaiian Bagel ★$ This modest bagel factory bakes them as fresh as they get. Sandwiches, quiche, and a limited selection of deli items are also available. ◆ Bagels/Deli ◆ Daily breakfast and lunch. No credit cards accepted. 753-B Halekauwila St (between Ward Ave and Cooke St). 596.0638 ♿

90 Yanagi Sushi ★★★$$ Serving some of the freshest sashimi and sushi in Hawaii, this shoji-screened restaurant packs in locals as well as tourists and celebrities (photos and autographs of the latter adorn the walls). ◆ Sushi bar ◆ Daily lunch and dinner. Reservations recommended. 762 Kapiolani Blvd (between Ward Ave and Cooke St). 537.1525 ♿

91 Columbia Inn ★$ Every city has a spot that caters to the media, and this is Honolulu's. Adjacent to the **News Building,** which houses both of the state's daily papers, the restaurant and bar opened the day the Japanese bombed Pearl Harbor. Journalists and public relations people choose from the mixed menu of basic American and Japanese cuisine, with assorted local favorites thrown in for good measure. Order a burger, saimin, or the sizzling steak platter. Kids eat free on Monday and Tuesday. ◆ Japanese/American ◆ Daily lunch and dinner. 645 Kapiolani Blvd (between Cooke and South Sts). 596.0757 ♿

92 News Building Home of Hawaii's two daily newspapers, this green building with a red-tile roof is also a gallery where local artists' work is shown. Liberty Newspapers runs the *Honolulu Star-Bulletin,* the afternoon publication, and Gannett Corporation owns the *Honolulu Advertiser,* the more successful morning paper. Free tours are available; call advance. ◆ M-F. 605 Kapiolani Blvd (at South St). 525.8000 &

93 Mission Houses Museum The first frame house **(Frame House)** in the islands was built here in 1821 for newly arrived Congregationalist missionaries. Two coral-block buildings were soon added to the prim white-frame structure: the **Chamberlain House** (1831) was for the mission's purchasing agent; and the **Printing Office** (1841) is where printer Elisha Loomis established Hawaii's first press. Now operated by the Hawaiian Mission Children's Society (descendants of the missionaries), the museum is a repository of mementos from Hawaii's early history. A visitors' center houses a gift shop, a library holds a substantial collection of Hawaiiana, and a 14-minute video tells the story (part of it, anyway) of Hawaii's past. ◆ Admission

(includes a 45-minute guided tour). Tu-Sa. 553 S King St (at Kawaiahao St). 531.0481

94 Restaurant Row The selection of trendy restaurants and bars near the Honolulu waterfront make this is an "in" place for discriminating singles and yuppies. ◆ 500 Ala Moana Blvd (at Punchbowl St)

Within Restaurant Row:

Sunset Grill ★★$$$ The noise level tends to get out of hand in this high-ceilinged restaurant, but that hasn't made it any less popular, especially for lunch. The menu offers a pleasant selection of pasta, salads, grilled fish, and meat, with tempting appetizers to start. The Anaheim peppers or roasted garlic and goat cheese are both outstanding. ◆ Pacific Rim ◆ M-F lunch and dinner; Sa-Su dinner. 521.4409 &

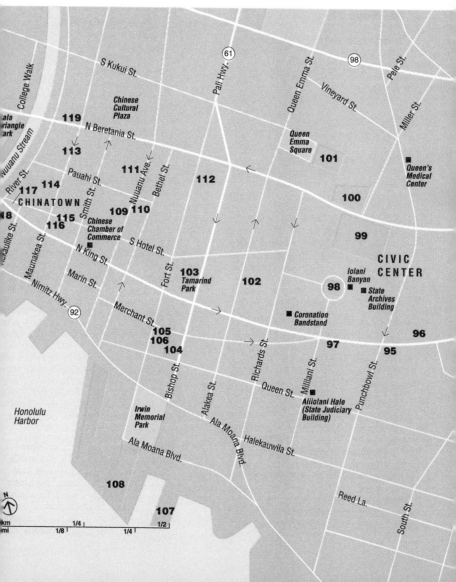

Ruth's Chris Steak House ★★$$$$
Twenty-four-ounce T-bone steaks and 16-ounce rib eyes as well as other entrées like chicken breast broiled with lemon and herbs are served in an atmosphere enhanced by padded booths and white linen. Everything is à la carte, so dinner can get pricey real quick. ◆ Steak ◆ Daily dinner. Reservations recommended. 599.3860 ♿

COURTESY OF KAWAIAHAO CHURCH

95 **Kawaiahao Church** Completed in 1842, more than 20 years after the first New England missionaries arrived aboard the *Thaddeus,* this handsome structure took 5 years to build, using 14,000 coral blocks that the congregation cut from ocean reefs. The walls of **Kawaiahao,** which means "freshwater pool of Hao" (the ancient spring), have witnessed royal marriages, coronations, and funerals. The Sunday 10:30AM service, conducted in Hawaiian and English, is noted for its stirring sermons, first-rate choir, and organ music. Visitors may take a self-guided tour. ◆ Call for hours. 957 Punchbowl St (at S King St). 522.1333

On the grounds of the Kawaiahao Church:

King Lunalilo's Tomb This tomb can be seen near the entrance to the church. Lunalilo was the only Hawaiian monarch who refused to be interred in the **Royal Mausoleum** in Nuuanu Valley, asking on his deathbed to be buried closer to his people at **Kawaiahao.** The churchyard is also the resting place of several missionaries and converts.

96 **Honolulu Hale (Honolulu City Hall)**
The gracious California Spanish–style design of the city hall, built in 1929, provides a nice contrast to **Iolani Palace** and the **State Capitol** (see below). Italian sculptor Mario Valdastri designed the bronze-sheeted front doors, which weigh 1,500 pounds each; the 4,500-pound chandeliers in the terra-cotta–tiled courtyard, patterned after one in the 13th-century Palazzo Bargello in Florence, Italy; and the columns and balconies made of coral and crushed Hawaiian sandstone. Two three-story wings in the original style were added in the early 1950s. A belt of green space links the city hall to the colonial-style **Mission Memorial** buildings and the gray concrete **Honolulu Municipal Building.** ◆ 530 S King St (between Alapai and Punchbowl Sts). 523.4385

97 **King Kamehameha I Statue** The gold-and-black statue of the spear-carrying chief wearing a feather cloak and helmet stands outside **Aliiolani Hale** (the State Judiciary Building). King Kamehameha I, who conquered and then united the islands, is regarded as Hawaii's greatest warrior. This statue is a replica, however; the original stands in front of the **Kapaau Courthouse** in Kohala on the Big Island (see page 25), where Kamehameha was born and reared and where he first came to power. Visit here in June during the King Kamehameha Day celebration when the statue's outstretched arms are filled with dozens of leis. ◆ 417 S King St (between Punchbowl and Mililani Sts)

98 **Iolani Palace** In an attempt to keep the highly polished Douglas fir floors scuff-free, America's only royal palace (pictured above) provides guests with booties to cover their shoes. The palace, whose name means "the hawk of heaven," epitomizes King Kalakaua's preoccupation with emulating the royal courts of Europe. Aptly nicknamed "The Merry Monarch," Kalakaua had a penchant for surrounding himself with material goods. With construction costs topping $360,000, the palace was completed in 1882, 8 years after Kalakaua was crowned king. The design, the work of architects **Thomas J. Baker, Isaac Moore,** and **C.J. Wall,** provided the perfect backdrop for Kalakaua's elaborate court life. The palace was filled with period furniture shipped around Cape Horn or painstakingly

copied by local artisans. Royal guards were outfitted in dazzling uniforms that weighed entirely too much for the tropics.

Following Kalakaua's death in 1891 and the coup that toppled the monarchy in 1893, the palace became Hawaii's seat of government. Until 1969, when the new **State Capitol** (see below) was built, the Senate met in the palace's royal dining room and the House of Representatives in the throne room. Some $6 million has been spent over the years restoring the palace to its former glory. The nonprofit Friends of Iolani Palace conducts 45-minute tours that include the viewing of a video on palace history. ◆ Admission. Tours: Tu-Sa 9AM-2:15PM every 15 minutes. Reservations recommended. 364 S King St (between Punchbowl and Richards Sts). 522.0822 ዼ

On the grounds of Iolani Palace:

Iolani Banyan What appears to be a massive tree is really two banyans that have been intertwined for a century. Said to have been planted by Queen Kapiolani, the banyan provides a shady canopy for passersby.

Coronation Bandstand King Kalakaua wanted a fitting site for his coronation, so in 1883 he built this gazebo and crowned himself and Queen Kapiolani in a lavish ceremony. The copper dome of the wedding cake–like pavilion is the original, but the rest of the structure was rebuilt of concrete after termites had weakened it. Eight pillars symbolizing Hawaii's major islands support the dome. Kalakaua was the only king crowned here, but the bandstand also serves as a stage for gubernatorial inaugurations and weddings. In 1993 it was the site of a Hawaiian sovereignty rally, which drew thousands of spectators. Each Friday, the Royal Hawaiian Band, established in 1836 by King Kamehameha II, gives a free concert at noon.

99 State Capitol Designed to take advantage of the views of the ocean, city, and mountains, the capitol features a four-story atrium that lets natural light fill the center of the structure. The interior trim, paneling, and furnishings are koa wood, and the courtyard is paved with Molokai sand, a nice Hawaiian touch. The state legislature and the governor moved into the $24.5-million building in 1969, after being headquartered in **Iolani Palace.** The sign on the governor's doors reads *E komo mai* (Please come in). Visitors are free to sit in on regular sessions of the Senate and the House of Representatives, which are held

from January through April. While the laws of parliamentary procedure are followed on the floor, proper English tends to crumble in favor of local Pidgin (Hawaiian slang) during heated debates. The capitol's most festive occasion is the traditional opening of the legislature the third Wednesday of every January. On that day, both the legislators and their desks are covered with flowers and leis. Morning festivities include hula dancing, songs, and even comedy routines by leading island entertainers. At noon, everyone adjourns to lavish buffets. ◆ Building: M-F; Courtyard: daily 24 hours. 415 S Beretania St (between Punchbowl and Richards Sts). 586.2211 ዼ

At the entrance to the State Capitol:

Queen Liliuokalani Statue Hawaii's last monarch is memorialized in an eight-foot bronze sculpture. Unveiled in 1982, the statue by Marianne Pineda shows the queen standing erect, her left hand holding the proposed constitution of 1893 (which cost her the throne) and a page of "Aloha Oe," the islands' traditional song of farewell. Her right hand is extended in friendship.

In the State Capitol courtyard:

Father Damien Statue Belgian priest Damien Joseph de Veuster lived and worked among the lepers of Molokai for 16 years before dying of leprosy (now called Hansen's disease) in 1889. He is memorialized in this bronze statue by Marisol Escobar. The work drew a great deal of criticism when it was unveiled in 1969 because it portrays the priest in his dying days, when his features were deformed by the disease.

100 Washington Place When the American naval captain who built this estate (named after George Washington) in 1846 was lost at sea, his son, John Dominis, moved into the mansion with his wife, Lydia Kapaakea, the future Queen Liliuokalani. After Dominis's death and the overthrow of the monarchy in 1893, Liliuokalani came here to live until her death in 1917. The governor of Hawaii now resides in the stately two-story mansion, and the ground floor, most of which has been restored to look as it did originally, is used for state receptions. Past governors have hosted dinners here for visiting dignitaries, including Queen Elizabeth and the late Emperor of Japan. The upstairs rooms are private quarters for the governor and his family. The building is closed to the public except on such special occasions such as inauguration celebrations. ◆ S Beretania and Miller Sts. 538.3113

The most common name in the Oahu phone directory is "Lee." It takes up 200 inches.

101 St. Andrew's Cathedral Shortly after the traumatic death of his four-year-old son Albert, King Kamehameha IV converted to the Church of England and founded **St. Andrew's.** The king died a year later at age 29, but construction of this Episcopalian headquarters began in 1867 under the direction of his widow, Queen Emma. The uniformed students on the premises go to **St. Andrew's Priory,** at the back of the cathedral. ♦ Queen Emma Sq (just southeast of Queen Emma St). 524.2822 &

102 Young Sing ★$$ Lunch conversations reverberate off the high ceiling of this popular and crowded Chinese restaurant. The extensive menu includes outstanding dim sum. ♦ Chinese ♦ Daily lunch and dinner. 1055 Alakea St (between S Hotel and S King Sts). 531.1366 &

103 Tamarind Park Bring a brown-bag lunch and enjoy one of the frequent noontime concerts held in this green, open space fronting the **Pauahi Tower** office building. Henry Moore's *Upright Motive No. 9,* an 11-foot bronze statue in the reflecting pool, was executed in 1979. Loosely based on the human form, it draws its inspiration from the prehistoric monoliths at Stonehenge, North American Indian totem poles, and Polynesian sculpture. ♦ Bishop St (between S Hotel and S King Sts)

104 Alexander & Baldwin Building This distinctive corporate headquarters (pictured above) opened in 1929. Alexander and Baldwin founded the youngest of the "Big Five" companies (the others are C. Brewer & Company, Theo. H. Davis & Company, Amfac Inc., and Castle & Cooke Inc.), a group of corporations that ruled the islands economically until Hawaii became a state (and that still have quite a bit of influence). Architects **C.W. Dickey** and **Hart Wood** designed the structure with Dickey's trademark Hawaiian roof; the subtle Chinese influence was Wood's signature. At the time, the building was one of only two Honolulu structures made completely of concrete and steel. Admirers praised its workmanship and details, particularly the murals, terra-cotta ornamentation, and black Belgian marble in the first-floor reception area. A floating mezzanine has been added to the building, but many original details remain. ♦ M-F. 822 Bishop St (between Merchant and Queen Sts). 525.6611 &

105 Stangenwald Building Few people know that this six-story building, now dwarfed by those surrounding it, was the tallest structure in Honolulu when it went up in 1901. Designed by **Ripley and Vickey,** the monument to simpler times is today filled with offices. ♦ M-F. 119 Merchant St (between Bishop and Fort Sts)

106 C. Brewer Building Constructed in 1930, this last and smallest of the "Big Five" headquarters built in downtown Honolulu looks more like a mansion than a corporate office. Chief architect **Hardie Phillips** gave the two-story structure a Mediterranean flavor with Hawaiian motifs. Details include wrought-iron rails and grillwork that represent sugarcane and light fixtures that recall sugar cubes. ♦ M-F. 827 Fort St (between Merchant and Queen Sts)

107 Hawaii Maritime Center Trace the role of the sea in life on the islands, from Polynesian migration by canoe to the whaling days and the era of Matson steamships, at this museum. Three thousand years of maritime history are displayed. The ship docked outside, *Falls of Clyde,* is part of the one-hour tour. ♦ Admission. Daily. Pier 7, just southwest of Ala Moana Blvd and Bishop St. 536.6373 &

At the Hawaii Maritime Center:

Falls of Clyde The last of its kind, this square-rigged, four-masted, iron-hulled ship used to sail into Honolulu Harbor more than a century ago, at a time when the docks were lined with similar vessels and sailors could virtually step from one ship to another. Built in Scotland, the wooden ship was purchased in 1898 by the Matson cruise line to serve on the route between San Francisco and Hawaii. The ship was restored in 1963 and is now a museum.

Tropical Treasures

Chances are your first introduction to the Hawaiian Islands will include a gift of flowers, since many guests are greeted with leis either at the airport or their hotel. Hawaiians take great pride in their flowers; here's a brief guide to some of their finest flora:

Anthurium *(Anthurium andraeanum)* This heart-shaped flower grows in many colors, including white, greenish white, pink, red, lavender, and pink-streaked. The surface of the bloom has a waxy shine that looks almost artificial. When anthuriums are cut and placed in a vase, they last for weeks.

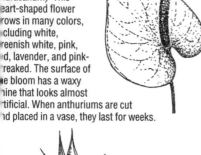

Lobster-claw Heliconia *(Heliconia humilis)* A member of the same family as the bird of paradise, this plant has leaves the color and shape of cooked lobster claws. Cradled within these leaves are small green flowers.

Bird of Paradise *(Strelitzia reginae)* Originally from South Africa, this ostentatious flower is easy to identify—just look for plumage (bright orange and blue petals) topping a long gray-green stalk. Each flower blooms in six stages, a new one every couple of days.

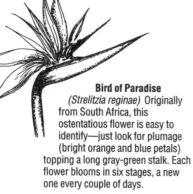

Night-blooming Cereus *(Hylocereus undatus)* A nocturnal beauty, this cactus blooms from June through October. The fragrant yellow blossoms open at dusk and close when the sun rises.

Ginger *(Zingiberaceae)* This large-leafed plant is known for its fragrant smell and comes in 47 different varieties that are used the world over as a spice, in medicine, and as ornaments.

Plumeria *(Meli; Frangipani)* A favorite of lei-makers, the plumeria is a fragrant, durable flower.

Hibiscus *(Hibiscus rosa-sinensis; Hibiscus koki'o)* Hibiscus shrubs grow easily on all the islands and come in several colors and shapes. They're rarely used in leis, because the large showy flowers are so fragile.

Silversword *(Argyroxiphium sandwicense)* This plant grows in Maui's **Haleakala National Park** and on the **Big Island** in rocky or volcanic soil at altitudes of 6,000 to 12,000 feet. Its silver spike leaves grow on a six-foot-tall stalk, which is capped in August by tufts of flowers.

ALOHA TOWER MARKETPLACE

108 Aloha Tower Marketplace Passengers who sailed Matson steamships to Hawaii decades ago will remember the **Aloha Tower** as an imposing architectural landmark—it was the tallest structure on the waterfront. The 10-story, 184-foot-high tower, designed in 1921 by **Arthur Reynolds,** doesn't seem tall at all any more compared to the steel-and-glass high-rises of downtown Honolulu. But it's the centerpiece of one of Honolulu's trendy gathering places, a $100-million collection of 120 shops and restaurants designed to attract visitors to the historic port area of town. ♦ Pier 9, just southwest of Ala Moana Blvd and Fort St. 537.9260 ♿

Within the Aloha Tower Marketplace:

Big Island Steak House ★★$$$ This restaurant was transplanted from the Big Island and looks to have survived the move fairly well, except that, unlike the original, it doesn't metamorphose into a nightclub at 10PM. A romantic interlude over lobster or filet mignon is the specialty of the house. ♦ Steak/Seafood ♦ Daily lunch and dinner. 537.4446 ♿

Gordon Biersch Brewery Restaurant ★★★$$$ Like its San Francisco and Palo Alto branches, this place has become popular with the thirtysomething crowd. Folks drift in to knock back a few of the restaurant's five kinds of microbrewed beers and gobble down a plate of seafood Napoleon (alternating layers of marinated seafood and wontons, topped with papaya salsa and avocado sour cream) or Marzen-barbecued baby back ribs with Asian slaw and garlic fries. Hold out for a booth in the dining room decorated in contemporary style; or, better yet, a harbor-view outside table. ♦ Pacific Rim ♦ Daily lunch and dinner. Reservations recommended. 599.4877 ♿

109 Lai Fong Inc. Low rents and interesting storefronts and spaces have attracted art dealers to Honolulu's Chinatown, resulting in a number of galleries clustered within several blocks of Nuuanu Avenue. This is one of our favorites. While you could easily mistake it for a thrift shop, what with the musty mounds of Chinese bric-a-brac, real treasures lurk in the shadows here: carved jade buttons, *cheongsams* (fitted Chinese dresses), funky ivory jewelry from pre-statehood days, and garish Chinese statues of folk gods. ♦ M-F; Sa 11AM-3PM. 1118 Nuuanu Ave (between N Pauahi and N Hotel Sts). 537.3497 ♿

110 Hawaii Theater This restored 1,400-seat beaux-arts theater hosts art shows and theatrical and musical performances in an auditorium that features mosaics, columns, and bas-reliefs with Shakespearean themes. ♦ 1130 Bethel St (at S Pauahi St). 528.0506

111 Pegge Hopper Gallery One of Hawaii's best-known artists, Pegge Hopper paints canvases of huge Hawaiian women in Gauguin colors. Their various poses create a feeling of calm serenity. You can also buy greeting cards, calendars, and T-shirts featuring her work. ♦ Tu-F; Sa 11AM-3PM. 1164 Nuuanu Ave (between N Beretania and N Pauahi Sts). 524.1160 ♿

112 Cathedral of Our Lady of Peace The first Catholic priests came to Hawaii in 1827 from France, but this cathedral wasn't dedicated until 1843, when opposition to Catholicism had died down. Three years later, the first pipe organ on the islands was played here. Mass is held daily. ♦ Bishop St (between S Hotel and Beretania Sts). 536.7036 ♿

113 Maunakea Street Lei Stands Along a few blocks of Maunakea Street are small storefronts selling leis, with workrooms behind the refrigerated flower cases. The scents of carnation, maile, puakinikini, ginger, pikake, and tuberose fill the air as women string the leis with long, thin needles. These shops offer some of the best prices and selections of leis. **Cindy's Lei and Flower Shoppe** (1034 Maunakea St, 536.6538) is a family-run landmark that has been around for generations. Also recommended are **Lita's Lei and Flower Shoppe** (59 N Beretania St, 521.9065), **Jenny's** (65 N Beretania St, 521.1595), and **Sweetheart's** (69 N Beretania St, 537.3011). ♦ Maunakea St (between N Beretania St and Nimitz Hwy)

114 Maunakea Marketplace If you're cruisin' through Chinatown, don't miss this market-place and don't eat before you come here. A permanent conglomeration of stands, set up county-fair style, sells food from all over the world—the Philippines, Japan, Singapore, Malaysia, China, Hawaii, Thailand, Korea, Italy, India, and Vietnam. After you're filled to the brim, waddle through the huge Asian market and gaze upon the myriad foodstuffs for sale. ♦ Daily. Maunakea St (between N Pauahi and N Hotel Sts)

115 Hotel Street Hawaii's version of skid row isn't what it was during World War II, when servicemen frequented the area's red-light establishments. James Jones documented the seediness of these few downtown blocks in his novel *From Here to Eternity*. You can still buy a cold beer at any of the bars, and ladies of the night continue to beckon from the street corners, but the city is making an effort to clean up the area (as is indicated by the police station on one of the side streets). Restaurants and groceries operated mainly by immigrants from Southeast Asia are gradually replacing the bars and X-rated businesses. ♦ Between Bishop and River Sts

16 Wong and Wong Restaurant ★★$ Wonderful down-home cooking characterizes this modest restaurant. The trick is to order the specials, listed on signs hanging from the walls. The steamed fish, especially the mullet, is prepared Chinese style with a soy-sauce, ginger, and green-onion sauce. ♦ Chinese ♦ Daily lunch and dinner. Reservations recommended. 1023 Maunakea St (between N Hotel and N King Sts). 521.4492

17 Ba-le Sandwich Shop 1 ★$ Some of the best French baguettes in the islands (and great French coffee, too) are made and sold by the Vietnamese owners of the **Ba-le** concessions around Honolulu. This little coffee shop—the **Ba-le** headquarters—serves spring rolls, 20 noodle dishes, and sandwiches that hint of the flavors of Saigon. ♦ Vietnamese ♦ Daily breakfast and lunch. No credit cards accepted. 150 N King St (between Kekaulike and River Sts). 521.3973 ♿

18 Oahu Market Every morning this large, bustling market illustrates how busy Chinatown was before supermarkets came into existence. The regular customers obviously prefer to select their fresh fish and roasted pork from butchers who know their names. You'll hear Cantonese, Vietnamese, and other Asian languages as prices are agreed upon. When in season, mangoes and litchis are sold here, but you'll have the most fun buying *char siu* (barbecued pork). The butcher will chop the meat into bite-size pieces so you can nibble as you browse. ♦ M-Sa 6:30AM-4:30PM; Su 6:30AM-noon. 145 N King St (at Kekaulike St). 841.6924

19 Doong Kong Lau-Hakka Restaurant ★★$ The food here (ginger chicken, shrimp with broccoli, etc.) is as superb as the decor is simple. Hakka cuisine isn't as spicy as Szechuan, but it's just as good. Some of the more popular selections arrive at your table on sizzling platters. ♦ Chinese ♦ Daily breakfast, lunch, and dinner. 100 N Beretania St (at Maunakea St), Suite 110. 531.8833 ♿

120 Foster Botanic Gardens Feel free to picnic and wander in this 13.5-acre green domain at the edge of downtown Honolulu. A plethora of orchids and other plants (5,000 species of tropical flora in all) flourishes in the oldest botanical garden in the state. A gallery and bookstore also are on site. ♦ Nominal fee. Daily. Tours: M-F 1PM. Reservations required for tours. 50 N Vineyard Blvd (between Nuuanu Ave and Aala St). 522.7065 ♿

121 Punchbowl Crater (National Memorial Cemetery of the Pacific) Centuries ago, human lives were sacrificed here to appease the gods (hence the dormant volcano's Hawaiian name, *Puowaina*, which means "Hill of Sacrifice"). The crater's 114-acre floor is now the final resting place for veterans of World Wars I and II, the Korean and Vietnam Wars, and the Persian Gulf War, as well as their dependents. Some 34,000 white pillars in neat rows line the velvet expanse. The first rays of sun that probe the rim of the crater at dawn create a powerful effect, especially during the sunrise service on Easter Sunday. World War II journalist Ernie Pyle is buried here among the soldiers he immortalized, as is Ellison Onizuka, the astronaut from Hawaii who was killed in the *Challenger* space-shuttle disaster in 1986. ♦ Free. Daily. 2177 Puowaina Dr (off Lusitana St). 566.1430 ♿

122 Tantalus Drive If you start to get the feeling that the Honolulu area is short on natural beauty, make your way down this scenic route. Start on Puowaina Drive (on the north side of Punchbowl Crater), which eventually turns into Tantalus Drive and winds through some incredible real estate almost to the top of Mount Tantalus (2,013 feet), with pull-offs every mile or so to let you admire the view of Honolulu. At the top of Tantalus Drive, pull over and wander along the trails that meander through the valley, then head back down Round Top Drive, stopping at the **Puu Ualakaa State Wayside** to snap a few photos.

123 The Contemporary Museum A cultural oasis in a city where cartoonlike portraits of flippers, fins, and sunsets often pass for art, this museum in a stunning 3.5-acre setting exhibits works by artists of international reputation, including David Hockney and George Rickey. The main building, a former estate of Mrs. Charles Montague Cooke, consists of five interconnected galleries and a separate pavilion, although some of the most interesting works—large contemporary sculptures by Rickey, Robert Arneson, Tom Klesselmann, Charles Analdi, and others—are displayed on the impeccably landscaped grounds. The prints sold at the adjacent **Museum Shop** make wonderful gifts.

♦ Admission. Tu-Sa; Su noon-4PM. 2411 Makiki Heights Dr (between Makiki St and Tantalus Dr). 526.0232 ♿

Within The Contemporary Museum:

The Contemporary Cafe ★★$ If you are anywhere near the Makiki Heights area, stop at this chic cafe and choose from a wide selection of salads, gourmet sandwiches, daily specials (hope for escargot mezzanine, with sun-dried tomatoes, pesto butter, and wine sauce), and homemade desserts. On a sunny day, the outdoor seating surrounded by sculpture is unbeatable. ♦ Cafe ♦ Tu-Su lunch. Reservations recommended. 523.3362 ♿

124 Royal Mausoleum The most important burial place in the islands holds the remains of Kings Kamehameha II, III, IV, and V, King Kalakaua, Queen Liliuokalani, and other royalty and favored friends of their courts. (King Kamehameha I's body has never been discovered, though historians presume it's hidden in a secret burial cave on the Big Island, where he died in 1891.) The other Hawaiian monarch who isn't buried here is King Lunalilo, who requested a private tomb on the grounds of **Kawaiahao Church** (see page 140). King Kamehameha V chose the mausoleum's three-acre site in 1865, and royal remains were moved from an old, overcrowded tomb on the **Iolani Palace** grounds. The cross-shaped chapel was designed by the islands' first professional architect, **Theodore Heuck.** ♦ Free. M-F. 2261 Nuuanu Ave (between Judd St and Pali Hwy)

125 Queen Emma Summer Palace This cool summer retreat in Nuuanu Valley belonged to Queen Emma and her husband, King Kamehameha IV. When the Duke of Edinburgh visited Hawaii in 1869, Emma had the elegant **Edinburgh Room** built to accommodate a lavish gala for him (a party that he, unfortunately, failed to attend). The Hawaiian government purchased the palace in 1890, after Emma's death, and the Daughters of Hawaii have maintained it as a museum since 1915. The grand rooms contain many personal belongings of the royal family, including the koa wood cradle of Emma and Kamehameha's son, Albert, heir to the throne and Queen Victoria's godson, who died at the age of four. Self-guided tours are available. ♦ Admission. Daily. 2913 Pali Hwy (between Laimi and Puiwa Rds). 595.3167

126 Alexander Cartwright's Tomb The man who some believe invented baseball (others credit Abner Doubleday) was buried in Honolulu on 12 July 1892, and his pink granite tomb is in **Oahu Cemetery** (to the right of the road, a few hundred feet from the entrance). Alexander Cartwright was chairman of the committee that drew up the rules for baseball in 1845, and he fixed the base paths at 90 feet. He also umpired in the first official game, held 19 June 1846 between the **New York Knickerbockers Baseball Club** (which later became the basketball team that plays today) and the **New York Nine** in Hoboken, New Jersey. Later, on a trip to the islands, Cartwright became so enamored of Honolulu that he moved here and began to teach baseball. (He also founded the city's first volunteer fire department.) **Cartwright Playground** in Makiki is where he is said to have laid out Hawaii's first baseball diamond. ♦ 2162 Nuuanu Ave (between Judd St and Kawananakoa Pl). 538.1538

127 Dole Cannery Outlet Center In the old days, the cloying smell of pineapple filled the air as you neared the cannery in the Iwilei District. Two million pineapples a day were processed here, each inspected by women in white aprons, gloves, and caps. Now the buildings house brand-name outlet stores, including **Levi Strauss, Big Dog Sportswear,** and **Hawaiian Island Gems,** along with photos and artifacts from the pineapple's heyday. The shopping center has expanded exponentially and is hard to miss—it's painted seven shades of yellow. A free multimedia show on the history of pineapple production in Hawaii goes on every half hour from 9:30AM to 3:30PM. At press time there were plans to build a $40-million aquarium on the property. ♦ Free. Daily. 650 Iwilei Rd (between Sumner and Pacific Sts). 528.2236 ♿

128 Hilo Hattie Garment Factory Every month, more than 30,000 aloha garments (shirts, dresses, shorts, and the like) are cranked out here. Busloads of tourists come to watch the garments being made by dozens of workers toiling at their machines. The outlet store, Hawaii's largest, is a great place for alohawear souvenirs. An artificial lei and a cup of pineapple juice are given to all visitors. ♦ Free. Daily. 700 Nimitz Hwy (at Pacific St). 537.2926 ♿

129 Tamashiro Market Look for a hot-pink building and the faded landmark sign (a pinkish-orange crab), and start hoping for a parking space. The market is worth a visit, especially if you love seafood, as it offers a wide selection of fresh island fish as well as favorites from the mainland and other parts of the world. The kids will enjoy watching the live crabs, frogs, and lobsters crawling around in tanks, and you'll marvel at the extraordinary beauty of some of the sea's strange bounty. A huge board hanging over one of the fish counters lists the Hawaiian and mainland names for fish. If you're not squeamish, there's a first-rate selection of *poke*. ♦ Daily. 802 N King St (at Palama St). 841.8047 ♿

30 Bishop Museum When Charles Reed Bishop founded this museum in 1889 in honor of the Hawaiian heritage of his wife, Princess Bernice Pauahi, he hoped it would rank among the great museums on earth. No doubt he would be proud to know that it now not only houses the world's greatest collection of Hawaiian cultural and natural-history artifacts but is a highly regarded center for Pacific-area studies. The museum's success is largely attributable to its director, W. Donald Duckworth, who came to Honolulu in the early 1980s and continues to expand the exhibition and publication programs.

The museum's centerpiece is **Hawaiian Hall**—three floors of carved war gods and feather cloaks, mementos of the 19th-century monarchs, valuable Polynesian artifacts, and more. The **Hall of Hawaiian Natural History** offers fascinating displays on the islands' geological origins, including a lava tube with its own ecosystem. Children can touch lava or try making a grass hut in the **Hall of Discovery,** across the lawn from the main gallery building. Next door is the **Planetarium** and the **Shop Pacifica,** which stocks numerous books on Hawaiian and Polynesian history. You can also purchase authentic reproductions of museum pieces, such as bags and hats woven from *lauhala* (the leaves of the pandanus tree), and Hawaiian quilts. A branch of **Native Books & Beautiful Things** (848.4119) is also here. ♦ Admission. Daily. Tours: M-F 10AM, noon. Planetarium shows: M-Th, Su 11AM, 2PM; F-Sa 11AM, 2PM, 7PM. Observatory: F-Sa 7-9PM, weather permitting. 1525 Bernice St (between Houghtailing St and Likelike Hwy). 847.3511; planetarium reservations 847.8201

31 LaMariana Sailing Club ★$$ Situated on the docks on a peninsula outside a visitor's ordinary travel pattern, this dining spot is just the place to go to get off the Waikiki tourist trail. It's kitschy, with tiki statues and glass fishing floats of all description (the piano player and other staffers and regulars worked at the kitschy **Tahitian Lanai** before that restaurant closed in 1998), and the food runs to steak and lobster plates, shrimp scampi, grilled *ahi,* and other fairly standard items— but the conversation around the piano is often worth the trip. ♦ American ♦ Daily lunch and dinner. 50 Sand Island Access Rd (south of Pahounui Dr). 848.2800 ♿

132 Moanalua Gardens Huge monkeypod trees dominate this sprawling 26-acre playground that is open to the public. The Prince Lot Hula Festival is held here each July to honor the prince (who became King Kamehameha V) for reviving the ancient hula during his 1863-72 reign, after more than four decades of a missionary-imposed ban. The only remaining buildings are a cottage where Kamehameha V used to entertain his friends and the **Chinese Hall** built in the early 1900s by Samuel Mills Damon. Nearby Moanalua Valley features petroglyphs and other historic sights. ♦ Daily 7AM-6PM. Nature hikes into the valley twice monthly; call for dates and reservations. Moanalua Fwy and Jarrett White Rd. 833.1944

133 Honolulu International Country Club Designed in part by Arnold Palmer, this 18-hole course (par 71, 5,987 yards) is private. ♦ Expensive greens fees. Daily. Members and guests only. 1690 Ala Puumalu (just west of Ala Hahanui). 833.4541

Southeast Oahu

Not far from the hurly-burly of Honolulu, the southeast section of Oahu is a quiet, natural region of uncrowded white-sand beaches, dramatic lava rock coastline, and jagged cliffs. In the late 1980s public outcry halted proposed development there, and thus far the area has escaped encroaching civilization. **Sandy Beach** and **Makapuu Beach** are considered two of the best bodyboarding spots on the island, and the calm, clear waters of **Hanauma Bay** make it easy for snorkelers to observe the colorful residents of the underwater state park here.

134 Swiss Inn ★★$$$ Fans of Martin Wyss's cooking love this restaurant for its affordable menu and first-rate cuisine. Red napkins top white tablecloths at this out-of-the-way "in" spot; go early to snag one of the wooden booths lining the walls. The veal dishes (Wiener schnitzel, veal medaillons, Holstein schnitzel) are very popular, and there's also pasta, chicken, seafood, and fondue. ♦ Continental ♦ W-Sa dinner; Su brunch and dinner. Niu Valley Shopping Center, 5730 Kalanianaole Hwy (at Halemaumau St). 377.5447 ♿

The reef runway at Honolulu International Airport was designed as an alternate landing site for space shuttles.

135 Roy's Restaurant ★★★$$$ Roy Yamaguchi was a leader in establishing a regional Hawaiian/California cuisine, and his consistently innovative creations keep it interesting. He calls his cuisine "Euro-Asian," and specialties include seafood pot stickers; ravioli of lamb, goat cheese, and pesto; lobster in macadamia-nut butter sauce; and rack of Niihau lamb. The hundreds of other selections change regularly, depending on what's in season. The place is wildly successful, although the noise level in the trendy dining room is distracting to conversationalists, and the restaurant is in an odd location on the outskirts of the Hawaii Kai neighborhood. Jazz is performed on Friday and Saturday after 8PM, and Hawaiian music is on tap on Sunday at the same time. ♦ Euro-Asian ♦ Daily dinner. Reservations recommended. 6600 Kalanianaole Hwy (between Keahole St and Hawaii Kai Dr). 396.7697 &

136 Hanauma Bay Nestled in a volcanic crater that's missing a chunk on one side, this bay is a beautiful snorkeling spot, with waves so gentle even nonswimmers feel safe. The fish in this underwater state park are protected by law from spearhunters and anglers, which means snorkelers often find themselves nose-to-nose with brilliantly colored reef fish boldly going about their business (they're accustomed to stares). Food for the fish can be purchased at the concession stands, where snorkel gear is rented too. The best spot for swimming (but not snorkeling) here is the **Keyhole,** a sandy-bottomed section at the far end of the park. Nonswimmers will enjoy the **Toilet Bowl,** a hole in the rock where waves shoot out at regular intervals. The bay's downside is that it gets pretty crowded; try to avoid the afternoon rush. The preserve is closed on Tuesday to give the marine life some private time. This bay may look familiar to film buffs; this is where Elvis Presley starred in *Blue Hawaii,* and directors used it for beach scenes in *From Here to Eternity* (the Burt Lancaster–Deborah Kerr clincher, however, was shot near Makapuu Beach). ♦ Hanauma Bay Rd (southwest of Kalanianaole Hwy)

Bette Midler was born and schooled in Honolulu, and worked as a pineapple packer at the Dole Plantation.

---

137 Halona Blowhole A powerful gush of water spews into the air whenever ocean waves shooting through the lava tube here cause enough pressure to build. (You may hear a honking sound too.) On clear days, the islands of Molokai and Lanai are visible on the horizon, and on those rare, exceptionally fine days, you may see Maui between them. ♦ Kalanianaole Hwy (east of Hanauma Bay Rd)

137 Sandy Beach You may see people playing in the surf, but it can be dangerous to swim at this beach because the waves break in shallow water. While they offer some of the island's best tubes for bodysurfing, only experts should tackle these waves—many swimmers and bodysurfers have suffered broken necks throughout the years. A safer activity is kite flying. Picnic and public facilities are available and a lifeguard is on the lookout. ♦ Off Kalanianaole Hwy (east of Hanauma Bay Rd)

138 Makapuu Beach Park Although this is a dangerous swimming spot, there is excellent bodysurfing for experts. The lookout point above Makapuu offers a breathtaking view of the windward coastline, outlying Sharkfin and Rabbit Islands, and bodysurfers in the waves below. Public facilities and lifeguards are here too. ♦ Kalanianaole Hwy (southeast of Bell St)

139 Sea Life Park Paying to see fish and sea mammals in tanks and pools seems ridiculous when you're surrounded by water full of these saltwater denizens. But this park (see map on page 149) is well worth the price of admission for anyone who likes to watch dolphins, not to mention schools of tropical fish, monk seals, penguins, and other marine life—more than 4,000 creatures in all. The **Rocky Shores Exhibit** re-creates the surfswept intertidal zone of Hawaii's shoreline, and the **Hawaiian Reef Exhibit** simulates an offshore reef three fathoms below sea level, with live sharks, eels, sea turtles, and fish. A Pacific bottle-nosed dolphin rides a boogie board at the **Hawaiian Ocean Theater,** where you can also meet Kekaimalu, the world's only "wholphin" (a cross between a whale and a dolphin) on the guided tour. The park's setting is perfect for swimming, sunbathing, and picnicking. ♦ Admission. Daily. 41-202 Kalanianaole Hwy (southeast of Bell St). 259.7933 &

140 Bellows Field Beach Park You can ride the gentle bodysurfing waves at this rural beach, which is part of the Bellows Air Force Station, but only from noon Friday to Sunday evening, since war games are played here the rest of the week. ♦ Tinker Rd (northeast of Kalanianaole Hwy)

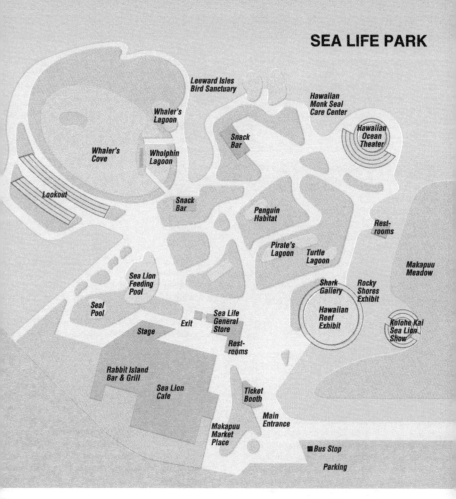

Map labels:

- Leeward Isles Bird Sanctuary
- Whaler's Lagoon
- Whaler's Cove
- Wholphin Lagoon
- Snack Bar
- Hawaiian Monk Seal Care Center
- Hawaiian Ocean Theater
- Lookout
- Snack Bar
- Penguin Habitat
- Restrooms
- Pirate's Lagoon
- Turtle Lagoon
- Makapuu Meadow
- Sea Lion Feeding Pool
- Shark Gallery
- Rocky Shores Exhibit
- Seal Pool
- Hawaiian Reef Exhibit
- Kolohe Kai Sea Lion Show
- Exit
- Sea Life General Store
- Stage
- Restrooms
- Rabbit Island Bar & Grill
- Sea Lion Cafe
- Ticket Booth
- Main Entrance
- Makapuu Market Place
- ■ Bus Stop
- Parking

Windward Oahu

An excursion to Windward Oahu is an enjoyable change of pace for people vacationing in Waikiki and elsewhere in Honolulu. Most people on this side of the island live in **Kailua,** a Honolulu bedroom community, or **Kaneohe,** an attractive suburb that's home to the Kaneohe Marine Corps Air Station. Kailua's main attraction is its wide, sandy beach—perfect for swimming and a top windsurfing spot. Kaneohe has a number of beachside and cliffside houses and an offshore reef where numerous colorful creatures hang out. Both towns have some good restaurants. To get an overview of the vast green arena known as Windward Oahu—Kailua and Kaneohe, the ocean, farms, and cliffs—stop at the **Nuuanu Pali Lookout,** about 15 minutes from downtown Honolulu. The area also features a number of tourist attractions.

141 Olomana Golf Links Waimanalo boasts a short, relatively easy 18-hole course (par 72, 6,326 yards) as well as a small restaurant on Oahu's northeast shore. ♦ Expensive greens fees. Daily. 41-1801 Kalanianaole Hwy, Waimanalo. 259.7926

142 Koolau Farmers Stop at this nursery on the outskirts of Kailua for freshly cut flowers and potted plants. Colorful hibiscus, bougainvillea, heliconia, anthuriums, and orchids contribute to the fragrance in the air. ♦ Daily. 1127 Kailua Rd (at Ulumanu Dr), Kailua. 263.4414 &

143 Buzz's Original Steak House ★$$$
One of Oahu's first surf-and-turf restaurants, this branch is the original **Original Steak House.** At lunch order off the menu, and for dinner there's a selection of specials, including the usual fresh fish and steaks, and a salad bar that's better than most.
♦ Steak/Seafood ♦ M-F lunch and dinner; Sa-Su dinner. Reservations recommended. 413 Kawailoa Rd (between Alala and Popoia Rds), Kailua. 261.4661 & Also at: 98-751 Kuahao Pl (just west of Kaahumanu St), Pearl City. 487.6465 &

Child's Play

Entertaining a youngster usually isn't hard in Hawaii, since the beach is only a short drive away from almost everywhere. But should you want a change of pace from the surf and sand, here are 10 alternative activities sure to delight everyone in the family:

1 Swim with the dolphins at the **Hilton Waikoloa Village** on the **Big Island.**

2 Visit **Sea Life Park** on **Oahu.** Children small and large will love Kekaimalu, the only "wholphin" (which is a cross between a whale and a dolphin) in captivity.

3 Spend a day at the **Waimea Valley Adventure Park** on Oahu, where not only is there an interactive butterfly exhibit, treehouse, cliff divers, and maze, but a race track for radio-controlled cars that may well prove a highlight of your child's trip.

4 Bike down **Haleakala.** Kids have to be at least 4 feet, 8 inches tall to take on the 10,023-foot-high dormant volcano on **Maui,** but all those who qualify will love the 38-mile ride, downhill all the way.

5 Tour **Iolani Palace,** the only royal palace in America, located in **Honolulu,** Oahu. Older children (and their parents) will be intrigued by stories about the Hawaiian royals, including the extravagant King Kalakaua and the beloved Queen Liliuokalani, who was made a prisoner in her own home.

6 Hike to the top of **Diamond Head,** the volcanic crater just outside Honolulu. It's supposed to take an hour, but the kids will probably run up in half that time. This is a fun excursion for all ages, but the smallest hikers may be scared by the tunnel that stretches for a few hundred feet en route, so bring a flashlight.

7 Walk the **Kau Desert Trail** at **Hawaii Volcanoes National Park** on the Big Island. The two-hour hike leads to footprints in lava made by 18th-century Hawaiian warriors trying to escape a 1790 eruption of **Kilauea.** The trail also winds through the Big Island's only desert; be sure to bring water.

8 Go to the **USS Arizona Memorial,** which memorializes those who died in the Japanese raid on **Pearl Harbor,** Oahu, on 7 December 1941. A free boat tour is given daily by the US Navy, but young history buffs will also be interested in the documentary film shown at the visitors' center. Also stop in at the **USS Missouri Memorial Museum** for a series of exhibits on the ship on which the treaty that ended World War II was signed.

9 Ride the waves on **Waikiki Beach.** Several beachfront outfitters offer surfing and body-boarding lessons.

10 Take a ghost tour of **Waikiki.** Kids of all ages will be thrilled to hear about the dozens of spirits that are said to haunt this modern metropolis. **Honolulu Time Walks** (922.5277) offers this and other walking tours.

144 Kailua Beach Park A family-oriented windward beach with generous stretches of white sand, this spot is safe for swimming and bodysurfing, but look out for windsurfers recklessly zipping about. The beach continues to the southeast as Lanikai Beach, which fronts the tony Lanikai neighborhood. Picnic and public facilities are available, and there's a lifeguard on duty. ◆ Lihiwai Rd (just northeast of S Kalaheo Ave), Kailua

145 Casablanca ★$$ The Benalis, two brothers from Morocco with experience at a number of local restaurants, including **Rex's Black Orchid** and the now-defunct **Hajiibaba's,** took over a neighborhood Mexican restaurant and transformed it into Kailua's (and Hawaii's) only Moroccan dining establishment. This is about as culinarily adventurous as the bedroom community of Kailua gets; *pastilla* (chicken pie) and couscous with vegetables are menu highlights. ◆ Moroccan/North African ◆ M-Sa dinner. 19 Hoolai St (at Kihapai St), Kailua. 262.8196 ♿

145 Bueno Nalo ★★$ Forced to move by a plumbing nightmare, this insanely popular restaurant relocated from Waimanalo to the more upscale town of Kailua in 1997. Neither management nor diners have any regrets. The restaurant formerly seated 20; it can now take up to 6 times that, in a substantially cleaner, more attractive setting (the command-performance sombreros, piñatas, and photos of the staff and clientele are still around, though), and it's no longer BYOB, as evidenced by the 18-ounce margaritas. Specials include New York steak fajitas and chicken chimichangas. ◆ Southwestern/Mexican ◆ Daily lunch and dinner. 20 Kainehe St (at Kihapai St), Kailua. 263.1999 ♿

146 Nuuanu Pali Lookout Follow the signs or the busloads of tourists along Pali Highway to this lookout and hold on to your hat. It's one of the most blustery spots in Hawaii—a place where gentle trade winds turn into formidable gusts. Civilization hasn't improved the panorama (that's the **Pali Golf Course** you're looking at). Still, at 1,000 feet, it's a great place to view Windward Oahu. Legend has it that the Battle of Nuuanu Valley was fought here in 1795, with Kamehameha the Great and his forces pushing the opposing army over the palisades to their deaths. ◆ Nuuanu Pali Dr (off Pali Hwy)

Byodo-in Temple

MATT MORROW/NORTH MARKET STREET GRAPHICS

146 Pali Golf Course This verdant 18-hole course (par 72, 6,524 yards) is located at the foot of the Koolau Mountains. ♦ Inexpensive greens fees. Daily; call a week ahead for reservations or try being a walk-on. 45-050 Kamehameha Hwy (between Pali Hwy and I-H3), Kaneohe. 266.7610

Haiku Gardens

147 Haiku Gardens Pathways wind through the landscaped grounds of this tropical garden at the base of the misty Koolau Mountains. Site of the occasional wedding, it's also a favorite spot for pleasant strolls. ♦ Haiku Rd (southwest of Kahekili Hwy), Kaneohe

Within Haiku Gardens:

Chart House ★$$$ The food isn't the best at this member of the steak-and-seafood chain, but romantics could certainly do worse than book a table in the atmospheric garden dining room and put in a couple of orders for coconut crunchy (tempura-fried) shrimp or a 20-ounce prime rib with Santa Fe spice and firecracker onions. ♦ Steak/Seafood ♦ Daily dinner. Reservations recommended. 46-335 Haiku Rd. 247.6671 &

148 Byodo-in Temple Built in 1968 to honor Hawaii's first Japanese immigrants, the replica of a 900-year-old Buddhist temple in Japan (illustrated above) is situated serenely in the **Valley of the Temples Memorial Park,** a huge cemetery at the foot of the Koolau Mountains. A Buddha statue near a pond filled with swans and carp is an imperturbable presence as peacocks stroll by and visitors ring the three-ton bronze bell. ♦ Nominal admission. Daily. 47-200 Kahekili Hwy (at Hui Iwa St), Ahuimanu. 239.8811 &

149 Kahaluu Drive Route 836, from Kaneohe to Kahaluu, is a pleasant coastline detour around Kahekili Highway (Route 83). If you don't wish to see the **Haiku Gardens** or **Byodo-in Temple,** take this alternative scenic route.

150 Senator Fong's Plantation and Gardens Former US Senator Hiram Fong retired to devote more time to this 725-acre botanic garden, which opened to the public several years ago. There are more than a hundred varieties of fruits and flowers, and sweeping ocean views from a 200-acre section of the garden, which visitors explore on a guided tram tour. Lei-making lessons are offered for an additional charge. The gift shop features a selection of Hawaiian-made souvenirs. ♦ Admission. Daily; last tram tour 3PM. 47-285 Pulama Rd (west of Kamehameha Hwy), Kaalaea. 239.6775

151 Crouching Lion Inn ★★★$$$ Named after a rock formation that sits atop the mountain behind the restaurant, this dining spot has pulled in visitors and locals alike on the circle-island drive for decades. The draws: a drop-dead view of the Pacific, cozy gas fireplaces, and alfresco dining on the lanai. Kailua pork and rotisserie chicken are enjoyable entrées, but the signature dish is Slavonic steak, and justifiably so. ♦ American ♦ Daily lunch and dinner. Reservations recommended. 51-666 Kamehameha Hwy, Kaaawa. 237.8511 &

Hawaiians believe that the spirits of the dead leave an island from its northernmost point.

North Shore

The drive along the northern coast of Oahu is memorable. On one side of the road are small ranches and farms hauling with banana trees, papayas, taro, orchids, and anthuriums backed by the green **Koolau Mountains.** On the other side is the **Pacific,** often roiled in the awe-inspiring waves, several stories high, that make this the most famous surf spot in the world. Many wealthy residents of Honolulu and the mainland own vacation homes along the North Shore beaches.

152 Ahi's ★★$$ At one time this hacienda-style establishment was a truck stop for cane truckers hauling their goods between Kahuku and Punaluu and was owned by none other than Don Ho. Now the inviting restaurant under the banyan trees is home to a business transplanted from a hole-in-the-wall location farther up the North Shore. The 30-shrimp special plate here pulls in visitors and locals alike, as does the local lobster served boiled, broiled, fried, or grilled. ♦ Seafood ♦ Daily lunch and dinner. 53-146 Kamehameha Hwy, Punaluu. 293.5650 ঠ

153 Polynesian Cultural Center If you haven't been to the South Seas, this is a good introduction to the cultures of Polynesia: Hawaii, Fiji, Tonga, Samoa, Tahiti, and the Marquesas. It's a kind of Disney-goes-Pacific, with each culture's traditions demonstrated by students from the nearby **Brigham Young University (BYU)** campus, many of them Polynesian. Watch as they pound poi, string leis, husk coconuts, and make tapa cloth from mulberry bark. Set aside a whole day to drive from Waikiki (it's about 1.5 hours each way), tour the various areas devoted to individual islands and island groups, and take in all the demonstrations (the canoe pageant is at 2:30PM; the evening show is at 8PM). You may be exhausted and overwhelmed, but the narration is as entertaining as it is corny. Each evening there's a buffet dinner show. (You can buy a general admission ticket, which includes daytime activities and the dinner show, or an admission-only ticket, which doesn't include the evening buffet.) With more than 30 million guests, the center has been one of Hawaii's leading visitor attractions since the **Church of Jesus Christ of Latter-day Saints** opened it in 1963. And though there's controversy about the integrity of the production, which has provided more than $100 million for **BYU,** it's still an educational experience. ♦ Admission. M-Sa 12:30PM-9:30PM. 55-370 Kamehameha Hwy (just south of Naniloa Loop), Laie. 293.3333 ঠ

154 Mormon Temple Since 1864, the Mormon headquarters has occupied 6,000 acres in the community of Laie, where 95 percent of the population is Mormon. The **Church of Jesus Christ of Latter-day Saints** built the temple, a comely white edifice on impeccably landscaped grounds, in 1919. Visitors are not allowed to enter the structure, but are welcome to tour the surroundings, which are dotted with reflecting pools. A visitors' center features a large statue of Christ, a genealogy center, and several films. ♦ Free. Grounds: daily 9AM-8PM. 55-600 Naniloa Loop (at Lanihuli St), Laie. Visitors' Center 293.2427 ঠ

154 Tiare Puroto Pareus Just down the street from the **Mormon Temple** is the home and business of Ura Behling, a charming and talented designer and fabricator of colorful pareus (wraparound skirts). You can't miss the place when it's in full operation; dozens of brightly colored sheets stretch across the driveway as solar power and patterned cutouts create tropical impressions. The prices here are the best around, and the service can't be beat, which explains the occasional tourist bus unloading at the doorstep. ♦ Daily. 55-533 Naniloa Loop (between Kamehameha Hwy and Lanihuli St), Laie. 293.5893 ঠ

155 Malaekahana State Recreation Area Just past Laie, right before you reach the former plantation town of Kahuku, you'll find postcard-perfect Malaekahana. On weekdays the arc-shaped beach is usually empty except for a few fishers casting their nets. There's good swimming and bodysurfing, but no lifeguard on duty. Remember to lock your car and keep valuables out of sight, then take your time strolling down the wide white-sand beach or picnicking under the ironwood trees on the south end. There's a bathhouse with cold showers, and camping by permit. ♦ Kamehameha Hwy (between Naniloa Loop and Adams Rd)

156 Turtle Bay Hilton Golf and Tennis Resort $$$$ More than an hour's drive from Waikiki, this 808-acre resort is for people who really want to get away from everything. There's not much to do here but test your skill on the two Arnold Palmer–designed golf courses (one 18 holes and one 9), sunbathe by the 2 pools, hit the beach, or lounge in one of the hotel's 2 bars or 3 restaurants. It can get pretty windy at Kuilima Point, where the hotel's 374 guest rooms, 26 suites, and 85 cabanas are located, but that makes the beach next door popular with surfers. Sit back and watch them ride the waves, or roust yourself to play tennis, ride horses, or windsurf. If you rent a car, Waimea Bay,

Sunset Beach, or the town of Haleiwa are nice day trips. ♦ 57-091 Kamehameha Hwy (at Kuilima Dr). 293.8811, 800/445.8667; fax 293.9147; www.hilton.com ♿

Within the Turtle Bay Hilton Golf and Tennis Resort:

The Cove ★★★$$$ The ocean view and the salted prawns are at the top of the list of reasons to eat at the resort at least one night of any stay, or to stop in on a circle-island tour. Farther down the list are this quiet restaurant's broiled *opakapaka* brought in fresh from Haleiwa Harbor and the intimate candlelit atmosphere. ♦ Seafood/Steak ♦ F-Sa dinner. Reservations recommended. 293.8811 ♿

Sea Tide Room ★$$$$ The Sunday brunch buffet here draws local residents for the bountiful selection, including the omelette bar, fish table, and dessert station, and the fine beach view. ♦ Continental ♦ Su brunch. 293.8811 ♿

Turtle Bay Hilton Golf Courses These oceanside courses are known for their ferocious winds, but that doesn't keep golfers away from the 18 holes of the championship **Kuilima** course (par 72, 7,199 yards) or the regulation nine-hole course (par 36, 3,164 yards). Legend says that Mickey Mantle, with the wind at his back, drove a ball over the 357-yard fourth hole using a No. 4 wood, though George Fazio designed the course with wind in mind. ♦ Expensive greens fees. Daily. Preferred starting times and rates for Turtle Bay Hilton Golf and Tennis Resort guests. 293.8811

57 Sunset Beach It's a world-famous North Shore site for winter surfing contests, but year-round high waves and strong currents make this beach dangerous for swimmers. When the sets of 10-story-high waves come in, head this way and join the mesmerized crowd. It's a good beach for strolling and sunbathing during spring and summer, but don't ever turn your back on the winter waves. ♦ Kamehameha Hwy, Sunset Beach

58 Ke Iki Hale $$ This is the Hawaii everyone dreams of—palm trees silhouetted against the sunset, golden beaches stretching for miles, whales cavorting in the winter, and cozy little cottages with large picture windows to take it

all in. Only 8 duplexes occupy this 1.5-acre oceanfront property, from single bedrooms on the street side to 1- and 2-bedroom adjoining units facing the ocean. Simplicity and serenity are the operative words here, with a deliberate absence of modern-day luxuries: no Jacuzzi, room service, restaurant, maid service, TVs, or telephones (there's a pay phone nearby, though, and the amenities of Haleiwa are only minutes away). The exteriors of the hotel buildings could use a new coat of paint, but the cottages are immaculate inside, with full kitchens and patios. The property is on Ke Iki, one of Oahu's best beaches, a broad expanse of white sand and palm trees that partially recedes during the winter, when thundering 10-foot waves crash on the reefy shoreline. Rinse off under a shower that's been fastened to a palm tree, then lie in a hammock or picnic at tables near the sand. You could easily stay in your swimsuit all day, "talking story" with aloha-spirited owner Alice Tracy and not caring one whit about the rest of the world. ♦ 59-579 Ke Iki Rd (west of Kamehameha Hwy), Waimea. 638.8229, 388.9490, 800/377.4030

159 Puu-o-Mahuka Heiau (Escape Hill Temple) For an incredible view of the North Shore and Waimea Bay, drive up Pupukea Road to this *heiau* (ancient temple), where humans once were sacrificed as part of the Hawaiian religion. The temple remains a sacred place, and offerings of ti leaves and stones are still made here. ♦ Pupukea Rd (east of Kamehameha Hwy), Waimea

159 Waimea Valley Adventure Park The lush grounds of the 1,800-acre park across the street from Waimea Beach include an arboretum and more than 30 botanical gardens, with thousands of tropical and subtropical species. Ride through the park in an open-air tram or take a self-guided walking tour. Be sure to see the cliff divers jumping 4 times daily from the 45-foot falls that give the park its name, and **Halau o Waimea,** the park's resident hula troupe, which performs the *kahiko* (ancient hula) in the upper meadow immediately following each dive. **The Butterfly Encounter** features hundreds of kinds of butterflies in captivity. **The Jungle Trek** is a giant tree house featuring an anaconda slide, a maze, and a racing area for radio-controlled cars; the kids will adore it. There's also a snack bar and picnic area—and plenty of peacocks. ♦ Admission. Daily. 59-864 Kamehameha Hwy (at Waimea Valley Rd), Waimea. 638.8511 ♿

Waimea Beach Park

MARK AMMERMAN/NORTH MARKET STREET GRAPHIC

160 Waimea Beach Park The waters are calm during the summer, when local kids play "king of the mountain" on the huge rock in the bay. But it's an entirely different beach in November, when enormous waves pound the shore. This is one of the world's premier surfing spots, lined with spectators in the winter when the expert surfers are out. There are lifeguards and public facilities. ◆ Kamehameha Hwy (between Waimea Valley Rd and Iliohu Way)

161 Haleiwa Beach Park There's good swimming and snorkeling here during the spring and summer, but surfing should be left to the experienced. ◆ 62-449 Kamehameha Hwy (at Kahalewai Pl)

162 Jameson's by the Sea ★★$$$ This is *the* roadside stop for seafood and pasta at sunset. Baked stuffed shrimp and fresh *opakapaka* are served in the upstairs dining room. Downstairs, at the informal open-air lanai, *pupus* are offered and drinks flow all day. ◆ Seafood ◆ Downstairs: daily lunch and dinner. Upstairs: W-Su dinner. Reservations recommended for both restaurants. 62-540 Kamehameha Hwy (between Emerson Rd and Kahalewai Pl). 637.4336 &

163 Haleiwa Joe's Seafood Grill ★★$$$ With indoor and outdoor dining right next to Haleiwa Harbor, this seafood-and-steak dining room is a local hot spot. Hawaiian fish (including mahimahi, *opakapaka, ahi,* and *ono*) are brought in daily from the neighboring harbor, and served blackened, broiled, grilled, fried, and baked. The prime rib is a specialty of the house. ◆ Steak/Seafood ◆ M-Th, Sa-Su dinner; F lunch and dinner. 66-011 Kamehameha Hwy, Haleiwa. 637.8005 &

163 H. Miura Store & Tailor Shop Walking into this store is like stepping back in time to the days when Haleiwa was a plantation town. The friendly family—now in its third generation of shopkeeping—can tell you about that era because they opened their place in 1918. The secret to their success is making swim trunks and walking shorts for the surfers who frequent the North Shore every winter. The names and measurements of their regular customers are kept in a ledger, but the Miuras never forget a face. ◆ Daily. 66-057 Kamehameha Hwy, Haleiwa. 637.4845 &

163 S. Matsumoto Shave Ice Store For generations, Haleiwa has been the home of a favorite local treat: finely shaved ice flavored with fruit syrups served modestly in a paper cone. Comparing "shave ice" to a snow cone would be an injustice, though; even the finest snow cone couldn't compete. The best establishments, like this place, make their own syrups and offer variations with vanilla ice cream (delicious) and sweet *azuki* beans. Three flavors in one cone is the norm. ◆ Daily. 66-087 Kamehameha Hwy, Haleiwa. 637.482

163 Rosie's Cantina ★$ Surfers meet here for the hefty breakfasts, good margaritas, standard Mexican cuisine, and friendly environment. Order a margarita and a plate of sizzling fajitas or a "Triple Crown" (one beef, one chicken, and one cheese enchilada) and let the hassles of everyday life recede. ◆ Mexican ◆ Daily breakfast, lunch, and dinner. Haleiwa Shopping Plaza, 66-165 Kamehameha Hwy, Haleiwa. 637.3538 &

163 Pizza Bob's $ With small booths and a bustling surfer atmosphere, this is a typical beer and pizza joint. ◆ Pizza/Pasta ◆ Daily lunch and dinner. Haleiwa Shopping Plaza, 66-165 Kamehameha Hwy, Haleiwa. 637.5095 & Also at: Restaurant Row, 500 Ala Moana Blvd (at Punchbowl St), Honolulu. 532.4602 &

164 Kua Aina Sandwich Shop ★★$ The hamburgers here are so juicy they'll literally drip down your elbows, the french fries actually taste like potatoes, and the sandwiches are *onolicious,* especially those with creamy avocados. The only thing that needs work is the less-than-amiable service. ◆ Sandwiches ◆ Daily lunch and dinner. No credit cards accepted. 66-214 Kamehameha Hwy, Haleiwa. 637.6067 &

164 Coffee Gallery ★★$ We wouldn't drive here from Honolulu for a cup of java, but if you're in Haleiwa you'd be insane not to stop in for the olfactory rush, an "aesthetically correct cup of coffee" (according to the business card), and a pesto-veggie sandwich. Soup, desserts, sandwiches, and bagels are served in a covered patio setting, with Grateful Dead tunes in the background. ♦ Coffeehouse ♦ M-F breakfast, lunch, and dinner; Sa-Su lunch and dinner. 66-250 Kamehameha Hwy, Haleiwa. 637.5355 &

65 Sugar Bar A cool, blue oasis in a desert of tourist traps, this bar may be Oahu's last bastion of local beer-guzzling solidarity. Described as your basic down-home country bar by owner Peter Birnbaum, a patron of the arts and possessor of what must be Hawaii's only bust of Beethoven, this place is a second home to the people of sleepy Waialua. Packs of bikers tether their hogs here on the weekends and proceed to gorge on the sausages and drinks, always under the watchful, scowling eye of ol' Ludwig V. Rumor has it that somewhere on the memorabilia-lined walls—if you look hard enough and drink long enough—you'll find the answer to the meaning of life. ♦ Daily 11AM-2AM. 67-069 Kealohanui St (west of Kupahu St), Waialua. 637.6989 &

Central Oahu

...nd in the center of Oahu is devoted to agriculture ...d the military. Pineapple and sugarcane fields ...retch as far as the eye can see, and ensconced in ...ose fields are **Schofield Barracks,** headquarters for ...e US Army's 25th Infantry Division. **Wahiawa,** near ...e military base, was once a picturesque plantation ...wn. Now it's a seedy spot with a few grocery ...ores, fast-food outlets, and rough bars.

66 Dole Pineapple Plantation Sink your teeth into a piece of pineapple while viewing the display on the fruit's history. The pavilion is in the heart of Hawaii's pineapple country, surrounded by neat pineapple fields and red soil so rich it'll stain your white sneakers. The gift shop carries replicas of old Dole labels, now collector's items. Self-guided tours take about 45 minutes. ♦ Daily. 64-1550 Kamehameha Hwy (just north of Poamoho). 621.8408 &

Within the Dole Pineapple Plantation:

Pineapple Garden Maze Eleven thousand, four hundred endemic plants, including hibiscus, plumeria, gardenia, anthurium, orchid, puakinikini, and bougainvillea comprise this two-acre maze, recognized in the *1998 Guiness Book of World Records* as the world's largest. ♦ Daily. 621.8408

COURTESY OF THE DOLE PLANTATION

167 Schofield Barracks The US Army's 25th Infantry Division headquarters are here, right beside the sugarcane and pineapple fields that Japanese bombers flew over to raid Pearl Harbor. The barracks are named for Major General John M. Schofield, the Army's Pacific military division commander, who came to Hawaii in the 1870s on the pretext of vacationing but spent his time around the Pearl River Lagoon, as Pearl Harbor was then called, investigating its suitability as an American military enclave.

168 Mililani Golf Club Located in the suburbs of leeward Oahu, this course (par 72, 6,455 yards) is shaded by trees on former sugarcane fields. ♦ Expensive greens fees. Daily. 95-176 Kuahelani Ave (west of Kamehameha Hwy), Mililani. 623.2254

Leeward Oahu

This is the least touristy section of Oahu—in fact, you won't find any hotels, fancy restaurants, or tourist-oriented shops here at all. A large community of native Hawaiians and other Pacific Islanders lives here, working small farms in the broad valleys. West coast residents have a reputation for being unfriendly to the people they consider intruders, and in the past there have been incidents of vandalism and even violence against tourists, although the situation has improved in recent years. This is the dry, leeward side of the island, where the days are usually hot and dusty. The beaches can be dangerous for swimmers from October through April, with strong currents and undertows, but they are great for surfing. **Makaha Beach,** the most famous on the **Waianae Coast,** has been the site of the **Makaha World Surfing Championships** since 1952.

169 Keaau Beach Park It's easy to find—just keep driving until you run out of road. A popular surf spot (called "Yoke's"), this is also a great beach for soaking in the rays. The waves are too big to allow swimming in winter; snorkeling here isn't recommended because of poor visibility year-round. ♦ 83-431 Farrington Hwy (between Lawaia St and Keaau Homesteads Rd)

170 Makaha Beach Park Professional surfing originated here. It subsequently shifted to the North Shore, but Makaha still hosts the annual **Makaha World Surfing Championships,** which include the **Buffalo Big Board Surfing Classic,** a championship tournament for surfers whose long, elegant boards first put the sport on the map. The competition is held in February or March, depending on when the surfing conditions are best. As with most other beaches along the Waianae Coast, this isn't the most hospitable place for tourists, so keep a low profile and lock your car. ♦ Farrington Hwy and Kili Dr, Makaha

---

Restaurants/Clubs: Red   **Hotels:** Blue
Shops/ ⊤ Outdoors: Green   **Sights/Culture:** Black

171 Sheraton Makaha West Course This uncrowded, 18-hole championship golf course (par 72, 7,077 yards) is set against the green cliffs of the Waianae range. The fairways have great views of the Pacific coastline, especially at sunset. Shuttle service from **Sheraton** hotels in Waikiki is available. ♦ Expensive greens fees. Daily. 84-626 Makaha Valley Rd (northeast of Farrington Hwy), Makaha. 695.9544

172 Pokai Bay Beach Park Being the only fully sheltered beach along the Waianae Coast makes this place unique. Unfortunately, this part of the island doesn't cater to tourists. To avoid vandalism, be sure to lock your car. Picnic and public facilities are available, and lifeguards are on duty. ♦ Waianae Valley Rd and Pokai Bay St, Waianae

Kapolei and Pearl City

In the southwest corner of Oahu, Kapolei is an urban area that stands where there were acres of gently waving sugarcane for many decades, until the 1990s. Developers had high hopes of someday rivaling Waikiki dollar for visitor-industry dollar, but years into development, Kapolei still consists of a hotel, restaurant, and golf course in the middle of nowhere.

East of this new resort area is middle-class Pearl City, on the shores of **Pearl Harbor.** The **USS Arizona Memorial,** which honors those who died in the Japanese attack of the harbor on 7 December 1941, has drawn respectful visitors for decades, and the new **USS Missouri Memorial Museum** is expected to entice more people into the area.

173 Koolina Resort With a hotel, a classy Mediterranean restaurant, and an 18-hole golf course, this $3-billion development is located in the fairly isolated resort area of Kapolei. ♦ Off Aliinui Dr (southwest of Farrington Hwy)

Within the Koolina Resort:

Ihilani Resort and Spa $$$$ This resplendent 387-room hotel is removed from the usual visitor attractions, but it offers many of its own, including a white-sand beach, 2 pools, a spa, 5 restaurants, and 6 tennis courts. Rooms come equipped with CD players and three phones. ♦ 92-1001 Olani St. 679.0079, 800/626.4446; fax 679.0295; reservations@ihilani.com; www.ihilani.com &

Within the Ihilani Resort and Spa:

Azul ★★$$$$ No children under age seven are allowed in this elegant and intimate cherry wood–adorned dining room. Select from such specialties as marinated rack of lamb, veal tenderloin, and ragout *onaga* (red snapper in a saffron and white-wine sauce). ♦ Mediter-ranean ♦ M, W, F-Sa dinner. Reservations required; shirts with collars required for men. 679.0079 &

Koolina Golf Course Cascading waterfalls and ocean views add to the appeal of this Ted Robinson–designed 18-hole course (par 72, 6,867 yards). There's a free shuttle for guests of the **Ihilani Resort and Spa.** ♦ Expensive greens fees, discounted for resort guests. Daily. 676.5300

174 Waikele Center Lots of great outlet stores are on tap here, including **The Sports Authority** (677.9933), **The Saks Fifth Avenue Clearinghouse** (676.1773), **OshKosh B'Gosh** (676.8080), and other well-known names like **Borders Books & Music** (676.6699). ♦ M-F 9AM-9PM; Sa. Lumiaina St (just west of Kamehameha Hwy), Waipahu. 671.7337 &

175 Pearl Country Club A country club in name only, this public 18-hole course (par 72, 6,23 yards) overlooks Pearl Harbor; a forest of trees patiently awaits your hooks and slices. ♦ Expensive greens fees. Daily. 98-535 Kaonohi St (north of Moanalua Rd), Aiea. 487.3802

176 Pearlridge Center The two sections of this air-conditioned mall are connected by monorail. **Liberty House, JC Penney,** and **Sears** are the anchor stores; there are also more than 170 boutiques and specialty shop, 16 movie screens, and numerous restaurant, including **Bravo Restaurant and Bar** (487.5544) for pizza and **Monterey Bay Canners** (483.3555) for grilled fish at affordable prices. On the corner of the busy intersection leading to the mall is **Anna Miller's** (487.2421), a coffee shop with winning pies; look for a circular building separate from the center. There's also a miniature golf course called **Jungle River** (488.8808) that keeps nonshoppers busy. ♦ Daily. 98-1005 Moanalua Rd (at Kaonohi St), Aiea. 488.0981 &

ALOHA STADIUM

177 Aloha Stadium Charles Luckman & Associates designed the 50,000-seat stadium, home of the **University of Hawaii Rainbows,** the state's only college football team. The real excitement is when the **Aloha Bowl** and **Pro Bowl** football games are televised from here every winter. The stands can be moved to transform the football field a baseball field. Unfortunately, it seems that the stadium is slowly rusting because of the salty environment. ♦ 99-500 Salt Lake Blvd (between Kahuapaani St and Kamehameha Hwy). 486.9300 &

Within Aloha Stadium:

Aloha Stadium Flea Market Every Wednesday and weekend the stadium parking lot is a giant flea market, with new and second-hand goods. Vendors sell jewelry, kids' clothes, food, muumuus, aloha shirts, slippers, and toys, among other things. Shuttles pick up passengers at the major hotels for a fee. ♦ Nominal entry fee. W, Sa-Su 6AM-3PM. 955.4050 &

78 USS Bowfin Submarine & Park Explore the living and working spaces of a restored World War II US submarine, one of fewer than 20 still in existence, on a 40-minute self-guided tour. There is also an impressive collection of sub-related artifacts, and a small theater screens submarine-themed videos. ♦ Admission (no children under age four allowed). Daily. 11 Arizona Memorial Dr (west of Kamehameha Hwy). 423.1341

78 USS Arizona Memorial It was early Sunday morning, 7 December 1941, and most of Honolulu was still sleeping when the **Pearl Harbor Naval Base** was bombed by Japanese planes. The attack caught the US Pacific fleet by surprise, leaving it devastated: 2,395 military personnel and civilians died, 188 planes were destroyed, and 18 major warships were sunk. The *USS Arizona* sank at its mooring blocks in 40 feet of water, becoming the tomb for 1,177 officers and sailors.

In 1962, a gracefully arched white structure (illustrated on page 181) was built over the *USS Arizona*. Designed by Honolulu architect **Alfred Preis,** the memorial is a national shrine, with the names of the 1,177 US Navy men and Marines killed on the *Arizona* engraved on a marble plaque. This site has also become one of Hawaii's most popular tourist attractions.

Before boarding a Navy shuttleboat to the memorial, walk through the $5-million **Visitors' Center,** where the "day of infamy" is recounted. The National Park Service tour, including a documentary film and shuttle to the memorial, lasts about 75 minutes. ♦ Free. Tickets to the day's launches are issued on a first-come, first-served basis; before noon there's often a one- to three-hour wait. Visitors' Center: daily 7:30AM-5PM. Shuttleboat: 8AM-3PM (weather permitting). Shirts and shoes required. Arizona Memorial Dr (just west of Kamehameha Hwy). 422.0561 &

179 USS Missouri Memorial Museum This 887-foot-long battleship, which saw action in World War II, the Korean War, and the Persian Gulf War before being decommissioned in 1992 and moored in the state of Washington, opened as a museum in 1999. It covers the period of US Pacific involvement in World War II from 7 December 1941 to the Japanese surrender agreement was signed aboard the ship in Tokyo Bay on 2 September 1945. ♦ Admission (pay at USS Bowfin Submarine & Park, see above). Daily. Off Lexington Blvd, Ford Island, US Naval Reservation (shuttle buses leave from USS Bowfin Submarine & Park, see above). 423.2263

Bests

Revé Shapard
Editor, The Bess Press

Don't miss **The Contemporary Museum.** Even after other memories of Hawaii have faded, you'll remember the striking art and the serenity of the setting.

Whether it's breakfast on your hotel lanai, lunch by the beach, or a dinner cruise, eat at least one meal a day outside, with a view of the ocean.

For tasteful, locally produced books, clothing, and gifts, visit **Native Books & Beautiful Things** at one of its three locations.

Michelle Calabro Hubbard
Author/Freelance Writer/President, Aloha Chapter Romance Writers of America

Even though I'm a local, I always take along a copy of *This Week* magazine on my tour for special guests. The maps come in handy for me, and my guests love the discounts they get with the coupons.

The tour leaves **Kailua** on the windward side of Oahu and takes **Kamehameha Highway** to just outside of

Kaneohe where **Byodo-in Temple** and **Valley of the Temples Memorial Park** are interesting. I like to stop at **Crouching Lion Inn** and art gallery.

Continuing the drive to the town of **Laie** which hosts the **Polynesian Cultural Center, Brigham Young University,** and the **Mormon Temple.**

Turtle Bay Hilton Golf and Tennis Resort is located at the highest point of the island. **Sunset Beach** is a surfer's dream, especially during winter months when waves are huge. Nearby are **Waimea Beach Park** and **Waimea Valley.**

A few minutes away is the **North Shore** town of **Haleiwa,** a must stop. Many galleries and shops feature the work of local artists, plus there are a lot of great restaurants.

Afterwards, it's back to Kam Highway and down the center of the island. **Dole Plantation** is home of the world's largest maze (it's shaped like a pineapple).

After leaving **Wahiawa,** the H2 goes to the **Waikele Center** with its premium designer outlets; or just keep going to **H1** and turn off at **Pali Highway** going toward Kailua. The final stop is **Nuuanu Pali Lookout** for a panoramic view of the windward side of Oahu.

Kauai

A rainbow rising over a sugarcane field. A trio of laughing girls riding riding their horses through a small town. A Japanese man with a weathered face selling produce from his fields. These are the sorts of memorable vistas and vignettes seen around every other bend on the 553-square-mile island of Kauai (Kuh-wah-*ee*).

Nicknamed "The Garden Island," Kauai can lay claim to many superlatives. It's the oldest major island in the Hawaiian chain, believed to have been the original home of the volcano goddess Pele. Its cliffs and canyons, unduplicated on any of the other islands, are the result of the persistent workings of streams and ocean waves on once-bleak volcanic craters and cinder cones. At the dead center of this roughly circular isle, 5,148-foot **Mount Waialeale** draws the most rainfall of anywhere in the world, an average of 440 inches a year. It's here (some believe) that a race of tiny people called "menehune" fashioned impossibly intricate structures overnight. Kauai was also the first island visited by English explorer Captain James Cook in 1778 (with tragic results). This island has many more miles of sandy beach (40) than any other in the Hawaiian chain—and, finally, Kauai is the only Hawaiian island from which no other land can be seen.

But it isn't just the island's historical, geographical, or geological attributes that distinguish it from its counterparts. Kauai's people are extraordinary too. When Hurricane Iniki hit in September 1992, there were few criminal incidents; instead, the island's 50,000 residents pooled their energy and skills to put the island back together—and to make it better than before. A Mayor's Conference on Tourism was held, and islanders set about creating a structure for planned growth that focuses on ecotourism and Hawaiian cultural programs rather than megaresorts and golf courses.

The result is a place where the atmosphere is a trifle less westernized than the rest of the larger islands and more than a trifle slower paced. There are hundreds of side roads to explore; big-hearted people to talk to; and local-style shops, restaurants, and attractions at which to spend slow and sun-drenched days.

Kauai has much to attract a traveler's interest and admiration. On the island's verdant **North Shore**, there's the nouveau-chic town of **Hanalei**; the deluxe **Princeville Resort; Lumahai Beach**, where Mitzi Gaynor endeavored to wash a man out of her hair in the movie *South Pacific*; the mythical island of Bali Hai, actually a series of misty mountain peaks seen from **Haena State Beach Park** and transformed by clever camera angles in that same movie; and the postcard-perfect cliffs of **Na Pali Coast**. On Kauai's dramatically different southern coast, sun lovers bask on the beach in the **Poipu** resort area. And in the heart of the isle, there's the awe-inspiring 10-milelong, two-mile-wide **Waimea Canyon**, where meandering rivers and earth-colored canyon walls rob even the veteran traveler of facile descriptions.

If you're determined to find your way to the "real" Hawaii, consider this magical place.

Valley of the Lost Tribe

Kalalau Valley Lookout

Kokee Lodge/ Kokee Natural History Museum

Kokee Rd.

29 Polihale State Park

Canyon Lookout

Kokee Rd.

Waimea River

Waimea Canyon Dr.

Kaumualii Hwy.

50

55

550

550

Kekaha

25 Waimea

24

Waimea Bay

Kaulakahi Channel

26

28

State

Wa Ca

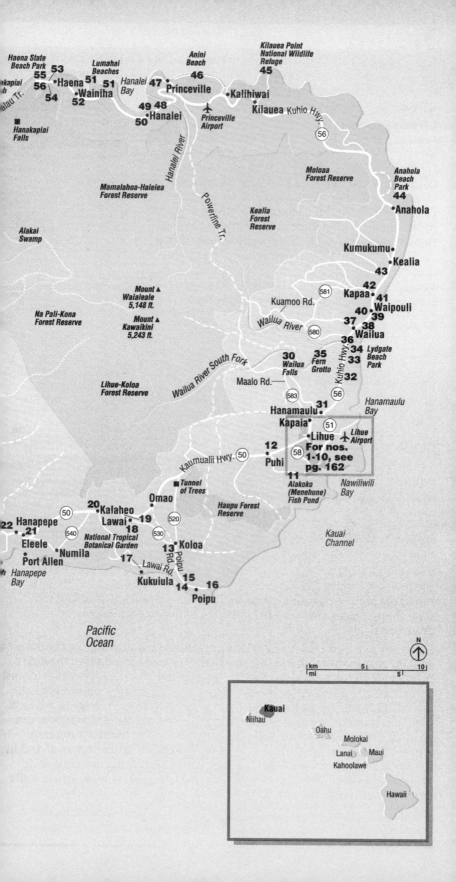

Haena State
Beach Park
nakapiai
h
55
53
56
Haena 51 51
54 52 Wainiha
Hanakapiai
Falls

Lumahai
Beaches
Hanalei
Bay
49 48
50 Hanalei

Anini
Beach
46
47 Princeville

Princeville
Airport

Kilauea Point
National Wildlife
Refuge
45

Kalihiwai

Kilauea Kuhio Hwy.

56

Hanalei River

Powerline Tr.

Moloaa
Forest Reserve

Anahola
Beach
Park
44

Anahola

Alakai
Swamp

Mamalahoa-Haleiea
Forest Reserve

Kealia
Forest
Reserve

Kumukumu

Kealia

43

Na Pali-Kona
Forest Reserve

Mount ▲
Waialeale
5,148 ft.

Mount ▲
Kawaikini
5,243 ft.

581

Kuamoo Rd.

Wailua River

580

Kapaa

42

41 Waipouli
40 39
37 38
36 Wailua
34 Lydgate
33 Beach
Park
32

Lihue-Koloa
Forest Reserve

Wailua River South Fork

Maalo Rd.

30
Wailua
Falls

35
Fern
Grotto

Kuhio Hwy.

56

583

31

Hanamaulu
Kapaia

51

Lihue
Kapaia

58

12
Puhi

Kaumualii Hwy. 50

11

Hanamaulu
Bay

Lihue
Airport

For nos.
1-10, see
pg. 162

Alakoko
(Menehune)
Fish Pond

Nawiliwili
Bay

Tunnel
of Trees

Haupu Forest
Reserve

Kauai
Channel

20
Kalaheo
19
Lawai
18

Omao

520

530

13
Koloa

Poipu Rd.

Lawai Rd.

Hanapepe
22
21
Eleele
Numila
Port Allen

50

540

National Tropical
Botanical Garden

17

Kukuiula
14

15
Poipu

16

Hanapepe
Bay

Pacific
Ocean

N

km
mi
5
10
5

Kauai

Niihau

Oahu

Molokai

Lanai Maui

Kahoolawe

Hawaii

Area code 808 unless otherwise noted.

Getting to Kauai

Airports
Lihue Airport
A mile-and-a-half east of **Lihue,** this small, island-style airport has an open-air terminal and car-rental booths—period. All arrivals and departures are interisland, except for a daily **United Airlines** flight from and to Los Angeles.

Airport Services
Information 246.1440

Lost and Found 246.0253

Parking...245.8716

Airlines
Aloha..................................245.3691, 800/367.5250

Hawaiian 800/882.8811
   from the mainland...........................800/367.5320

United 800/241.6522

Getting to and from Lihue Airport
By Car
To get to Lihue from the airport, head west on **Ahukini Road (Route 570)** or south on **Kapule Highway (Route 51).** Reverse the directions to get to the airport from Lihue.

The following car-rental firms have booths at **Lihue Airport.**

Alamo................................246.0646, 800/327.9633

Avis 245.3512, 800/331.1212

Budget 245.1901, 800/527.0700

Dollar 245.3651, 800/800.4000

Hertz 245.3356, 800/654.3031

National 245.5636, 800/CAR.RENT

By Taxi
There's a cab stand across from the baggage claim area. The fare to Lihue is about $7, to the **Wailua/ Kapaa** area, about $16, and to Poipu resorts, $30.

Princeville Airport
Two miles east of **Princeville** on Kauai's North Shore, this small airport has one terminal (no phone). At press time no commercial planes were allowed to fly in and out of the airport, but a couple of helicopter tour operators often use it as a base.

Interisland Carriers
Aloha Airlines makes direct hops to **Lihue Airport** from **Honolulu International Airport** on Oahu and **Kahului Airport** on Maui, while **Hawaiian Airlines** flies nonstop to Lihue from **Honolulu International.**

Getting Around Kauai

Bicycles
Although some of the roads tend to be a bit narrow on the North Shore, Kauai is a great place to travel on two wheels. **Pedal and Paddle** in Hanalei (Ching Young Shopping Village, Aku Rd and Kuhio Hwy, 826.9069) rents mountain bikes and Kauai cruisers (old, beaten-up bikes) on a daily and weekly basis, with locks and helmets included.

Buses
The **Kauai Bus** (241.6410) travels between **Kekaha** and Lihue or Hanalei and Lihue Monday through Saturday from 5:30AM to 6PM.

Driving
One main road follows the island's coastline. From Lihue west it is called **Kaumualii Highway (Route 50);** from Lihue north it is called **Kuhio Highway (Route 56).** Roads are generally good and drivers normally courteous.

Avoid driving between Lihue and Kapaa during rush hours. Otherwise, driving on the island is easy; the road that skirts the coast will get you almost everywhere you want to go. Be sure to explore some of those intriguing side roads that extend off the highway, however. Some of Kauai's most beautiful and untouched spots are off the beaten path but well worth seeking out.

Hiking
Some of the finest hiking trails in Hawaii can be found on Kauai. Headliners include treks across Waimea Canyon, and the 13-mile **Powerline Trail,** a ridge trail that connects the North Shore with Wailua. But the quintessential Kauai hike is the 11-mile **Kalalau Trail** from **Kee Beach** along the Na Pali Coast to an unparalleled stretch of white sand. For the lowdown on this and other trails, order *Hiking Kauai* by Robert Smith (Booklines Hawaii; $10.95).

Parking
Parking in Kauai is easy. Rarely will you have to feed a meter. There are no parking garages.

Taxis
Cabs aren't easily hailed here, but they come (eventually) when called. Try **Kauai Cab Service** (246.9554) or **North Shore Cab** (826.6189).

Tours
Kauai doesn't suffer from any shortage in the tour department, from adrenaline-producing adventures to tame rides in horse-drawn carriages. No roll call of tours would be complete without a mention of **Waialeale Boat Tours** (822.4908), which offers departures every hour on slow-moving power boats to the well-known, if over-commercialized, **Fern Grotto.** For those interested in a retreat from the madding crowd, **Polynesian Adventure Tours** (246.0122) runs full- and half-day tours of Waimea Canyon, **Wailua River,** and the North Shore. **Outfitters Kauai** (742.9667) provides bike tours

down **Waimea Canyon Drive,** and kayaks, equipment, and guides for coastal tours in lightweight boats. **Princeville Stables** (826.6772) on the island's North Shore offers horseback tours. **Holoholo Charters** (335.0815) operates half-day snorkel tours on the 65-foot *Holoholo* (which translates to something like AWOL). Included is an hour's boat ride to the reefs off the shores of Niihau, an island on which visitors are barred from setting foot. History buffs will enjoy the tours offered by **Plantation Carriages** (246.9529); participants hear how sugar was and is cultivated on the island during a 60-minute cane-field ride in a wagon pulled by Clydesdales. Flight-seeing tours are offered by many, including **Jack Harter Helicopters** (245.3774) and **Na Pali Helicopters** (245.6959).

Walking

Walking is the transportation mode of choice in small towns like Hanalei, Kapaa, **Koloa,** and **Hanapepe,** but between towns, something a bit faster-moving is in order.

FYI

Shopping

The biggest mall is **Kukui Grove Center** (245.7784) in Lihue, with branches of **Liberty House** (245.7751), the state's largest department store; **Paradise Fun** (241.7050), which has entertainment for kids; and **Kauai Products Store** (246.6753), featuring goods made by local artisans. The **Coconut Plantation Marketplace** (822.3641) in Kapaa is home to 69 stores, among them **Tropic Casuals** (823.8327), which stocks island attire for women, and **Island Surf Shop** (822.6955), with ocean gear for all ages. The **Poipu Shopping Village** (742.2831) is a small assortment of alohawear boutiques, shops showcasing local art, and surf-style stores. But the place that's the most fun to shop is probably Hanalei town, site of more unusual enclaves like the **Ching Young Shopping Village** (826.7222), where the merchandise runs to Indonesian beads and koa wood figurines.

Visitors' Information Centers

The **Kauai Visitors' Bureau** (**KVB;** 3016 Umi St, Lihue, HI 96766, 245.3971; fax 246.9235; www.kauaivisitorsbureau.com) is open Monday through Friday.

Phone Book

Emergencies

Ambulance/Fire/Police 911

Dental Emergency 246.8811

Hospital (Wilcox Memorial Hospital) 245.1100

Locksmith 823.0957

Pharmacy...822.4918

Poison Control 800/360.3585

Police (nonemergency) 241.6711

Lihue

On the southeast coast of Kauai, Lihue is the commercial and governing center of the island and the point of arrival for most visitors. Although it in many ways remains a quiet old plantation town (there's still an operating sugar mill here), restoration of portions of the town, renovation of the **Lihue Shopping Center** as a civic center, new housing, and a shopping center have given Lihue a somewhat more modern aspect in recent years. The town's streets reflect its changing nature, with banged-up old pickups parked behind shiny new sports cars. The heart of "downtown" Lihue is a little square lined with government offices, a small museum, and the county court. **Nawiliwili,** the island's main harbor, and **Kalapaki Beach** are both a mile-and-a-half southeast of the town center. Lihue offers some interesting sights, good restaurants, and a quirky charm.

1 **Hamura's Saimin Stand** ★$ If you haven't experienced the saimin sensation, hunker over a bowl of the traditional Hawaiian noodle soup (the ethnic equivalent of burgers and fries) here with the locals. A modest place with narrow Formica counters, this eatery spoons out some of the best saimin on Kauai. Try the teriyaki beef version. ♦ Hawaiian/Japanese ♦ Daily breakfast, lunch, and dinner. No credit cards accepted. 2956 Kress St (between Kalena and Rice Sts). 245.3271

2 **Kauai Museum** The story of the islands of Kauai and Niihau, from the first volcanic eruptions more than 6 million years ago through the 19th century, is told in a permanent exhibit in the **William Hyde Rice Building,** named for the last appointed governor of Kauai under the Hawaiian monarchy. In the **Albert Spencer Wilcox Building** (illustrated above), named for the son of missionary teachers, you'll find changing exhibits of Kauai art and historical artifacts. Or to see some of the generally inaccessible sights of the island without boarding a chopper, watch the film called *Flight of the Canyon Bird,* which was shot during a helicopter tour. ♦ Admission. M-Sa. Tours M throughout the day. 4428 Rice St (at Eiwa St). 245.6931 ♿

TIP TOP

3 **Tip Top** ★$ Known by locals and visitors from the outer islands as *the* breakfast place

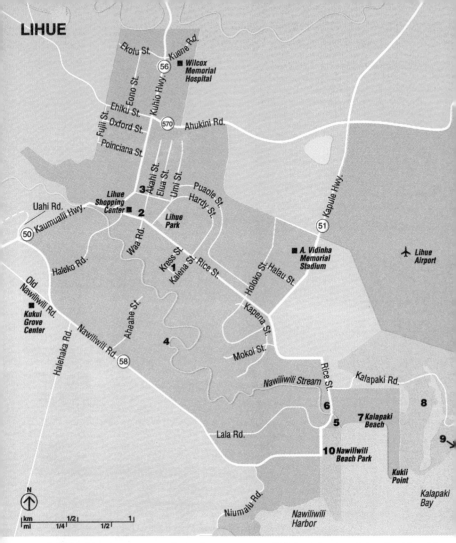

LIHUE

in Lihue, this eatery serves up stacks of macadamia nut and banana pancakes, side orders of spicy Portuguese sausage, and eggs with papaya. A favorite meeting place of Kauai's movers and shakers, it's also renowned for its fresh-baked cookies, cakes, and pies. The cafe is connected with a low-budget motel, but that isn't recommended. ◆ Japanese/American ◆ Tu-Su breakfast, lunch, and dinner. 3173 Akahi St (at Hardy St). 245.2333 ♿

4 Grove Farm Founded in 1864 by George N. Wilcox, a descendant of New England missionaries, this self-contained sugar plantation is a slice of the real Kauai. When Mabel Wilcox, George's niece and the last Wilcox to live on the plantation, died in 1978, it became a nonprofit educational organization dedicated to preserving the history of plantation life on the island. Well-versed guides conduct tours of the main plantation home, the cottages in which George lived and guests stayed, and the workers' camp houses. Miss

Mabel's clothes hang in her closet, her sister Elsie's silver-handled hairbrushes remain on her dresser, and their uncle's collection of canes and hats is in his cottage. Housekeepers dust the furniture, replace the flowers, bake cookies, and make iced tea for visitors. This is one of the most fascinating attractions on Kauai. ◆ Admission. Tours M, W-Th 10AM, 1PM. Reservations required (sometimes one week in advance). 4050 Nawiliwili Rd (between Lala Rd and Aheahe St). 245.3202

5 JJ's Broiler ★★$$$ Even *Gourmet* magazine couldn't wrest the recipe for the secret sauce on this eatery's famous garlic-flavored Slavonic steak from owner Jim Jasper. Mahimahi and lobster join the beefy stars served in this handsome establishment. ◆ Steak/Seafood ◆ Daily lunch and dinner. Reservations recommended. Anchor Cove Complex, 3416 Rice St (at Waapa Rd). 246.4422 ♿

6 Kauai Chop Suey ★★$ The enormous menu here has a following among the lunchtime crowd hungry for chow mein, shrimp with black beans, or one of the dozens of other Cantonese offerings. Kauai chow mein—a steaming plate of noodles, chicken, shrimp, *char siu* (barbecue pork), and lots of vegetables on cake noodles—is the house specialty. ♦ Chinese ♦ Tu-Su lunch and dinner. No credit cards accepted. Pacific Ocean Plaza, 3501 Rice St (between Lala Rd and Mokoi St). 245.8790 &

6 Cafe Portofino ★★$$$ Wood beams, ceiling fans, and an open-air terrace overlooking Kalapaki Beach all contribute to this eatery's charm. The gourmet Italian menu features such unusual dishes as rabbit in wine sauce with black olives, and veal Portofino—sautéed with shrimp and scallops in a lemon sauce. Treat yourself to an afternoon cocktail or an espresso at the bar or stop by for one of the occasional live jazz or harp performances in the lounge. ♦ Italian ♦ M-F lunch and dinner; Sa-Su dinner. Reservations recommended. Pacific Ocean Plaza, 3501 Rice St (between Lala Rd and Mokoi St). 245.2121 &

7 Kauai Marriott $$$$ Formerly the **Westin Kauai,** the island's largest hotel underwent a $28-million refurbishment in the mid-1990s that placed special emphasis on things Hawaiian, from the plants used to landscape the grounds to the animals living on islands created by a 2.1-acre reflecting lagoon in the center of the 800-acre property. There are 5 towers with 356 well-appointed guest rooms and suites, 232 one- and two-bedroom time-share units, 4 restaurants, a health spa, meeting space, and cabanas on the beach. The swimming pool is the largest in Hawaii, with 26,000 square feet of water surface and a lining of 1.8 million blue-and-white mosaic tiles. It's decadent in the most pleasant of ways. ♦ Kalapaki Rd (just east of Rice St). 245.5050, 800/228.9290; fax 245.5049; www.marriott.com &

Within the Kauai Marriott:

Duke's Canoe Club ★★$$ The theme of this statewide restaurant chain is Hawaii's "Ambassador of Goodwill," surf star Duke Kahanamoku. At this branch, the walls are made of elegant koa wood, photos of the Duke adorn the walls, and there's a spectacular ocean view. The steak and lobster or shrimp scampi over linguine aren't half bad either. Check out the bands that play Wednesday through Saturday after the dinner hour. ♦ American ♦ Daily lunch and dinner. Reservations recommended. 245.5050 &

8 Kauai Lagoons Golf Club The championship 18-hole **Kiele Course** (par 72, 6,674 yards) was created for tournament play, and the traditional links-style 18-hole **Kauai Lagoons Course** (par 72, 6,578 yards) is for all levels; all 36 holes were designed by Jack Nicklaus. The club also has health spas and eight tennis courts, including a stadium court. ♦ Expensive greens fees. Daily. Just east of Kalapaki Rd. 241.6000, 800/634.6400

9 Whaler's Brew Pub ★$$$ This casual microbrewery serves eight kinds of beer made on the premises, including Wild Wahine (Woman) Wheat and Tutu's Lilikoi, as well as a fair plate of blackened chicken and a 20-ounce hamburger that would put any meat lover in his or her place. ♦ Brew Pub/American ♦ Daily lunch and dinner. 3132 Ninini Point St (east of Kalapaki Rd). 245.2000 &

10 Nawiliwili Beach Park The beach here is superb for swimming, thanks to its sheltered cove and sandy bottom, and the waves are suitable for novice surfers. Old-timers will remember the days when Hawaiian beachboys steered their canoes through the surf here. ♦ Nawiliwili and Waapa Rds

South Shore

Hot and nearly always sunny, with broad, white beaches, generally calm seas, and a profusion of tropical plants and trees, the southern coast of Kauai has long been one of the island's most popular destinations; vacationers flock to the resorts at **Poipu** to enjoy tennis, good restaurants, and luxurious lodgings as well as excellent swimming, snorkeling, scuba diving, and surfing.

Beyond the Poipu resorts and the gentrified plantation town of **Koloa,** southern Kauai is a quiet, rural place where people depend on sugarcane rather than tourism for their livelihoods.

11 Alakoko Fish Pond (Menehune Fish Pond) According to folk legend, the menehune were two-foot-tall people who occupied Kauai long before the Polynesians and accomplished enormous physical feats, the remains of which are still visible. The menehune are credited with making this mullet pond by building a 900-foot-long wall to cut off a bend in Huleia Stream. Legend has it that a princess and her brother asked the menehune to undertake this task, and they agreed as long as the two didn't watch them build it. Naturally, they did watch, and, quite unnaturally, they were turned to stone as a result. The twin pillars near the fish pond are said to be the curious siblings. ♦ Hulemalu Rd (between Niumalu and Puhi Rds)

12 Kilohana Estate Gaylord Parke Wilcox, a relative of **Grove Farm** founder George N. Wilcox (see page 162) and at one point head of the **Grove Farm** plantation, probably never imagined that the Tudor-style dream house he built in 1935 would one day be a shopping complex. The original woodwork and furnishings now adorn an Art Deco gallery, shops, and restaurants. The master bedroom is a gallery featuring the works of leading Hawaiian artists. Carriage rides and sugarcane tours are available for a fee. ♦ Daily. 3-2087 Kaumualii Hwy (southwest of Uahi Rd). 245.5608 &

Within Kilohana Estate:

Gaylord's Restaurant ★★$$$$
Named after Gaylord Wilcox of the prominent missionary family, this restaurant offers alfresco dining in some of the most pleasing surroundings on the island. A courtyard overlooks the sprawling lawns of the estate while a private dining room retains the luxury and splendor of its plantation-era heyday. Continental specialties include fresh seafood, prime rib, and lamb with exotic chutneys. ♦ Continental ♦ M-Sa lunch and dinner; Su brunch and dinner. Reservations recommended. 245.9593 &

13 Old Koloa Town Bodysurfing and sun worshiping aren't the only attractions in the Poipu area. This $2-million restoration project was the brainchild of Robert H. Gerell of Koloa Town Associates. Gerell negotiated a 67-year lease from the Mabel P. Waterhouse Trust and acquired three acres and about a thousand feet of frontage road in Koloa, then set to work refurbishing the weathered, termite-ridden storefronts that creaked from one end of Koloa to the other, outfitting them in 19th-century style. Some of the historical structures that were restored are a stone mill stack from **Grove Farm;** the **Koloa Hotel,** Kauai's first hostelry, built in 1898; and the 1900 **Yamamoto Store.** There are more than a dozen businesses here in renovated storefronts, including **Lappert's** (742.1272) for ice cream and **Crazy Shirts** (742.7161). ♦ Koloa and Poipu Rds, Koloa

Within Old Koloa Town:

Don Ho is only 25 percent Hawaiian.

Hawaii residents have the longest life expectancy of all US citizens.

Koloa Broiler ★$$ Save some money and broil your own steaks and burgers at this casual, quaint little restaurant. Fish and chicken are also reasonably priced. Meals include salad bar, rice, and baked beans. ♦ Steak ♦ Daily lunch and dinner. 5412 Koloa Rd. 742.9122 &

14 Poipu A trip to the sunny South Shore and Poipu Beach is a popular excursion from the Wailua or Lihue areas. The **Tunnel of Trees,** a grove of eucalyptus trees that forms a natural archway along Route 520, is a distinctive landmark along the way. **Poipu Beach Park** (see below) attracts sun lovers and whale watchers, and quality bodysurfing can be found at Brennecke Beach. The area's most famous natural attraction, beyond the fine beaches, is **Spouting Horn** (see page166), a geyserlike lava tube.

Within Poipu:

Sheraton Kauai $$$$ More than $100 million was spent to restore this hotel (actually rebuild, from slab to shingle) in the wake of Hurricane Iniki in 1992, and the result is dazzling. There are 413 rooms and 14 suites, all with air-conditioning, lanais, and a decorating scheme that runs to pastels and floral prints. Guests either lounge on Poipu Beach or by one of the resort's two swimming pools. Other activities include tennis (three courts), golf (three nearby courses), windsurfing (nowhere finer on Kauai than the beach that fronts the hotel), kayaking, diving, and biking. Those less sports-minded can make the rounds of the hotel's four restaurants and one lounge and wash their cares away with Cabernet and cioppino. ♦ 2440 Hoonani Rd (off Lawai Rd). 742.1661, 800/325.3535; fax 742.9777; www.sheratonhawaii.com &

Within the Sheraton Kauai:

The Shells Restaurant ★★★★$$$$
This highly acclaimed dining spot has had two constants since the hotel's 1968 opening—a shell chandelier that survived two hurricanes, and chef Bert Matsuyoka who continues to

turn out such delicacies as baby rack of lamb, and fresh fish, prawns, and spicy pineapple. Top billing goes to the oceanside seating—be sure to request a table on the water, especially in the winter and at sunset when whale sightings are not infrequent. The seafood buffet on Friday is not to be believed. ♦ American ♦ Daily dinner. Reservations recommended. 742.1661 &

Outrigger Kiahuna Plantation Condominiums $$$$ Plantation-style buildings right beside Poipu Beach make up the accommodations at this first-class resort. The 36-acre property is generously landscaped with broad, manicured lawns, trees, and bougainvillea, with pathways and tiny Japanese-style bridges leading to the beach. While the most popular of the 200 units are those on the shore, the ones fronted by lawns are equally pleasant. There's a pool, restaurant, and 10 tennis courts. Each unit has a full kitchen and is equipped with a TV and VCR. It is an excellent place to settle while enjoying Kauai's sunniest shoreline. ♦ 2253 Poipu Rd (between Hoowili and Kapili Rds). 742.6411, 800/688.7444 &

Poipu Beach Park Considered the best swimming beach on the island and one of the most beautiful on Kauai, this beach is also good for snorkeling and whale watching (in winter). ♦ Hoone and Hoowili Rds

Poipu Kai Condominiums $$$ This comfortably appointed condominium resort has 235 units (100 managed by Colony Hotels & Resorts) on 110 lavishly landscaped acres adjacent to the beach. Each unit comes equipped with a full kitchen, washer/dryer, TV set, and fans; there's also a restaurant that serves dinner. Six swimming pools, two Jacuzzis, nine tennis courts, an activity booth, and two championship golf courses are on opposite sides of the property. ♦ 1941 Poipu Rd (between Pee and Hoowili Rds). 742.6464, 800/367.8020; fax 742.9121; mail@suite-paradise.com; www.suite-paradise.com

15 Roy's Poipu Bar and Grill ★★★$$$ This was Midas-fingered restaurateur Roy Yamaguchi's fourth eatery (there are now about a dozen scattered throughout the Pacific Rim). The place is packed with diners putting away meals like *kiawe*-grilled hibachi-style salmon and herb-grilled fillet of beef. ♦ Euro-Asian ♦ Daily dinner. Reservations recommended. 2360 Kiahuna Plantation Dr (between Poipu Rd and Pau A Laka St). 742.5000 &

15 Kiahuna Golf Course Poipu's first championship 18-hole course (par 70, 6,336 yards), designed by Robert Trent Jones Jr., was completed in 1983. It's since been

eclipsed by several island courses, but is less expensive and challenging, so it still attracts eager golfers. A weekly pass is available for real addicts. ♦ Moderate greens fees. Daily. 2545 Kiahuna Plantation Dr (between Poipu Rd and Pau A Laka St). 742.9595

16 Hyatt Regency Kauai $$$$ Kauai's second-largest resort sits on 48 acres of choice oceanfront property. Although Iniki inflicted $55 million worth of damage, the completely restored hotel reopened only six months after the 1992 hurricane. Designed by Honolulu architects **Wimberly, Allison, Tong and Goo** and Santa Monica interior decorators Hirsch-Bedner & Associates, the structure is splendidly landscaped with a re-created shipwreck and a five-acre lagoon that faces Keoniloa Bay, commonly called "Shipwreck Beach." The remarkable architecture draws inspiration from island homes, with gorgeous, hand-crafted koa wood furnishings. Five restaurants are on the property. Scuba diving, snorkeling, tennis, and catamaran sailing are among the many sports guests can enjoy, plus there's an 18-hole Robert Trent Jones Jr. golf course and a driving range. Sailing, horseback riding, kayak excursions, and helicopter tours are all nearby. In addition, the hotel's "Discover Kauai" program, run under the auspices of the Kauai Historical Society and Na Hula o Kaohi Kukapulani, offers a range of activities (free to guests), including presentations on the history and lore of hula (with demonstrations) and a dune walk focusing on the endemic plants and sea life of the Poipu Beach area. ♦ 1571 Poipu Rd (east of Pee Rd). 742.1234, 800/742.2353; fax 742.6265; www.hyatt.com &

Within the Hyatt Regency Kauai:

Dondero's ★★★$$$$ The locals come for miles for the veal scallopini at this attractive, ocean-view establishment (the porcini mushroom crepes and *spaghettini alla pescatora*—with seafood—are equally good). Green tiles, yellow tablecloths, and elegant open windows give the place a relaxed feel, and celebrity sightings are not unknown. ♦ Northern Italian ♦ M-Sa dinner. 742.1234 &

Tidepools ★★★$$$$ Picture this. You're sitting in a thatched hut by the ocean. A waiter is bringing you fresh-caught mahimahi grilled with sunrise papaya or mango relish. Your dinner companion is getting sautéed *ahi* (yellowfin tuna) with *lilikoi* lemon butter. You're wearing shorts and an aloha shirt and are warm from a day on the beach. Is this your vision of Hawaii? It's just another night at this dining spot. ♦ Seafood ♦ Daily dinner. Reservations recommended. 742.1234 &

17 The Beach House ★★★$$$ At a table overlooking the water at sunset, with a sizable order of *ahi au poivre* (with pepper) or wok-charred, sesame-crusted tiger-eye sashimi, even the most craven holiday cynic would be hard-pressed not to enjoy him- or herself. ♦ Pacific Rim/Mediterranean ♦ Daily dinner. Reservations recommended. 5022 Lawai Rd, Kukuiula. 742.1424 ♿

17 Spouting Horn The Poipu area's top tourist attraction is a gush of ocean water that explodes through a lava tube when the waves roll in, sometimes causing a moaning sound. Legend has it that the groan is from a lizard trapped in the tube. Note: The lava tube's reputation far exceeds its actual performance. ♦ Lawai Rd, Kukuiula

18 National Tropical Botanical Garden
Since it opened in 1971, this garden has survived several storms, and Hurricane Iniki proved no exception. Restored to its original splendor, this 186-acre botanical jewel continues to protect and propagate plants that otherwise might become extinct, adding some 1,000 plants to its inventory each year.

In 1938, Robert Allerton, the son of a pioneer Chicago cattleman, and his son, John Gregg Allerton, began to transform the **Allerton Estate** (formerly a vacation domicile of Queen Emma, wife of Kamehameha IV) into a garden showplace. With the help of hired gardeners, Allerton and his son spent 20 years clearing jungle growth to create sweeping gardens around reflecting pools, fountains, and statues. Kauai's *kamaaina* (locals) gave them cuttings and seeds, and the Allertons scoured the islands of the South Pacific for varieties never before seen on Kauai. Today visitors are able to tour the garden and **Allerton Estate**. ♦ Admission. Tours Tu-Sa 9AM, 1PM. Reservations required (sometimes six months in advance); call 332.7361 or write to PO Box 340, Lawai, HI 96765. Hailima Rd (south of Koloa Rd), Lawai

19 Mustard's Last Stand ★★$ If you're anywhere near the area, stop at this red-and-yellow kiosk for hot dogs, hamburgers, or fish-and-chips. Surfboard benches, daily specials, and friendly service are enough to keep the joint busy. ♦ American ♦ Daily. Kaumualii Hwy and Koloa Rd, Lawai. 332.7245 ♿

20 Brick Oven Pizza ★$$ It's the best-known name in pizza on the island and one of the few places to eat on the way to Waimea Canyon. Selections include pineapple and vegetarian

pizza on whole-wheat dough (made fresh daily). Sandwiches, salads, and take-out orders are also available. ♦ Pizza/Deli/Takeout ♦ Tu-Su lunch and dinner. 2-2555 Kaumualii Hwy, Kalaheo. 332.8561 ♿

21 Green Garden Restaurant ★★$$
Sue Hamabata and her daughter Gwen continue a family tradition started in 1948 of serving abundant amounts of delicious Asian, American, and Hawaiian food in the greenery-filled dining room that was once the family's home. Draped in her signature cascade of Niihau-shell leis, Sue greets guests, helps with the serving, and offers advice on meals tailored to your taste and budget. Start with a fresh *lilikoi* daiquiri, indulge in butter-brushed filet mignon or broiled peppercorn chicken, and don't dare leave without finishing a piece of the famous *lilikoi* chiffon pie. ♦ Asian/American/Hawaiian ♦ M, W-Su breakfast, lunch, and dinner. Hana Rd (between Kaumualii Hwy and Hanapepe Rd), Eleele. 335.5422 ♿

22 Lappert's The Kauai-pie ice cream—a concoction of coffee and fudge with a hint of coconut and macadamia—is one of the irresistible flavors created by ice-cream wizard Walter Lappert, who came to Kauai to retire in 1981 and instead found himself churning out this creamy dessert. Soon the hobby snowballed into a 13,000-gallon-a-month business. His sweet success is spreading to local merchants as well, who supply him with crates of papayas, guavas, coconuts, pineapples, and mangoes, and about 8,000 pounds of macadamia nuts a month, not to mention the pure cane sugar, which he whips into more than 70 flavors of ice cream. You can buy Lappert's ice cream from this small white factory and shop, as well as throughout the islands. ♦ Daily. 1-3555 Kaumualii Hwy (just west of Hanapepe Rd). 335.6121, 800/356.4045 ♿

23 Salt Pond Beach Park This beach is named for the nearby ancient ponds where the Hawaiians harvested salt from drying beds. Every year the Hui Hana Paakai o Hanapepe (Hanapepe Association of Salt Workers) lets ocean water dry in the ponds, collecting the prized salt crystals for use at home or for gifts. Sometimes referred to as "Hanapepe salt," it has a reddish tint and is coveted by Hawaiians, who consider the colored salt superior for healing and seasoning. However, because of state health regulations, it can't be sold commercially. There is also good swimming, fishing, and shelling at the beach, as well as picnic and public facilities. ♦ Lokokai Rd (west of Lele Rd)

West Kauai

The main attractions on the western side of Kauai are natural ones. The highlight is **Waimea Canyon,** a spectacular 10-mile-long gash cut by the **Waimea River.** Just north of the canyon is **Kokee State Park,** a 4,345-acre nature reserve that delights picnickers, hikers, campers, and others who just appreciate nature at its purest. Also pristinely beautiful are the white-sand beaches at **Polihale State Park.**

In recent times, West Kauai's economy has benefited from a change in venue for the departure point of boat tours of the **Na Pali Coast. Port Allen** has become the center for these expeditions since a change in restrictions caused operators to leave the North Shore.

24 Russian Fort (Fort Elizabeth) In 1817 a German doctor named Georg Anton Schaeffer was sent to Kauai as a Russian agent. His mission was to negotiate the return of some furs lost in a Russian shipwreck off Kauai, and while he was at it, to convince Kauai's King Kaumualii to allow Russia to establish a military presence on the island in return for military assistance. The plan was eventually derailed by Kamehameha I, the ruler of the other Hawaiian isles. Wary of Russia, he forced Kaumualii to send Schaeffer away, but not before this star-shaped Russian-style fort, named for Czar Nicholas's daughter, was built on the banks of the Waimea River. Remnants of the lava stone fort are buried in the brush. ♦ Just south of Kaumualii Hwy

25 Waimea Plantation Cottages $$$ If you wanted to immerse yourself in the real island lifestyle, you would get yourself one of the 48 1- to 5-bedroom cottages (oceanfront, if possible) here and settle into a rocking chair on the lanai. The Aston-owned property, comprising 27 acres in laid-back Waimea, is recommended for true R&R seekers only, as there isn't much in the way of entertainment nearby (unless you include Waimea Canyon). However, there is a pool on the premises and a restaurant serving dinner on Friday and Saturday. One caveat: There's no air-conditioning and Waimea is hot in the summer. ♦ 9400 Kaumaulii Hwy (west of Pokole Rd), Waimea. 338.1625, 800/9.WAIMEA; www.waimea-plantation.com &

26 Menehune Ditch Kauai schoolchildren learn shortly after they can talk that if they don't want to be held responsible for some-thing that goes wrong, they can always blame it on the menehune. Some say the menehune were a pygmy-size class of Polynesian laborers brought to Kauai by the old Hawaiians. Others say they are only a myth, the Hawaiian version of the leprechaun. True romantics credit the mysterious, mis-chievous people with magical powers and maintain that the ones who left Kauai did so on a floating island. This prodigious work is probably the menehune's most famous. The fitted stonework, not found anywhere else in Hawaii, is said to be the remains of an aqueduct built by the menehune at the request of a Kauai king who wanted to irrigate nearby taro patches. Legend holds that the king was so pleased with their work he rewarded the menehune with a feast of shrimp, along with their favorite foods: sweet potatoes and *haupia* (coconut pudding). ♦ Menehune Rd (north of Gay Rd)

27 Waimea Canyon Plummeting 3,657 feet at its deepest point, the 10-mile-long canyon is a rough, inhospitable cut—only goats and birds can manage the jagged terrain. For lack of a better comparison, it is often called the "Grand Canyon of the Pacific"—a worn-out exaggeration that Mark Twain was supposed to have said, but didn't (Twain never even visited Kauai). Although no match for the Grand Canyon, it is still one of Hawaii's most photographed attractions. The main overlook offers a sprawling landscape, where white-tailed birds soar overhead and the echoes of bleating feral goats can often be heard. Colors range from gold to purple, red, and green, and when the canyon depths are clouded by mist, the effect is even more dramatic.

Hardy hikers may want to tackle the trails that zigzag down the canyon's wall, while the **Iliau Nature Loop** south of the lookout is a nice path for casual strollers. If you're staying in Lihue or Poipu, set aside an entire day for this excursion; although the canyon is only about 35 miles from Lihue, there are interesting towns along the way and slow-moving traffic occasionally causes delays. Once there, you'll want to continue on to **Kokee State Park** (see page 169) for a peek into the verdant and mysterious Kalalau Valley. Check your gas gauge before heading up to the out-of-the-way canyon, and bring a sweater—it's cool because of the higher elevation. ♦ Canyon lookout: Kokee Rd (north of Waimea Canyon Dr)

Mokihana, a rare, fragrant plant that grows only on Kauai, is used to make exotic leis; however, *mokihana* leis cannot be worn against bare skin because the berry-size fruit is so potent it can burn your flesh.

When Hurricane Iniki hit Kauai in 1992, one of those trapped on the island without electricity or water for several days was Steven Spielberg, on location here to film *Jurassic Park.*

Missionaries, the Moana, and Modernization: The Evolution of Hawaiian Music

From ancient times through the 17th century, the *mele* was the primary musical expression in the Hawaiian islands. This repetitive chant, commonly used to accompany hula dancing and most often sung outdoors during religious ceremonies, told a story using only a few notes. The conch shell and nose flute, also played while the hula was danced, were the predominant instruments of the day.

The next musical era was influenced by the missionaries who arrived on the islands in 1820. Although historically they have been castigated for their negative effect on certain areas of Hawaiians' lives, their impact on island music was unequivocally positive. The Hawaiians took to melody and harmony as if they had been singing since they learned to talk. The first hymns, sung that year, caused such excitement that the missionaries lost no time in founding a singing school and translating the words for the Christian music into Hawaiian. It wasn't long, however, before the Polynesians began replacing the religious words with secular lyrics. They were often sad, talking about a longing for a distant place or person, probably as a result of King Kamehameha I uniting the island nation by forcibly scattering the population across the chain.

The next period of musical development was in the 1870s, when three things happened. First, Spanish *vaqueros* (cowboys) were brought in to teach the people of the **Big Island** how to punch cattle, and in the process, taught the wet-behind-the-ears *paniolos* ("Hawaiian cowboys," from the word *español*) a thing or two about playing the guitar. The Hawaiians then took it upon themselves to loosen the strings, leading to the birth of the now-famous "slack key" guitar. Second, Portuguese immigrants began to arrive in the islands to work the fields, and they brought with them several novel instruments, among them the raga. The Hawaiians who first watched Portuguese fingers strumming the reinvented guitar thought the whole business looked like a dog scratching a flea, so they called the instrument the ukulele, or "jumping flea." Third, at the end of the decade, a German musician, Henri Berger, was invited in as the royal family's musician and asked to lead the fledgling Royal Hawaiian Band, which, with the help of King Kamehameha V, Queen Liliuokalani, and others, became prestigious and popular. (Amazingly, the band still puts on a free concert every Friday afternoon from 12:15PM to 1:15PM at the **Coronation**

Bandstand on the grounds of the **Iolani Palace** in downtown **Honolulu**.)

The next Hawaiian musical phase occurred in the 1890s when a comb was allegedly dropped onto a set of guitar strings by a student at **King Kamehameha School.** This led, after the construction of a steel bar to slide over some new steel strings, to the invention of the steel guitar.

These instruments kept Hawaii's aspiring musicians pretty well occupied for decades. A new era came about in 1935 when the posh **Moana Hotel** in **Waikiki** instituted a live radio program, "Hawaii Calls," from its courtyard. The show aired for 40 years, on as many as 700 stations around the world at its peak in the 1950s. Songs like "The Hawaiian Wedding Song," "Aloha Oe," and "Lovely Hula Hands" were suddenly heard in living rooms from San Francisco to Singapore.

But in the 1960s, Hawaii's music industry found itself in a slump. Compared to rock 'n' roll, local music suddenly seemed corny and provincial. Nevertheless, lounge acts performed by the likes of Don Ho, Al Harrington, and Danny Kaleikini remained popular, albeit with an older crowd.

What's known today as contemporary Hawaiian music originated in the early 1980s with groups that scorned the old names—Waikiki Beachboys, Royal Hawaiian Serenaders—in favor of such Hawaiian names as Hui Ohana and Na Keonimana. These bands, whose young, energetic members had never known a pre-statehood Hawaii, combined lilting Hawaiian harmonies with mainland pop, R&B, and country, and came up with the style of music played not only in the islands but to eager mainland audiences everywhere from Vegas lounges to Radio City Music Hall. Leading local talent, like The Brothers Cazimero, Hapa, Cecilio and Kapono, Kapena, Willy K., the late Israel Kamakawiwoole (more often known simply as "Iz"), The Makaha Sons of Niihau, and Kealii Reichel, were the main people playing this music.

There's no indication yet what direction Hawaiian music will take in the new millennium, but for now, the genre is thriving. One particularly good vantage from which to experience a local band's performance is the open-air amphitheater **Waikiki Shell** (2805 Monsarrat Ave, between Paki and Kalakaua Aves, 591.2211) in **Kapiolani Park.**

ILLUSTRATIONS BY KEELY EDWARDS

Polihale State Park

MATT MORROW/NORTH MARKET STREET GRAPHICS

28 Kokee State Park Three miles from the Waimea Canyon lookout, the park has a cool climate that attracts islanders tired of the same perfect weather day in and day out. At a 3,600-foot elevation, the 4,345-acre park is a brisk, nature-lover's bonanza, with rare honeycreepers, native flora, and burbling streams. The hiking trails are abundant (they cover 45 miles), and there's one for just about every level of expertise. From the end of June through August, the park's island-famous plums are free for the picking, and anglers (with licenses) can fish for rainbow trout in Kokee's cool streams from August through September. The fish eggs were flown in from the mainland, hatched on Oahu, and released for sportfishing here. You'll also find **Kokee Lodge** (see below), a gift shop, a bar and restaurant, and an information center in this idyllic forest setting. ♦ Kokee Rd (north of Waimea Canyon Dr)

Within Kokee State Park:

Kokee Lodge $ These 12 rustic cabins sleep 4 to 6 people in extremely simple style. There's one bathroom per cabin, and each bed has a blanket and a sheet, but that's about it for amenities. The restaurant is open daily for breakfast and lunch. Book well in advance by writing to: Kokee Lodge, PO Box 819, Waimea, HI 96796. ♦ 335.6061 &

Kokee Natural History Museum
Informative and well managed, the museum features displays, videos, and photographs about Waimea Canyon and **Kokee State Park**. Trail information also is available. ♦ Donation. Daily. 335.9975; fax 335.6131 &

Kalalau Valley Lookout Timing is everything at this 4,000-foot-high vantage point, where the vista is usually clear in the early morning but obscured by mist and clouds by afternoon. Sightseers often make the long ascent to Kalalau only to find the fabled view hidden by the clouds. But when the clouds part, even if just for a moment, the effect is startlingly beautiful. Honeycreepers feed on lehua blossoms; waterfalls and fluted cliffs stand before you. Until early this century, the valley—the largest on the Na Pali Coast—was occupied by hundreds of Hawaiians who lived on the abundant fruits and vegetables grown here. No one lives in this remote area now. Experienced hikers can reach Kalalau from Haena on the North Shore, but there is no trail from the lookout because of the dangerous terrain.

29 Polihale State Park This is the most remote beach on Kauai that can be reached by car. There's good summer swimming, but it's rough the rest of the year. Rest rooms, showers, and barbecue grills are provided. ♦ North of Lower Saki Mana Rd

Kauai didn't get its first traffic lights until 1973, when they were installed in Lihue at the intersection of Rice and Umi Streets, near the Kauai Museum.

East Kauai

Midway up the east coast of Kauai are the resort areas of **Wailua** and **Kapaa**. Once the private preserve of Hawaii's *alii* (royalty), this is now the most popular tourist area on the island (and the only place that has any traffic to speak of). It offers a superb beach, a river that winds through tropical forests hiding grottoes and waterfalls, and dependable weather all year. In recent years the two towns of Wailua and Kapaa have grown together, linked by development along **Kuhio Highway (Route 56)**. Both have some fairly good restaurants, numerous souvenir and dive shops, and hotels and condominiums that line miles of white-sand beach.

30 Wailua Falls If there's been substantial rain, you'll see two exquisite falls (*wailua* means "twin waters") tumbling over the 80-foot cliff. Hawaiian chiefs used to dive down this precipice to prove their courage. Skip the lookout for the falls, which is four miles west of Kapaa, unless you don't mind the monotonous ride to get there. ♦ Maalo Rd (northwest of Kuhio Hwy)

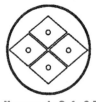

31 Hanamaulu Cafe & Tea House ★★$$ Kick the Kauai salad-bar habit and spend a unique island evening in one of the garden rooms at this Japanese/Chinese restaurant, a local favorite since 1923. The nine-course dinners (including snow-crab claws, spare-ribs, and ginger-seasoned fried chicken) are memorable, and the lobster—baked in a rich butter sauce with bread crumbs—has a unique flavor. ♦ Japanese/Chinese ♦ Tu-F lunch and dinner; Sa-Su dinner. Reservations required for the garden rooms. 3-4291 Kuhio Hwy, Hanamaulu. 245.2511 ♿

32 Outrigger Kauai Beach Hotel $$ Although it rests on a Hawaiian burial site (which is considered unlucky), this property rode out Hurricane Iniki relatively unscathed. In 1996, a $1.8-million renovation polished the rooms further. The series of five-story buildings is oriented toward the ocean and a long strip of sandy beach, which is suitable only for sunning because of the undertow. Three swimming pools more than

compensate, though; the main pool is particularly elaborate, with caves, trickling waterfalls, fountains, and lots of greenery. The hotel has 341 guest rooms with lanais, cable TV, and refrigerators. The **Hale Kipa Terrace** serves breakfast, lunch, and a signature buffet supper nightly; **Gilligan's** lounge offers Latin dance music on Thursday, 1970s tunes on Friday, and Top 40 on Saturday until 2AM. The **Wailua Golf Course** (see below) is a short ride away. ♦ 4331 Kauai Beach Dr (east of Kuhio Hwy). 245.1955, 800/688.7444; fax 245.3956; okb@outrigger.com; www.outrigger.com ♿

33 Wailua Golf Course The low greens fees make this one of the best golf bargains in Hawaii. Extending more than a mile along the beach, the 18-hole course (par 72, 6,585 yards) was built in 1920 among sand dunes and ironwood trees. The ocean comes into play on three holes, and the demanding back nine is highlighted by the famous Sea Beach Hole at the par-three 17th, where too much club will guarantee a Pacific-bound ball. ♦ Inexpensive greens fees. Daily. 3-5350 Kuhio Hwy (between Kauai Beach and Leho Drs). 241.6666

34 Aston Kaha Lani Condominiums $$ Secluded on nine acres of beachfront property, the 74 individually owned and decorated units have ocean-view lanais and are managed by the always reliable Aston Resorts. There's a pool and a tennis court (but no restaurant) on the premises; a golf course is nearby. ♦ 4460 Nehe Rd (just southeast of Leho Dr). 822.9331, 888/524.2526; fax 822.2828

34 Lydgate Beach Park Local families and visitors enjoy this pleasant combination of beach, protected pools, the multimillion-dollar **Kamalani Playground**, picnic pavilions, and a tree-shaded park beside the Wailua River. There are public facilities on the premises. ♦ Leho Dr and Nalu Rd

35 Fern Grotto The Wailua River, the best-known river in Hawaii, leads to this visitor attraction that has achieved the status of a "must-do" (it's a "must-not-do" if you don't like crowds or a circuslike atmosphere). The grotto is reached via boxy cruise boats that glide upriver as entertainers do the hula and perform standard Hawaiian tunes to ukulele accompaniments. After the boats land, you'll walk through jungle to a truly impressive cave filled with giant cascading ferns. Inside, the hired help recount legends with background music. The return trip is highlighted by a Hawaiian sing-along. The grotto is a popular site for weddings, complete with the traditional "Hawaiian Wedding Song." ♦ Fee. Boats leave from Wailua Marina, 5971 Kuhio Hwy, Wailua. Smith's Motor Boat Service 821.6892; Waialeale Boat Tours 822.4908 ♿

36 Wailua Marina Restaurant $$ Crowded with **Fern Grotto** tourists during the day, this huge, very touristy place has a little more breathing room during dinner hours. Such dishes as baked stuffed pork chops, fried chicken, and *ahi* filled with crabmeat carry reasonable price tags. ♦ American/Asian ♦ Tu-Su lunch and dinner. Wailua Marina, 5971 Kuhio Hwy (just south of Kuamoo Rd), Wailua. 822.4311 ⅙

37 Kintaro ★★$$$ Sleek, elegant, and authentically decorated with kimonos and Japanese screens, this restaurant offers an impressive selection of sashimi, sushi, *zaru soba* (buckwheat noodles), *nabemono* (seafood soup), *teppanyaki* (items grilled at tableside), and other exquisite delicacies. Be adventurous and try freshwater eel grilled with sweet sauce over rice. ♦ Japanese ♦ M-Sa dinner. Kuhio Hwy, Wailua. 822.3341 ⅙

38 Coconut Plantation This resort development comprises four hotels and the **Coconut Plantation Marketplace,** with some 70 shops (most of them touristy), several restaurants, and a movie theater. ♦ Kuhio Hwy (between Papaloa Rd and Kamoa St). 822.3641

Within Coconut Plantation:

Aston's Kauai Beachboy Hotel $$ The highlight of this establishment is its setting on a milelong stretch of Waipouli Beach, which is actually better suited for wading and beachcombing than for swimming. The 243 lackluster rooms have refrigerators and lanais with ocean or mountain views. Serious shoppers are well located here, within walking distance of the **Coconut Plantation Marketplace.** There's also a pool, tennis court, and a spartan restaurant on the premises. ♦ 4-484 Kuhio Hwy. 822.3441, 800/922.7866; fax 822.0843 ⅙

Kauai Coconut Beach Resort
COCONUT PLANTATION

Kauai Coconut Beach Resort $$$ Set in nearly 11 acres of coconut trees along Waipouli Beach, all 311 rooms and suites in this resort have lanais, most with ocean views. Stained-glass windows and tapestries in the public areas are accented by a 40-foot waterfall cascading into a reflecting pool. The beach is scenic but often windy, and swimming isn't recommended because of the rocks; the Jacuzzi at poolside is a good alternative. The restaurant on the grounds is only fair (though a deal for families, as kids under 12 eat free), but the nearby town of

Kapaa offers appealing dinner options. ♦ 822.3455, 800/222.5642; fax 822.1830; www.hawaiihotels.com ⅙

39 The Bull Shed ★$$$ Many swear by it and others swear at it, but there's no argument over the choice location on the windy eastern shore, with the waves marching toward the windows. A heroic cut of prime rib stands out on the short menu of beef, lamb, chicken, and fish dishes; there's also a salad bar. This local favorite is usually crowded; service can be haphazard. ♦ American ♦ Daily dinner. 796 Kuhio Hwy (Hwy 56, across from McDonald's), Waipouli. 822.3791 ⅙

40 Kauai Village This shopping center houses a sorely needed **Safeway** grocery store plus **Waldenbooks** and a **Longs** drugstore. There are also a few restaurants, including **Papaya's Natural Foods** (823.0190) and **Panda Garden Chinese Restaurant** (822.0092). ♦ Kuhio Hwy (between Pouli and Hoi Rds), Waipouli. 822.4904

Within Kauai Village:

A PACIFIC CAFE

A Pacific Cafe ★★★$$$ When owner/chef Jean-Marie Josselin, formerly of the **Hotel Hana-Maui** and the **Coco Palms Resort,** opened this stylish restaurant, he lost no time boosting his already considerable reputation. Pacific Rim cuisine takes on new life in his able hands; try the wok-charred mahimahi with garlic-sesame crust and lime-ginger sauce or sea scallops in caramelized pineapple vinaigrette. Local farmers truck in the fresh produce daily—all the vegetables served here are grown on the island. The decor is tropical, with ceramic plates made by Josselin's wife, Sophaonia. ♦ Pacific Rim ♦ Daily dinner. Reservations recommended. 822.0013 ⅙

40 Aloha Diner ★$ Strictly local style, this small diner serves the best saimin and Hawaiian food on Kauai. The small family operation is an institution—folks line up for fried *akule* (scad), *lomilomi* salmon (chopped with tomato), *laulau* (pork in taro and ti leaves), and poi (taro root). ♦ Hawaiian ♦ M-Sa lunch and dinner. No credit cards accepted. Waipouli Complex, 971-F Kuhio Hwy (between Hoi and Panihi Rds), Waipouli. 822.3851 &

41 Ono Family Restaurant ★$ Famous first for its charburgers, this popular place has expanded its offerings. The prices are low (compared to the resort areas), and the food is American, from fresh fish to meat loaf. There's takeout too. ♦ American ♦ Daily breakfast and lunch. 4-1292 Kuhio Hwy (south of Kukui St), Kapaa. 822.1710 &

42 Kountry Kitchen ★$ From the Polynesian omelette with Portuguese sausage and kimchee (spicy, pickled cabbage) to the quarter-pound burgers on sesame-seed buns, this dependable little diner keeps big eaters happy without devouring their wallets. ♦ Country-style ♦ Daily breakfast and lunch. 4-1485 Kuhio Hwy (between Kukui St and Mailihuna Rd), Kapaa. 822.3511 &

43 Kapaia Trading Company How about this one, cigar lovers: a stogie hand made in Kapaa from tobacco grown in the Dominican Republic? And, even better, a $7,000 humidor to store it in? You get the point: This store has everything a cigar smoker could wish for. ♦ 4-1621 Kuhio Hwy (at Mailihuna Rd), Kapaa. 822.7972. Also at: Kuhio Hwy, Hanamaulu. 246.6792 &

44 Anahola Beach Park Because of Anahola's shallow waters, the swimming is excellent here. It's a popular spot for families and fishers, and the northern end is Hawaiian Homestead land (set aside for people who are at least 50 percent Hawaiian). Picnic facilities are available. ♦ Anahola Rd (east of Kuhio Hwy)

North Shore

Beautiful and remote, the northern coast of Kauai ha an embarrassment of riches: white-sand beaches; luminous **Hanalei Bay;** numerous waterfalls; a wide fertile valley of taro fields; funky resort communities with lots of unusual shops and interesting restaurants; luxurious resort hotels; and places to camp, hike, swim, surf, snorkel, sail, fish, golf, play tennis, and ride horses. Movie aficionados may recognize some spots here—parts of *Jurassic Park* were filmed on the North Shore, and this was also th setting for *South Pacific.* In the northwest is the extravagantly beautiful and nearly inaccessible **Na Pali Coast,** 14 miles of cliffs so rocky and valleys so steep and narrow that the road that follows the perimeter of the island can't traverse them.

On the down side, the towns of **Princeville** and **Hanalei** are decidedly quiet, and the weather can be wet in winter. But if you take the time to explore the area's character—on one of its uncrowded beaches or in one of the laid-back pubs, or by taking any one of a hundred back roads—this less-traveled region will yield rich secrets.

45 Kilauea Point National Wildlife Refuge Lighthouses are usually found in rugged, unspoiled areas, and this one is no exception When this lighthouse, which is on the Nation Register of Historic Places, was built in 1913 it could be seen 20 miles from shore. The US Coast Guard stopped operating it when an automated light was installed in 1974; the US Fish and Wildlife Service now runs the 106-acre preserve. A $6-million renovation was done after Hurricane Iniki hit in 1992, sprucing up the visitors' center with new exhibits and building a half-mile trail to a volcanic crater. Look for red-footed boobies and wedge-tailed shearwaters soaring above from the lookout point, try to spot sea turtles

Kilauea Point Lighthous

MATT MORROW/NORTH MARKET STREET GRAPHIC

and porpoises. Nene geese, Hawaii's endangered state bird, and the Laysan albatross are to be found here too. From December through April, this nature-lover's refuge is a wonderful vantage point for humpback-whale watching. ♦ Nominal admission. Daily. Kilauea Rd (northeast of Kolo Rd). 828.1413 &

46 Anini Beach There's a protective reef 200 yards offshore, making this white-sand beach safe for swimming and a favorite with beginning windsurfers. The picnic area makes the beach popular with families, and shell seekers also find it rewarding. Polo matches are held here on summer weekends and **Anini Beach Windsurfing** (826.9463) offers three-hour-long introductory and advanced windsurfing lessons, as well as equipment rental. On either side of the main beach are numerous secluded coves. ♦ Anini Rd (north of Kalihiwai Rd)

Princeville Resort
K A U A I

47 Princeville Resort In the summer of 1969, Eagle County Development Corporation was breaking ground on what two decades later would be a 9,000-acre resort area, complete with beaches, two golf courses, two hotels, a shopping center, health club, airport, condominiums, and numerous restaurants. ♦ Princeville

Within Princeville Resort:

Chuck's Steak House ★$$$ A notch or two above the Surfer Joe ambience of the chain's earlier restaurants, this place has a smart design and an interesting menu. Ask for a table on the lanai and settle in for a fish sandwich or an enchilada at lunch; sautéed *opakapaka* (pink snapper) and prime rib are the specialties at night. ♦ Steak/Seafood ♦ M-F lunch and dinner; Sa-Su dinner. Princeville Shopping Center, 5-3420F Kuhio Hwy (between Ka Haku and Hanalei Plantation Rds). 826.6211 &

Princeville Condominiums $$$ Although the **Princeville Hotel** (see below) garners more attention, some of these

condominiums on the bluffs above Hanalei Bay are exceptionally roomy. The main attractions here are the **Makai** and the **Prince Golf Courses**, as well as the gorgeous beaches and dramatic mountain scenery of the Hanalei area. All of the condominiums have pools, plus there are two tennis courts, riding stables, and good beaches nearby (though access to them is somewhat difficult). Many real estate companies handle vacation rentals of condos and homes in the Princeville area. ♦ Ka Haku Rd (west of Punahele Rd). Pacific Paradise Properties 826.7211, 800/800.3637; fax 826.9884; www.pacific-paradise.com &

Within the Princeville Condominiums:

Winds of the Beamreach ★★$$
Mountain views and expertly prepared Hawaiian fare await at this eatery. The casual, airy decor is accented by nature's art outside the large windows. Try the Hawaiian fish (steamed in ginger and sesame oil), macadamia-nut chicken, or stir-fried vegetables with either chicken or beef. Don't miss the smooth-as-silk guava chiffon pie. ♦ Steak/Seafood ♦ Daily dinner. 826.6143 &

Princeville Hotel $$$$ In 1985 Sheraton decided to venture where others feared to tread: the extraordinary setting but sometimes unreliable climate of Kauai's North Shore. Situated on the Hanalei Bay lookout point, the hotel holds the plum location in the Princeville development.

The architects originally designed a simple hotel, which descended the face of Puu Poa Point in a series of three terraces. But the Sheraton corporation wanted more upscale accommodations and more ocean views, so the architects came up with a $100-million renovation, which was completed in 1991. All 252 rooms, 44 suites, and public areas, including the lobby, lounge, and restaurants, now offer a clear view of the 23-acre site. Each of the **Prince Suites,** about 1.5 times the size of the king and double rooms, boasts a formal entry hall, living room, oversized bathroom with a spa tub, a bedroom with floor-to-ceiling bronze mirrors, and 18th-century Italian-style furniture throughout. Special extras include butler and valet service, 24-hour room service, and complimentary transportation to the 2 nearby golf courses, health spa, and 6 tennis courts.

Also on site are an Italian restaurant, luxurious pool, exercise room, beauty salon, and beach kiosks for snorkeling and windsurfing. Guests have preferred starting times and charge privileges at the adjacent **Princeville Resort** facilities, including the tennis courts and **Makai** and **Prince Golf Courses**. ♦ 5520 Ka Haku Rd (west of Punahele Rd). 826.9644, 800/826.4400; fax 826.1166; www.princeville.com &

Top Waterfalls

Hawaii's tropical terrain is the perfect setting for some wonderful waterfalls and pools. Unfortunately 99 percent of the islands' waterfalls are accessible only after a risky and involved helicopter dropoff. But the tiny percentage that can be reached by car or foot (with the advantage of trekking on some enchanting hiking trails along the way) is enough to keep annual visitors engaged for the rest of their days. The following are at least two vacations' worth of aquatic entertainment.

Akaka Falls, Big Island

The one-hour hike to these 420-foot falls is easy, the half-mile trail is well maintained (with steps on the steeper portions), and there are rain-forest flowers and plants (red ginger, banana plants, birds of paradise, hapu ferns, and plumeria blossoms, for example) around nearly every bend in the trail. Hikers will also see the lesser-known 100-foot **Kahuna Falls** en route. ♦ Rte 220 (west of Mamalahoa Hwy)

Hanakapiai Falls, Kauai

These 750-foot falls are a 3.5-mile hike from the end of Kuhio Highway, partly along the **Kalalau Trail**—one of the finest treks in the islands, known for its spectacular views and gusty winds. Hike through a valley once thickly settled, passing house foundations, the ruins of a coffee mill, and abandoned taro patches before arriving at the main pool below the waterfall. *Warning*: It's often raining in this area, and a high water level can make the requisite stream crossings difficult and dangerous. ♦ South of Kalalau Tr

Hiilawe Falls, Big Island

In order to get to the trailhead leading to these falls, hikers will have to navigate the mile-long, four-wheel-drive only, 45° drop into **Waipio Valley,** and make their way up the valley's eastern branch. There are several fords en route, including the one-of-a-kind, quarter-mile-wide "Stream Highway." And all of that before the trek even begins. Then it's a half-day, 4.5-mile round-trip journey that alternately follows a stream bed and the stream itself, to the often-deserted falls (nudity is sometimes an option here). At 1,300 feet, this is Hawaii's highest free-falling waterfall. ♦ Waipio Valley, Waipio

Jackass Ginger Pool, Oahu

The one-hour loop to this pool makes a wonderful family excursion. Children will be entranced by the opportunity to slide down the smooth rock faces adjacent to the pool on ti leaves. Grownups will be awed by the diversity of the botanical life, which includes Norfolk Pine, bamboo, guava, eucalyptus, and turpentine groves. It is recommended that you bring along a picnic on this 1.3-mile round-trip hike. ♦ Nuuanu Pali Dr (just east of Poli Hiwa Pl), Honolulu

Sacred Falls, Oahu

A good place to bring the kids, the 4.5-mile hike to this 800-foot waterfall is relatively easy to manage. Plan to spend an afternoon negotiating the trail, picnicking at the end on a sun-warmed boulder next to the enormous pool that lies at the bottom of the falls. And don't be afraid if you feel a nibble at your legs while bathing; it's only a Black Malay prawn checking out a new life form in the ecosystem. ♦ Sacred Falls State Park, Kamehameha Hwy (between Puhuli St and Pokiwai Pl)

Waimoku Falls, Maui

Variously called "Seven Pools," "Seven Sacred Pools," and "Oheo Gulch," this 500-foot waterfall near **Hana** is pristine. The 4-mile, 4-hour jaunt leads over bridge and boardwalk and through a thicket of taro and bamboo before winding up at the falls. Don't go if it's raining hard; flash floods are quite common here. ♦ Piilani Hwy, Haleakala National Park

Waipoo Falls, Kauai

Kokee State Park in northwest Kauai has hundreds of miles of hiking trails that go through striking **Waimea Canyon.** One such trail begins on **Halemanu Road** as **Cliff Trail,** then branches off and becomes **Canyon Trail,** continuing for 1.5 miles before stopping at the 500-foot waterfall. The trail then winds back out of the canyon, concluding at **Kumuwela Lookout;** hikers will need to hitchhike back to Kokee Road and their starting place unless they are able to bring two cars along with them. Note: Water is essential; the canyon can get very hot. ♦ Kokee State Park, Kokee Rd (north of Waimea Canyon Dr)

Akaka Falls

Hanalei Bay Resort and Suites $$$

Originally built as an exclusive condominium project, this 200- to 300-unit property was converted into a hotel complete with a full-service restaurant, stunning landscaping, and all the romance of Bali Hai. Two- and three-story buildings with one- to three-bedroom suites overlook Hanalei Bay. The spacious units offer all the conveniences of home—living room, dining room, full kitchen, and washer/dryer. With eight tennis courts, an on-site tennis pro, and the Princeville golf courses nearby, this is an attractive choice for golf and tennis buffs. There are two pools, daily maid service, and air-conditioning. ◆ 5380 Honoiki Rd (west of Liholiho Rd). 826.6522, 800/827.4427; fax 826.6680; www.hanaleiresort.com &

Within the Hanalei Bay Resort and Suites:

Bali Hai ★★$$$$ The airy dining room, beautifully embellished with batik banners, overlooks the tennis courts, with the Pacific Ocean in the distance. Baked salmon, grilled chicken with raspberry sauce, scampi, and smoked tofu stir-fry are among the extensive selections. ◆ Pacific Rim ◆ Daily breakfast, lunch, and dinner. Reservations required. 826.6522 &

Princeville Golf Courses These sensationally scenic 45 holes of golf (18 holes at the **Prince Course,** 27 holes at the **Makai Course**) were designed by Robert Trent Jones Jr., who owns a home in nearby Hanalei. The courses are spread out on a lush plateau high above Hanalei Bay with a view of Mount Waialeale, plunging waterfalls, and the ocean. The ocean holes are the most spectacular, but the lake and woods holes offer superb blends of golf and scenery. The only drawback is the threat of rain, especially during winter and spring. The **Prince Course** is par 72, 7,309 yards. The **Makai Course** consists of the **Ocean Course** (9 holes, 3,157 yards), the **Lake Course** (9 holes, 3,149 yards), and the **Woods Course** (9 holes, 3,208 yards); play 2 for a full par 72 round. The **Prince Golf and Country Club,** which serves the **Prince Course,** has its own restaurant, health spa, and lounge. ◆ Expensive greens fees. Daily. Preferred starting times and rates for Princeville Resort guests. Lei o Papa Rd (between Hanalei Plantation and Ka Haku Rds). 826.5000

48 Hanalei to Haena Drive The drive begins when you cross the Hanalei River on the Hanalei Bridge (built in 1912) and dead-ends eight miles later at **Haena State Beach Park** (see page 177). Along the way you'll rumble across 10 little bridges, some of them wooden and most only one lane wide. Taro fields fan out across the valley, then the road swings closer to the steep cliffs. The Na Pali Coast is rich with eucalyptus, paperbark, giant tree ferns, and banana and coconut trees. You'll also see a succession of sandy beaches nuzzled by foamy waves, and waterfalls plunging hundreds of feet down the mountain slopes. Cattle graze in green valleys that extend from the base of the mountains, and side roads dart off through tunnels of trees leading to silent beaches. There are wet caves and dry caves, tumbledown green clapboard houses with saddles straddled across porch rails, and chalet-style vacation homes trying to hide in the thickly wooded areas that guard the long, empty beaches. The only consolation in reaching the end of the road is that you'll get to turn around and drive the same beautiful route all over again.

49 Tahiti Nui ★★$$$ If you're in Hanalei on a Wednesday or Saturday night, don't even consider going anywhere else. Just plunk down your $40 and indulge in a practically authentic Hawaiian/Tahitian all-you-can-eat luau, complete with *kalua* pig cooked in the traditional *imu* (underground oven). The rest of the week the menu features such Asian items as Thai chicken and beef with garlic sauce. ◆ Polynesian/Asian ◆ Daily breakfast, lunch, and dinner. Reservations recommended. 5-5134 Kuhio Hwy (east of Aku Rd), Hanalei. 826.6277 &

49 Zelo's Beach House Restaurant and Grill ★★$$$ One of the "in" places in the "in" town on Kauai, this restaurant charms diners with alfresco seating, as well as shellfish tacos, sun-dried tomato pesto rigatoni, beer-battered fish-and-chips, and the like. ◆ Nouvelle ◆ Daily lunch and dinner. Kuhio Hwy and Aku Rd, Hanalei. 826.9700 &

49 Ching Young Shopping Village This eclectic collection of shops gets top marks for its ingenious array of goods; plan to fritter away at least an hour here. ◆ Daily. 5-5190 Kuhio Hwy (between Aku and Malolo Rds), Hanalei. 826.7222 &

Within the Ching Young Shopping Village:

On the Road to Hanalei Character oozes from every pore of this 1,000-square-foot emporium, where anything from a *pareu* (wraparound Polynesian outfit) to locally made jewelry, to Hawaiian antiques, to a child's toy may be found. The real secret to the place, though, is that the fun is in the looking. ◆ Daily. 826.7360 &

Damage caused by Hurricane Iniki on Kauai and Oahu in 1992 was estimated at $1.6 billion, making it the third most expensive natural disaster in US history.

Kauai was the first Hawaiian island discovered by Captain James Cook, who anchored here in 1778.

Hail to the Whale

Each winter, more than a thousand humpback whales (*megaptera novaeangliae*) turn up in the Hawaiian islands after having traveled from the waters around Alaska. They come here to breed and calf, living off blubber gained from feeding in Alaska during the summer months. The whales are called "humpbacks" because they raise their backs around the dorsal fins high above the water before diving.

Beginning in late November, a few humpbacks appear, crooning to one another in an underwater serenade. By January, they are coming in by the hundreds and calves originating from the previous year's mating are being born. In February, the number of humpbacks in the waters around Hawaii reaches its peak. From the vantage point of a boat, and sometimes even from shore, whale lovers can watch these nonmonogamous animals playfully pursuing each other. Tour boats large and small make trips from **Oahu,** the **Big Island, Kauai,** and **Maui.** The largest concentration of humpbacks, however, can be seen in the area near Maui, **Lanai, Molokai,** and **Kahoolawe.**

Baby whales grow very quickly, weighing about two tons at birth and expanding to four before migrating to higher latitudes in March. Fully grown, a 45-foot-long humpback weighs about 45 tons. A calf a year is, understandably, as much as a mother whale can produce; more commonly, she will give birth every two or three years.

The life span of a humpback is 30 to 40 years. Only in the past few decades, however, have these awe-inspiring animals been allowed to die of old age, rather than being killed by human predators. Whaling had been Hawaii's primary industry in the 1800s, and **Lahaina,** Maui evolved into the center of global operations, probably because it was located at the hub of the world's winter whaling grounds. During the peak of the whaling industry (1820-60), nearly a thousand sailing ships were devoted to tracking down and annihilating the great beasts. By the early 1900s, this marine mammal population, which had once numbered over a hundred thousand, had been decimated.

Today, humpback whales are protected from hunting and harassment (it is illegal to swim within 500 feet of the creatures) by Hawaii state law and a 1964 international treaty prohibiting the hunting of these creatures. The humpback whale is considered an endangered species; it became the official state mammal in 1979.

Sushi & Blues ★★$$$ If you're twentysomething, try this: Sit down at a copper-topped table on a weekend night when the blues are cooking and order a plate of mahimahi grilled with garlic-sake cream, a pile of coconut shrimp, or a California sushi roll—and rid yourself of the notion that nothing's happening on Kauai. ♦ Seafood/Sushi ♦ Tu-Su dinner. Second level. 826.9701

49 Hanalei Bay Beach A stunning, picture-perfect arc of sand cradled by the sharp flanks of Mount Waialeale, this beach is popular for picnics, sunbathing, and local beach gatherings, and sought after by Hollywood, which caught it in all its splendor in the movie *South Pacific.* Swimming is dangerous here during the winter. There are public facilities and a quaint pier. ♦ Off Weke Rd, Hanalei

50 Hanalei Gourmet ★★$$ Teachers at the old **Hanalei Elementary School** might have been surprised to know that students' desks would someday be replaced by elegant tables and the head of their classrooms morphed into a long bar facing a series of mountain water falls in what is now one of the town's most popular restaurants. Menu highlights here include such fare as eggplant sandwiches, shrimp boil, and artichoke dip. ♦ American ♦ Daily breakfast, lunch, and dinner. 5-5161 Kuhio Hwy, Hanalei. 826.2524 &

50 Waioli Mission House Museum This two-story cottage was brought to Hawaii in prefabricated sections in 1836 by New England missionaries who didn't want to go native. Period furniture fills all of the rooms. There used to be a pole-and-thatch meeting house on this site in the early 1830s, when traditional, prehistoric tools were still used and made in Hanalei. Lovely gardens flourish in the back. ♦ Admission. Tu, Th, Sa 9AM-3PM. Kuhio Hwy, Hanalei. 245.3202

51 Lumahai Beach It's one of the most photographed beaches in Hawaii, and you probably won't be able to resist taking your own snapshot of the place where Mitzi Gaynor washed that man out of her hair in *South Pacific*. There are actually two beaches; the one farther west is more dangerous, especially if the surf is up. ♦ Kuhio Hwy (to get to the first swimming area, turn right after Hanalei Bay, then follow the unmarked trail; the second beach is farther west by Lumahai River)

52 Wainiha General Store "The Last Store on the North Shore" is alive and well and still selling snacks and sodas at "last store" prices. Check out the T-shirts or rent snorkeling gear. ♦ Daily. 5-6607 Kuhio Hwy, Wainiha. 826.6251 &

53 Hanalei Colony Resort $$$ Spread along four acres of coastline, this scenic, isolated hideaway has 48 2-bedroom condominiums, a pool, Jacuzzi, beach, TVs, phones, and air-conditioning, but no restaurant. ♦ 5-7130 Kuhio Hwy, Haena. 826.6235, 800/628.3004; fax 826.9893; hcr@aloha.net; www.hcr.com

Lumahai Beach

MATT MORROW/NORTH MARKET STREET GRAPHICS

54 Maniniholo Dry Cave The first of a trio of caves on the south side of the highway, it is actually a milelong lava tube running under a cliff. ♦ Kuhio Hwy, Haena

55 Haena State Beach Park A set designer couldn't create a more beautiful beach than this one, curving sensuously among palm trees backed by mountains—used for the Bali Hai setting in the movie *South Pacific.* Swimming is unsafe here in the winter because of strong currents. There are picnic and camping facilities, though. ♦ Kuhio Hwy (west of Haena)

55 Kee Beach Kauai's famous "end of the road" also marks the beginning of the hiking trail into spectacular Kalalau Valley. This is a good place to swim year-round, and during summer months, when the waters are calm, the snorkeling is excellent. At the end of the road near the beach are the ruins of the **Hula Heiau,** a spot sacred to the ancient Hawaiians and the former site of a traditional Hawaiian school. ♦ Kuhio Hwy (west of Haena)

56 Waikapalae and Waikanaloa Wet Caves According to Hawaiian legend, the fire goddess Pele made a vain attempt to find a home on the North Shore of Kauai, but all she found were these two wet caves. Water was the last thing she needed, so she packed her flames and went to Kilauea on the Big Island. Some people swim in the caves—or even scuba dive—but it can be dangerous. It's worth a quick stop to see their exteriors, though. Kuhio Hwy (west of Haena)

57 Hanakapiai Beach The mildly arduous two-mile hike from Kee Beach offers spectacular views at every turn. Pandanus, wild watercress, guava, fragrant *lauae* ferns, *kukui,* and countless other plants are fed by

mountain streams and tiny springs. White-tailed tropic birds circle against the cliffs and dolphins can sometimes be seen when the trail is close to sea level. This trail reveals the marvels of erosion and the beauty of Na Pali, one of Hawaii's unforgettable natural sights. Be careful of the strong riptides at the beach; swimming is not recommended here for less than strong swimmers and at any other time but summer. Also: In the winter, Mother Nature robs the beach of sand, which she graciously returns around the end of April. ♦ Kalalau Tr (west of Kuhio Hwy)

58 Na Pali Coast State Park The history of the area is as fascinating as the hike to it. Hawaiians lived here in large numbers from the 1400s through the 1800s. Later, a leprosy victim named Koolau hid from officials with his wife and child in these precipitous hills. And in the 1960s, flower children maintained the tradition by hiding from their families and the law in remote corners of the Na Pali Coast, building love shacks in which to turn on, tune in, and drop out. Today the area is a state park, but it's still a place to go when you want to feel far away from the world as you know it. **Whitey's Boat Cruises** (826.6853) and **Captain Sundowner** (826.5585) both offer a hiker's drop-off raft service for the 11-mile hike to Kalalau in the calmer summer months. Be forewarned that the **Kalalau Trail** isn't a cakewalk—even the first two miles require a lot of uphill walking. No prior arrangements are needed to hike the first two miles to Hanakapiai Beach, but hiking the remaining nine miles and camping requires a permit. For more information about hiking and camping permits, contact the **Department of Land and Natural Resources,** 3060 Eiwa St (at Hardy St), Lihue, 274.3444. ♦ Kalalau Tr (west of Kuhio Hwy)

Niihau

The mysterious island of Niihau (*Nee*-ee-how), located 17 miles off the leeward coast of Kauai, holds as much intrigue for the residents of Hawaii's neighboring islands as it does for tourists, both of whom are denied access. Strict controls on travel to and even information about this privately owned, 73-square-mile island have given rise to its nickname, "The Forbidden Island."

Niihau operates on a very simple doctrine, established by its owners, the Robinson family, to maintain the island's role as a haven for indigenous Hawaiians: No one is allowed on the island unless invited, and though residents are free to travel off the island with permission from the Robinsons, those who leave the island to marry may not return with their spouses and can arbitrarily be refused access.

By modern standards, life on Niihau would best be described as primitive, and that's how the residents intend to keep it. The island's 200 inhabitants, most of them pure-blooded Hawaiians, have an abundance of transistor radios and a couple of generators, but few modern appliances and no hotels, telephones, indoor plumbing, or jails. They spend their days fishing, swimming, shelling, and herding cattle or sheep on horseback. A few pick-up trucks provide the only modern modes of transportation, and entertainment occasionally includes gathering around a portable television. Most of the residents born and raised on Niihau speak fluent Hawaiian, and the children attend the island's one public school, then move to Kauai for the upper grades. Ironically, few Niihau students return to live here permanently once they've experienced the modern world.

The history of Niihau reads like a James Michener novel. In 1863, Eliza Sinclair, the daughter of a wealthy Scottish merchant and widow of a New Zealand rancher, loaded her family and all their possessions (including sheep, cattle, and prize Arabian horses) aboard a 300-ton bark canoe and set out to

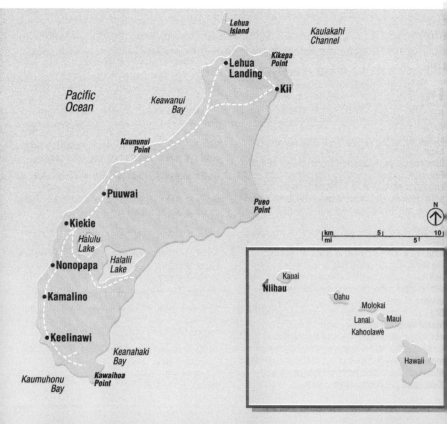

find an island for her clan. After turning down an invitation to purchase a swampy area later known as Waikiki, she persuaded King Kamehameha IV to sell Niihau to her for $10,000 and proceeded to build a rambling 20-room house, as well as barns for her animals. Her ranch flourished, and Hawaiian laborers hired from nearby Kauai quickly established a small community. These ranch hands are the ancestors of Niihau's current residents.

Sinclair's descendants, the Robinson family (who reside on nearby Kauai but still own Niihau), have refused all offers by outside agencies, including the state, to buy the island (in the general plebiscite of 1959, Niihau was the only precinct in Hawaii to reject statehood). Aside from a few modest bungalow-type dwellings, the island remains in its natural state, with miles of white-sand beaches, mostly arid land, and two large natural lakes. The people of Niihau are employed by the Robinsons to work on the ranch lands. In return, they pay no rent, do no grocery shopping (food and other supplies are brought to the island regularly by boat), and have little to worry about. A traditional pastime among the women is the gathering of tiny, rare shells that wash up only on Niihau's windward beaches and are fashioned into the famous Niihau shell leis. These delicate, ornate, and very expensive leis are often of museum quality and coveted by private collectors. In fact, Niihau shell leis are some of the most treasured possessions of the Hawaiian people.

Since the profit the ranch produces is inconsequential compared to the amount the Robinsons could make selling the island for commercial development, it is apparent that their motive for sustaining its unique lifestyle is not monetary. Yet because no newcomers are allowed to settle on Niihau, and the children seldom return to live out their lives on this archaic isle, the future of Niihau seems uncertain at best.

In 1998, for the first time in the island's history, Keith Robinson—said to be land rich but cash poor—talked about selling this unique tract of land. The US military expressed interest in purchasing Niihau and installing a missile launching site that it claimed would employ many residents and thus improve the island's economy. But this was so removed from both reality on Niihau and the Robinsons' wishes that the idea was dropped. At press time the island's future prospects remained unknown.

Paddling Paradise

Not many places in the world are better suited to sea kayaking than Hawaii. There are no significant tides, strong currents, life-threatening temperatures, or open-water crossings here. The only months that have any off-putting waves are December through February, and even then, the sea is often calm enough to get a boat in, particularly on the islands' south shores. The sun is close to constant in many places, and the rains are warm.

Some of the most popular put-in points (starting places, in kayakese) for self-guided tours on each major island are the **Wailua River** on **Kauai** (one of the few navigable rivers in Hawaii, this waterway delivers paddlers to the overly touristy **Fern Grotto**, with at least one stop recommended for a dunk under a riverside waterfall); **Kealakekua Bay** on the **Big Island** (kayakers can both visit the **Captain Cook Monument** and paddle through the school of dolphins that normally frolics here); **Kailua Bay** on **Oahu** (sea turtles are common and paddlers can make their way to a couple of offshore islands called **Mokulua** where thousands of birds nest); and **Kaanapali** and points north on **Maui**.

Kayak Operators

Fun Hogs Hawaii (PO Box 424, Hoolehua, HI 96729; 552.2761) offers guided treks on **Molokai**'s south coast, as well as rentals to the experienced.

Go Bananas (799 Kapahulu Ave, at Winam Ave, Honolulu, Oahu, 737.9514) rents boats and equipment as well as running custom-guided trips on Oahu and elsewhere.

Hawaii Pack and Paddle (87-3187 Honu Moe Rd, Captain Cook, HI 96704; 328.8911; specializes in combination kayak-camping trips of the **South Kona Coast, Waipio Valley,** and elsewhere on the Big Island. Equipment rental also is available.

Kayak Kauai (PO Box 508, Hanalei, HI 96714; 826.9844) is the undisputed top-drawer company on Kauai to approach for gear rental, a day tour, or a longer trip.

South Pacific Kayaks (2439 S Kihei Rd (between Keonekai and Kanani Rds), Kamaole, Maui, 575.4848) leads both day and camping kayak tours of Maui's coastline.

History

Hawaii's history, packed with kings, queens, hurricanes and volcanic eruptions, reads like a fairy tale. What follows are highlights in the state's colorful past.

In the beginning According to *Kumulipo* (the Hawaiian version of Genesis), in the beginning of time there was darkness. Out of the darkness, Wakea (father sky) and Papa (mother earth) united and gave birth to **Hawaii**, then **Maui, Kahoolawe,** and the other islands. Plant and animal life were placed on the islands in preparation for the appearance of Kumulipo (the first man) and Po'ele (the first woman). Happy with the fruits of their labor, Wakea and Papa bestowed royal titles on the children of Kumulipo and Wakea and made them rulers of the islands. All subsequent Hawaiian *alii* (royalty) claim their legitimacy as rulers from Wakea and Papa.

300-750 AD Polynesians from islands 2,000 miles to the south discover and eventually settle in the Hawaiian Islands. They abandon cannibalism and human sacrifice and develop a farming culture built around the worship of Lono, the fertility god.

1100 A wave of Tahitian warriors invades the islands, causing profound changes in the Hawaiian religious and social system. The practice of human sacrifice resurfaces (cannibalism does not), and a rigid social and religious system called *kapu* is introduced. Like European feudalism, *kapu* requires allegiance of peasants to local chiefs who control the land. In return, the chiefs protect the peasants from other chiefs. This system lasts 700 years. Over the years, upper, middle, and lower classes form. The *alii* are the ruling class, the *kahuna* (doctors, navigators, and other professionals) make up the middle class, and fishermen and laborers are at the bottom of the social order.

1778 While searching for the fabled Northwest Passage across the North American continent, English explorer Captain James Cook of the *HMS Resolution* sails into **Kauai's Waimea Bay.** Cook is mistaken for the god Lono, who is expected to return to earth in a vessel with a tall crossbeam hung with great white sheets. Cook names the archipelago the **Sandwich Islands** after his patron, John Montague, fourth Earl of Sandwich, then sails for Alaska.

1779 Frustrated by the Alaskan winter and his fruitless search, Cook returns to Hawaii. Cook's officer, William Bligh (of *HMS Bounty* fame), draws the first maps of Maui's coastline. Soon the *kahuna* conclude that, if not Cook, certainly most of the English sailors are mere mortals. Following a series of mishaps, Cook is killed by a Hawaiian mob. Hawaii's population is estimated at about 300,000.

1784 The Hawaiian Islands are divided into three kingdoms. Kalaniopuu controls Hawaii and part of Maui; Kahekili rules most of Maui, **Lanai,** and **Oahu;** his brother, Kaeo, controls **Kauai.** The three kingdoms are constantly at war with one another.

1788 In his dying days, Kalaniopuu names his nephew Kamehameha heir to his throne.

1790 Captain Simon Metcalfe of the US merchant ship *Eleanora* kills scores of Hawaiians in the Olowalu Massacre on Maui. Kamehameha captures the *Fair American* and two sailors, Isaac Davis and John Young. Using the *Fair American*'s cannons and the military expertise of Davis and Young, Kamehameha begins a bloody campaign to unite the islands.

1810 After years of war and thousands of deaths, Kamehameha captures Kauai, the last island not under his control. For the first time, all of Hawaii is ruled by one king, with **Lahaina** on Maui the capital.

1819 Kamehameha I dies. His son and heir Liholiho adopts the title Kamehameha II and begins to dismantle the *kapu* system. At a gathering of island royalty and foreign dignitaries, Kamehameha II violates one of the oldest and most sacred *kapu* by having women at his table and allowing them to eat freely. The feast becomes known as *Ai Noa* (free eating) and signals the collapse of the old order.

1820 Fourteen Calvinist missionaries arrive from Boston. Kamehameha II grants them permission to establish a mission. The missionaries establish schools and develop the Hawaiian alphabet; their impact on Hawaiian life will be profound and lasting.

1823 Kamehameha II's mother converts to Christianity. Following her lead, most of the island's royalty converts.

1824 Kamehameha II dies on a state trip to England and is succeeded by his nine-year-old son, who is crowned Kamehameha III.

1825 The first coffee seedlings are planted in **Manoa Valley.**

1831 **Lahainaluna School** is established. It is the first American school west of the Rockies.

1834 *The Torch of Hawaii*, the first Hawaiian-language newspaper, is printed.

1840 Kamehameha III replaces his absolute rule with a constitutional monarchy.

1845 The capital is moved to **Honolulu.**

1846 Lahaina is the undisputed whaling capital of the world. Almost 600 whaling ships anchor in its port each year.

1848 Kamehameha III introduces the practice of private ownership of land. He divides Hawaii into three land groupings: crown land belonging to the king; government land belonging to the chiefs; and public land belonging to the peasants who cultivate it. Hawaiians are unaccustomed to the concept of private property, and much of these lands will be sold by their owners in the next decade.

1849 The first sugar refinery is built in Maui.

1850 The Masters and Servants Act allows the importation of foreign labor to work on the new sugar plantations. Chinese laborers are the first immigrants to arrive, followed a decade later by Japanese. The stage is set for the growth of large commercial sugar estates with strong links to the US. Meanwhile, the influx of diseases previously unknown on the islands has taken a toll on the natives, whose population has been reduced to about 50,000.

1854 Kamehameha III, the last of the powerful monarchs, dies. His successor, Kamehameha IV

(Alexander Liholiho), resists pressure for annexation to the US. The plantation owners' increased influence accompanies a decline in the power of the crown and its Protestant advisors.

1863 Kamehameha IV dies childless. The throne passes to his brother, Lot Kamehameha, who becomes Kamehameha V.

1872 Kamehameha V dies without leaving a direct descendant, thus ending the Kamehameha dynasty. The next king, William Lunalilo, is elected by the legislature but soon dies childless.

1874 Kalakaua, known as the "Merry Monarch," is elected king. He pushes for even closer ties to the US. Kalakaua is also responsible for the compilation of the *mele*, Hawaii's great oral history tales.

1876 In exchange for long-term leasing rights to **Pearl Harbor,** the Reciprocity Act exempts Hawaiian sugar from US import duties, thus linking US strategic and Hawaiian commercial interests.

1891 Kalakaua dies during a visit to the US and is succeeded by his sister, Liliuokalani. A critic of American influence in Hawaii, she will be the last Hawaiian monarch.

1893 Liliuokalani is overthrown in a bloodless coup led by plantation owners and sanctioned by members of the US Congress. President Benjamin Harrison sends a Marine contingent to guarantee order. Sanford B. Dole heads the provisional government and seeks annexation by the US. However, the annexation treaty dies in the Senate and President-elect Grover Cleveland, a strong opponent of expansionism, threatens to reinstate Liliuokalani.

1894 The provisional government of Hawaii drafts a constitution placing strict property requirements on voting rights, thus limiting the native vote. On 4 July 1894 Sanford B. Dole reads the proclamation declaring Hawaii a republic.

1898 The Spanish-American War and fears of Japanese expansionism feed a surging expansionist sentiment in the US. On 7 July President William McKinley signs an agreement to annex the Hawaiian Islands. Five weeks later, the formal transfer of sovereignty takes place and Sanford B. Dole becomes the first official governor of the newly established territory of Hawaii (population 154,000).

1901 The **Moana,** the first hotel in **Waikiki,** opens.

1903 The **Hawaii Visitors and Convention Bureau** opens its first office on Oahu.

1906 James Dole purchases Lanai and establishes the world's largest pineapple plantation and fruit cannery.

1911 **Pearl Harbor** is officially inaugurated. The US military presence in Hawaii grows steadily.

1936 **Pan American Airlines** flies to Hawaii from California. The trip takes 20 hours. Commercial air service spurs the growth of tourism.

1941 The Japanese bomb the **Pearl Harbor Naval Base** on Oahu on 7 December. The US enters World War II; martial law is declared in Hawaii.

1945 During World War II, Hawaii's population grows from 400,000 to 900,000.

1959 Hawaiians vote 17-to-1 in favor of statehood in an islands-wide referendum. In March, Congress ratifies the Hawaiian State Bill. President Eisenhower signs the bill on 21 August, making Hawaii the 50th state. Owen Douglas Jr., the winner of the first **Hawaiian Open International Golf Tournament,** receives a $150 award.

1964 The average number of tourists in Hawaii on any given day is 16,037.

1973 The first **Honolulu Marathon** is held; in less than a quarter-century it will be the third-largest 26.2-mile race in the country.

1983 The long-dormant **Kilauea** volcano erupts on the **Big Island.** Hawaii's population reaches one million; the annual tourist count, five million.

1985 Japanese investment in Hawaiian real estate explodes. By the end of the decade, Japanese investment accounts for 80 percent of the total foreign investment in Hawaii.

1989 The average number of tourists in Hawaii on any given day is 169,670.

1990 Democrat John D. Waihee III is elected the first native Hawaiian governor in the United States.

1991 Tourism accounts for one-third of Hawaii's $30-billion economy. Carolyn Suzanne Sapp is the first Miss Hawaii to be named Miss America.

1992 On 11 September, Hurricane Iniki ravages Kauai, causing $2.5 billion dollars in damage.

1993 The US Congress issues an official apology for its involvement in the coup that overthrew Queen Liliuokalani 100 years earlier.

1994 Democrat Benjamin Cayetano is elected the first Filipino governor in the United States.

1996 Hawaii's court rules there is no compelling interest to deny the rights of marriage to same-sex partners.

1998 Hawaii residents vote for a constitutional amendment banning same-gender marriage.

USS Arizona Memorial

Index

Index

Hotels

The hotels listed below are grouped according to their price ratings; they are also listed in the main index. The hotel price ratings reflect the base price of a standard room for two people for one night during the peak season.

$$$$ Big Bucks ($251 and up)
$$$ Expensive ($176-$250)
$$ Reasonable ($100-$175)
$ The Price Is Right (less than $100)

$$$$